BIG ROAD ATLAS
BRITAIN
AND NORTHERN IRELAND

Contents

Collins

Published by Collins
An imprint of HarperCollins Publishers
Westerhill Road, Bishopbriggs, Glasgow G64 2QT

www.harpercollins.co.uk

Copyright © HarperCollins Publishers Ltd 2020

Collins® is a registered trademark of HarperCollins Publishers Limited

Mapping generated from Collins Bartholomew digital databases

Contains Ordnance Survey data © Crown copyright and database right (2020)

The grid on the maps is the National Grid used on Ordnance Survey mapping, except in Northern Ireland. The National Grid is taken from the Ordnance Survey map with the permission of the Controller of her Majesty's Stationery Office.

Printed in China

Paperback ISBN 978 0 00 837436 5   10 9 8 7 6 5 4 3 2 1
Spiral   ISBN 978 0 00 837437 2   10 9 8 7 6 5 4 3 2 1

e-mail: roadcheck@harpercollins.co.uk facebook.com/collinsref @collins_ref

© Natural England copyright. Contains Ordnance Survey data © Crown copyright and database right (2019)

Information for the alignment of the Wales Coast Path provided by ©Natural Resources Wales. All rights reserved. Contains Ordnance Survey data. Ordnance Survey licence number 100019741. Crown copyright and database right (2013).

Information for the alignment of several Long Distance Trails in Scotland provided by © walkhighlands

With thanks to the Wine Guild of the United Kingdom for help with researching vineyards.

For the latest information on Blue Flag award beaches visit www.blueflag.global

MIX
Paper from
responsible sources
FSC™ C007454

Promotional gifts and data sales
The mapping in this Collins Road Atlas is also available for use in promotional gifts or for sale as digital data. For details of products and services visit our website at www.collinsbartholomew.com or contact us at:

Promotional gift enquiries – collins.reference@harpercollins.co.uk

Data sales enquiries – collins.bartholomew@harpercollins.co.uk

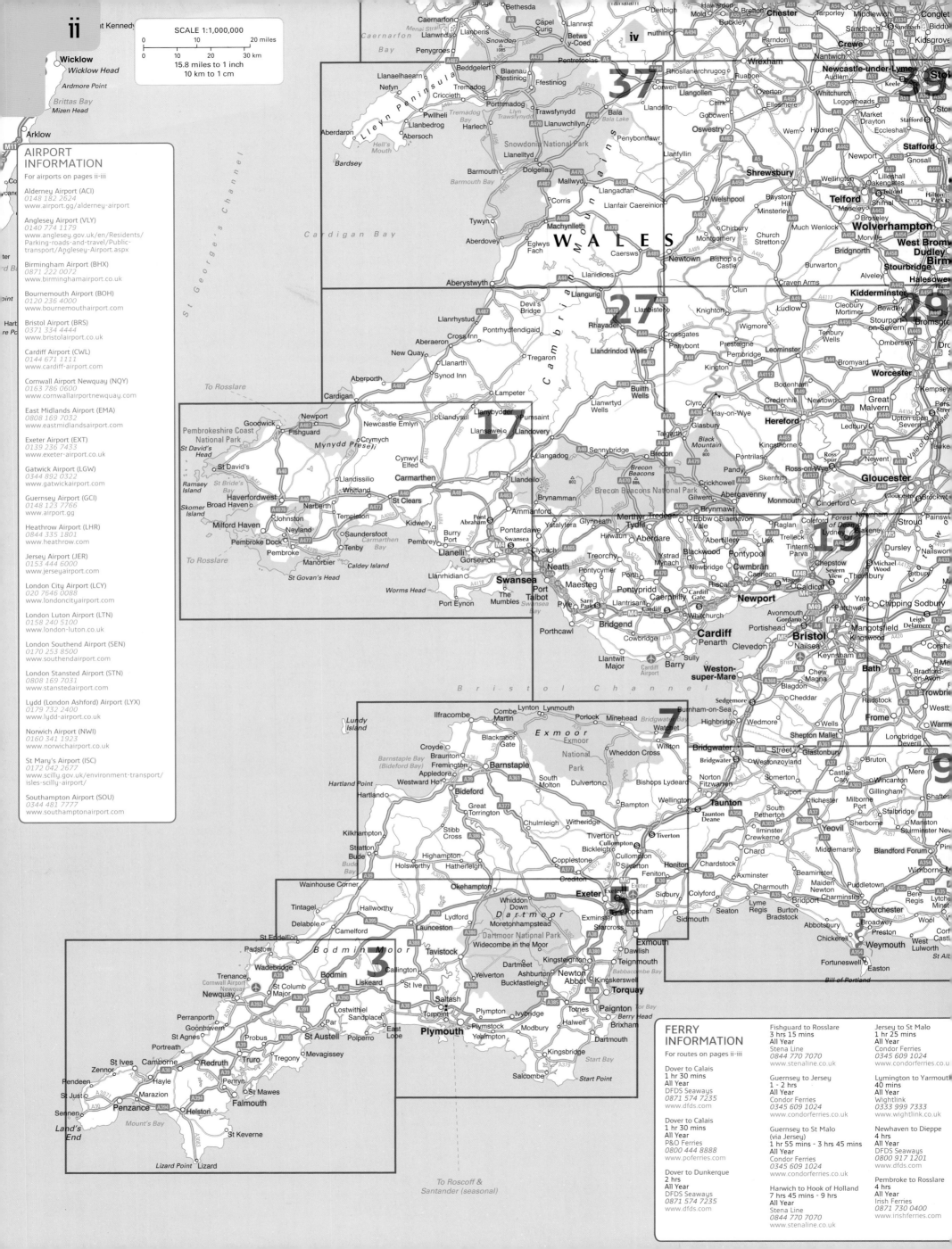

ii

SCALE 1:1,000,000

| 0 | 10 | 20 miles |
| 0 | 10 | 20 | 30 km |

15.8 miles to 1 inch
10 km to 1 cm

AIRPORT INFORMATION

For airports on pages ii-iii

Alderney Airport (ACI)
0148 182 2624
www.airport.gg/alderney-airport

Anglesey Airport (VLY)
0140 774 1179
www.anglesey.gov.uk/en/Residents/
Parking-roads-and-travel/Public-
transport/Anglesey-Airport.aspx

Birmingham Airport (BHX)
0871 222 0072
www.birminghamairport.co.uk

Bournemouth Airport (BOH)
0120 236 4000
www.bournemouthairport.com

Bristol Airport (BRS)
0371 334 4444
www.bristolairport.co.uk

Cardiff Airport (CWL)
0144 671 1111
www.cardiff-airport.com

Cornwall Airport Newquay (NQY)
0163 786 0600
www.cornwallairportnewquay.com

East Midlands Airport (EMA)
0808 169 7032
www.eastmidlandsairport.com

Exeter Airport (EXT)
0139 236 7433
www.exeter-airport.co.uk

Gatwick Airport (LGW)
0344 892 0322
www.gatwickairport.com

Guernsey Airport (GCI)
0148 123 7766
www.airport.gg

Heathrow Airport (LHR)
0844 335 1801
www.heathrow.com

Jersey Airport (JER)
0153 444 6000
www.jerseyairport.com

London City Airport (LCY)
020 7646 0088
www.londoncityairport.com

London Luton Airport (LTN)
0158 240 5100
www.london-luton.co.uk

London Southend Airport (SEN)
0170 253 8500
www.southendairport.com

London Stansted Airport (STN)
0808 169 7031
www.stanstedairport.com

Lydd (London Ashford) Airport (LYX)
0179 732 2400
www.lydd-airport.co.uk

Norwich Airport (NWI)
0160 341 1923
www.norwichairport.co.uk

St Mary's Airport (ISC)
0172 042 2677
www.scilly.gov.uk/environment-transport/
isles-scilly-airport/

Southampton Airport (SOU)
0344 481 7777
www.southamptonairport.com

FERRY INFORMATION

For routes on pages ii-iii

Dover to Calais
1 hr 30 mins
All Year
DFDS Seaways
0871 574 7235
www.dfds.com

Dover to Calais
1 hr 30 mins
All Year
P&O Ferries
0800 444 8888
www.poferries.com

Dover to Dunkerque
2 hrs
All Year
DFDS Seaways
0871 574 7235
www.dfds.com

Fishguard to Rosslare
3 hrs 15 mins
All Year
Stena Line
0844 770 7070
www.stenaline.co.uk

Guernsey to Jersey
1 - 2 hrs
All Year
Condor Ferries
0345 609 1024
www.condorferries.co.uk

Guernsey to St Malo
(via Jersey)
1 hr 55 mins - 3 hrs 45 mins
All Year
Condor Ferries
0345 609 1024
www.condorferries.co.uk

Harwich to Hook of Holland
7 hrs 45 mins - 9 hrs
All Year
Stena Line
0844 770 7070
www.stenaline.co.uk

Jersey to St Malo
1 hr 25 mins
All Year
Condor Ferries
0345 609 1024
www.condorferries.co.uk

Lymington to Yarmouth
40 mins
All Year
Wightlink
0333 999 7333
www.wightlink.co.uk

Newhaven to Dieppe
4 hrs
All Year
DFDS Seaways
0800 917 1201
www.dfds.com

Pembroke to Rosslare
4 hrs
All Year
Irish Ferries
0871 730 0400
www.irishferries.com

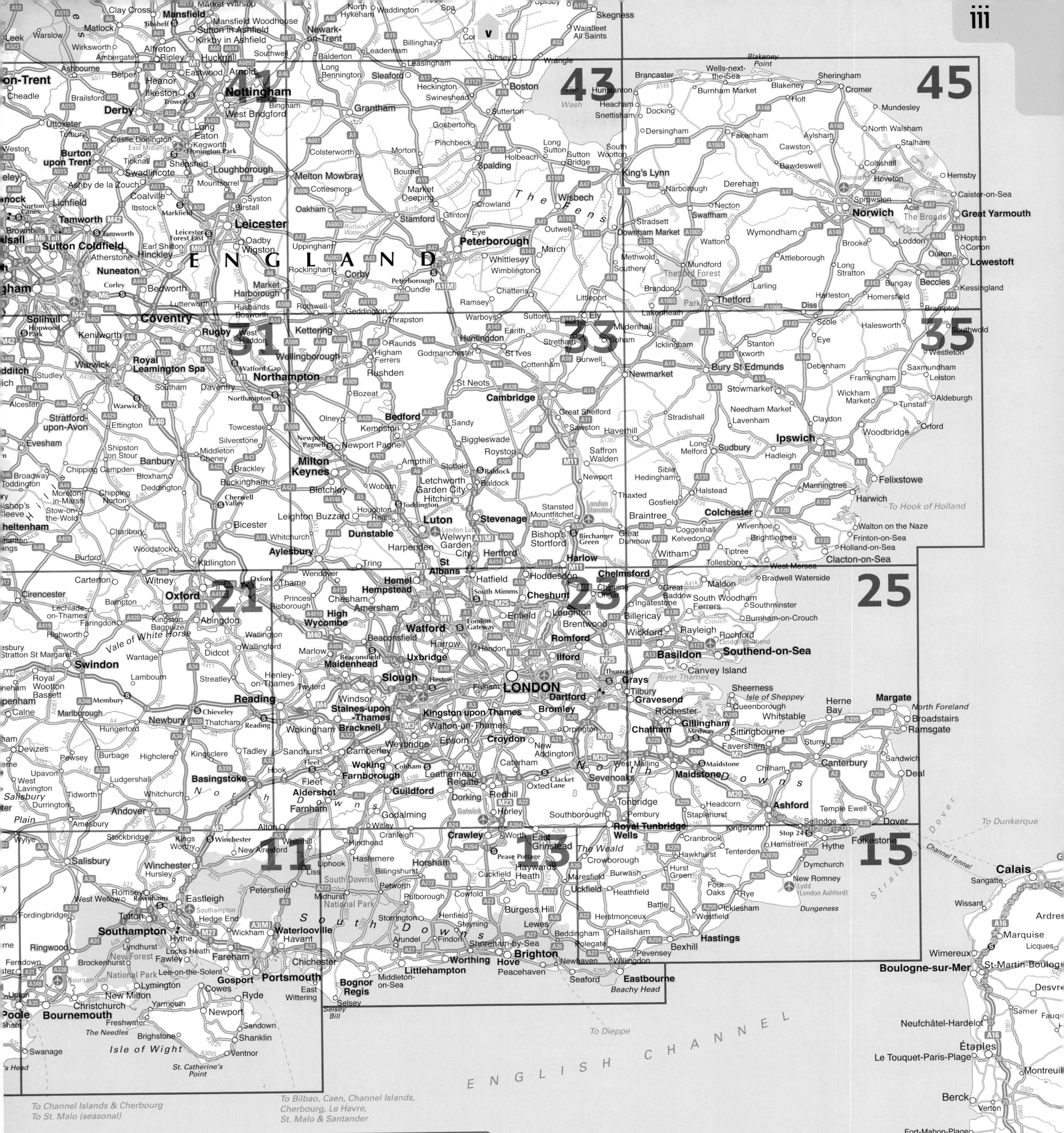

Plymouth to Roscoff
6 hrs - 8 hrs
All Year
Brittany Ferries
0330 159 7000
www.brittany-ferries.co.uk

Plymouth to Santander
22 hrs 30 mins
Seasonal
Brittany Ferries
0330 159 7000
www.brittany-ferries.co.uk

Poole to Cherbourg
4 hrs 30 mins
All Year
Brittany Ferries
0330 159 7000
www.brittany-ferries.co.uk

Poole to Guernsey
3 hrs
All Year
Condor Ferries
0345 609 1024
www.condorferries.co.uk

Poole to Jersey
4 hrs 30 mins
All Year
Condor Ferries
0345 609 1024
www.condorferries.co.uk

Poole to St Malo
(via Guernsey or Jersey)
6 hrs 40 mins -
11 hrs 55 mins
Seasonal
Condor Ferries
0345 609 1024
www.condorferries.co.uk

Portsmouth to Bilbao
24 hrs - 32 hrs
All Year
Brittany Ferries
0330 159 7000
www.brittany-ferries.co.uk

Portsmouth to Caen
6 hrs - 7 hrs
All Year
Brittany Ferries
0330 159 7000
www.brittany-ferries.co.uk

Portsmouth to Cherbourg
3 hrs
Seasonal
Brittany Ferries
0330 159 7000
www.brittany-ferries.co.uk

Portsmouth to Fishbourne
45 mins
All Year
Wightlink
0333 999 7333
www.wightlink.co.uk

Portsmouth to Guernsey
7 hrs
All Year
Condor Ferries
0345 609 1024
www.condorferries.co.uk

Portsmouth to Jersey
(via Guernsey)
8 hrs 5 mins -
12 hrs 55 mins
All Year
Condor Ferries
0345 609 1024
www.condorferries.co.uk

Portsmouth to Le Havre
5 hrs 30 mins - 10 hrs
All Year
Brittany Ferries
0330 159 7000
www.brittany-ferries.co.uk

Portsmouth to St Malo
10 hrs 30 mins -
12 hrs 5 mins
All Year
Brittany Ferries
0330 159 7000
www.brittany-ferries.co.uk

Portsmouth to Santander
24 hrs - 32 hrs
All Year
Brittany Ferries
0330 159 7000
www.brittany-ferries.co.uk

Southampton to East Cowes
55 mins
All Year
Red Funnel Ferries
0844 844 9988
www.redfunnel.co.uk

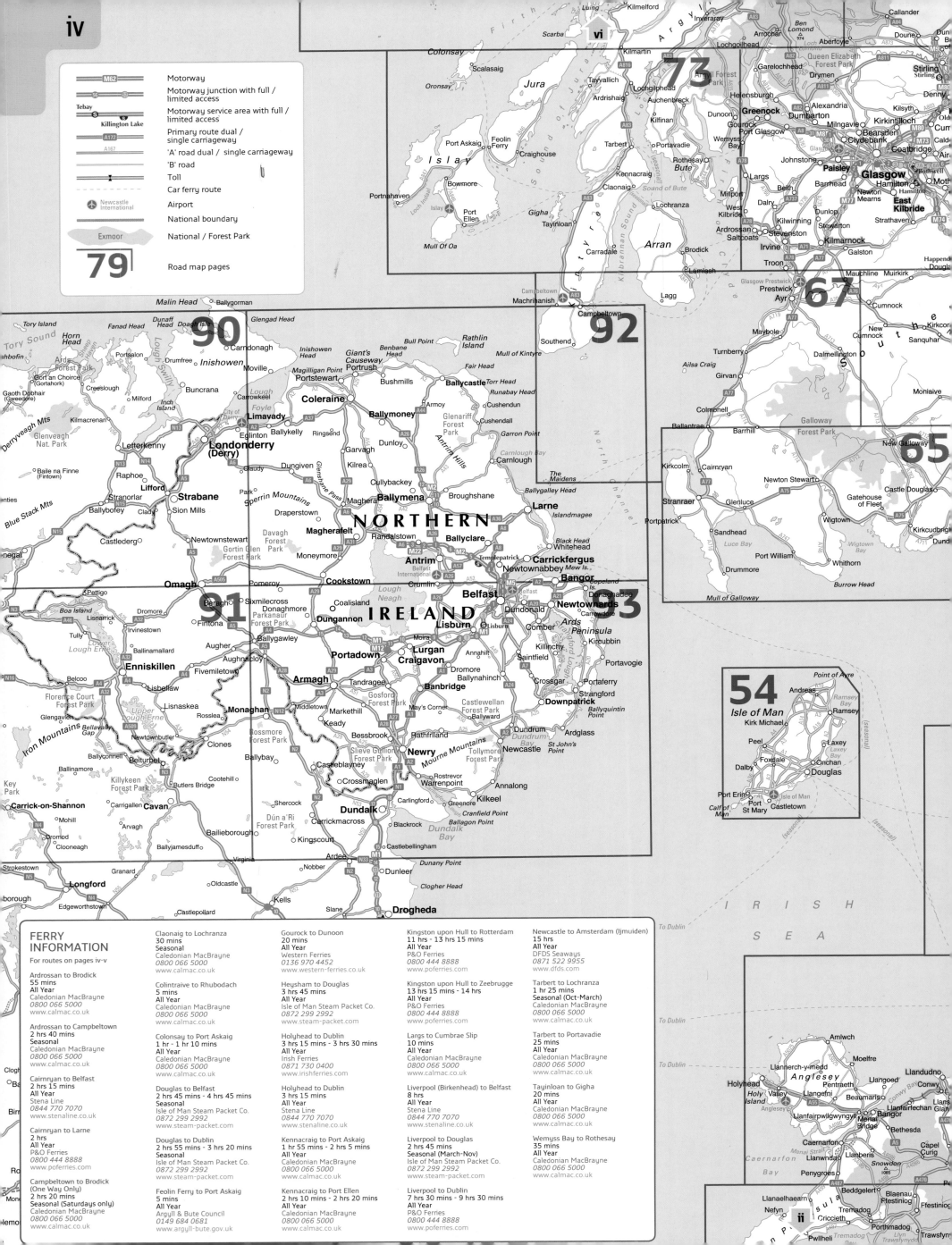

Legend

Motorway	
Motorway junction with full / limited access	
Motorway service area with full / limited access	
Primary route dual / single carriageway	
'A' road dual / single carriageway	
'B' road	
Toll	
Car ferry route	
Airport	
National boundary	
National / Forest Park	
Road map pages	

M62
Tebay
Killington Lake
A172
A167
Newcastle International
Exmoor
79

Map references

73 · vi · 92 · 67 · 65 · 90 · 91 · 93 · 83 · 54 · ii

FERRY INFORMATION

For routes on pages iv-v

Ardrossan to Brodick
55 mins
All Year
Caledonian MacBrayne
0800 066 5000
www.calmac.co.uk

Ardrossan to Campbeltown
2 hrs 40 mins
Seasonal
Caledonian MacBrayne
0800 066 5000
www.calmac.co.uk

Cairnryan to Belfast
2 hrs 15 mins
All Year
Stena Line
0844 770 7070
www.stenaline.co.uk

Cairnryan to Larne
2 hrs
All Year
P&O Ferries
0800 044 8888
www.poferries.com

Campbeltown to Brodick
(One Way Only)
2 hrs 20 mins
Seasonal (Saturdays only)
Caledonian MacBrayne
0800 066 5000
www.calmac.co.uk

Claonaig to Lochranza
30 mins
Seasonal
Caledonian MacBrayne
0800 066 5000
www.calmac.co.uk

Colintraive to Rhubodach
5 mins
All Year
Caledonian MacBrayne
0800 066 5000
www.calmac.co.uk

Colonsay to Port Askaig
1 hr - 1 hr 10 mins
All Year
Caledonian MacBrayne
0800 066 5000
www.calmac.co.uk

Douglas to Belfast
2 hrs 45 mins - 4 hrs 45 mins
Seasonal
Isle of Man Steam Packet Co.
0872 299 2992
www.steam-packet.com

Douglas to Dublin
2 hrs 55 mins - 3 hrs 20 mins
Seasonal
Isle of Man Steam Packet Co.
0872 299 2992
www.steam-packet.com

Feolin Ferry to Port Askaig
5 mins
All Year
Argyll & Bute Council
0149 684 0681
www.argyll-bute.gov.uk

Gourock to Dunoon
20 mins
All Year
Western Ferries
0136 970 4452
www.western-ferries.co.uk

Heysham to Douglas
3 hrs 45 mins
All Year
Isle of Man Steam Packet Co.
0872 299 2992
www.steam-packet.com

Holyhead to Dublin
3 hrs 15 mins - 3 hrs 30 mins
All Year
Irish Ferries
0871 730 0400
www.irishferries.com

Holyhead to Dublin
3 hrs 15 mins
All Year
Stena Line
0844 770 7070
www.stenaline.co.uk

Kennacraig to Port Askaig
1 hr 55 mins - 2 hrs 5 mins
All Year
Caledonian MacBrayne
0800 066 5000
www.calmac.co.uk

Kennacraig to Port Ellen
2 hrs 10 mins - 2 hrs 20 mins
All Year
Caledonian MacBrayne
0800 066 5000
www.calmac.co.uk

Kingston upon Hull to Rotterdam
11 hrs - 13 hrs 15 mins
All Year
P&O Ferries
0800 444 8888
www.poferries.com

Kingston upon Hull to Zeebrugge
13 hrs 15 mins - 14 hrs
All Year
P&O Ferries
0800 444 8888
www.poferries.com

Largs to Cumbrae Slip
10 mins
All Year
Caledonian MacBrayne
0800 066 5000
www.calmac.co.uk

Liverpool (Birkenhead) to Belfast
8 hrs
All Year
Stena Line
0844 770 7070
www.stenaline.co.uk

Liverpool to Douglas
2 hrs 45 mins
Seasonal (March-Nov)
Isle of Man Steam Packet Co.
0872 299 2992
www.steam-packet.com

Liverpool to Dublin
7 hrs 30 mins - 9 hrs 30 mins
All Year
P&O Ferries
0800 444 8888
www.poferries.com

Newcastle to Amsterdam (Ijmuiden)
15 hrs
All Year
DFDS Seaways
0871 522 9955
www.dfds.com

Tarbert to Lochranza
1 hr 25 mins
Seasonal (Oct-March)
Caledonian MacBrayne
0800 066 5000
www.calmac.co.uk

Tarbert to Portavadie
25 mins
All Year
Caledonian MacBrayne
0800 066 5000
www.calmac.co.uk

Tayinloan to Gigha
20 mins
All Year
Caledonian MacBrayne
0800 066 5000
www.calmac.co.uk

Wemyss Bay to Rothesay
35 mins
All Year
Caledonian MacBrayne
0800 066 5000
www.calmac.co.uk

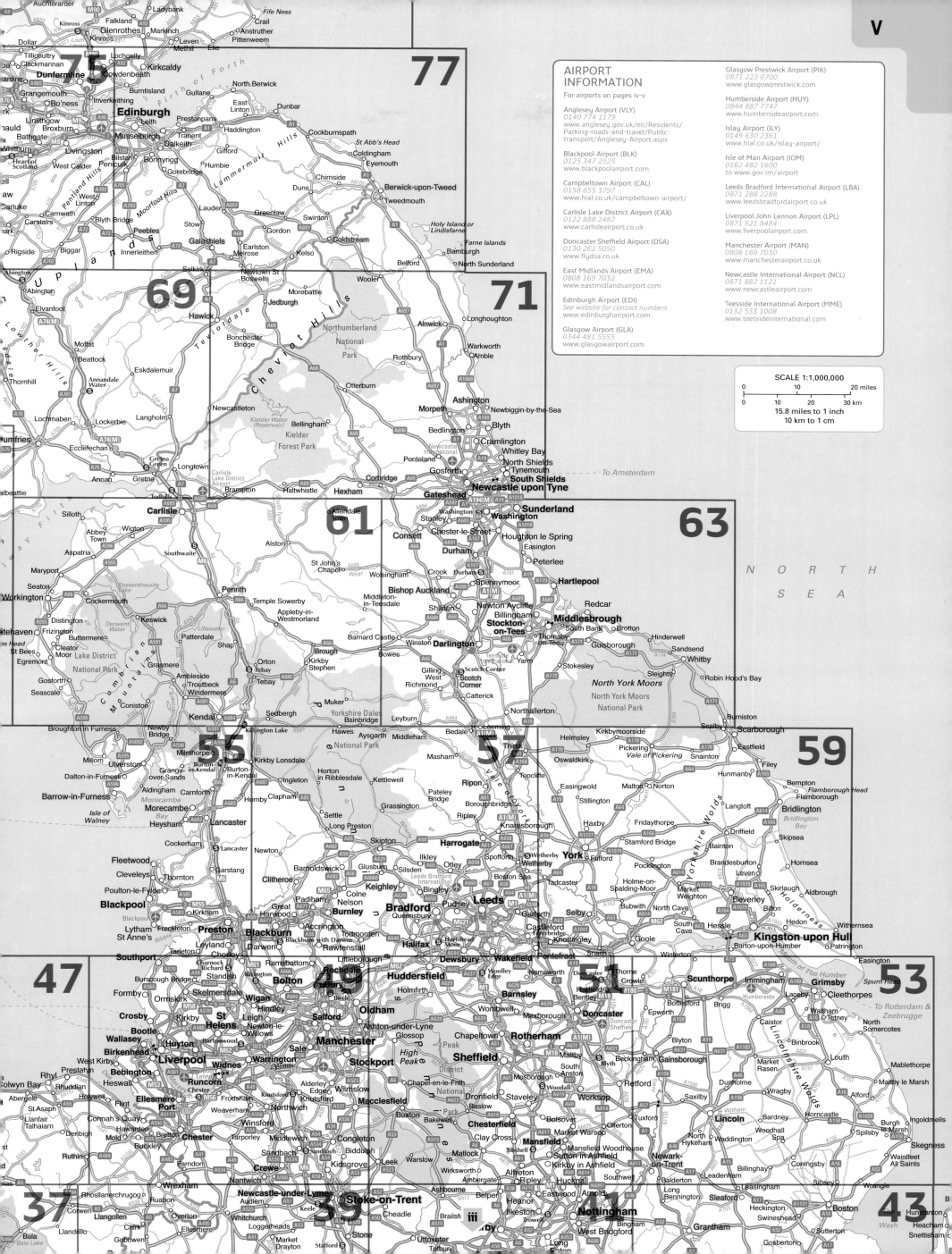

v

AIRPORT INFORMATION

For airports on pages iv–v

Anglesey Airport (VLY)
0140 774 1179
www.anglesey.gov.uk/en/Residents/
Parking-roads-and-travel/Public-
transport/Anglesey-Airport.aspx

Blackpool Airport (BLK)
0125 347 2525
www.blackpoolairport.com

Campbeltown Airport (CAL)
0158 655 3797
www.hial.co.uk/campbeltown-airport/

Carlisle Lake District Airport (CAX)
0122 888 2482
www.carlisleairport.co.uk

Doncaster Sheffield Airport (DSA)
0130 262 5050
www.flydsa.co.uk

East Midlands Airport (EMA)
0808 169 7032
www.eastmidlandsairport.com

Edinburgh Airport (EDI)
See website for contact numbers
www.edinburghairport.com

Glasgow Airport (GLA)
0344 481 5555
www.glasgowairport.com

Glasgow Prestwick Airport (PIK)
0871 223 0700
www.glasgowprestwick.com

Humberside Airport (HUY)
0844 887 7747
www.humbersideairport.com

Islay Airport (ILY)
0149 630 2361
www.hial.co.uk/islay-airport/

Isle of Man Airport (IOM)
0162 482 1600
to www.gov.im/airport

Leeds Bradford International Airport (LBA)
0871 288 2288
www.leedsbradfordairport.co.uk

Liverpool John Lennon Airport (LPL)
0871 521 8484
www.liverpoolairport.com

Manchester Airport (MAN)
0808 169 7030
www.manchesterairport.co.uk

Newcastle International Airport (NCL)
0871 882 1121
www.newcastleairport.com

Teesside International Airport (MME)
0132 533 1008
www.teessideinternational.com

SCALE 1:1,000,000

0   10   20 miles
0   10   20   30 km

15.8 miles to 1 inch
10 km to 1 cm

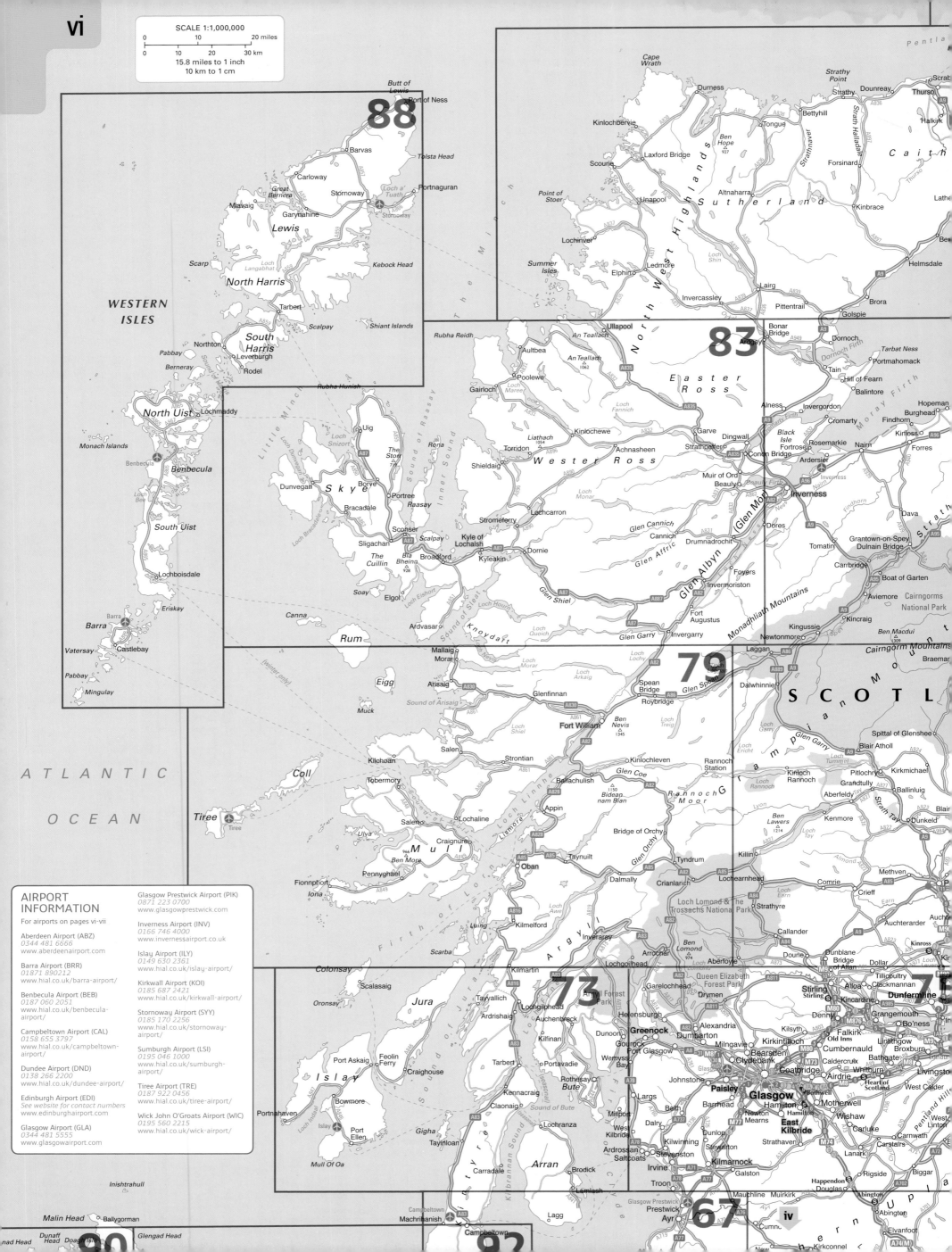

SCALE 1:1,000,000

0 10 20 miles
0 10 20 30 km

15.8 miles to 1 inch
10 km to 1 cm

AIRPORT INFORMATION

For airports on pages vi-vii

Aberdeen Airport (ABZ)
0344 481 6666
www.aberdeenairport.com

Barra Airport (BRR)
01871 890212
www.hial.co.uk/barra-airport/

Benbecula Airport (BEB)
0187 060 2051
www.hial.co.uk/benbecula-airport/

Campbeltown Airport (CAL)
0158 655 3797
www.hial.co.uk/campbeltown-airport/

Dundee Airport (DND)
0138 266 2200
www.hial.co.uk/dundee-airport/

Edinburgh Airport (EDI)
See website for contact numbers
www.edinburghairport.com

Glasgow Airport (GLA)
0344 481 5555
www.glasgowairport.com

Glasgow Prestwick Airport (PIK)
0871 223 0700
www.glasgowprestwick.com

Inverness Airport (INV)
0166 746 4000
www.invernessairport.co.uk

Islay Airport (ILY)
0149 630 2361
www.hial.co.uk/islay-airport/

Kirkwall Airport (KOI)
0185 687 2421
www.hial.co.uk/kirkwall-airport/

Stornoway Airport (SYY)
0185 170 2256
www.hial.co.uk/stornoway-airport/

Sumburgh Airport (LSI)
0195 046 1000
www.hial.co.uk/sumburgh-airport/

Tiree Airport (TRE)
0187 922 0456
www.hial.co.uk/tiree-airport/

Wick John O'Groats Airport (WIC)
0195 560 2215
www.hial.co.uk/wick-airport/

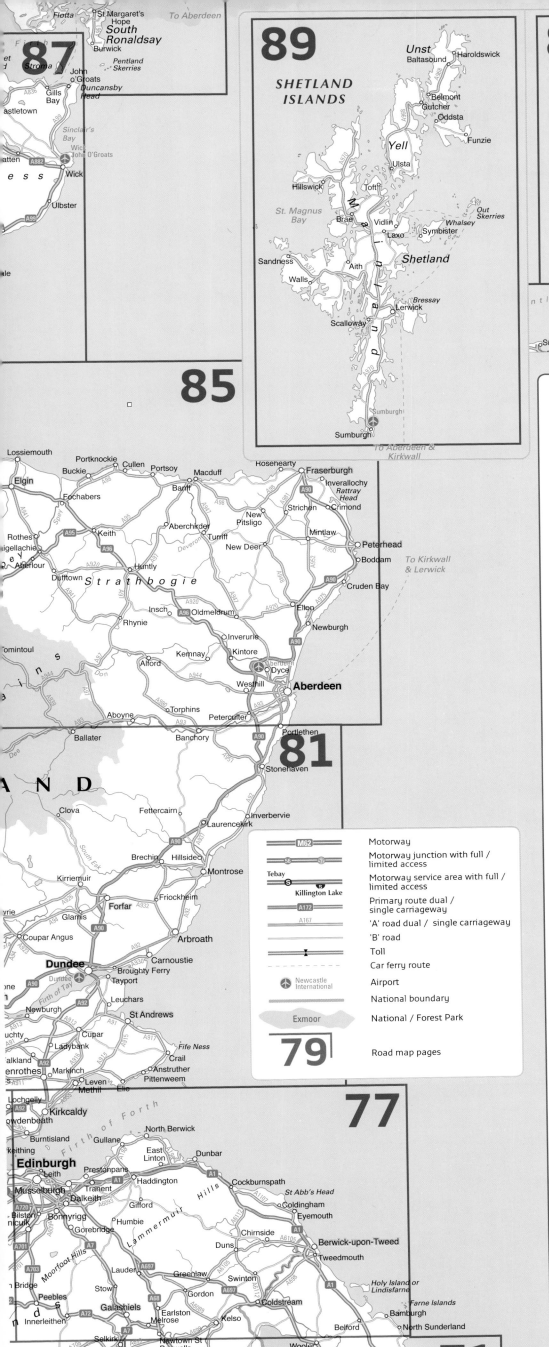
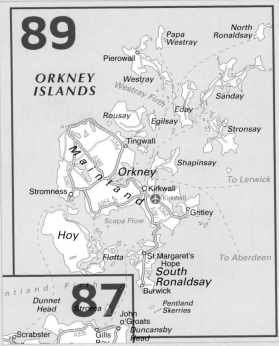

87

89 SHETLAND ISLANDS

89 ORKNEY ISLANDS

85

81

77

69

71

79

	Motorway
	Motorway junction with full / limited access
	Motorway service area with full / limited access
	Primary route dual / single carriageway
	'A' road dual / single carriageway
	'B' road
	Toll
	Car ferry route
Newcastle International	Airport
	National boundary
Exmoor	National / Forest Park
79	Road map pages

FERRY INFORMATION

For routes on pages vi-vii

Aberdeen to Kirkwall
6 hrs
All Year
North Link Ferries
0845 600 0449
www.northlinkferries.co.uk

Aberdeen to Lerwick
12 hrs 30 mins - 14 hrs 30 mins
All Year
North Link Ferries
0845 600 0449
www.northlinkferries.co.uk

Ardrossan to Brodick
55 mins
All Year
Caledonian MacBrayne
0800 066 5000

Ardrossan to Campbeltown
2 hrs 40 mins
Seasonal
Caledonian MacBrayne
0800 066 5000

Barra to Eriskay
40 mins
All Year
Caledonian MacBrayne
0800 066 5000
www.calmac.co.uk

Belmont to Gutcher
10 mins
All Year
Shetland Islands Council
0180 624 4200
www.shetland.gov.uk/ferries/

Belmont to Hamars Ness
25 mins
All Year
Shetland Islands Council
0180 624 4200
www.shetland.gov.uk/ferries/

Campbeltown to Brodick
(One Way Only)
2 hrs 20 mins
Seasonal (Saturdays only)
Caledonian MacBrayne
0800 066 5000

Claonaig to Lochranza
30 mins
Seasonal
Caledonian MacBrayne
0800 066 5000
www.calmac.co.uk

Coll to Tiree
55 mins - 1 hr
All Year
Caledonian MacBrayne
0800 066 5000

Colonsay to Port Askaig
1 hr - 1 hr 10 mins
All Year
Caledonian MacBrayne
0800 066 5000
www.calmac.co.uk

Cromarty to Nigg
5 mins
Seasonal
Highland Ferries
0746 841 7137
www.highlandferries.co.uk

Eday to Sanday
20 mins
All Year
Orkney Ferries
0185 687 2044
www.orkneyferries.co.uk

Eday to Stronsay
35 mins
All Year
Orkney Ferries
0185 687 2044
www.orkneyferries.co.uk

Egilsay to Rousay
15 mins - 30 mins
All Year
Orkney Ferries
0185 687 2044
www.orkneyferries.co.uk

Egilsay to Wyre
15 mins - 20 mins
All Year
Orkney Ferries
0185 687 2044

Gill's Bay to St. Margaret's Hope
1 hr
All Year
Pentland Ferries
0185 683 1226
www.pentlandferries.co.uk

Glenelg to Kylerhea
5 mins
Seasonal
Skye Ferry
0159 952 2700
www.skyeferry.co.uk

Gourock to Dunoon
20 mins
All Year
Western Ferries
0136 970 4452
www.western-ferries.co.uk

Gutcher to Hamars Ness
25 mins - 35 mins
All Year
Shetland Islands Council
0180 624 4200
www.shetland.gov.uk/ferries/

Houton to Flotta
35 mins - 1 hr 5 mins
All Year
Orkney Ferries
0185 687 2044
www.orkneyferries.co.uk

Houton to Lyness
35 mins - 1 hr 5 mins
All Year
Orkney Ferries
0185 687 2044
www.orkneyferries.co.uk

Kennacraig to Port Askaig
1 hr 55 mins - 2 hrs 5 mins
All Year
Caledonian MacBrayne
0800 066 5000
www.calmac.co.uk

Kennacraig to Port Ellen
2 hrs 10 mins - 2 hrs 20 mins
All Year
Caledonian MacBrayne
0800 066 5000
www.calmac.co.uk

Kirkwall to Eday
1 hr 15 mins - 2 hrs 55 mins
All Year
Orkney Ferries
0185 687 2044
www.orkneyferries.co.uk

Kirkwall to North Ronaldsay
2 hrs 40 mins
All Year
Orkney Ferries
0185 687 2044
www.orkneyferries.co.uk

Kirkwall to Papa Westray
1 hr 50 mins - 2 hrs 15 mins
All Year
Orkney Ferries
0185 687 2044
www.orkneyferries.co.uk

Kirkwall to Sanday
1 hr 25 mins - 2 hrs 25 mins
All Year
Orkney Ferries
0185 687 2044
www.orkneyferries.co.uk

Kirkwall to Shapinsay
25 mins
All Year
Orkney Ferries
0185 687 2044
www.orkneyferries.co.uk

Kirkwall to Stronsay
1 hr 35 mins - 2 hrs 35 mins
All Year
Orkney Ferries
0185 687 2044
www.orkneyferries.co.uk

Kirkwall to Westray
1 hr 25 mins
All Year
Orkney Ferries
0185 687 2044
www.orkneyferries.co.uk

Largs to Cumbrae Slip
10 mins
All Year
Caledonian MacBrayne
0800 066 5000
www.calmac.co.uk

Laxo to Symbister
30 mins
All Year
Shetland Islands Council
0180 624 4200
www.shetland.gov.uk/ferries/

Lerwick to Bressay
7 mins
All Year
Shetland Islands Council
0180 624 4200
www.shetland.gov.uk/ferries/

Lerwick to Kirkwall
5 hrs 30 mins - 7 hrs 45 mins
All Year
North Link Ferries
0845 6000 449
www.northlinkferries.co.uk

Lerwick to Skerries
2 hrs 15 mins
All Year
Shetland Islands Council
0180 624 4200
www.shetland.gov.uk/ferries/

Leverburgh to Berneray
1 hr - 1 hr 10 mins
All Year
Caledonian MacBrayne
0800 066 5000
www.calmac.co.uk

Lochaline to Fishnish
18 mins
All Year
Caledonian MacBrayne
0800 066 5000
www.calmac.co.uk

Longhope to Flotta
20 mins - 40 mins
All Year
Orkney Ferries
0185 687 2044
www.orkneyferries.co.uk

Longhope to Lyness
20 mins - 50 mins
All Year
Orkney Ferries
0185 687 2044
www.orkneyferries.co.uk

Luing to Seil
5 mins
All Year
Argyll and Bute Council
0185 230 0252
www.argyll-bute.gov.uk

Lyness to Flotta
15 mins - 20 mins
All Year
Orkney Ferries
0185 687 2044
www.orkneyferries.co.uk

Mallaig to Armadale
30 mins
All Year
Caledonian MacBrayne
0800 066 5000
www.calmac.co.uk

Mallaig to Lochboisdale
3 hrs 30 mins
All Year
Caledonian MacBrayne
0800 066 5000
www.calmac.co.uk

Oban to Castlebay
4 hrs 45 mins - 5 hrs 30 mins
All Year
Caledonian MacBrayne
0800 066 5000
www.calmac.co.uk

Oban to Coll
2 hrs 40 mins
All Year
Caledonian MacBrayne
0800 066 5000
www.calmac.co.uk

Oban to Colonsay
2 hrs 15 mins - 2 hrs 40 mins
All Year
Caledonian MacBrayne
0800 066 5000
www.calmac.co.uk

Oban to Craignure
46 mins
All Year
Caledonian MacBrayne
0800 066 5000
www.calmac.co.uk

Oban to Lismore
55 mins
All Year
Caledonian MacBrayne
0800 066 5000
www.calmac.co.uk

Oban to Lochboisdale
5 hrs 10 mins - 5 hrs 45 mins
Winter only
Caledonian MacBrayne
0800 066 5000
www.calmac.co.uk

Oban to Tiree
3 hrs 30 mins - 3 hrs 50 mins
All Year
Caledonian MacBrayne
0800 066 5000

Rousay to Wyre
5 mins - 10 mins
All Year
Orkney Ferries
0185 687 2044
www.orkneyferries.co.uk

Sconser to Raasay
25 mins
All Year
Caledonian MacBrayne
0800 066 5000
www.calmac.co.uk

Scrabster to Stromness
1 hr 30 mins
All Year
North Link Ferries
0845 6000 449
www.northlinkferries.co.uk

Tarbert to Lochranza
1 hr 25 mins
Seasonal (Oct-March)
Caledonian MacBrayne
0800 066 5000
www.calmac.co.uk

Tarbert to Portavadie
25 mins
All Year
Caledonian MacBrayne
0800 066 5000
www.calmac.co.uk

Tayinloan to Gigha
20 mins
All Year
Caledonian MacBrayne
0800 066 5000
www.calmac.co.uk

Tingwall to Rousay
25 mins - 40 mins
All Year
Orkney Ferries
0185 687 2044
www.orkneyferries.co.uk

Tobermory to Kilchoan
35 mins
All Year
Caledonian MacBrayne
0800 066 5000
www.calmac.co.uk

Toft to Ulsta
20 mins
All Year
Shetland Islands Council
0180 624 4200
www.shetland.gov.uk/ferries/

Uig to Lochmaddy
1 hr 45 mins
All Year
Caledonian MacBrayne
0800 066 5000
www.calmac.co.uk

Uig to Tarbert
1 hr 40 mins
All Year
Caledonian MacBrayne
0800 066 5000
www.calmac.co.uk

Ullapool to Stornoway
2 hrs 30 mins - 2 hrs 45 mins
All Year
Caledonian MacBrayne
0800 066 5000
www.calmac.co.uk

Vidlin to Skerries
1 hr 30 mins
All Year
Shetland Islands Council
0180 624 4200
www.shetland.gov.uk/ferries/

Wemyss Bay to Rothesay
35 mins
All Year
Caledonian MacBrayne
0800 066 5000
www.calmac.co.uk

Westray to Papa Westray
20 mins - 25 mins
All Year
Orkney Ferries
0185 687 2044
www.orkneyferries.co.uk

Wyre to Tingwall
25 mins - 45 mins
All Year
Orkney Ferries
0185 687 2044

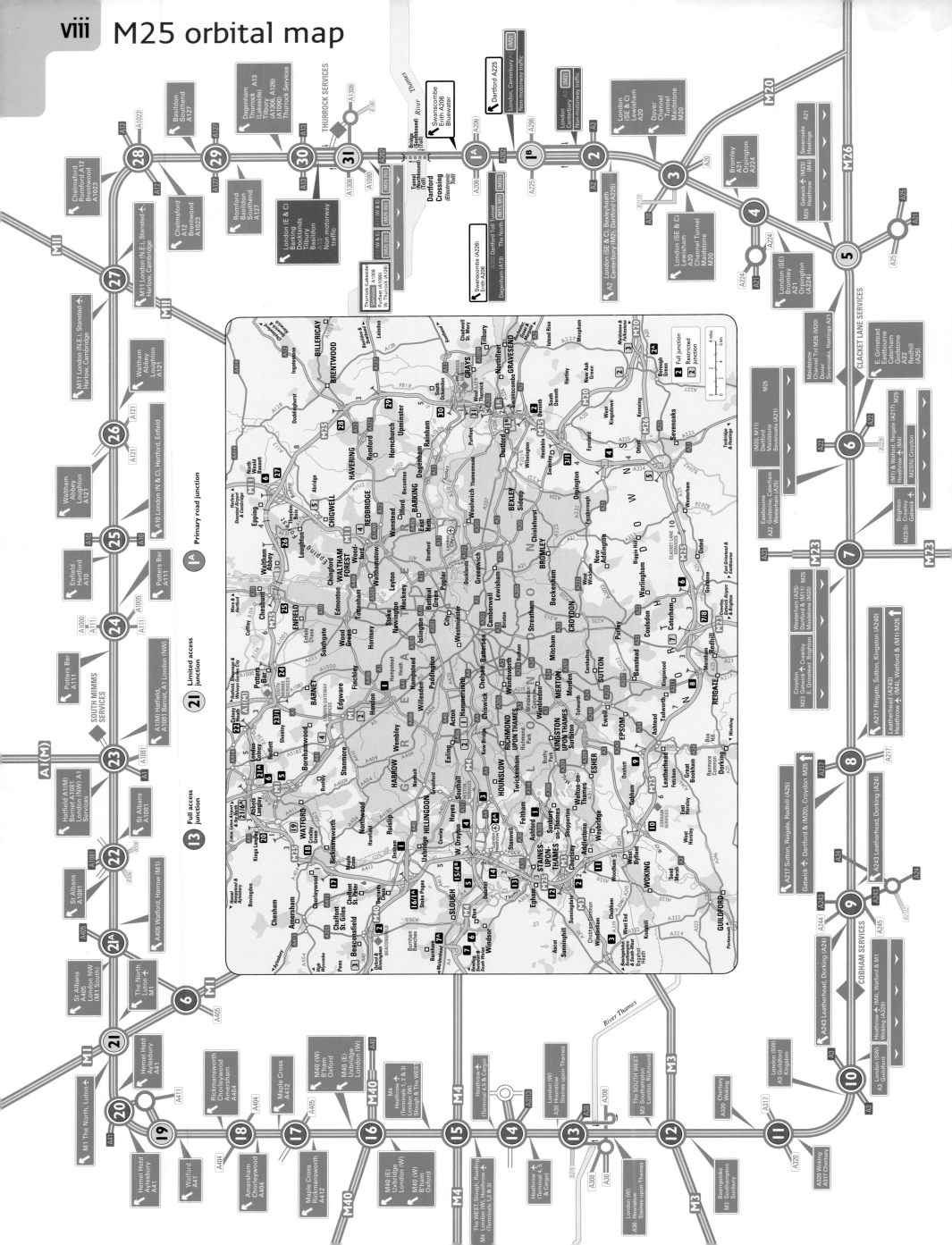

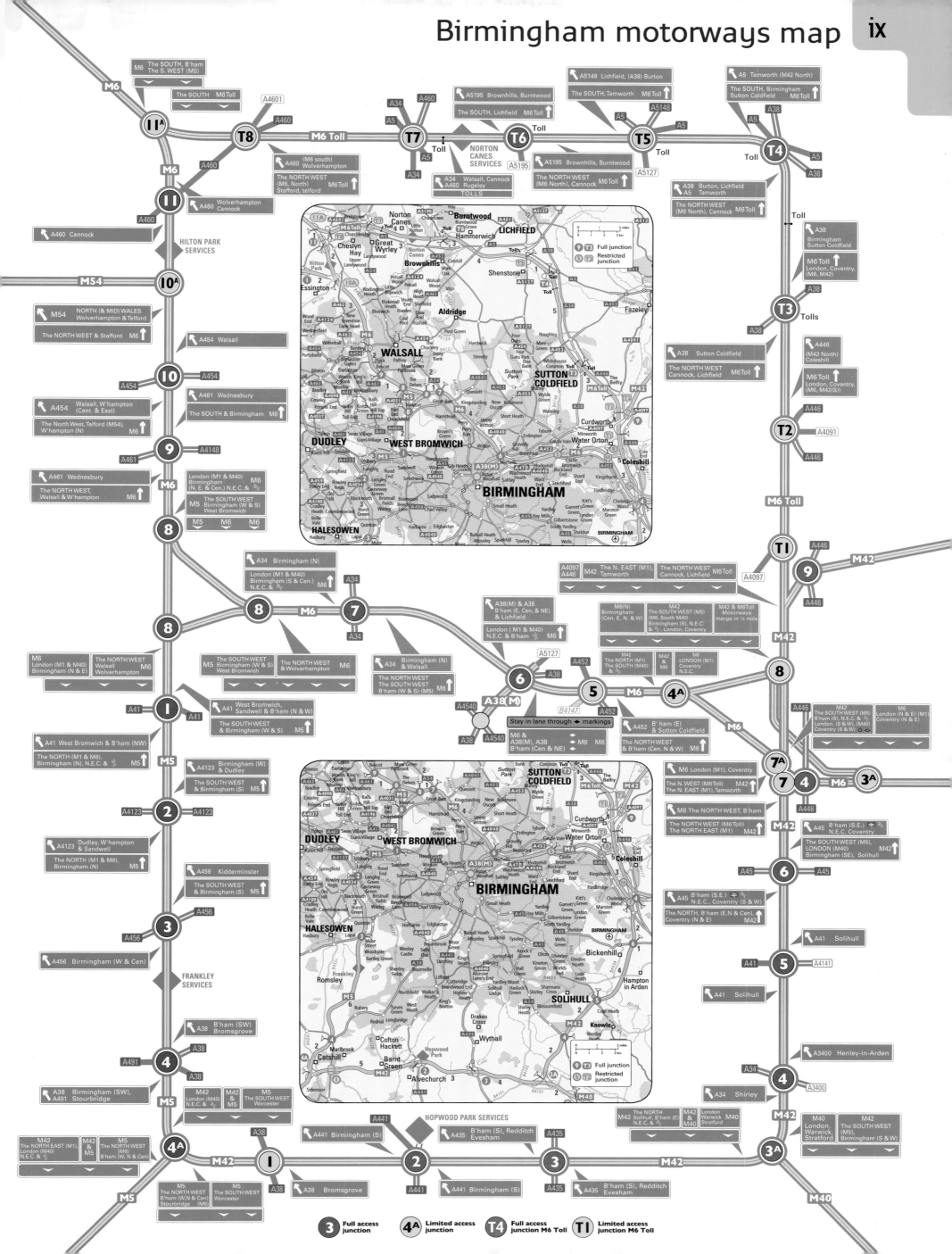

Motorway services information

All motorway service areas have fuel, food, toilets, disabled facilities and free short-term parking

For further information on motorway services providers:
Moto www.moto-way.com
Euro Garages www.eurogarages.com
RoadChef www.roadchef.com
Extra www.extraservices.co.uk
Welcome Break www.welcomebreak.co.uk
Westmorland www.westmorland.com

Motorway Services ½m
Petrol

Facility columns (left to right): Information, Accommodation, Conference facilities, Showers, M&S Simply Food, Waitrose, Costa Coffee, Starbucks, Burger King, KFC, McDonalds

Motorway	Junction	Service provider	Service name	Fuel supplier	Info	Accom	Conf	Showers	M&S	Waitrose	Costa	Starbucks	BK	KFC	McD
A1(M)	1	Welcome Break	South Mimms	BP	●	●	●	●		●		●	●	●	
	10	Extra	Baldock	Shell	●	●	●	●			●				●
	17	Extra	Peterborough	Shell	●	●		●		●				●	●
	34	Moto	Blyth	Esso	●	●		●		●		●			
	46	Moto	Wetherby	BP	●	●		●		●		●			
	53	Moto	Scotch Corner	Esso	●			●		●		●			
	61	RoadChef	Durham	Shell	●		●	●		●					●
	64	Moto	Washington	BP	●	●						●			
A74(M)	16	RoadChef	Annandale Water	BP	●	●			●						●
	22	Welcome Break	Gretna Green	BP	●	●		●		●	●		●	●	
M1	2-4	Welcome Break	London Gateway	Shell	●	●	●	●		●		●			
	11-12	Moto	Toddington	BP	●	●		●		●		●			●
	14-15	Welcome Break	Newport Pagnell	Shell	●	●		●		●		●			
	15A	RoadChef	Northampton	BP	●					●					●
	16-17	RoadChef	Watford Gap	BP	●	●	●	●		●					●
	21-21A	Welcome Break	Leicester Forest East	Shell	●	●		●				●			
	22	Euro Garages	Markfield	BP	●			●							
	23A	Moto	Donington Park	BP	●	●		●	●	●		●			
	25-26	Moto	Trowell	BP	●	●		●		●		●			
	28-29	RoadChef	Tibshelf	Shell	●	●		●		●					●
	30-31	Welcome Break	Woodall	Shell	●	●		●		●		●	●	●	
	38-39	Moto	Woolley Edge	BP	●	●		●		●		●			
M2	4-5	Moto	Medway	BP	●			●		●					
M3	4A-5	Welcome Break	Fleet	Shell	●	●	●	●		●		●	●	●	●
	8-9	Moto	Winchester	BP	●	●		●		●					
M4	3	Moto	Heston	BP	●	●	●	●		●		●			
	11-12	Moto	Reading	BP	●	●	●	●		●		●			●
	13	Moto	Chieveley	BP	●	●	●	●		●		●			●
	14-15	Welcome Break	Membury	BP	●	●		●	●			●			●
	17-18	Moto	Leigh Delamere	BP	●	●	●	●		●		●			
	23A	RoadChef	Magor	Esso	●	●				●					●
	30	Welcome Break	Cardiff Gate	Shell	●	●					●		●		
	33	Moto	Cardiff West	Esso	●	●		●		●					
	36	Welcome Break	Sarn Park	Shell	●	●		●		●					
	47	Moto	Swansea	BP	●	●				●					
	49	RoadChef	Pont Abraham	Esso	●					●					●
M5	3-4	Moto	Frankley	BP	●			●		●					
	8	RoadChef	Strensham (South)	BP	●										
	8	RoadChef	Strensham (North)	Texaco	●	●	●			●					
	11-12	Westmorland	Gloucester	Texaco	●										
	13-14	Welcome Break	Michaelwood	BP	●	●	●	●	●		●	●	●		
	19	Welcome Break	Gordano	Shell	●	●	●	●	●		●	●	●		
	21-22	RoadChef	Sedgemoor (South)	Shell	●			●		●					
	21-22	Welcome Break	Sedgemoor (North)	Shell	●	●	●	●		●		●			
	24	Moto	Bridgwater	BP	●	●		●		●					
	25-26	RoadChef	Taunton Deane	Shell	●	●		●		●					●
	27	Moto	Tiverton	Shell	●	●		●		●					
	28	Extra	Cullompton	Shell				●							
	29-30	Moto	Exeter	BP	●	●		●		●		●			
M6 Toll	T6-T7	RoadChef	Norton Canes	BP	●	●	●			●				●	●

Motorway	Junction	Service provider	Service name	Fuel supplier	Info	Accom	Conf	Showers	M&S	Waitrose	Costa	Starbucks	BK	KFC	McD
M6	3-4	Welcome Break	Corley	Shell	●	●		●		●	●	●	●	●	
	10-11	Moto	Hilton Park	BP	●	●		●		●		●			●
	14-15	RoadChef	Stafford (South)	Esso	●	●		●		●					●
	14-15	Moto	Stafford (North)	BP	●	●		●		●		●			
	15-16	Welcome Break	Keele	Shell	●	●		●		●		●			
	16-17	RoadChef	Sandbach	BP	●	●		●		●					●
	18-19	Moto	Knutsford	BP	●	●		●		●		●			●
	20	Moto	Lymm	BP	●	●		●		●					
	27-28	Welcome Break	Charnock Richard	Shell	●	●		●		●		●			
	32-33	Moto	Lancaster	BP	●	●		●		●		●			
	35A-36	Moto	Burton-in-Kendal (N)	BP	●	●		●		●					
	36-37	RoadChef	Killington Lake (S)	BP	●	●		●		●					
	38-39	Westmorland	Tebay	Total	●	●	●	●							
	41-42	Moto	Southwaite	BP	●	●		●		●		●			
	44-45	Moto	Todhills	BP/Shell	●										
M8	4-5	BP	Heart of Scotland	BP			●	●	●						
M9	9	Moto	Stirling	BP	●	●		●		●					
M11	8	Welcome Break	Birchanger Green	Shell	●	●	●	●			●	●		●	●
M18	5	Moto	Doncaster North	BP	●	●		●		●					
M20	8	RoadChef	Maidstone	Esso	●	●		●		●					●
	11	Stop 24	Stop 24	Shell	●	●							●		
M23	11	Moto	Pease Pottage	BP	●			●		●					
M25	5-6	RoadChef	Clacket Lane	BP	●			●		●					●
	9-10	Extra	Cobham	Shell	●	●		●			●			●	●
	23	Welcome Break	South Mimms	BP	●	●		●	●			●			
	30	Moto	Thurrock	Esso	●	●		●	●						
M27	3-4	RoadChef	Rownhams	BP	●	●									
M40	2	Extra	Beaconsfield	Shell	●	●	●	●		●	●		●	●	●
	8	Welcome Break	Oxford	BP	●	●	●	●		●	●		●		
	10	Moto	Cherwell Valley	Esso	●	●		●		●		●			
	12-13	Welcome Break	Warwick	BP	●	●	●	●		●		●			
M42	2	Welcome Break	Hopwood Park	Shell	●	●		●		●	●		●		
	10	Moto	Tamworth	Esso	●	●		●		●		●			●
M48	1	Moto	Severn View	BP	●	●		●		●					
M54	4	Welcome Break	Telford	Shell	●	●		●		●					
M56	14	RoadChef	Chester	Shell	●	●	●			●					●
M61	6-7	Euro Garages	Rivington	BP	●	●		●		●					
M62	7-9	Welcome Break	Burtonwood	Shell	●			●		●					
	18-19	Moto	Birch	BP	●	●		●		●		●			
	25-26	Welcome Break	Hartshead Moor	Shell	●	●		●		●		●			
	33	Moto	Ferrybridge	BP	●	●		●		●					
M65	4	Extra	Blackburn with Darwen	Shell	●	●		●			●				
M74	4-5	RoadChef	Bothwell (South)	Shell	●	●		●		●					●
	5-6	RoadChef	Hamilton (North)	Shell	●	●		●		●					●
	11-12	Cairn Lodge	Happendon	Shell	●			●							
	12-13	Welcome Break	Abington	Shell	●	●						●	●		
M80	6-7	Shell	Old Inns	Shell	●			●		●					
M90	6	Moto	Kinross	BP	●	●		●		●					

There are a number of operators of motorway service areas in Britain; RoadChef, Welcome Break and Moto being the biggest three. All motorway service areas are required by law to provide fuel, free toilets and free short term parking 24 hours a day. Details of other facilities provided at each service area are shown opposite, although most of these will not be open 24 hours a day.

As part of its *Think, don't drive tired* road safety campaign the Government has the following tips for drivers:

- If you are feeling tired, opening the window or turning up the radio does not work, instead find a safe place to stop.
- On long journeys take a 15 minute break every 2 hours.
- If feeling tired, a 15 minute nap will help as will drinking 2 cups of coffee or other high caffeine drink. The most effective solution is to have some caffeine and then take a short sleep which gives the caffeine time to kick in.
- Avoid making long trips between midnight and 6am when you are most susceptible to sleepiness.
- Don't begin a journey if you are already feeling tired.

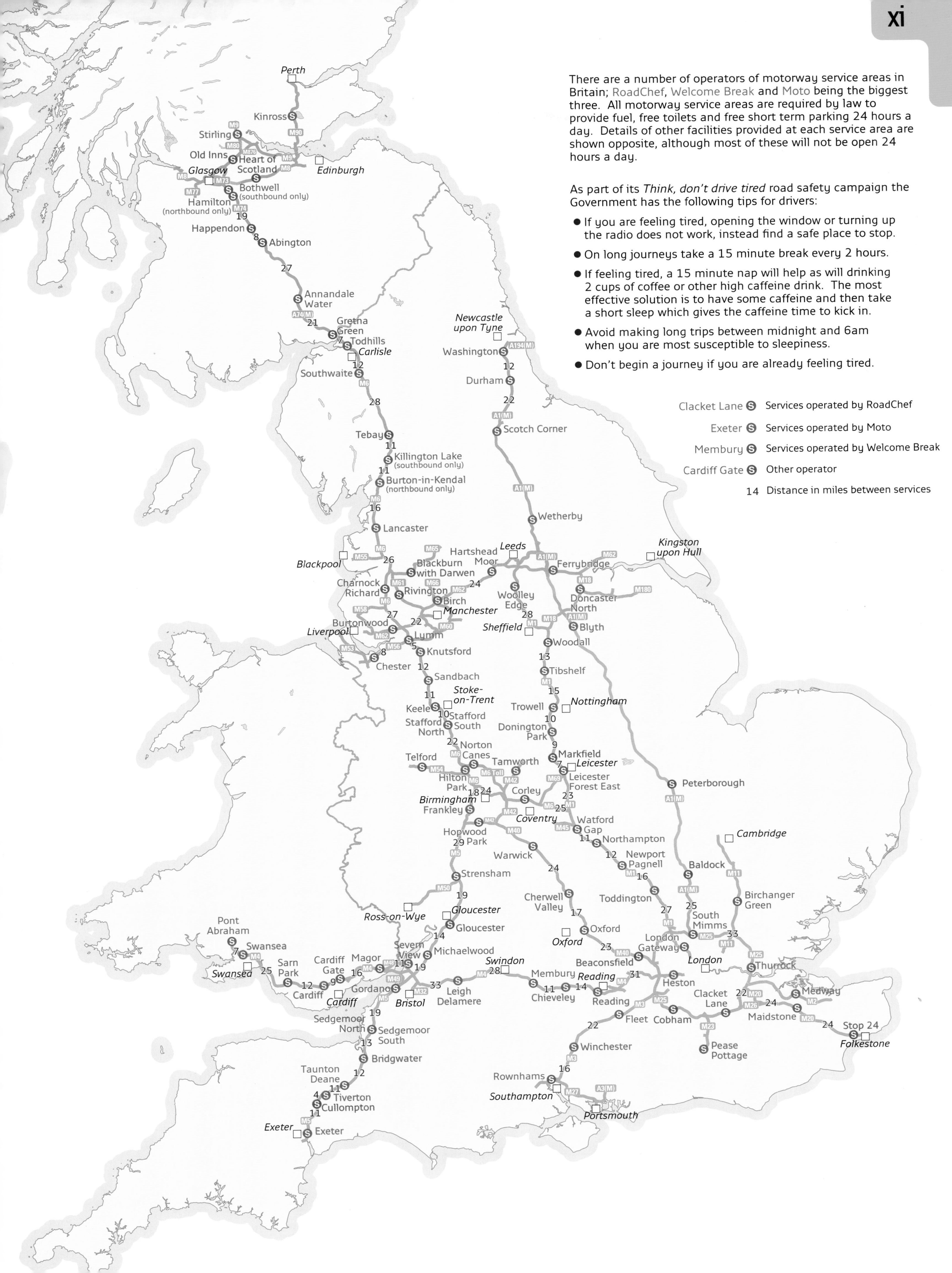

Clacket Lane ⓢ Services operated by RoadChef
Exeter ⓢ Services operated by Moto
Membury ⓢ Services operated by Welcome Break
Cardiff Gate ⓢ Other operator
14 Distance in miles between services

Perth
Kinross ⓢ
Stirling ⓢ M9
M80 M90
Old Inns ⓢ Heart of M9
Glasgow Scotland ⓢ M8 Edinburgh
M8 M73
M77 Bothwell (southbound only) ⓢ
Hamilton (northbound only) M74
19
Happendon 8 ⓢ Abington
27
Annandale Water ⓢ
A74(M) 21
Gretha Green ⓢ
7 Todhills ⓢ
Carlisle
12
Southwaite ⓢ M6
28
Tebay ⓢ
11
Killington Lake (southbound only) ⓢ
11
Burton-in-Kendal (northbound only) ⓢ
M6 16
Lancaster ⓢ
M65 Hartshead Leeds
Blackpool M55 26 Blackburn Moor ⓢ
with Darwen ⓢ 24
Charnock M61 Rivington ⓢ Woolley
Richard ⓢ Birch ⓢ Edge ⓢ
M58 27 Manchester 28
Burtonwood ⓢ 22 M60 Sheffield ⓢ
Liverpool Lymm ⓢ M62
M53 8 5 ⓢ Knutsford
Chester 12
Sandbach ⓢ
11
Keele ⓢ 10 Stafford ⓢ
Stafford ⓢ South
North 22 Norton
Telford ⓢ M6 Canes ⓢ
M54 Tamworth ⓢ
Hilton M6 M6 Toll
Park ⓢ 18 24 Corley
Birmingham M42
Frankley ⓢ
Hopwood M40
29 Park ⓢ
M5 Warwick
Strensham ⓢ
M50 19
Cherwell
Ross-on-Wye Gloucester Valley ⓢ
Gloucester ⓢ
14
Pont Michaelwood ⓢ
Abraham ⓢ Severn Swindon
Swansea View ⓢ 28
7 ⓢ M4 Magor ⓢ Membury ⓢ Reading
Sarn Cardiff 11 19
Swansea Park ⓢ Gate ⓢ 16 Chieveley
25 9 Reading
12 Gordano ⓢ
Cardiff M32 33 Leigh
Cardiff M5 Delamere ⓢ
Bristol
19
Sedgemoor ⓢ
North ⓢ Sedgemoor
13 South ⓢ
ⓢ Bridgwater
Taunton 12
Deane ⓢ
11 Rownhams ⓢ
4 ⓢ Tiverton 16
11 Cullompton Southampton
M5 M27 Portsmouth
Exeter ⓢ Exeter

Newcastle upon Tyne
Washington ⓢ A194(M)
12
Durham ⓢ
22
A1(M)
ⓢ Scotch Corner
A1(M)
ⓢ Wetherby
A1(M) M62 Kingston
Ferrybridge ⓢ upon Hull
M18
Doncaster M180
North ⓢ
M18 M1
Blyth ⓢ
Woodall ⓢ
13
Tibshelf ⓢ
M1
15
Trowell ⓢ Nottingham
10
Donington
Park ⓢ
9
Markfield ⓢ
7 Leicester
Leicester
Forest East ⓢ
M69 ⓢ Peterborough
23 A1(M)
M6 25
Coventry
Watford Cambridge
M45 ⓢ Gap ⓢ
11 ⓢ Northampton
12 Newport
Pagnell ⓢ Baldock
16 M11
A1(M) Birchanger
Toddington ⓢ 25 Green ⓢ
27 South M11
M1 Mimms ⓢ 33
London
Oxford Gateway ⓢ M25
23 M40 London M25
Beaconsfield ⓢ Thurrock ⓢ
31 Heston ⓢ
14 M4 Clacket 22 Medway ⓢ
Reading ⓢ M3 M25 Lane ⓢ 24
22 ⓢ Fleet Cobham ⓢ Maidstone M20
Winchester ⓢ M23 24 Stop 24
ⓢ Pease ⓢ Folkestone
Pottage

Restricted motorway junctions are shown on the maps as

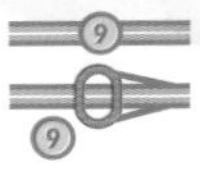

A1(M) LONDON TO NEWCASTLE

②
Northbound : No access
Southbound : No exit

③
Southbound : No access

⑤
Northbound : No exit
Southbound : No access
: No exit

④
Northbound : No exit to M62 Eastbound

④③
Northbound : No exit to M1 Westbound

Dishforth
Southbound : No access from A168 Eastbound

⑤⑦
Northbound : No access
: Exit only to A66(M) Northbound
Southbound : Access only from A66(M) Southbound
: No exit

⑤⑤
Northbound : No access from A1
Southbound : No exit to A1

A3(M) PORTSMOUTH

①
Northbound : No exit
Southbound : No access

④
Northbound : No access
Southbound : No exit

A38(M) BIRMINGHAM

Victoria Road
Northbound : No exit
Southbound : No access

A48(M) CARDIFF

Junction with M4
Westbound : No access from M4 ㉙ Eastbound
Eastbound : No exit to M4 ㉘ Westbound

㉙A
Westbound : No exit to A48 Eastbound
Eastbound : No access from A48 Westbound

A57(M) MANCHESTER

Brook Street
Westbound : No exit
Eastbound : No access

A58(M) LEEDS

Westgate
Southbound : No access
Woodhouse Lane
Westbound : No exit

A64(M) LEEDS

Claypit Lane
Eastbound : No access

A66(M) DARLINGTON

Junction with A1(M)
Northbound : No access from A1(M) Southbound
: No exit
Southbound : No access
: No exit to A1(M) Northbound

A74(M) LOCKERBIE

⑱
Northbound : No access
Southbound : No exit

A167(M) NEWCASTLE

Campden Street
Northbound : No exit
Southbound : No access
: No exit

M1 LONDON TO LEEDS

②
Northbound : No exit
Southbound : No access

④
Northbound : No exit
Southbound : No access

⑥A
Northbound : Access only from M25 ㉑
: No exit
Southbound : No access
: Exit only to M25 ㉑

⑦
Northbound : Access only from A414
: No exit
Southbound : No access
: Exit only to A414

⑰
Northbound : No access
: Exit only to M45
Southbound : Access only from M45
: No exit

⑲
Northbound : Exit only to M6
Southbound : Access only from M6

㉑A
Northbound : No access
Southbound : No exit

㉓A
Northbound : No access from A453
Southbound : No exit to A453

㉔A
Northbound : No exit
Southbound : No access

㉟A
Northbound : No access
Southbound : No exit

④③
Northbound : No access
: Exit only to M621
Southbound : No exit
: Access only from M621

④⑧
Northbound : No exit to A1(M) Southbound
: Access only from A1(M) Northbound
Southbound : No access from A1(M) Southbound
: Exit only to A1(M) Southbound

M2 ROCHESTER TO CANTERBURY

①
Westbound : No exit to A2 Eastbound
Eastbound : No access from A2 Westbound

M3 LONDON TO WINCHESTER

⑧
Westbound : No access
Eastbound : No exit

⑩
Northbound : No access
Southbound : No exit

⑬
Southbound : No exit to A335 Eastbound
: No access

⑭
Westbound : No access
Eastbound : No exit

M4 LONDON TO SWANSEA

①
Westbound : No access from A4 Eastbound
Eastbound : No exit to A4 Westbound

②
Westbound : No access from A4 Eastbound
: No exit to A4 Eastbound
Eastbound : No access from A4 Westbound
: No exit to A4 Westbound

㉑
Westbound : No access from M48 Eastbound
Eastbound : No exit to M48 Eastbound

㉓
Westbound : No exit to M48 Eastbound
Eastbound : No access from M48 Westbound

㉕
Westbound : No access
Eastbound : No exit

㉕A
Westbound : No access
Eastbound : No exit

㉙
Westbound : No access
: Exit only to A48(M)
Eastbound : Access only from A48(M) Eastbound
: No exit

㊳
Westbound : No access

㊴
Westbound : No exit
Eastbound : No access
: No exit

④①
Westbound : No exit
Eastbound : No access
: No exit

④②
Westbound : No exit to A48
Eastbound : No access from A48

M5 BIRMINGHAM TO EXETER

⑩
Northbound : No exit
Southbound : No access

⑪A
Northbound : No access from A417 Eastbound
Southbound : No exit to A417 Westbound

M6 COVENTRY TO CARLISLE

Junction with M1
Northbound : No access from M1 ⑲ Southbound
Southbound : No exit to M1 ⑲ Northbound

③A
Northbound : No access from M6 Toll
Southbound : No exit to M6 Toll

④
Northbound : No exit to M42 Northbound
: No access from M42 Southbound
Southbound : No exit to M42
: No access from M42 Southbound

④A
Northbound : No access from M42 ⑧ Northbound
: No exit
Southbound : No access
: Exit only to M42 ⑧

⑤
Northbound : No access
Southbound : No exit

⑩A
Northbound : No access
: Exit only to M54
Southbound : Access only from M54
: No exit

⑪A
Northbound : No exit to M6 Toll
Southbound : No access from M6 Toll

㉔
Northbound : No exit
Southbound : No access

㉕
Northbound : No access
Southbound : No exit

�30
Northbound : Access only from M61 Northbound
: No exit
Southbound : No access
: Exit only to M61 Southbound

㉛A
Northbound : No access
Southbound : No exit

M6 Toll BIRMINGHAM

T①
Northbound : Exit only to M42
: Access only from A4097
Southbound : No exit
: Access only from M42 Southbound

T②
Northbound : No exit
: No access
Southbound : No access

T⑤
Northbound : No access

T⑦
Northbound : No exit
Southbound : No access

T⑧
Northbound : No exit
Southbound : No access

M8 EDINBURGH TO GLASGOW

⑥A
Westbound : No exit
Eastbound : No access

⑦
Westbound : No exit
Eastbound : No access

⑦A
Westbound : No access
Eastbound : No exit

⑧
Westbound : No access from M73 ② Southbound
: No access from A8 Eastbound
: No access from A89 Eastbound
Eastbound : No access from A89 Westbound
: No exit to M73 ② Northbound

⑨
Westbound : No exit
Eastbound : No access

⑬
Westbound : No access
Eastbound : No access

⑭
Westbound : No exit
Eastbound : No access

⑯
Westbound : No access
Eastbound : No exit

⑰
Eastbound : Access only from A82, not central Glasgow
: Exit only to A82, not central Glasgow

⑱
Westbound : No access
Eastbound : No access

⑲
Westbound : Access only from A814 Eastbound
Eastbound : Exit only to A814 Westbound, not central Glasgow

⑳
Westbound : No access
Eastbound : No exit

㉑
Westbound : No exit
Eastbound : No access

㉒
Westbound : No access
: Exit only to M77 Southbound
Eastbound : Access only from M77 Northbound
: No exit

㉓
Westbound : No access
Eastbound : No exit

㉕A
Eastbound : No access
Westbound : No access

㉘
Westbound : No access
Eastbound : No exit

㉘A
Westbound : No access
Eastbound : No exit

㉙A
Westbound : No exit
Eastbound : No access

M9 EDINBURGH TO STIRLING

②
Westbound : No exit
Eastbound : No access

③
Westbound : No access
Eastbound : No exit

⑥
Westbound : No exit
Eastbound : No access

⑧
Westbound : No access
Eastbound : No exit

M11 LONDON TO CAMBRIDGE

④
Northbound : No access from A1400 Westbound
: No exit
Southbound : No access
: No exit to A1400 Eastbound

⑤
Northbound : No access
Southbound : No exit

⑧A
Northbound : No access
Southbound : No exit

⑨
Northbound : No access
Southbound : No exit

⑬
Northbound : No access
Southbound : No exit

⑭
Northbound : No access from A428 Eastbound
: No exit to A428 Westbound
: No exit to A1307
Southbound : No access from A428 Eastbound
: No access from A1307
: No exit

M20 LONDON TO FOLKESTONE

②
Westbound : No exit
Eastbound : No access

③
Westbound : No access
: Exit only to M26 Westbound
Eastbound : Access only from M26 Eastbound
: No exit

⑪A
Westbound : No exit
Eastbound : No access

M23 LONDON TO CRAWLEY

⑦
Northbound : No exit to A23 Southbound
Southbound : No access from A23 Northbound

⑩A
Southbound : No access from B2036
Northbound : No exit to B2036

M25 LONDON ORBITAL MOTORWAY

①B
Clockwise : No access
Anticlockwise : No exit

⑤
Clockwise : No exit to M26 Eastbound
Anticlockwise : No access from M26 Westbound

Spur of M25 ⑤
Clockwise : No access from M26 Westbound
Anticlockwise : No exit to M26 Eastbound

⑲
Clockwise : No access
Anticlockwise : No exit

㉑
Clockwise : No access from M1 ⑥A Northbound
: No exit to M1 ⑥A Southbound
Anticlockwise : No access from M1 ⑥A Northbound
: No exit to M1 ⑥A Southbound

㉛
Clockwise : No exit
Anticlockwise : No access

M26 SEVENOAKS

Junction with M25 ⑤
Westbound : No exit to M25 Anticlockwise
: No exit to M25 spur
Eastbound : No access from M25 Clockwise
: No access from M25 spur

Junction with M20
Westbound : No access from M20 ③ Eastbound
Eastbound : No exit to M20 ③ Westbound

M27 SOUTHAMPTON TO PORTSMOUTH

④ West
Westbound : No exit
Eastbound : No access

④ East
Westbound : No access
Eastbound : No exit

⑩
Westbound : No access
Eastbound : No exit

⑫ West
Westbound : No exit
Eastbound : No access

⑫ East
Westbound : No access from A3
Eastbound : No exit

M40 LONDON TO BIRMINGHAM

③
Westbound : No access
Eastbound : No exit

⑦
Eastbound : No exit

⑧
Northbound : No access
Southbound : No exit

⑬
Northbound : No access
Southbound : No exit

⑭
Northbound : No exit
Southbound : No access

⑯
Northbound : No access
Southbound : No exit

M42 BIRMINGHAM

①
Northbound : No exit
Southbound : No access

⑦
Northbound : No access
: Exit only to M6 Northbound
Southbound : Access only from M6 Northbound
: No exit

⑦A
Northbound : No access
: Exit only to M6 Eastbound
Southbound : No access
: No exit

⑧
Northbound : Access only from M6 Southbound
: No exit
Southbound : Access only from M6 Southbound
: Exit only to M6 Northbound

M45 COVENTRY

Junction with M1
Westbound : No access from M1 ⑰ Southbound
Eastbound : No exit to M1 ⑰ Northbound

Junction with A45
Westbound : No access
Eastbound : No access

M48 CHEPSTOW

M4
Westbound : No exit to M4 Eastbound
Eastbound : No access from M4 Westbound

M49 BRISTOL

⑱A
Northbound : No access from M5 Southbound
Southbound : No access from M5 Northbound

M53 BIRKENHEAD TO CHESTER

⑪
Northbound : No access from M56 ⑮ Eastbound
: No exit to M56 ⑮ Westbound
Southbound : No access from M56 ⑮ Eastbound
: No exit to M56 ⑮ Westbound

M54 WOLVERHAMPTON TO TELFORD

Junction with M6
Westbound : No access from M6 ⑩A Southbound
Eastbound : No exit to M6 ⑩A Northbound

M56 STOCKPORT TO CHESTER

①
Westbound : No access from M60 Eastbound
: No access from A34 Northbound
Eastbound : No exit to M60 Westbound
: No exit to A34 Southbound

②
Westbound : No access
Eastbound : No exit

③
Westbound : No exit
Eastbound : No access

④
Westbound : No exit
Eastbound : No access

⑦
Westbound : No exit
Eastbound : No access

⑧
Westbound : No exit
Eastbound : No access

⑨
Westbound : No exit to M6 Southbound
Eastbound : No access from M6 Northbound

⑮
Westbound : No access
: No access from M53 ⑪
Eastbound : No access
: No exit to M53 ⑪

M57 LIVERPOOL

③
Northbound : No access
Southbound : No access

⑤
Northbound : Access only from A580 Westbound
: No access
Southbound : No access
: Exit only to A580 Eastbound

M58 LIVERPOOL TO WIGAN

①
Westbound : No access
Eastbound : No exit

M60 MANCHESTER

②
Westbound : No exit
Eastbound : No access

③
Westbound : No access from M56 ①
: No access from A34 Northbound
: No exit to A34 Northbound
Eastbound : No access from A34 Southbound
: No exit to M56 ①
: No exit to A34 Northbound

④
Westbound : No access
Eastbound : No exit to M56

⑤
Westbound : No access from A5103 Southbound
: No exit to A5103 Southbound
Eastbound : No access from A5103 Northbound
: No exit to A5103 Northbound

⑭
Westbound : No access from A580
: No exit to A580 Eastbound
Eastbound : No access from A580 Westbound
: No exit to A580

⑯
Westbound : No access
Eastbound : No exit

⑳
Westbound : No access
Eastbound : No exit

㉒
Westbound : No access

㉕
Westbound : No access

㉖
Eastbound : No access
: No exit

㉗
Westbound : No exit
Eastbound : No access

M61 MANCHESTER TO PRESTON

②
Northbound : No access from A580 Eastbound
: No access from A666
Southbound : No exit to A580 Westbound

③
Northbound : No access from A580 Eastbound
: No access from A666
Southbound : No exit to A580 Westbound

Junction with M6
Northbound : No exit to M6 ㉚ Southbound
Southbound : No access from M6 ㉚ Northbound

M62 LIVERPOOL TO HULL

㉓
Westbound : No exit
Eastbound : No access

㉜A
Westbound : No exit to A1(M) Southbound

M65 BURNLEY

⑨
Westbound : No exit
Eastbound : No access

⑪
Westbound : No access
Eastbound : No exit

M66 MANCHESTER TO EDENFIELD

①
Northbound : No access
Southbound : No exit

Junction with A56
Northbound : Exit only to A56 Northbound
Southbound : Access only from A56 Southbound

M67 MANCHESTER

①
Westbound : No exit
Eastbound : No access

②
Westbound : No access
Eastbound : No exit

M69 COVENTRY TO LEICESTER

②
Northbound : No exit
Southbound : No access

M73 GLASGOW

①
Northbound : No access from A721 Eastbound
Southbound : No exit to A721 Eastbound

②
Northbound : No access from M8 ⑧ Eastbound
Southbound : No exit to M8 ⑧ Westbound

M74 GLASGOW

①
Westbound : No exit to M8 Kingston Bridge
Eastbound : No access from M8 Kingston Bridge

③
Westbound : No access
Eastbound : No exit

③A
Westbound : No exit
Eastbound : No access

⑦
Northbound : No exit
Southbound : No access

⑨
Northbound : No exit
Southbound : No access
: No exit

⑩
Northbound : No exit
Southbound : No access

⑪
Northbound : No exit
Southbound : No access

⑫
Northbound : Access only from A70 Northbound
Southbound : Exit only to A70 Southbound

M77 GLASGOW

Junction with M8
Northbound : No exit to M8 ㉒ Westbound
Southbound : No access from M8 ㉒ Eastbound

④
Northbound : No exit
Southbound : No access

⑥
Northbound : No exit to A77
Southbound : No access from A77

⑦
Northbound : No access
: No exit

⑧
Northbound : No access
Southbound : No access

M80 STIRLING

④A
Northbound : No access
Southbound : No exit

⑥A
Northbound : No exit
Southbound : No access

⑧
Northbound : No access from M876
Southbound : No exit to M876

M90 EDINBURGH TO PERTH

①
Northbound : No exit to A90

②A
Northbound : No access
Southbound : No exit

⑦
Northbound : No exit
Southbound : No access

⑧
Northbound : No access
Southbound : No exit

⑩
Northbound : No access from A912
: No exit to A912 Southbound
Southbound : No access from A912 Northbound
: No exit to A912

M180 SCUNTHORPE

①
Westbound : No exit
Eastbound : No access

M606 BRADFORD

Straithgate Lane
Northbound : No access

M621 LEEDS

②A
Northbound : No exit
Southbound : No access

⑤
Northbound : No access
Southbound : No exit

⑥
Northbound : No exit
Southbound : No access

M876 FALKIRK

Junction with M80
Westbound : No exit to M80 ⑤ Northbound
Eastbound : No access from M80 ⑤ Southbound

Junction with M9
Westbound : No access

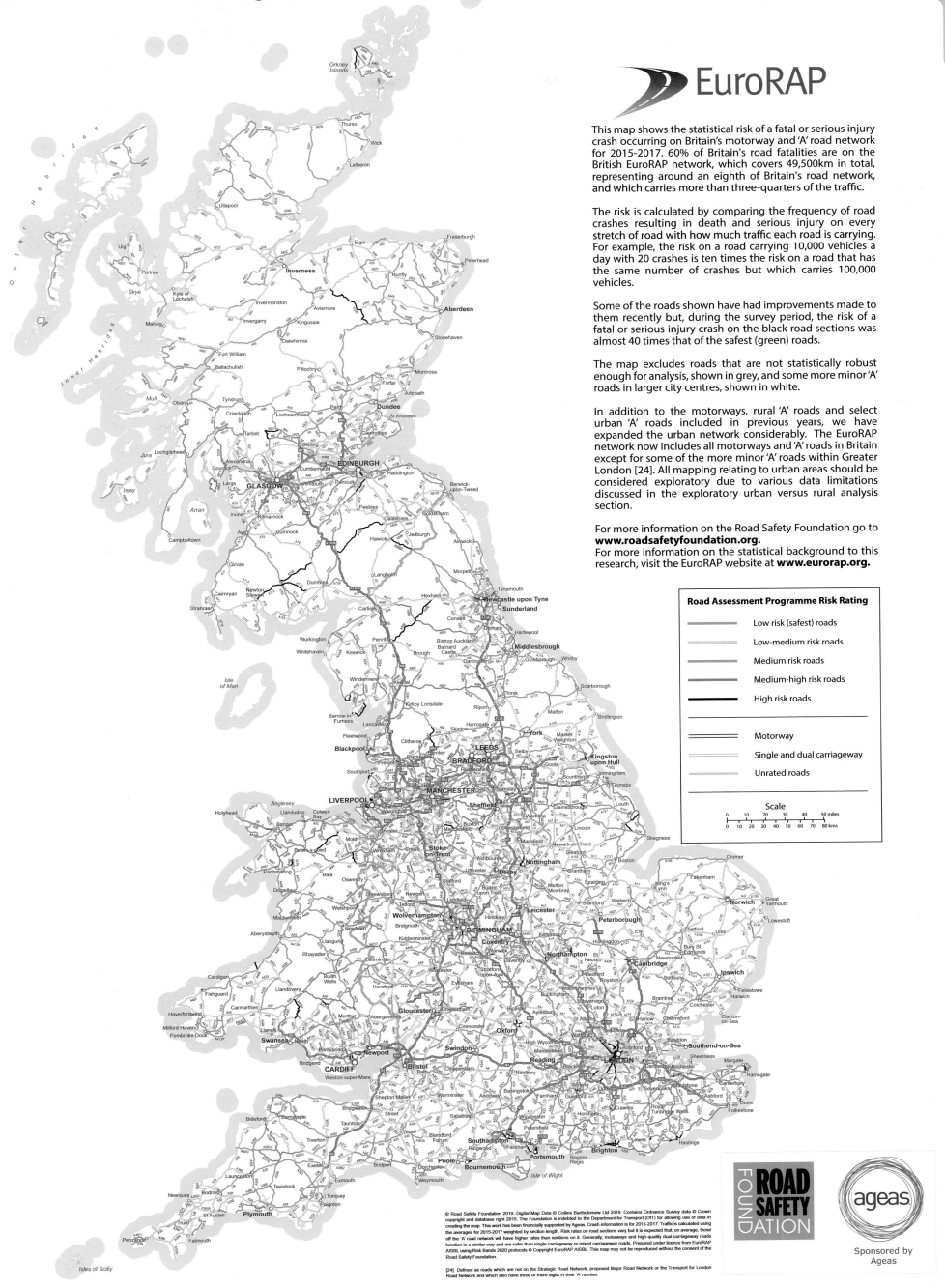

EuroRAP

This map shows the statistical risk of a fatal or serious injury crash occurring on Britain's motorway and 'A' road network for 2015-2017. 60% of Britain's road fatalities are on the British EuroRAP network, which covers 49,500km in total, representing around an eighth of Britain's road network, and which carries more than three-quarters of the traffic.

The risk is calculated by comparing the frequency of road crashes resulting in death and serious injury on every stretch of road with how much traffic each road is carrying. For example, the risk on a road carrying 10,000 vehicles a day with 20 crashes is ten times the risk on a road that has the same number of crashes but which carries 100,000 vehicles.

Some of the roads shown have had improvements made to them recently but, during the survey period, the risk of a fatal or serious injury crash on the black road sections was almost 40 times that of the safest (green) roads.

The map excludes roads that are not statistically robust enough for analysis, shown in grey, and some more minor 'A' roads in larger city centres, shown in white.

In addition to the motorways, rural 'A' roads and select urban 'A' roads included in previous years, we have expanded the urban network considerably. The EuroRAP network now includes all motorways and 'A' roads in Britain except for some of the more minor 'A' roads within Greater London [24]. All mapping relating to urban areas should be considered exploratory due to various data limitations discussed in the exploratory urban versus rural analysis section.

For more information on the Road Safety Foundation go to **www.roadsafetyfoundation.org.**
For more information on the statistical background to this research, visit the EuroRAP website at **www.eurorap.org.**

Road Assessment Programme Risk Rating

—————	Low risk (safest) roads
—————	Low-medium risk roads
—————	Medium risk roads
—————	Medium-high risk roads
—————	High risk roads
—————	Motorway
—————	Single and dual carriageway
—————	Unrated roads

Scale
```
0    10    20    30    40    50 miles
0  10  20  30  40  50  60  70  80 kms
```

ROAD SAFETY FOUNDATION

ageas

Sponsored by Ageas

Key to map symbols   🅿 Short stay car park   🅿 Mid stay car park   🅿 Long stay car park   🅿 Other car park   ▢ Airport terminal building

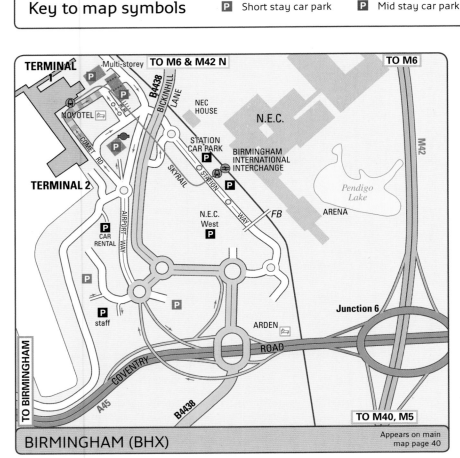

BIRMINGHAM (BHX)

Appears on main map page 40

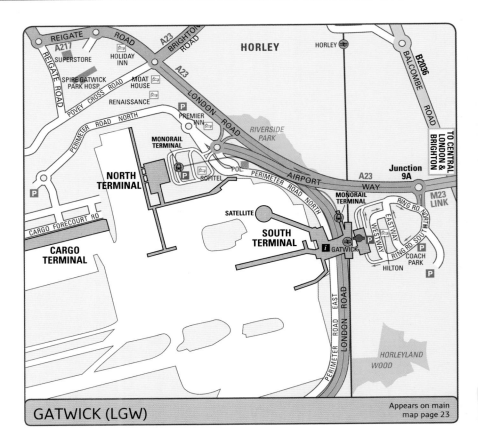

GATWICK (LGW)

Appears on main map page 23

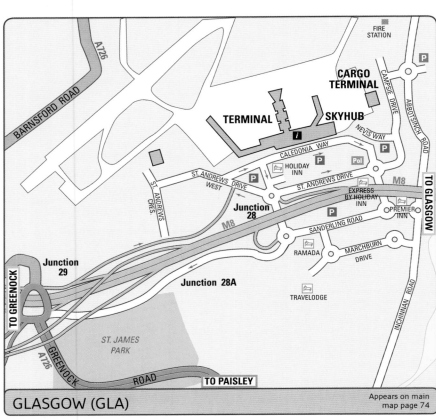

GLASGOW (GLA)

Appears on main map page 74

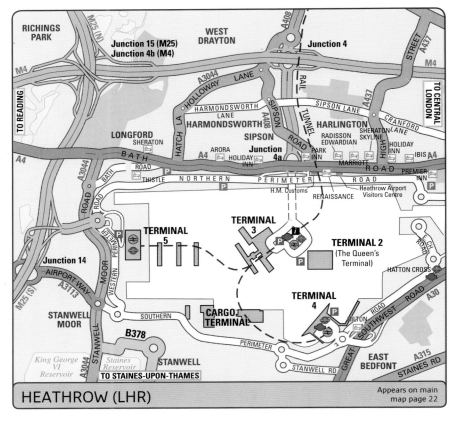

HEATHROW (LHR)

Appears on main map page 22

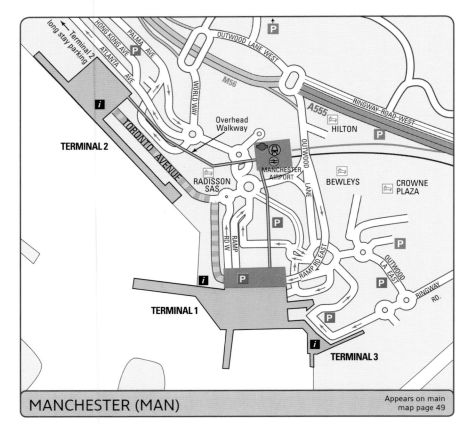

MANCHESTER (MAN)

Appears on main map page 49

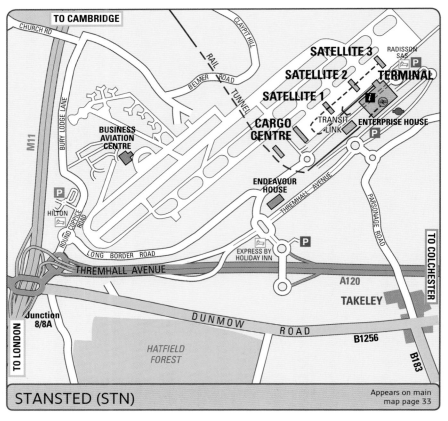

STANSTED (STN)

Appears on main map page 33

Road maps

Map scale

A scale bar appears at the bottom of every page to help with measurements.

```
0        2        4        6 miles
0    2    4    6    8    10 km
```

England, Wales & Southern Scotland are at a scale of 1:200,000 or 3.2 miles to 1 inch.
Northern Scotland & Northern Ireland are at a scale of 1:316,800 or 5 miles to 1 inch.
Orkney & Shetland are at a scale of 1:411,840 or 6.5 miles to 1 inch.

Symbols used on the map

M5	Motorway
M6 Toll	Toll motorway
8 9	Motorway junction with full / limited access (in congested areas there is just a numbered symbol)
Maidstone Birch / Sarn	Motorway service area with off road / full / limited access
A556	Primary route dual / single carriageway
S	24 hour service area on primary route
Peterhead	Primary route destination

Primary route destinations are places of major traffic importance linked by the primary route network. They are shown on a green background on direction signs.

A30	'A' road dual / single carriageway
B1403	'B' road dual / single carriageway
	Minor road
	Road with restricted access
	Roads with passing places
	Road proposed or under construction
33	Multi-level junction with full / limited access (with junction number)
	Roundabout
4	Road distance in miles between markers
	Road tunnel
	Steep hill (arrows point downhill)
Electronic Toll / Toll	Toll / Electronic Toll
	Level crossing
St Malo 8hrs	Car ferry route with journey times
	Railway line / station / tunnel
Wales Coast Path	National Trail / Long Distance Route

⊕ ✈	Airport with / without scheduled services
Ⓗ	Heliport
P&R P&R	Park and Ride site operated by bus / rail (runs at least 5 days a week)
	Built up area
□ □ □	Town / Village / Other settlement
Hythe ☀	Seaside destination
	National boundary
KENT	County / Unitary Authority boundary and name
	Heritage Coast
	National Park
	Regional / Forest Park boundary
	Woodland
Danger Zone	Military range
·468 ▲941	Spot / Summit height (in metres)
	Lake / Dam / River / Waterfall
	Canal / Dry canal / Canal tunnel
	Lighthouse
	Beach
SEE PAGE 91	Area covered by urban area map
190	National Grid reference figures
SY	National Grid reference letters

Places of interest

A selection of tourist detail is shown on the mapping. It is advisable to check with the local tourist information centre regarding opening times and facilities available.

Any of the following symbols may appear on the map in maroon ★ which indicates that the site has World Heritage status.

ℹ	Tourist information centre (open all year)
ℹ	Tourist information centre (open seasonally)
⬛	Ancient monument
	Aquarium
	Aqueduct / Viaduct
	Arboretum
⚔ 1643	Battlefield
	Blue flag beach
⚑	Camp site / Caravan site
	Castle
	Cave
	Country park
	County cricket ground
	Distillery
✝	Ecclesiastical feature
	Event venue
	Farm park
	Garden
	Golf course
	Historic house
	Historic ship

⚽	Major football club
£	Major shopping centre / Outlet village
	Major sports venue
	Motor racing circuit
	Mountain bike trail
⌂	Museum / Art gallery
	Nature reserve (NNR indicates a National Nature Reserve)
	Racecourse
	Rail Freight Terminal
	Ski slope (artificial / natural)
	Spotlight nature reserve (Best sites for access to nature)
	Steam railway centre / preserved railway
	Surfing beach
	Theme park
	University
	Vineyard
	Wildlife park / Zoo
	Wildlife Trust nature reserve
★	Other interesting feature
(NT) (NTS)	National Trust / National Trust for Scotland property

Reading our maps

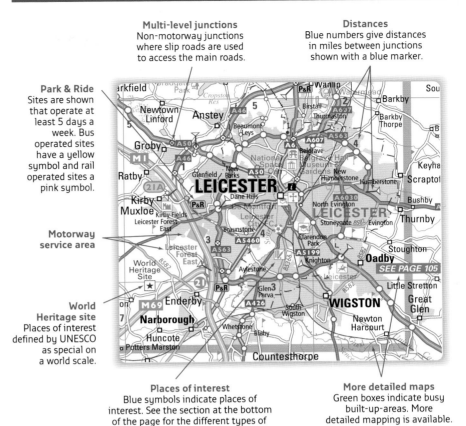

Multi-level junctions
Non-motorway junctions where slip roads are used to access the main roads.

Distances
Blue numbers give distances in miles between junctions shown with a blue marker.

Park & Ride
Sites are shown that operate at least 5 days a week. Bus operated sites have a yellow symbol and rail operated sites a pink symbol.

Motorway service area

World Heritage site
Places of interest defined by UNESCO as special on a world scale.

Places of interest
Blue symbols indicate places of interest. See the section at the bottom of the page for the different types of feature represented on the map.

More detailed maps
Green boxes indicate busy built-up areas. More detailed mapping is available.

Map pages

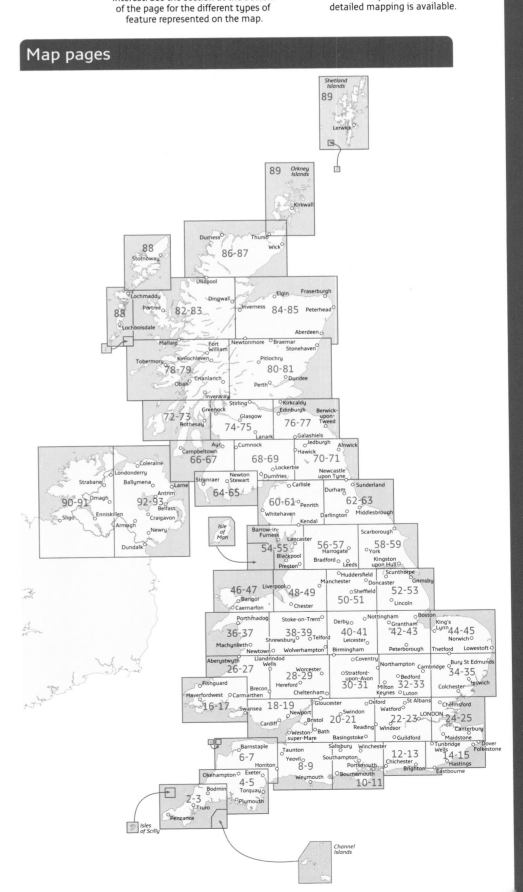

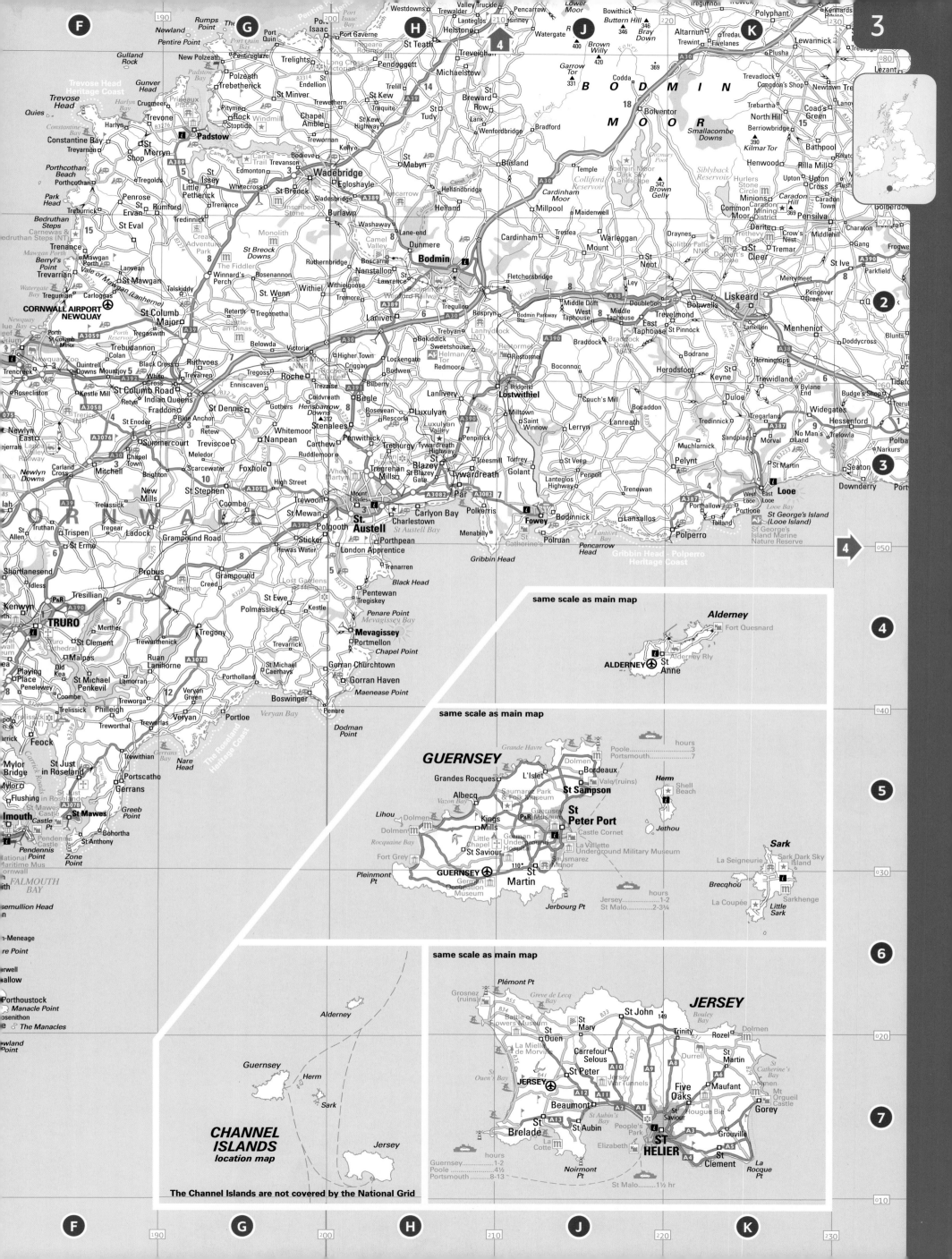

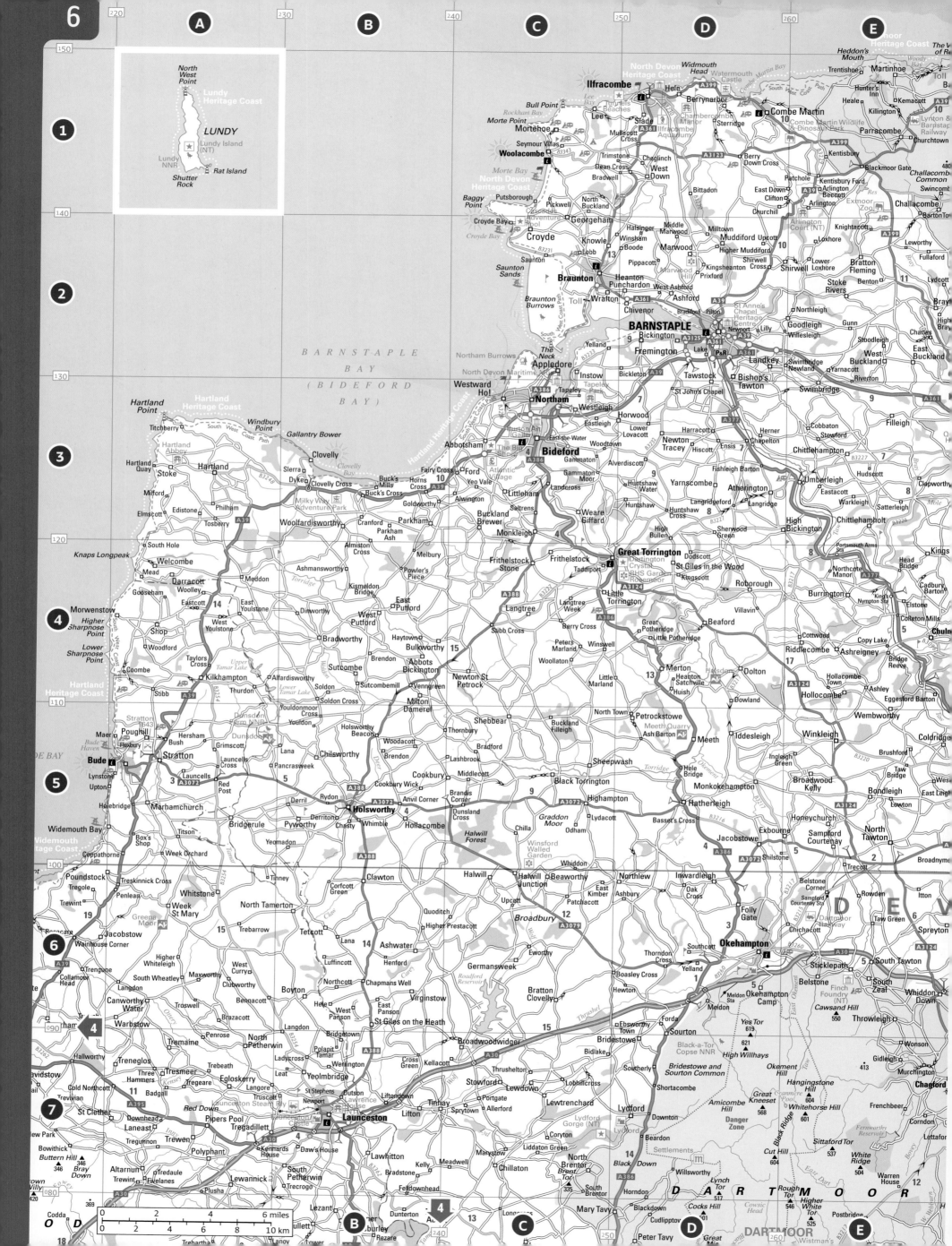

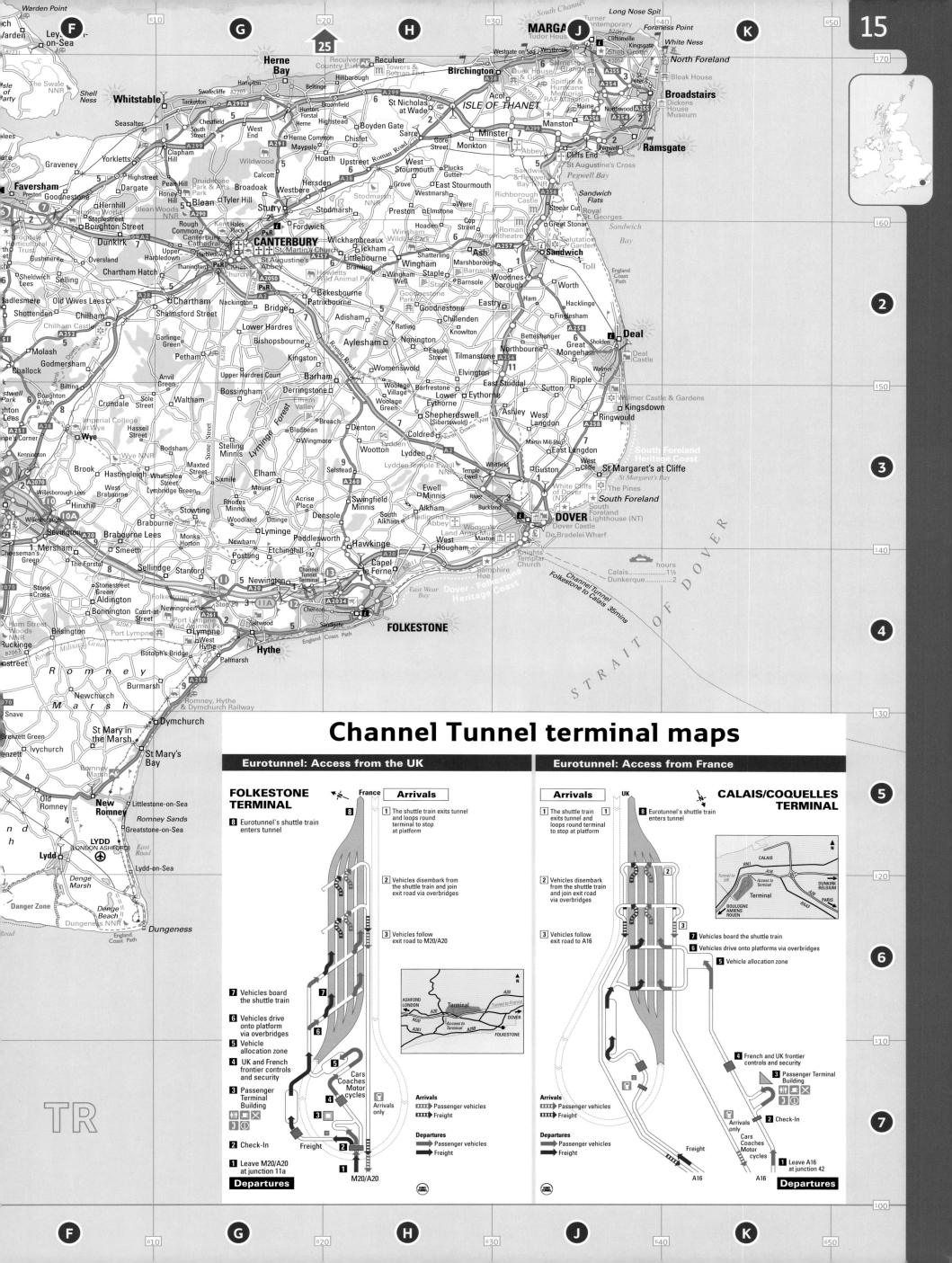

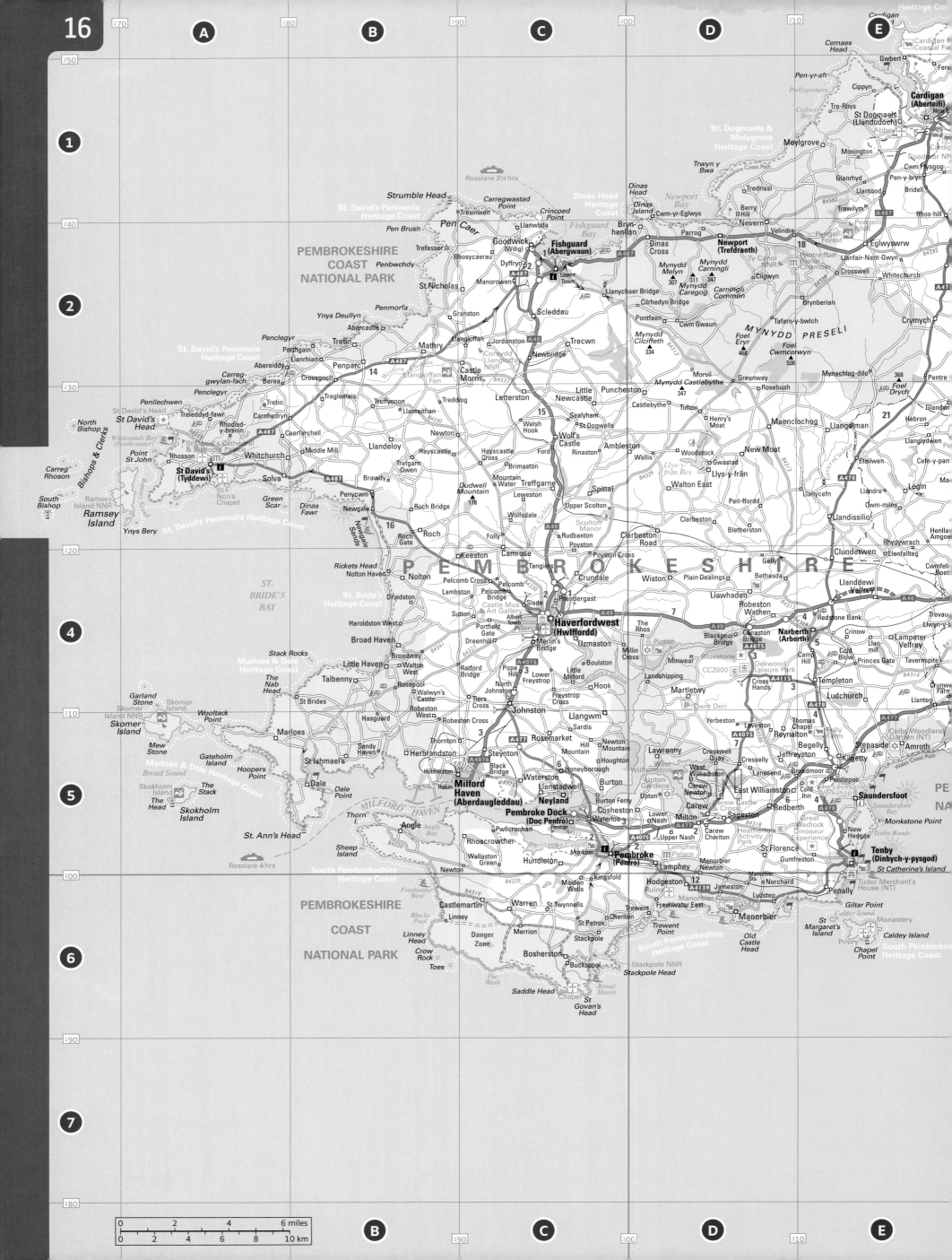

For a more detailed map of Bristol see page 100

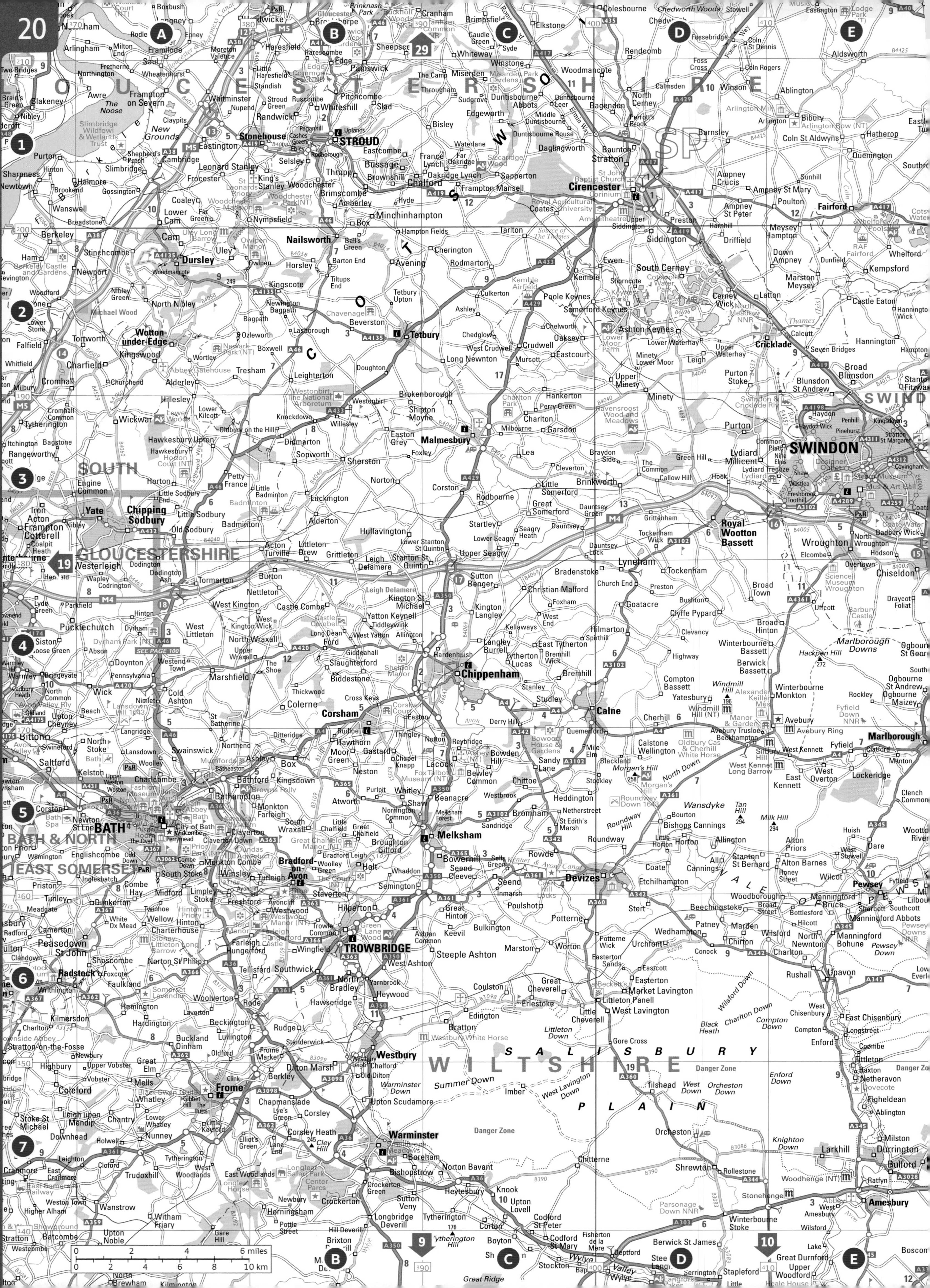

For a more detailed map of West Midlands see pages 106-107

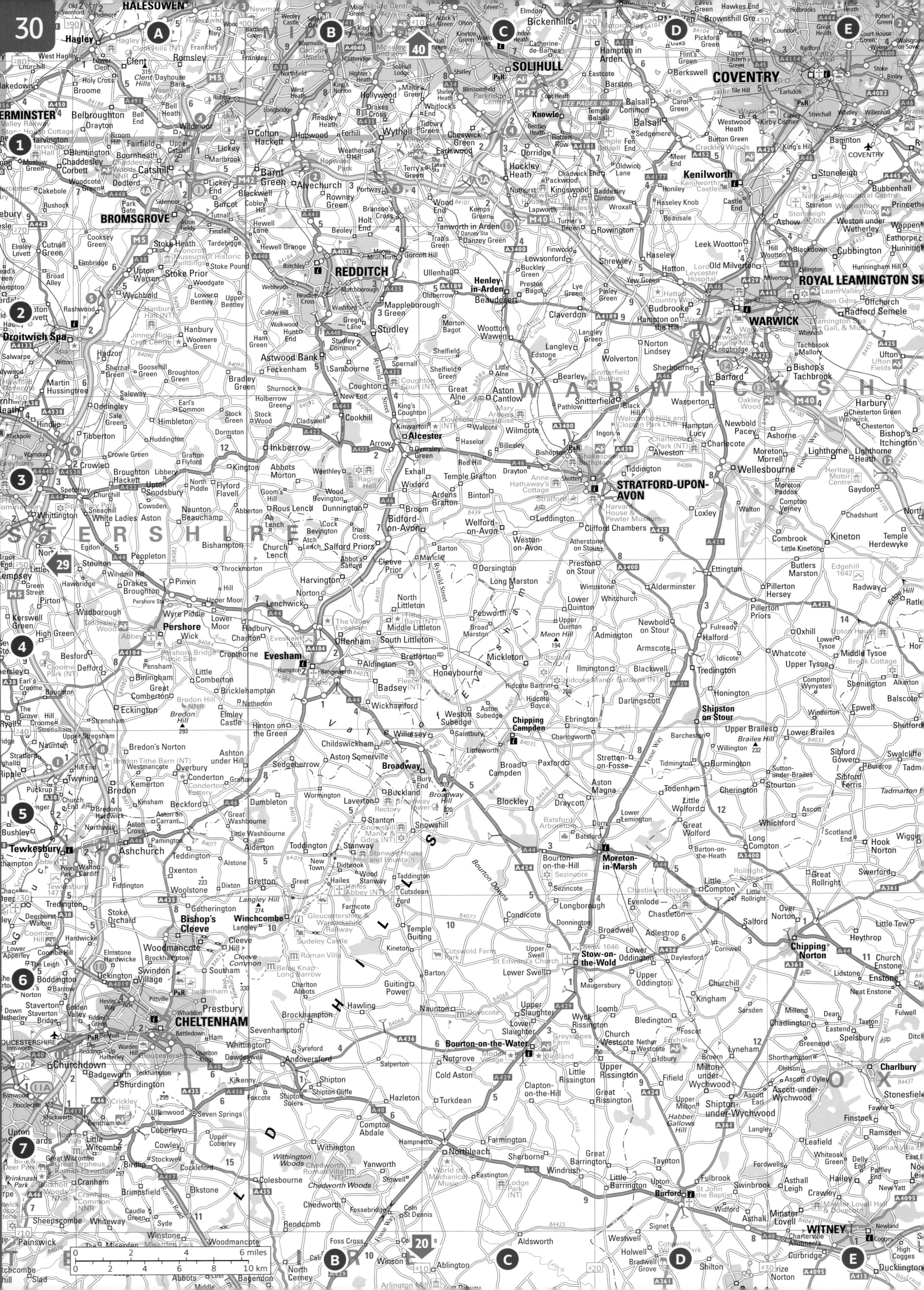

SEE PAGES 106-107

HALESOWEN · **SOLIHULL** · **COVENTRY**

KIDDERMINSTER · **BROMSGROVE** · **Droitwich Spa** · **Kenilworth**

REDDITCH · **Henley-in-Arden** · **ROYAL LEAMINGTON SPA** · **WARWICK**

Alcester · **STRATFORD-UPON-AVON**

Pershore · **Evesham** · **Chipping Campden** · **Shipston on Stour** · **Moreton-in-Marsh**

Tewkesbury · **Broadway** · **Chipping Norton**

Bishop's Cleeve · **Winchcombe** · **Stow-on-the-Wold**

CHELTENHAM · **Bourton-on-the-Water** · **Northleach** · **Burford** · **WITNEY**

WARWICKSHIRE · WORCESTERSHIRE · GLOUCESTERSHIRE · COTSWOLD HILLS

Grid references: A B C D E / 1 2 3 4 5 6 7

Scale: 0 – 6 miles / 0 – 10 km

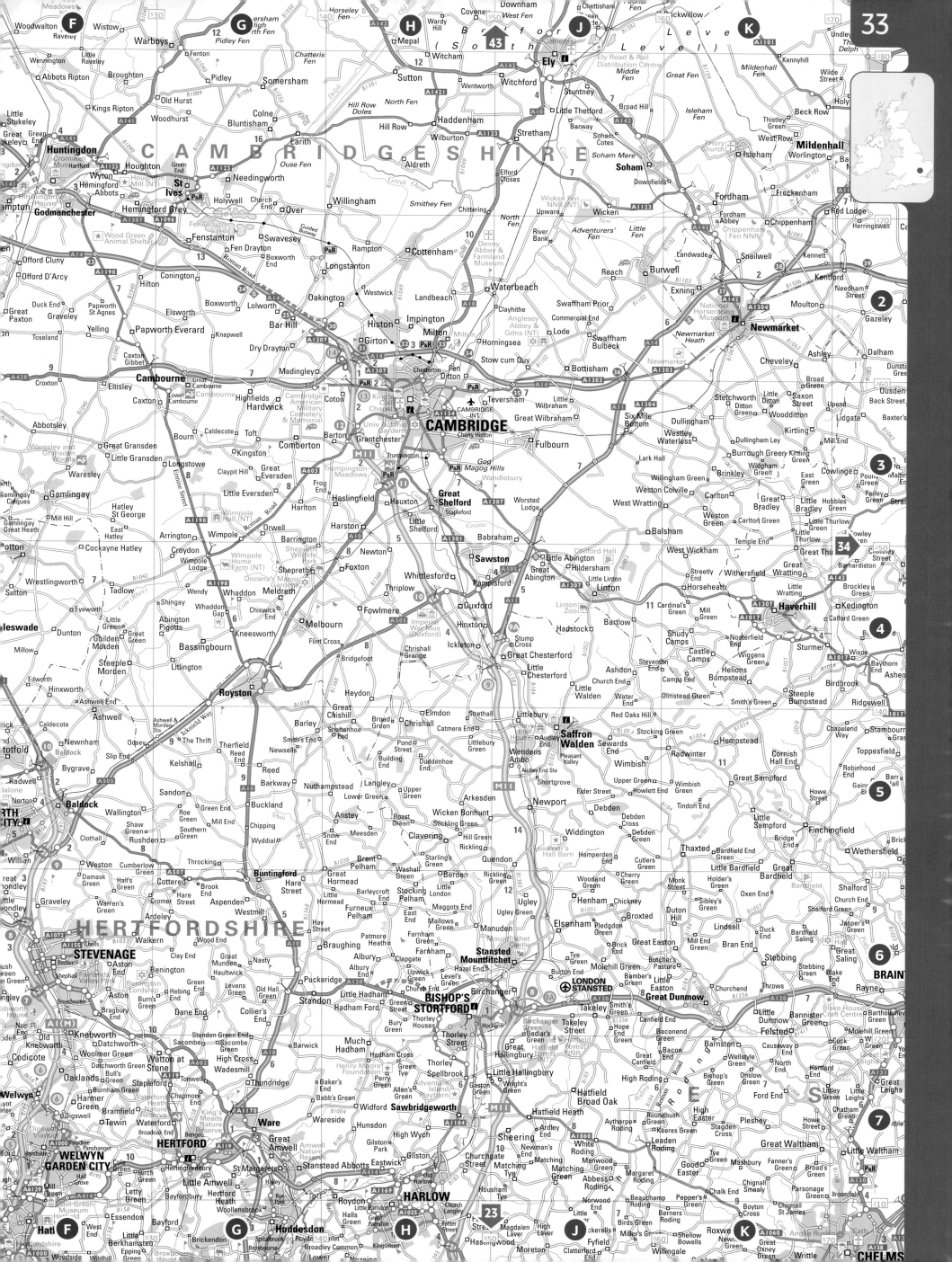

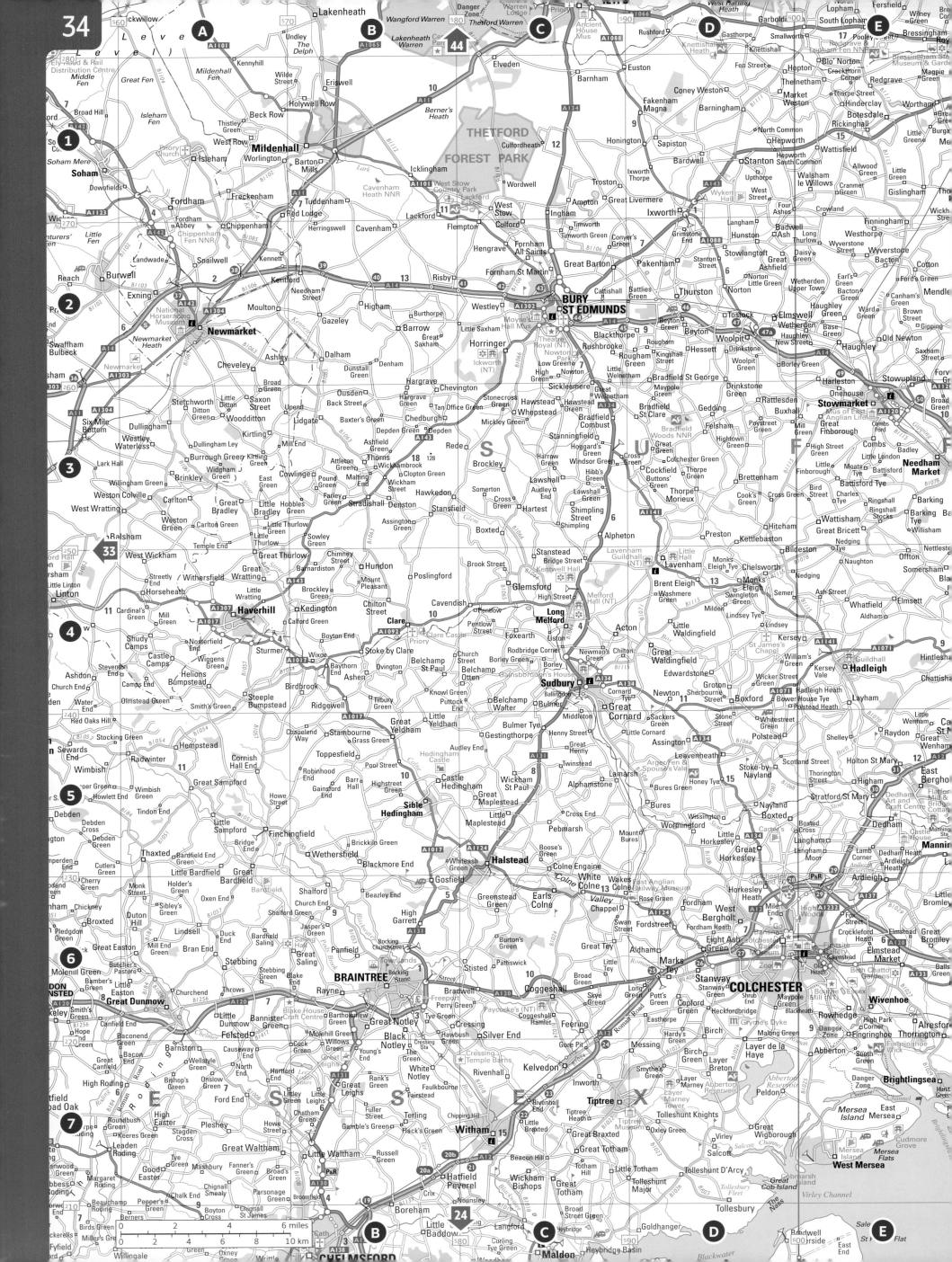

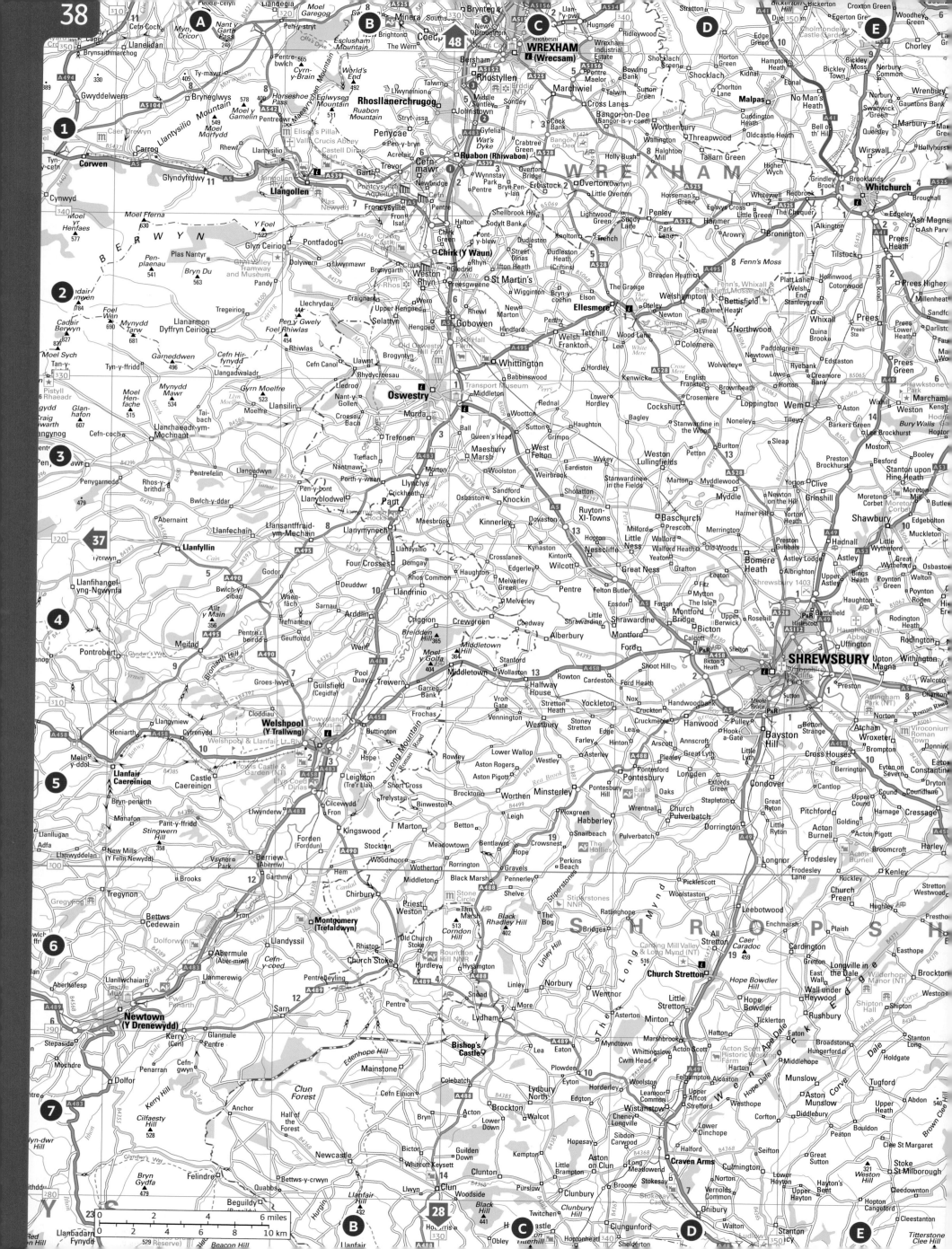

A B C E

LINCOLN

Rolleston · Brinkley · New Idderton · Sutton · Strathorpe · 19 · Leadenham · Temple Bruer · Brauncewell · Dorringt · North Kyme
Morton · Farndon · Beckingham · Fenton · 52 · Fulbeck · Cranwell · A153 · Ruskington · Anwick · South Kyme
Goverton · Fiskerton · Thorpe · Balderton · Claypole · Stubton · Caythorpe · Frieston · Lincoln · Leasingham · Howell · Ewerby · Ewerby Thorpe · South Kyme Fen
Thurgarton Priory · East Stoke · 11 · Hawton · Long Bennington · Westborough · Dry Doddington · Hough-on-the-Hill · Gelston · Normanton · North Rauceby · South Rauceby · Holdingham · Kirkby la Thorpe · Heckington
Epperstone · Thurgarton · Bleasby · Syerston · Elston · 14 · Staunton in the Vale · Marston · Hougham · Carlton Scroop · Sudbrook · Ancaster · Sleaford · Asgarby · 12 · Great Hale
Hoveringham · Kneeton · Flintham · Sibthorpe · Kilvington · Flawborough · Foston · Honington · Wilsford · Kelby · Quarrington · Silk Willoughby · Burton Pedwardine · Little Hale
Caythorpe · Gunthorpe · Screveton · Hawksworth · Shelton · Allington · Barkston · Syston · Culverthorpe · Swarby · Aswarby · Northbeck · Scredington
Bulcote · 4 · East Bridgford · Car Colston · Scarrington · Thoroton · Alverton · Normanton · Belton · Londonthorpe · Humby · Aunsby · Scott Willoughby · Spanby · Swaton
Newton · Seaundale · Aslockton · Orston · Barkston · St Peter & St Paul · Belton House (NT) · 6 · Welby · Oasby · Aisby · Dembleby · Osbournby
Bingham · Whatton · 15 · Bottesford · Sedgebrook · Muston Meadows NNR · Great Gonerby · Manthorpe · Gonerby Hill Foot · Heydour · Haceby · Newton · Threekingham · Bridge End · 13
Radcliffe on Trent · Cropwell Butler · Elton · Sutton · Easthorpe · Muston · Barrowby · GRANTHAM · Old Somerby · Ropsley · Sapperton · Pickworth · Folkingham · Horbling · Billingborough
Tithby · Barnstone · Granby · Redmile · Belvoir · Woolsthorpe · Harlaxton · Little Ponton · Boothby Pagnell · Hanby · Laughton · Birthorpe · Pointon
Cropwell Bishop · Langar · Plungar · Barkestone-le-Vale · Belvoir Castle · Denton · Harston · Ellys Manor House · Scotland · Ingoldsby · Walcot · Aslackby · Dowsby
Owthorpe · Colston Bassett · Kinoulton · Stathern · Knipton · Croxton Kerrial · Hungerton · Great Ponton · Bassingthorpe · Westby · Bitchfield · Keisby · Graby · Rippingale · Dunsby
Harby · Branston · Wyville · Stoke Rochford · Easton · Hawthorpe · Irnham · Hanby · Dunsby Fen
Hickling · Long Clawson · Eaton · Eastwell · Saltby · Skillington · Woolsthorpe by Colsterworth · Burton Coggles · Corby Glen · Bulby · Kirkby Underwood · Hacconby
Upper Broughton · Nether Broughton · Goadby Marwood · Wycomb · Waltham on the Wolds · Sproxton · Woolsthorpe Manor (NT) · Colsterworth · Birkholme · Swayfield · Stainfield · Morton · Morton Fen
Old Dalby · Scalford · Chadwell · Stonesby · Buckminster · Stainby · North Witham · Swinstead · Elsthorpe · Hanthorpe · Cawthorpe · Dyke · 14
Grimston · Saxelbye · Wartnaby · Holwell · Howell · Coston · Garthorpe · Sewstern · Gunby · Grimsthorpe Castle · Edenham · Bourne · Bourne North Fen
Asfordby · MELTON MOWBRAY · Thorpe Arnold · Freeby · Saxby · Wymondham · South Witham · Scottlethorpe · Eastgate · Twenty
41 · Kirby Bellars · Brentingby · Wyfordby · Edmondthorpe · Thistleton · Castle Bytham · Little Bytham · Obthorpe · Thurlby · Baston Common
Hoby · Frisby on the Wreake · Stapleford · Melton Carnegie Museum · Ye Olde Pork Pie Shoppe · Market Overton · Clipsham · Careby · Witham on the Hill · Manthorpe · North Drove
Rotherby · Burton Lazars · Teigh · Barrow · Stretton · Aunby · Carlby · Thetford · Cross
Brooksby · Great Dalby · Little Dalby · Whissendine · Greetham · Pickworth · Braceborough · Baston · Langtoft · Crowland
Gaddesby · Ashby Folville · Ashwell · Cottesmore · Essendine · Greatford · A1175
Goscote · Queniborough · Barsby · Pickwell · Somerby · Burrough on the Hill · Langham · Vale of Catmose · Exton · RUTLAND · Ryhall · Barholm · Market Deeping
South Croxton · Beeby · Twyford · Thorpe Satchville · Cold Overton · Barleythorpe · Burley · Barnsdale Gardens · Great Casterton · Belmesthorpe · Deeping Gate · Deeping St James
Hungarton · Baggrave Hall · Marefield · Owston · Knossington · Oakham Castle · Whitwell · Tickencote · Little Casterton · Northfields · West Deeping · Maxey · Northborough
Keyham · Lowesby · Cold Newton · Whatborough Hill 230 · Oakham · Rutland County Museum · Egleton · Upper Hambleton · Rutland Water · Empingham · Tinwell · Stamford · Burghley House · Bainton · Etton · Glinton · Peakirk
Tilton on the Hill · Halstead · Withcote · Braunston · Anglian Water Birdwatching Centre · Normanton · Collyweston · Pilsgate · Barnack · Helpston · PETERBOROUGH
Houghton on the Hill · Billesdon · Skeffington · Prior's Coppice · Brooke · Gunthorpe · Manton · Edith Weston · Ketton · Barnack Hills & Holes NNR · Ufford · Southorpe
Skinby · Tugby · East Norton · Loddington · Launde Abbey · Ridlington · Belton · Lyndon · North Luffenham · Easton on the Hill · Wittering · Thornhaugh · Upton · Marholm · Castor Hanglands NNR · Walton
Rolleston · Allexton · Wardley · Ayston · Preston · Wing · Pilton · South Luffenham · Morcott · Duddington · Bedford Purlieus NNR · Wansford · Water Newton · Longthorpe · Orton Longueville
King's Norton · Noseley · Goadby · Uppingham · Glaston · Bisbrooke · Barrowden · Tixover · Wakerley · Wittering · Thornhaugh · Sulehay · Yarwell · Sibson · Orton Waterville
Burton Overy · Carlton Curlieu · Shangton · Stockerston · Seaton · Shotley · Harringworth · Laxton · King's Cliffe · Apethorpe · Nassington · Alwalton · Chesterton
Illston on the Hill · Tur Langton · Stonton Wyville · Glooston · Hallaton · Horninghold · Lyddington Bede House · Harringworth Viaduct · Blatherwycke · Woodnewton · Fotheringhay · Peterborough
Kibworth Harcourt · Church Langton · Cranoe · Stoke Dry · Thorpe by Water · Bulwick · Deene · Deenethorpe · Cotterstock · Elton · Haddon · Morborne · Yaxley
Kibworth Beauchamp · Langton · Thorpe Langton · Blaston · Nevill Holt · Caldecott · Harringworth · Kirby Hall · Deene Hall · Southwick · Glapthorn · Big Sky Adventure Play
Smeeton Westerby · East Langton · Welham · Medbourne · Bringhurst · Gretton · Rockingham · Short Wood and Southwick Wood · Oundle · Ashton · Luddington in the Brook · Great Gidding
Foxton · Great Bowden · Slawston · Weston by Welland · Drayton · Rockingham Motor Speedway · Weldon · Upper Benefield · Barnwell · Polebrook · Denton · Sawtry
Lubenham · Market Harborough · Dingley · Little Bowden · Sutton Bassett · Ashley · Cottingham · Middleton · East Carlton · CORBY · Lower Benefield · Cotterstock · Tansor · Warmington · Folksworth · Stilton
Marston Trussell · Braybrooke · Brampton Ash · Stoke Albany · Wilbarston · Stanion · Brigstock · Stoke Doyle · Armston · Hemington · Caldecote
Great Oxendon · Clipston · Arthingworth · Dingley · Pipewell · Great Oakley · Little Oakley · Brigstock · Lyveden New Bield (NT) · Pilton · Wadenhoe · Wigsthorpe · Little Gidding · Winwick
Sibbertoft · Naseby 1645 · Kelmarsh · Rushton Triangular Lodge · Rushton · Newton · Geddington · Sudborough · Aldwincle · Achurch · Thurning · Steeple Gidding · Coppingford
Desborough · Rothwell · Thorpe Underwood · Harrington · Weekley · Warkton · Grafton Underwood · Lowick · Slipton · Thrapston · Titchmarsh · Hamerton Zoo · Upton
Thorpe Malsor · KETTERING · 32 · Cranford St Andrew · Cranford St John · Twywell · Islip · Woodford · Old Weston · Alconbury Weston · Buckworth

Barton Seagrave · Warkton · Naseby · Haselbech · Great Cransley

0   2   4   6 miles
0   2   4   6   8   10 km

NORFOLK
BROADS

THE
BROADS

NORWICH

Cromer
Sheringham

Aylsham

North
Walsham

GREAT YARMOUTH

Caister-on-Sea

LOWESTOFT

Beccles

Bungay

Loddon

Long
Stratton

Harleston

Diss

For a more detailed map of Merseyside see pages 112-113

55

SOUTHPORT

Horse Bank
Angry Brow
Southport Pier

Banks
Crossens
Marshside
Churchtown
Mere Brow
Croston
Eccleston

LEYLAND

CHORLEY

Tarleton
Bretherton
Rufford
Mawdesley
Burscough Bridge
Parbold
Appley Bridge
Standish

WIGAN

Birkdale
Ainsdale-on-Sea
Ainsdale
Southport Holiday Centre
Ainsdale Sand Dunes NNR

ORMSKIRK
Skelmersdale
Orrell

Liverpool (Birkenhead) to Belfast....8 hours
Liverpool to Douglas....2¾ (March-Nov) hours
Dublin....7½-9½

SEE PAGES 112-113

Formby
Formby Point

Cabin Hills (NT) NNR

Maghull
Lydiate

Rainford
Billinge

47

West Hoyle Bank

LIVERPOOL BAY

CROSBY
Litherland
BOOTLE
WALLASEY

MERSEYSIDE

Kirkby
ST HELENS
Newton-le-Willows
Haydock

Hoylake
East Hoyle Bank
Hilbre Island
Red Rocks Marsh
Point of Ayr

LIVERPOOL
Prescot
HUYTON

Greasby
BIRKENHEAD
West Kirby

WIDNES

Heswall
BEBINGTON

RUNCORN
Garston
Speke
LIVERPOOL JOHN LENNON

Frodsham

ELLESMERE PORT

Neston
Willaston

CHESHIRE WEST

FLINTSHIRE

Holywell (Treffynnon)
Greenfield
Flint (Y Fflint)

DELAMERE
FOREST PARK

CHESTER

Connah's Quay
Queensferry
Shotton

Mold (Yr Wyddgrug)
Buckley (Bwcle)
Hawarden (Penarlâg)

CHESTER

Ruthin (Rhuthun)

38

WREXHAM (Wrecsam)

0   2   4   6   8   10 km
0   6 miles

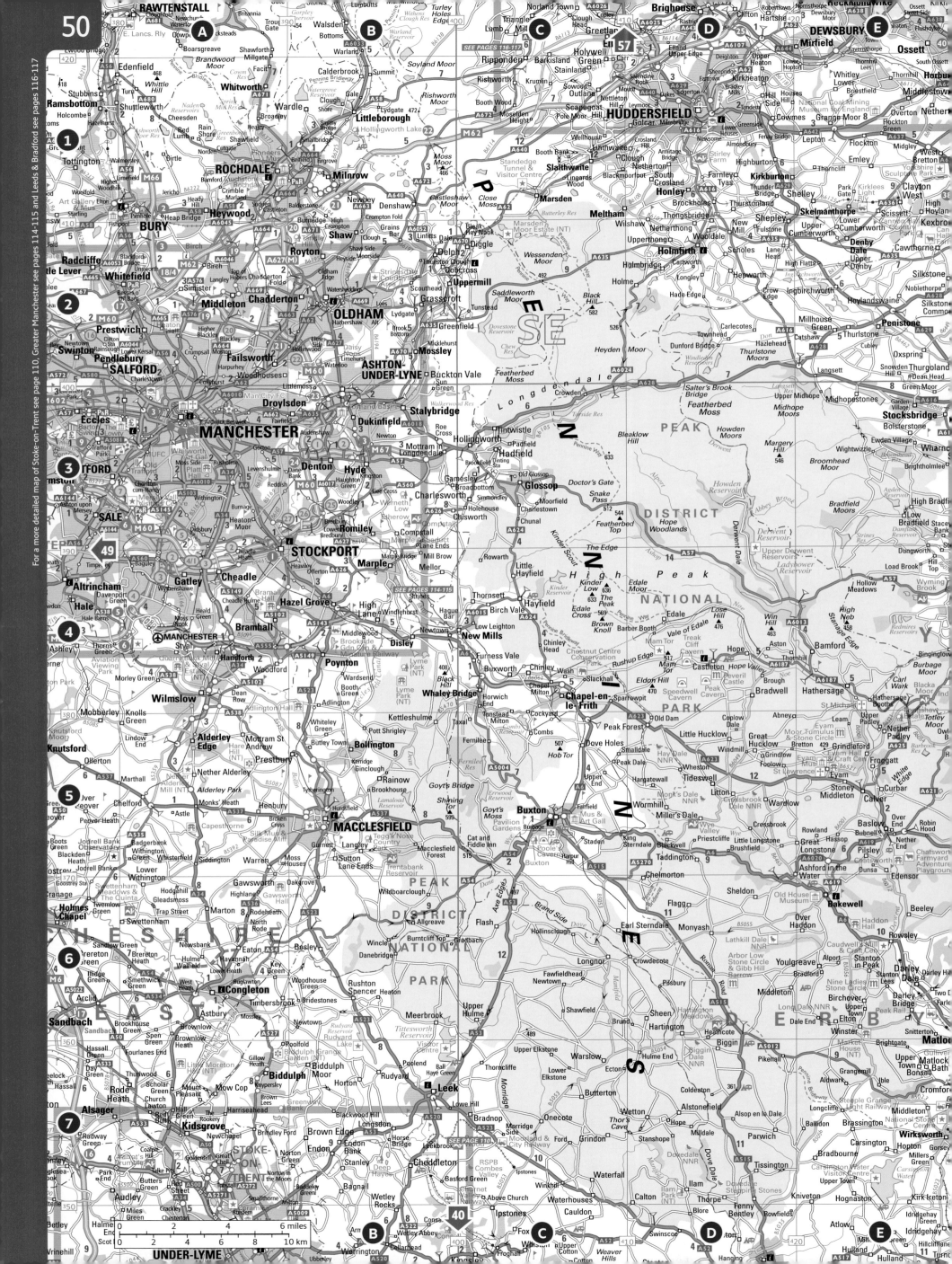

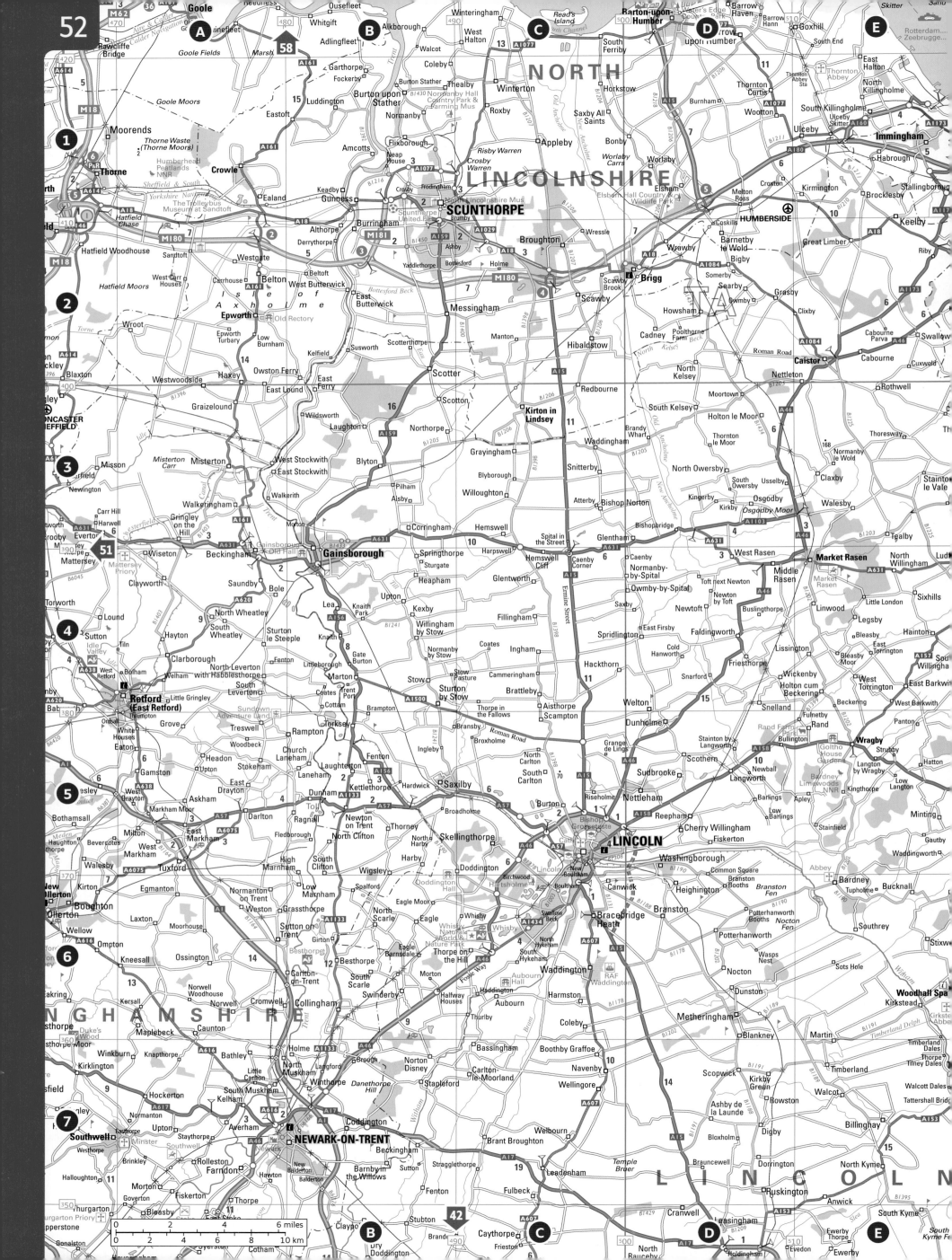

490
480

1

2

3

same scale as main map

4

ISLE
OF
MAN

5

6

7

500

490

480

470

Whitfell   Bigert Mire

A595
310   23

Corney
Prior Park   Ulph
Par
Stub Place

Selker Bay   Hycemoor
Stoneside Hill ▲422   Bootle
Hyton   Broadgate   4
Annaside   White Combe   Lady

Bootle
Fell   Duddon Bridg

Black Combe   417 The Green   Hallthw
▲600   3   Arn

Whitbeck   A5093   Strands
The Hill   4

Wicham   Millom Folk
Silecroft   Mus   Millom

Kirksanton   3   Steel   Borw
Green   Rails
Haverigg   Askam
Haverigg Point

Sandscale Ha
NNR
Duddon
Sands

North Scale
North Walney NNR   Dock Mu
Vickerstow
Tummer   A590
Hill Scar

Isle
of Walney

Point of
Ayre
Ayres Visitor
Centre and   The Ayres   A16
Nature Trail
Rue
Point   Ayres Visitor   Cranstal
Centre   3
CronkY Bing   13   The Lhen   Glentruan
A19   Dhowin   A17   Bride
Sartfield   A10   Jurby East   Andreas   A10   Shellag Point
Jurby Head   Jurby   6   A9   5
Jurby West   Sandygate   B7   Regaby
Ballasalla   A13   Ballachurry   Ramsey Bay
Crawyn   Close   St Judes   Fort   Dhoor
Sartfield   The   A13
The Cronk   Curraghs   Kella   4
Curraghs   Sulby   B14   Sulby   Ramsey
Wildlife   Churchtown   Port e Vullen
Orrisdale   3   Ballaugh   1079   Glen Auldyn   Maughold
Orrisdale Head   Ravensdale   6   Slieau Managh   7   Dreemskerry   A15   Maughold
383   565   North   Ballajora   Head
Kirk Michael   Slieau Curn   Barrule   Corrany   Port
351   Clagh   Glen   Mooar
T.T.   Slieau   Ouyr   Mona
Course   Dhoo   551   8   Glen
Cooildarry   424   Snaefell   Slieau   Mona   Manx
Slieau   621   Lhean   Electric Rly
Ballacarnane Beg   Freoaghane   469   Dhoon
A4   488   546   Laxey
Barregarrow   Sartfell   Beinn-   Wheel   Port Cornaa
6   454   Snaefell   y-Phott   Bulgham Bay
Gob y Deigan   A3   Mountain   Laxey
Knocksharry   Little   Rly   Glen   Laxey Head
6   Cronk-   London   Injebreck   Ballacannell
St German's Cath   y-Voddy   Colden   Laxey   Laxey
Peel   Ballaugh   Lambfell Moar   487   5   Ballaheannagh   Bay
St Patrick's Isle   Neb   Injebreck   Clay Head
Peel Castle &   Ballig   Reservoir   Baldrine   Garwick Bay
Round Tower   A20   Slieau   5
House of Manannan   Ruy   Sulby   A11
Contrary Head   A1   Greeba   478   Baldwin   Hillberry
Knockaloe Moar   Patrick   Tynwald   Mountain   B21   A2   Port Groudle
St   3   422   Crosby   A23
Dalby   John's   Glen Vine   Strang   Onchan   Onchan Head
Mountain   333   Lower   7   A22   Douglas
Glenmaye   Foxdale   Garth   Union Mills   A16   Bay
Dalby   7   Fairy   A24   Manx Mus
Point   Dalby   Foxdale   A24   DOUGLAS
Niarbyl   Mountain   483   Cooil   A37   Douglas
Island   280   South   Close   Stuggadhoo   Head
Barrule   Clark   Braaid   Belfast (seasonal)..........2¾-4¾   hours
Niarbyl   6   341   A27   Newtown   Quine's   Dublin (seasonal)............3-3¼
Bay   A36   Ballamodha   B30   Hill   Heysham...............3¼
Stroin   St Mark's   Little Ness   Liverpool (March-Nov)......2¾
Vuigh   Ronague   Grenaby   Ballaveare
Lingague   B42   A25   Isle of Man Steam Rly
Fleshwick Bay   A3   10   Santon Head
Ballakilpheric   Rushen
Bradda Head   Colby   Ballasalla
Bradda   Ballafesson   Ballabeg   Port
Croit e Caley   Ballabeg   Grenaugh   Santon Head
Port Erin   Ballasalla   Derby Fort
Meayll Circle   Ballaphetrick   ISLE OF MAN   St Michael's Island
Cregneash   Nautical Mus   Derbyhaven
Calf   Port   Castle
of Man   St Mary   Rushen   Castletown   Langness
The Howe   Cregneash Village   Castletown
Spanish   Perwick   Folk Museum   Bay
Head   Bay   Dreswick
Chicken   Point
Rock

220   230   240   250

0   2   4   6 miles
0   2   4   6   8   10 km

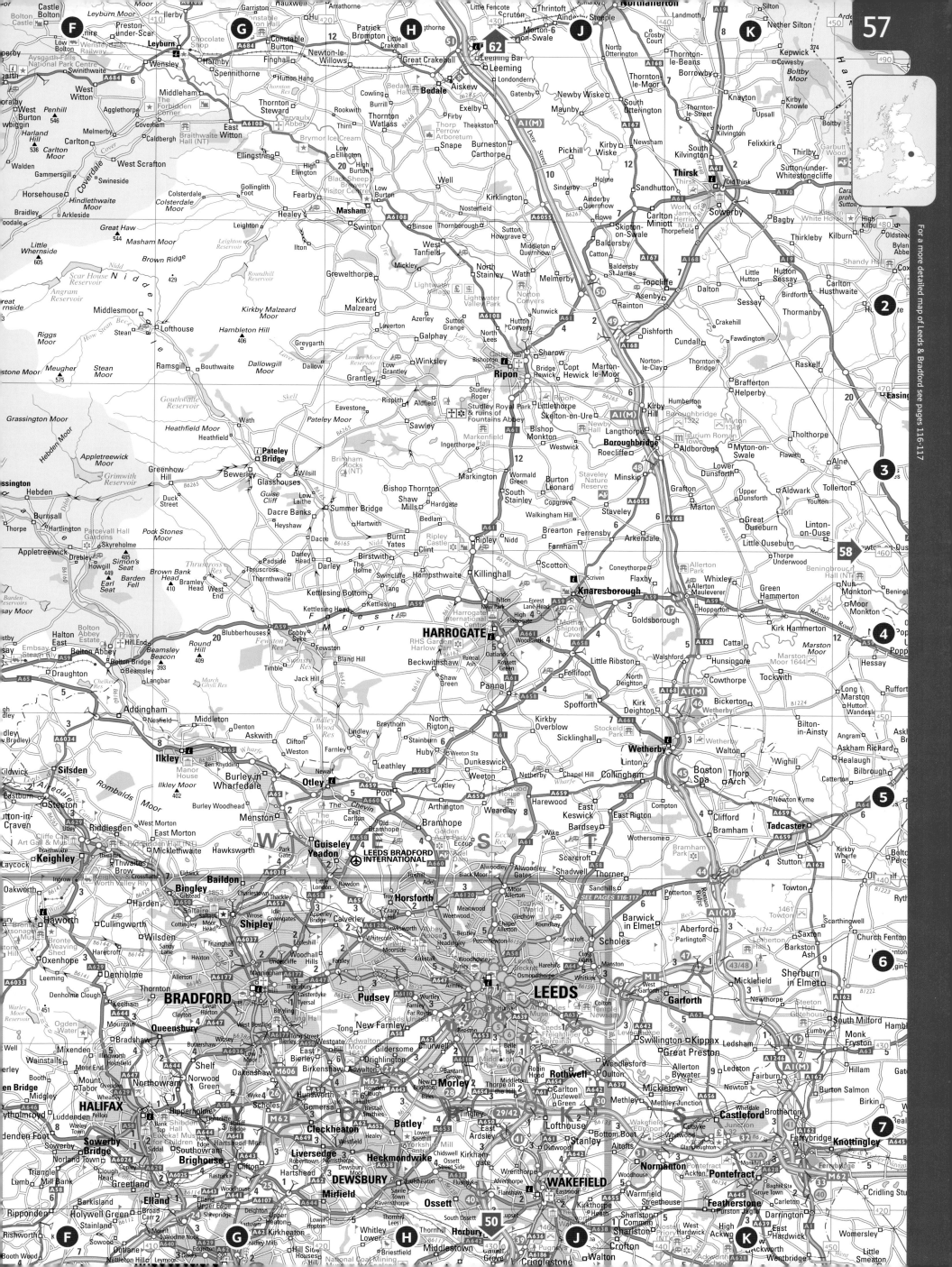

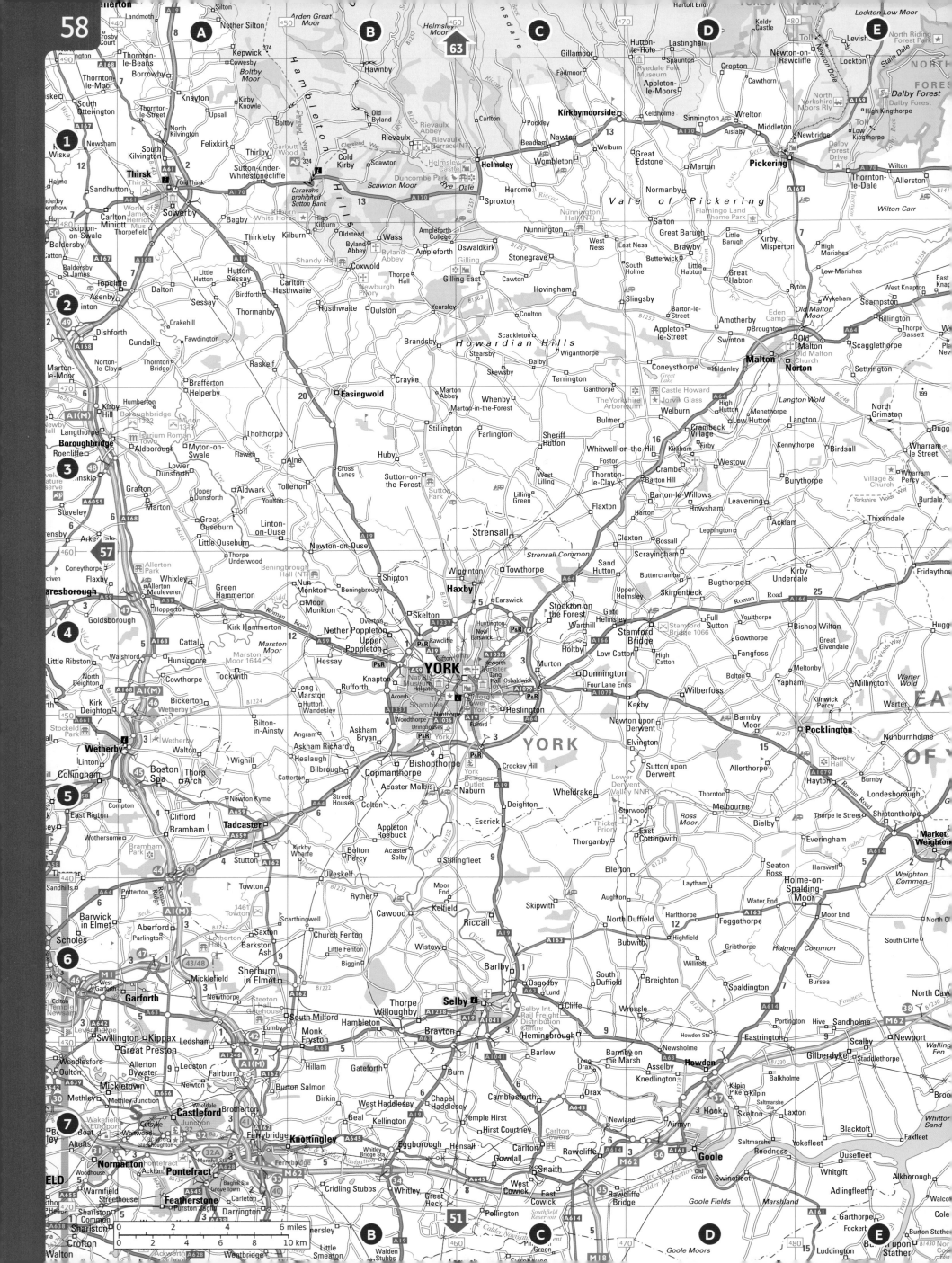

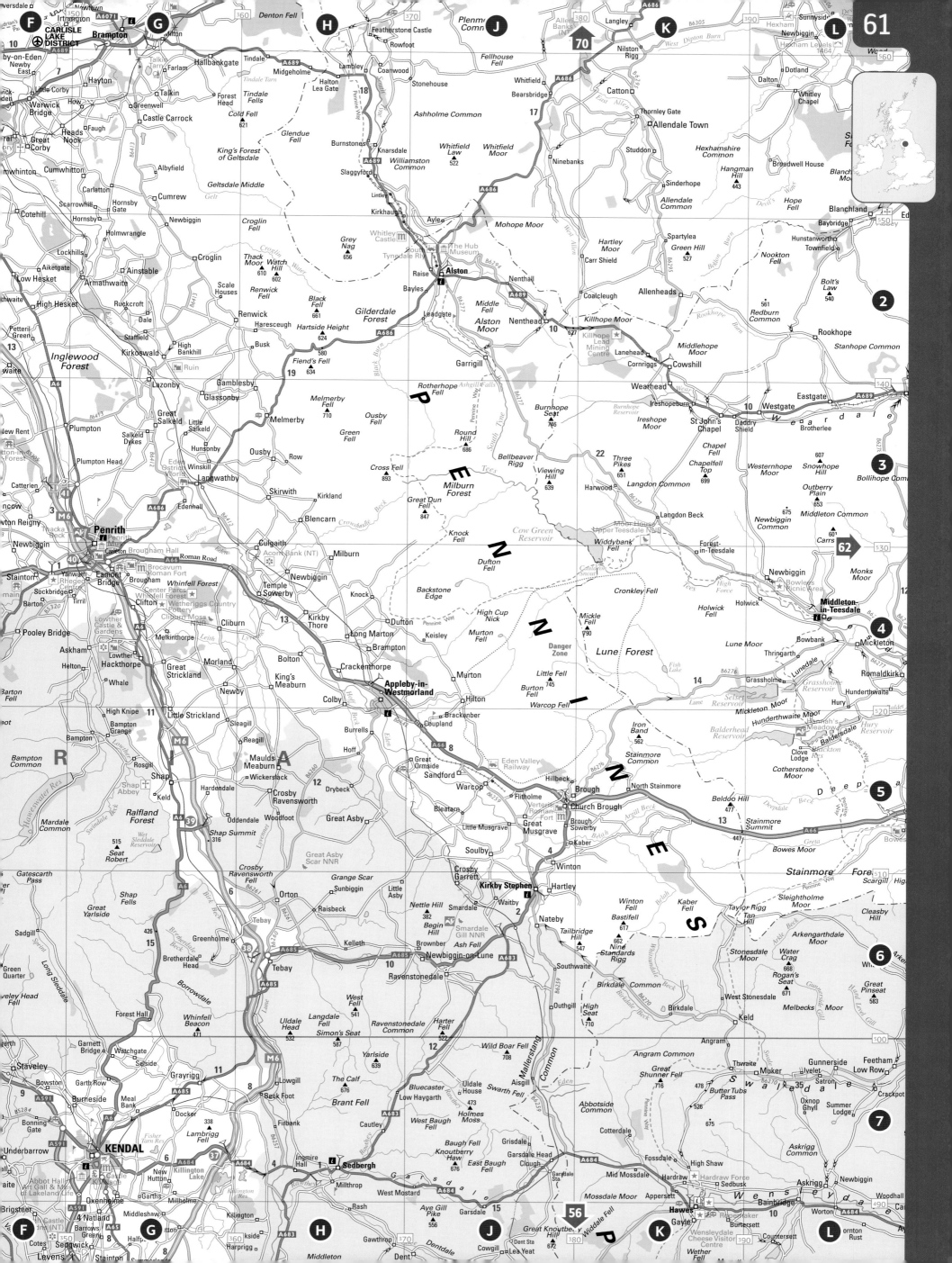

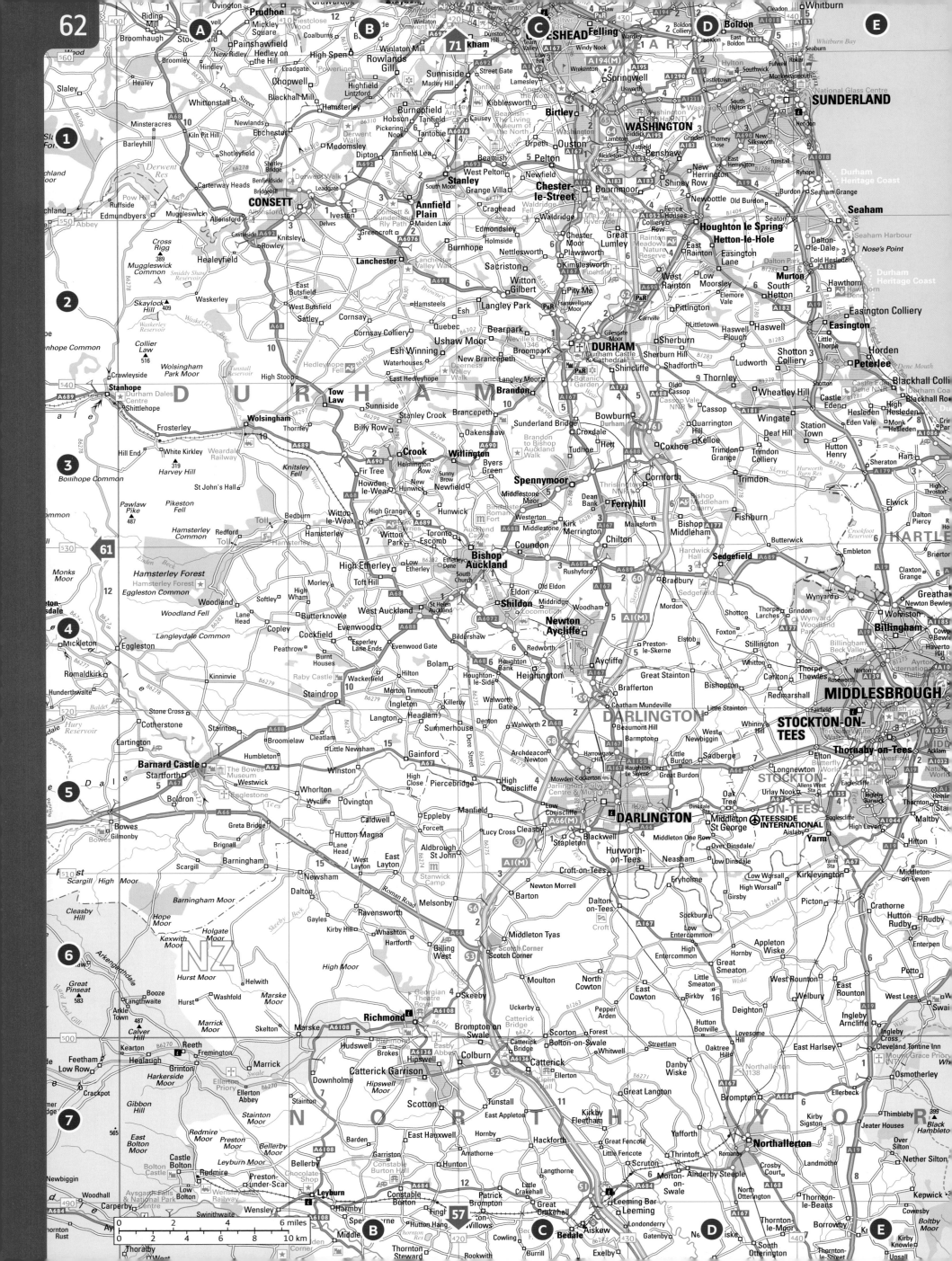

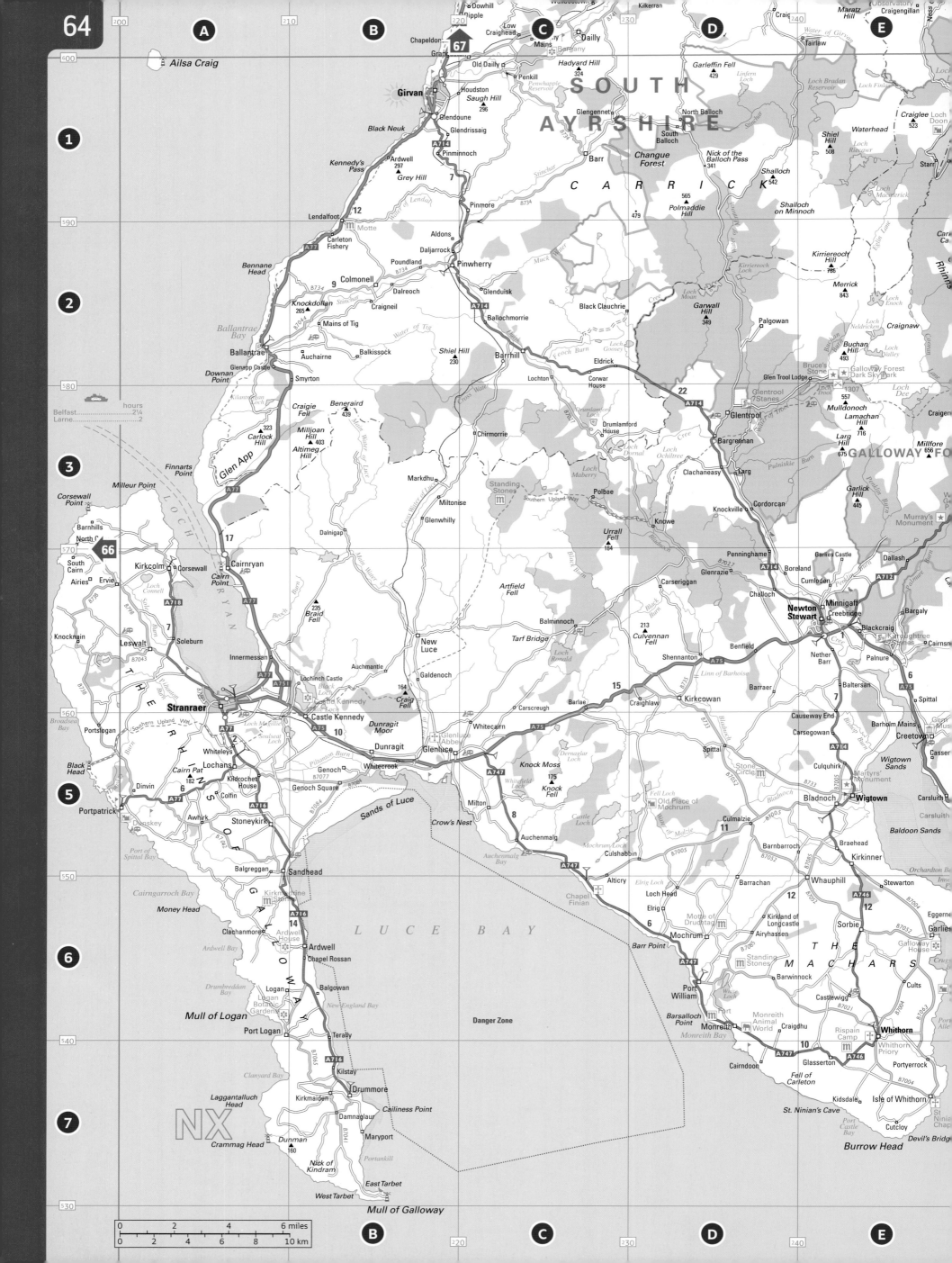

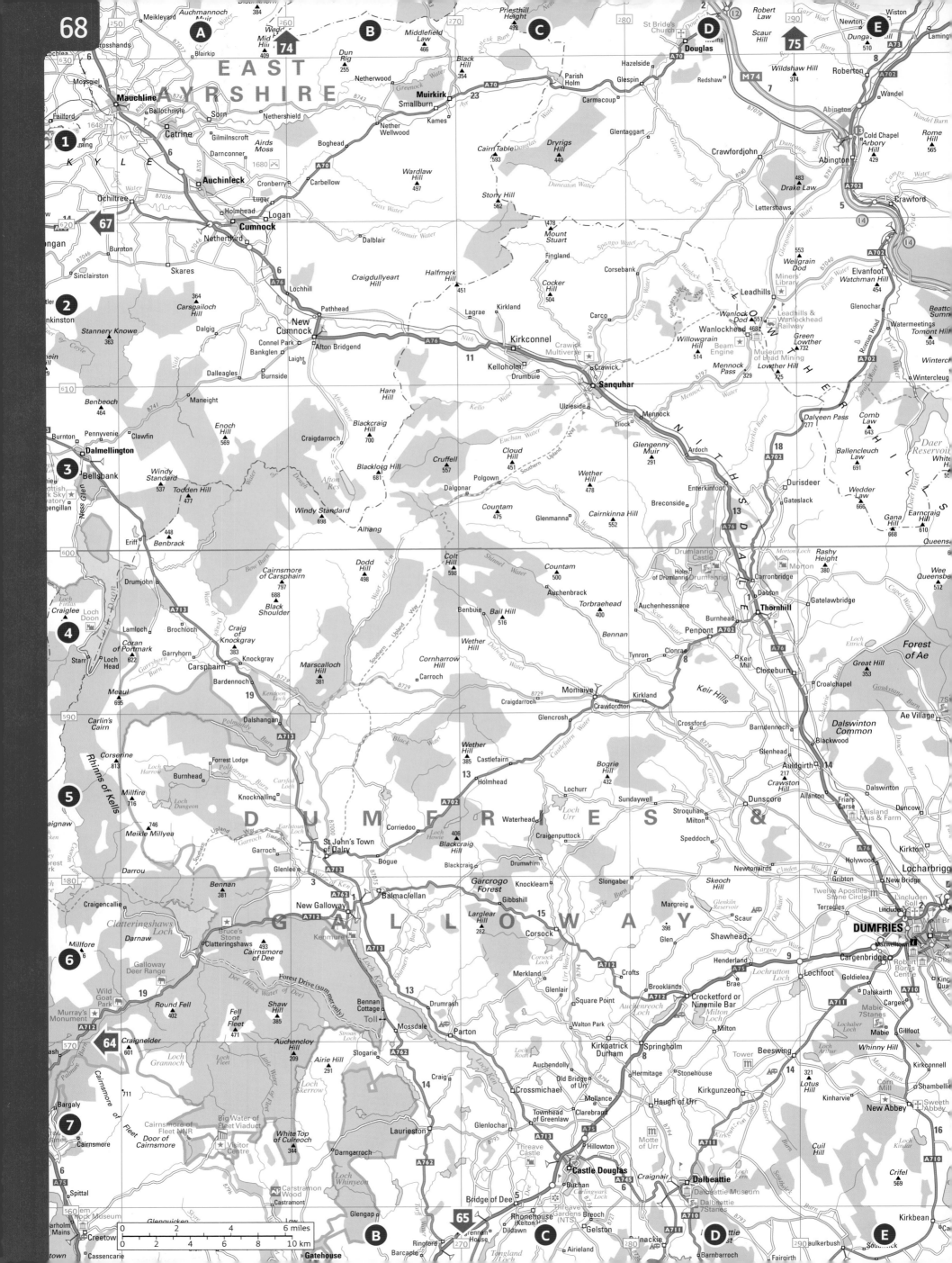

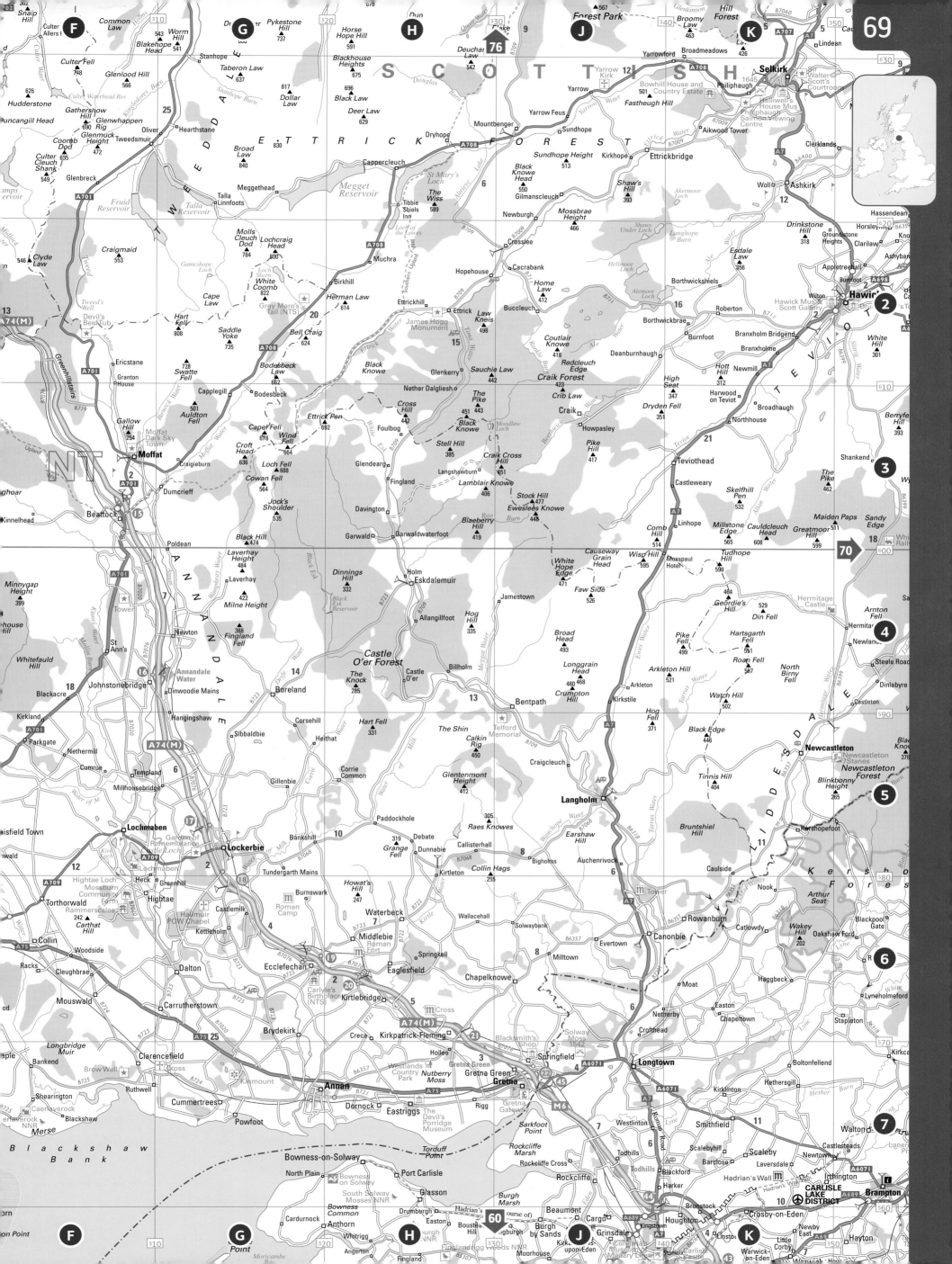

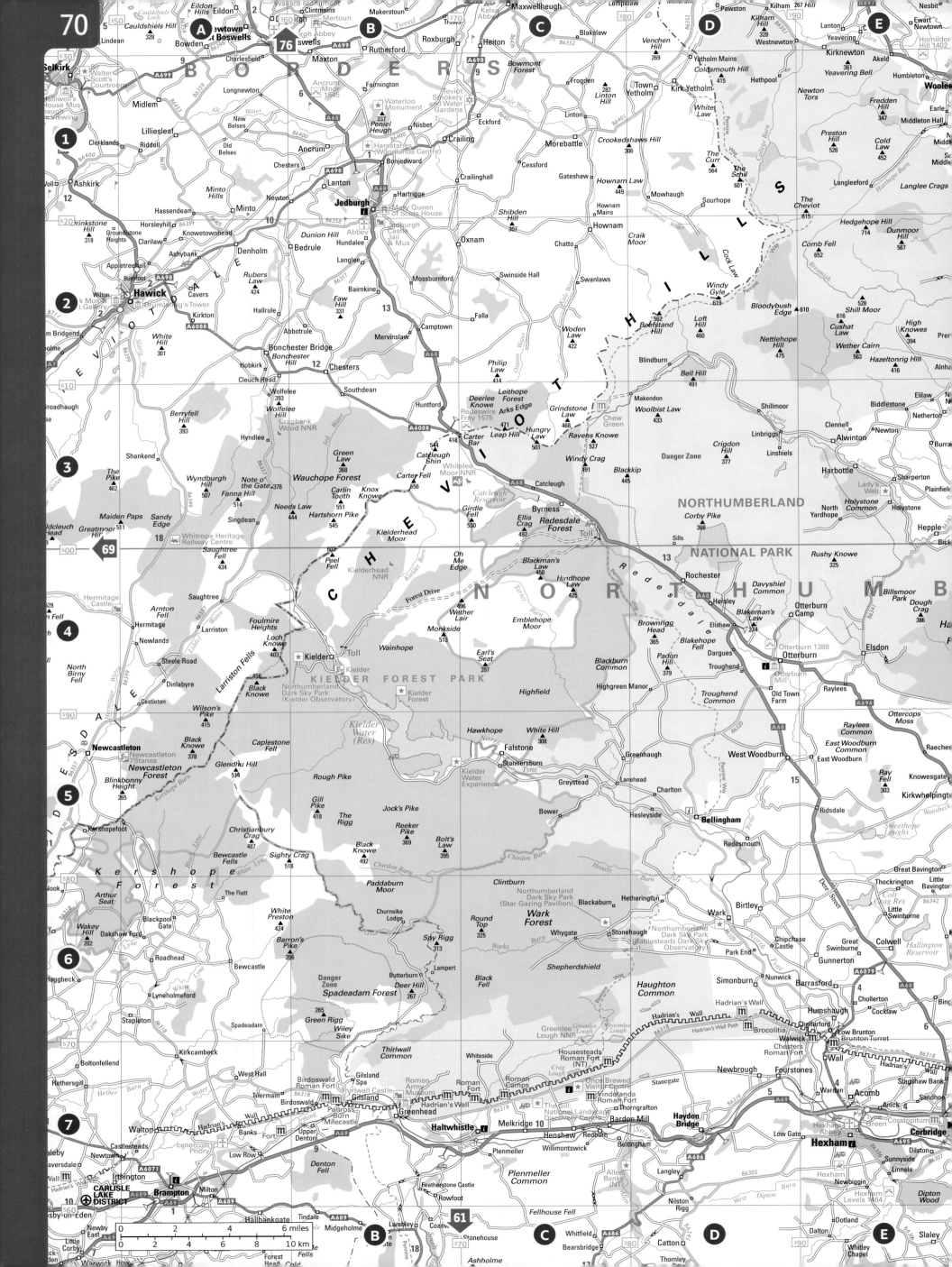

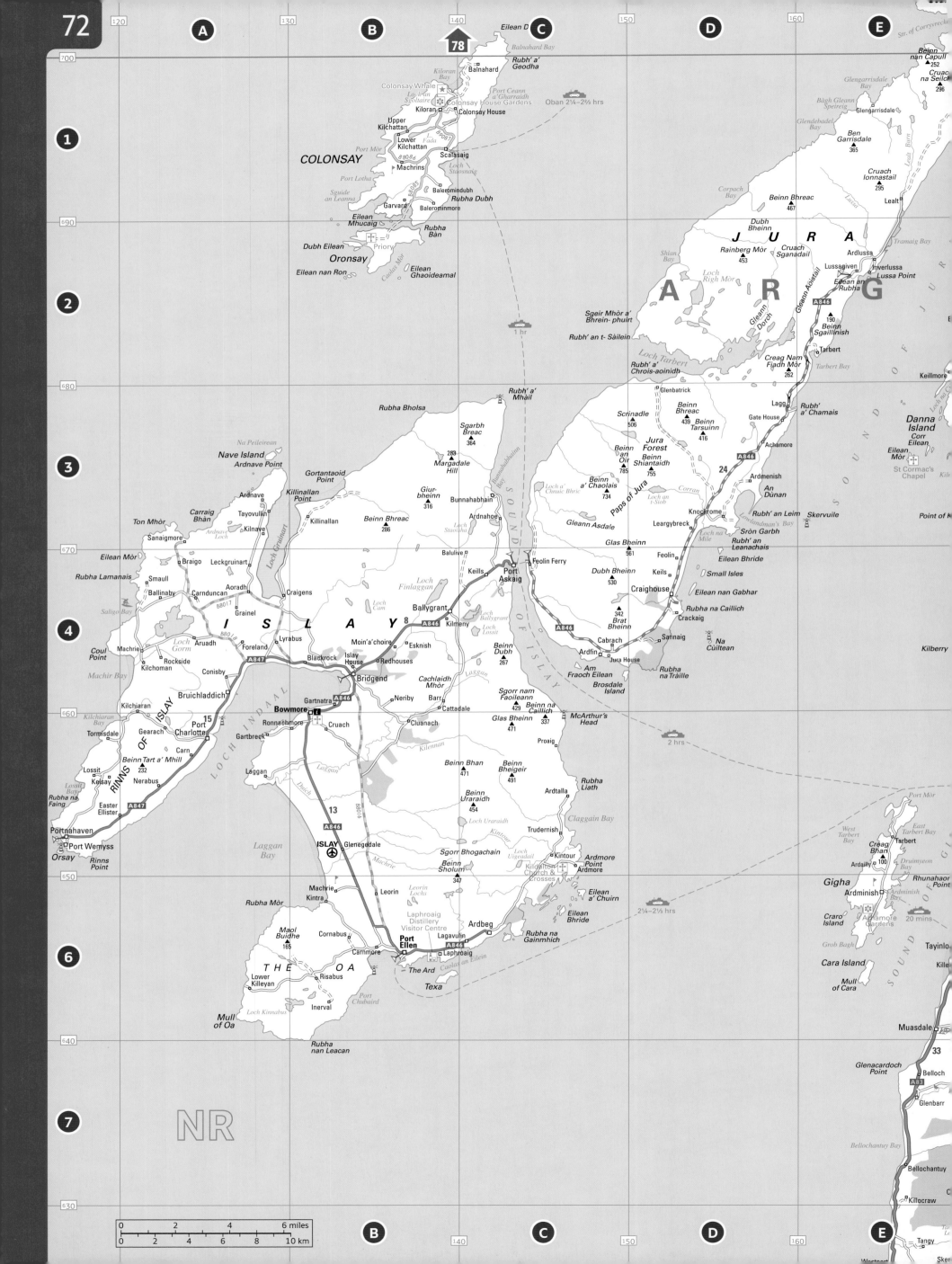

For a more detailed map of Glasgow see pages 118-119

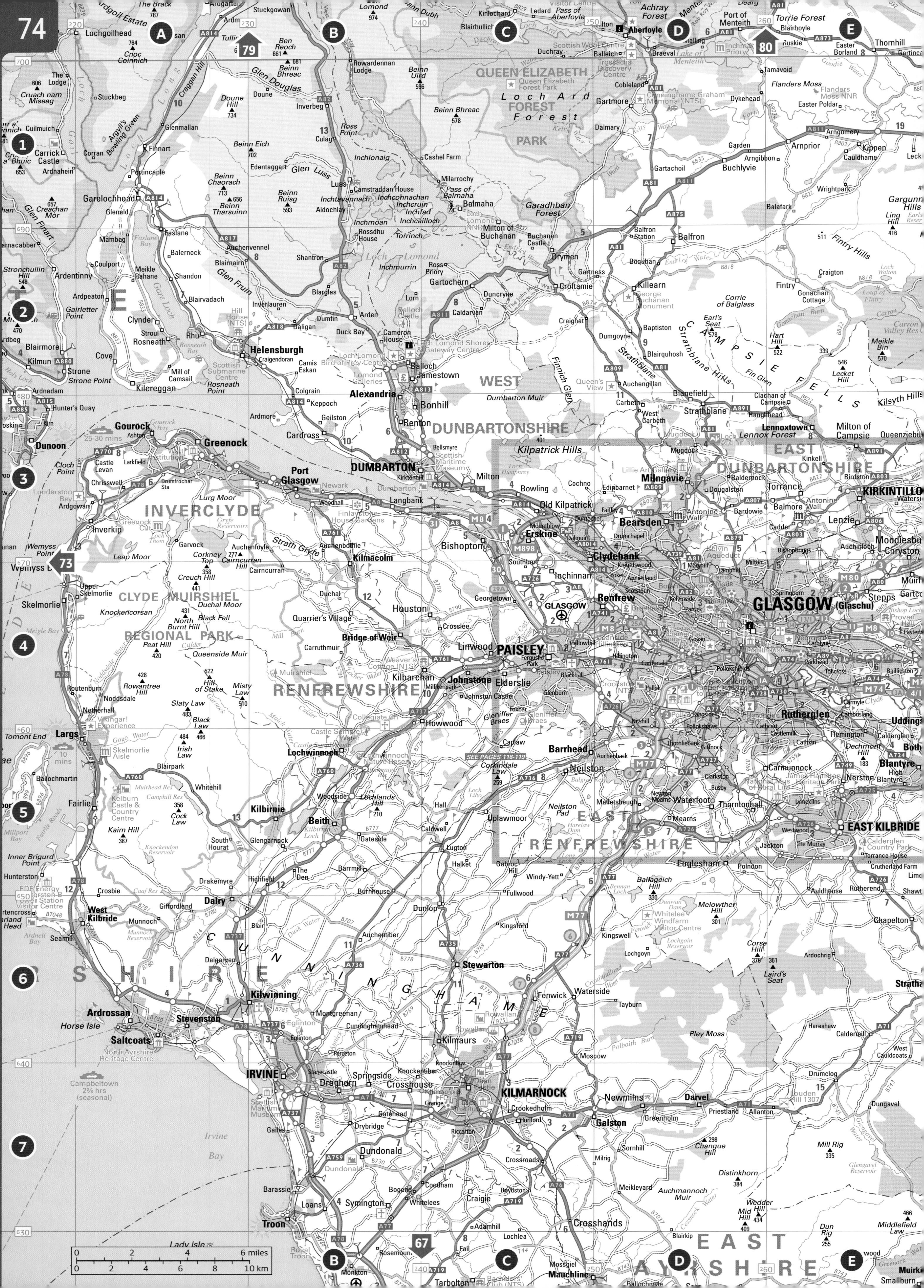

GLASGOW (Glaschu)
PAISLEY
KILMARNOCK
IRVINE
DUMBARTON
Helensburgh
Greenock
Port Glasgow
Gourock
Dunoon
Largs
Ardrossan
Saltcoats
Stevenston
Kilwinning
Kilbirnie
Beith
Dalry
West Kilbride
Troon
Barrhead
Renfrew
Clydebank
Bearsden
Milngavie
Erskine
Bishopton
Kilmacolm
Bridge of Weir
Johnstone
Linwood
Elderslie
Kilbarchan
Lochwinnoch
Rutherglen
East Kilbride
Blantyre
Uddingston
Kirkintilloch
Lenzie
Bishopbriggs
Stepps
Aberfoyle
Drymen
Balfron
Killearn
Strathblane
Blanefield
Lennoxtown
Milton of Campsie
Torrance
Balloch
Alexandria
Bonhill
Renton
Cardross
Lochgoilhead
Garelochhead
Rhu
Clynder
Cove
Kilcreggan
Rosneath
Stewarton
Fenwick
Waterside
Dunlop
Galston
Newmilns
Darvel
Crosshouse
Dreghorn
Springside
Kilmaurs
Dundonald
Symington
Crosshands
Eaglesham
Waterfoot
Thorntonhall
Neilston
Uplawmoor
Caldwell

QUEEN ELIZABETH FOREST PARK
LOCH ARD FOREST
Loch Lomond
Loch Long
Gare Loch
WEST DUNBARTONSHIRE
EAST DUNBARTONSHIRE
INVERCLYDE
RENFREWSHIRE
EAST RENFREWSHIRE
CLYDE MUIRSHIEL REGIONAL PARK
CAMPSIE FELLS
CAMPSIE HILLS
STRATHBLANE HILLS
Kilpatrick Hills
CUNNINGHAME
NORTH AYRSHIRE
EAST AYRSHIRE

SEE PAGES 118-119

Campbeltown 2¾ hrs (seasonal)

0   2   4   6 miles
0 2 4 6 8 10 km

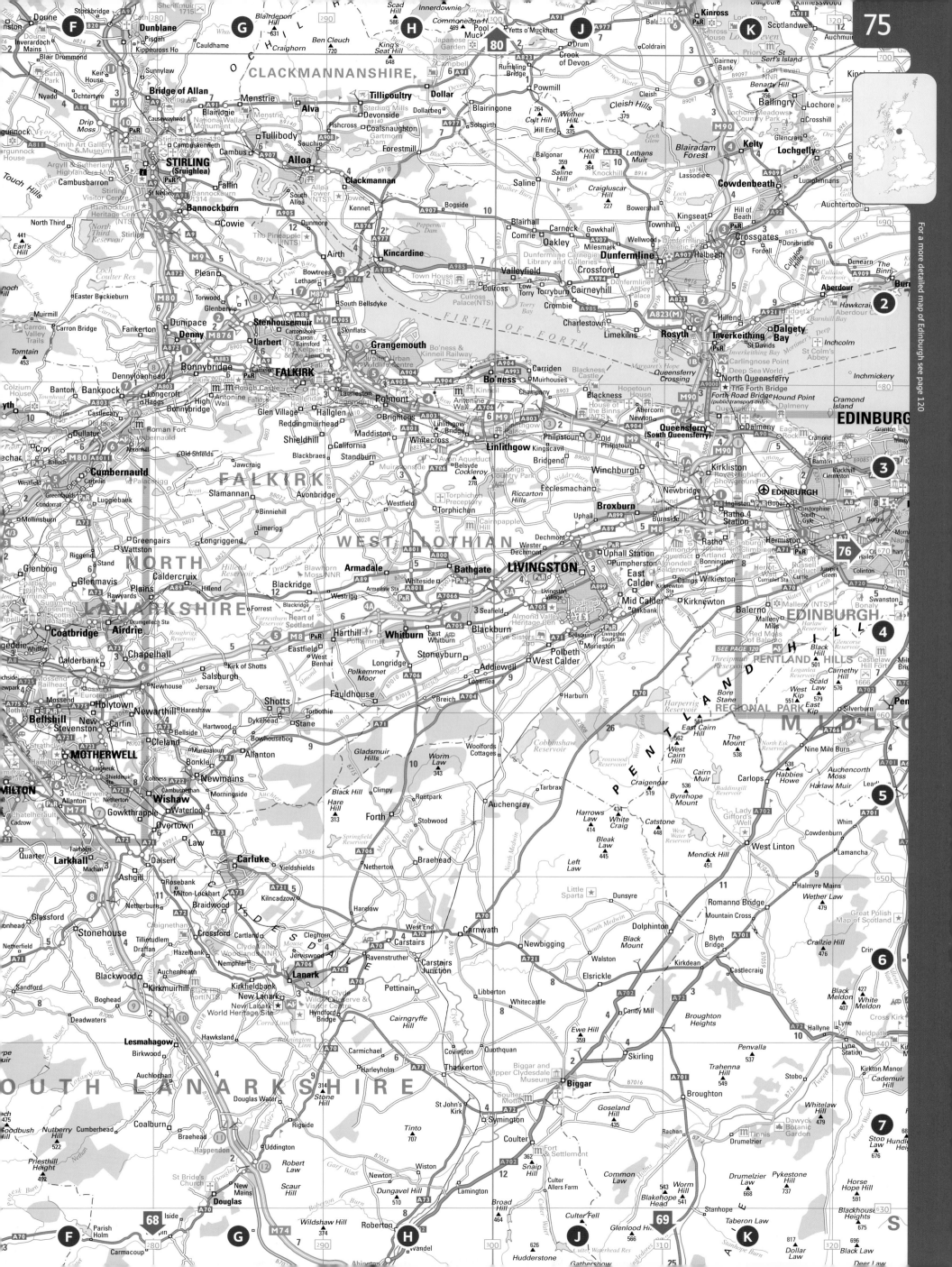

For a more detailed map of Edinburgh see page 120

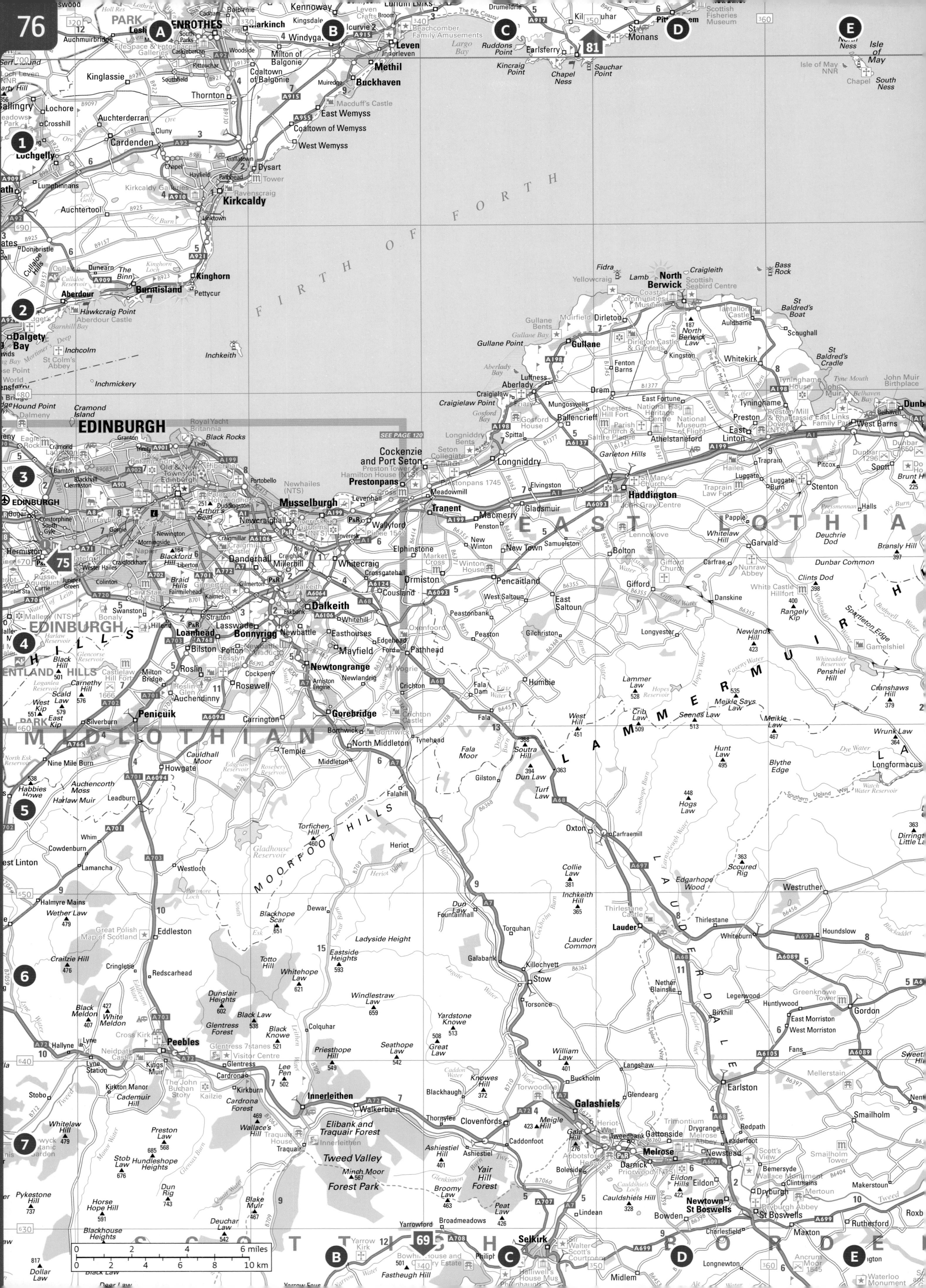

F 380 G 390 H 400 J 410 K 420

700

2

3

4

690

680

670

660

650

640

630

Barns Ness
Skateraw Harbour
Skateraw
erwick 11
Thorntonloch
Reed Point
Bilsdean
Cove
Pease Bay
Siccar Point & Hutton's Unconformity
Cocklaw Hill 319
Dunglass Church
Cockburnspath
Pease Dean
Siccar Point
Fast
Wheat Stack
Telegraph Hill 174
Oldhamstocks
Ecclaw
245
Meikle Black Law
St. Abb's Head NNR (NTS)
St Abb's Head
Heart Law 391
Ecclaw Hill 277
Blackburn Rig
Grantshouse
Coldingham Moor
Northfield
St Abbs
Laughing Law 307
Coldingham
Priory
Coldingham Bay
Abbey St Bathans
Houndwood
9
Cairncross
Mus
Eyemouth
Drakemire
Horseley Hill 262
Reston
Burnmouth
Ellemford
Cockburn Law 325
Marygold
Auchencrow
Ayton
Ayton
199
Ayton Hill 6
Hilton Bay
Lamberton Beach
Edin's Hall Broch
Millerton Hill 132
Preston
Lintlaw
Lamberton
Marshall Meadows
North Northumberland Heritage Coast
Blanerne
Chirnside
Mordington Holdings
Needles Eye
Edrom Norman Arch
Tithe Barn
Halidon Hill
Sharper's Head
Jim Clark Motorsport Museum
Edrom
Chirnsidebridge
16
Foulden
Clappers
163
Halidon Hill 1333
Highfields
Ravensdowne Barracks
Duns
Manderston
Allanton
Hutton
Paxton
Berwick
Berwick-upon-Tweed
Gavinton
Blackadder
Sunwick
Paxton House
Tweedmouth
Spittal
Choicelee
Whitelaw
Fishwick
Union Bridge
East Ord
3
Redshin Cove
Polwarth
Sinclair's Hill
Whitsome
Horncliffe
Longridge Towers
Scremerston
Fogo Church
Horndean
Cheswick Black Rocks
Greenlaw Moor
Fogo
Lady Kirk Church
Murton
North Northumberland Heritage Coast
Hule Moss
12
Thornton Park
Thornton
Cheswick
Holy Island (Lindisfarne)
Emmanuel Head
Greenlaw
Swinton
Ladykirk
Norham
West Allerdean
Cheswick Buildings
Goswick
Purves Hall
Swinton Quarter
Shoreswood
Shoresdean
Ancroft
Berrington
St Mary
St Aidan's Winery
Leitholm
Simprim
Upsettlington
Norham
13
Grindon
Felkington
Duddo
Bowsden
Haggerston
Beal
Lindisfarne NNR
Holy Island
Priory
Lindisfarne (NT)
Castle Point
Burrows Hole
Easter Howlaws
10
Lambden
Orange Lane
West Mains
13
Fenham
Guile Point
Humehall
Eccles
Castle Heaton
Barmoor Lane End
Lowick
West Kyloe
Holy Island Sands
Fenham Flats
Longstone
Legars
The Hirsel
Lennel
New Heaton
Crookham Eastfield
East Kyloe
Fenwick
Fenham
Farne Islands NNR
Coldstream
Coldstream Museum
Pallinsburn House
Etal
Buckton
Farne Islands
Stichill
Birgham
Carham
Wark
Cornhill on Tweed
Crookham
Ford
Holburn
Detchant
Elwick
Ross
Budle Bay
Budle Point
Grace Darling Museum
Ednam
Hendersyde Park
Hadden
West Learmouth
Branxton
Mardon
211
Low Middleton
Middleton
Easington
Budle
Bamburgh Castle
Monks House Rocks
Floors Castle
Kelso
Sprouston
Pressen
East Learmouth
Flodden 1513
Flodden
15
Kimmerston
Cockenheugh
Waren Mill
Bamburgh
Marine Life Centre & Fishing Museum
Kelso Abbey
Maxwellheugh
Downham
Howtel
Milfield
Fenton
North Hazelrigg
South Hazelrigg
Belford
Outchester
Spindlestone
Glororum
Burton
New Shoreston
Seahouses
Heiton
Mindrummill
Mindrum
Pawston
Kilham
Lanton
Nesbit
Doddington
Warenton
Bellshill
Adderstone
Lucker
East Fleetham
North Sunderland
Blakelaw
Venchen Hill 282
Kilham Hill 328
Westnewton
Ewart Newtown
West Horton
East Horton
10
Swinhoe
Newstead
Newham
East Fleetham
Bowmont Forest
70
Town Yetholm
Yetholm Mains
Coldsmouth Hill
Kirknewton
Akeld
Homildon Hill 1402
Greendykes
71
Warenford
Newham Hall
Benthall
Frogden
Kirk Yetholm
Hethpool
Newton Tors
Yeavering Bell 361
Humbleton
Wooler
Wandon
Chatton
Twizell House
Rosebrough
Chathill

A1 A1107 A6105 A6112 A6461 A6464 A697 A698 A1167 B6437 B6438 B6355 B6347 B6354 B6353 B6461 B6460 B6456 B6352 B6350 B6396 B6351 B6349 B6525 B1342

F 380 G 390 H 400 J 410 K 420

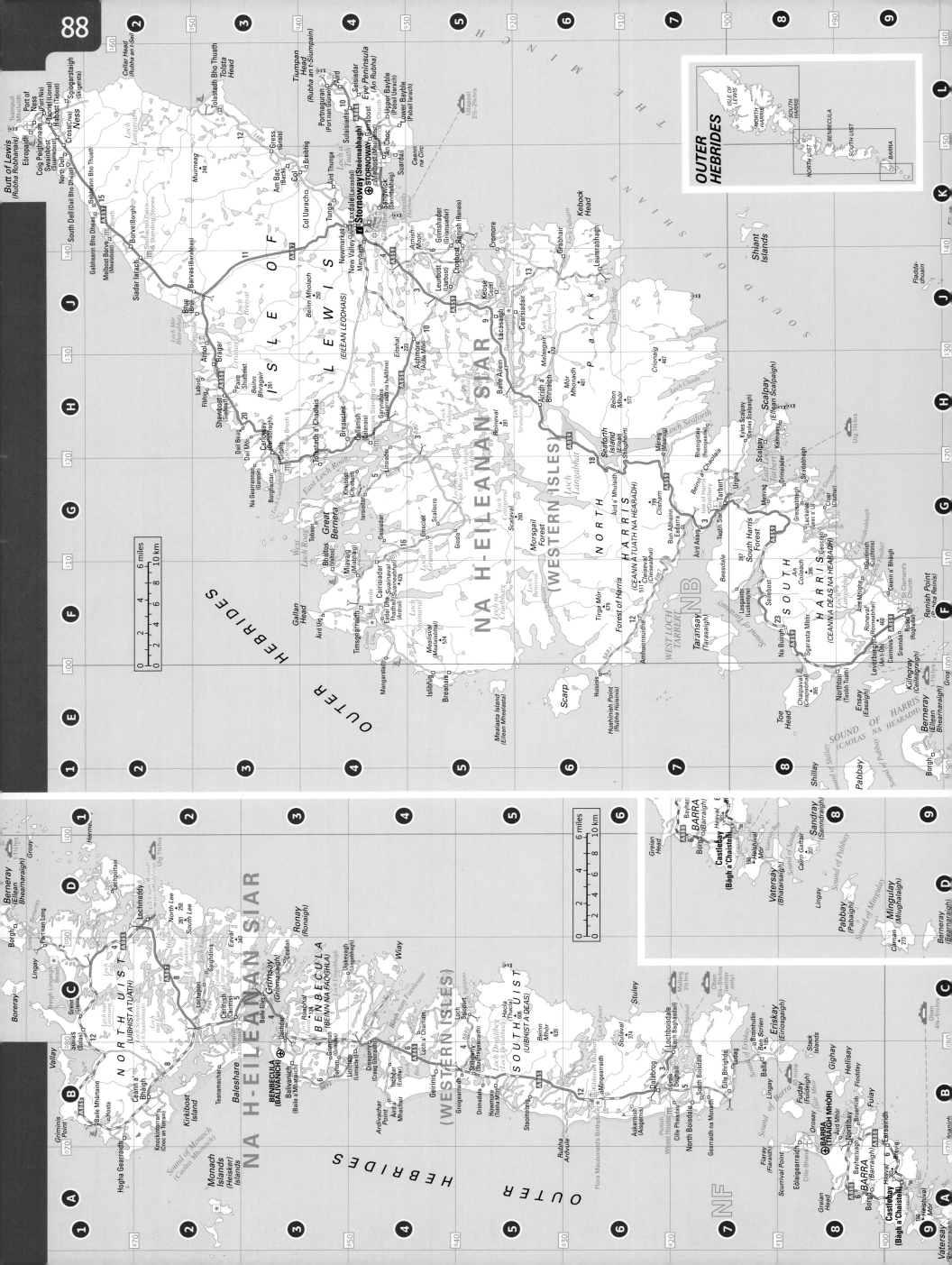

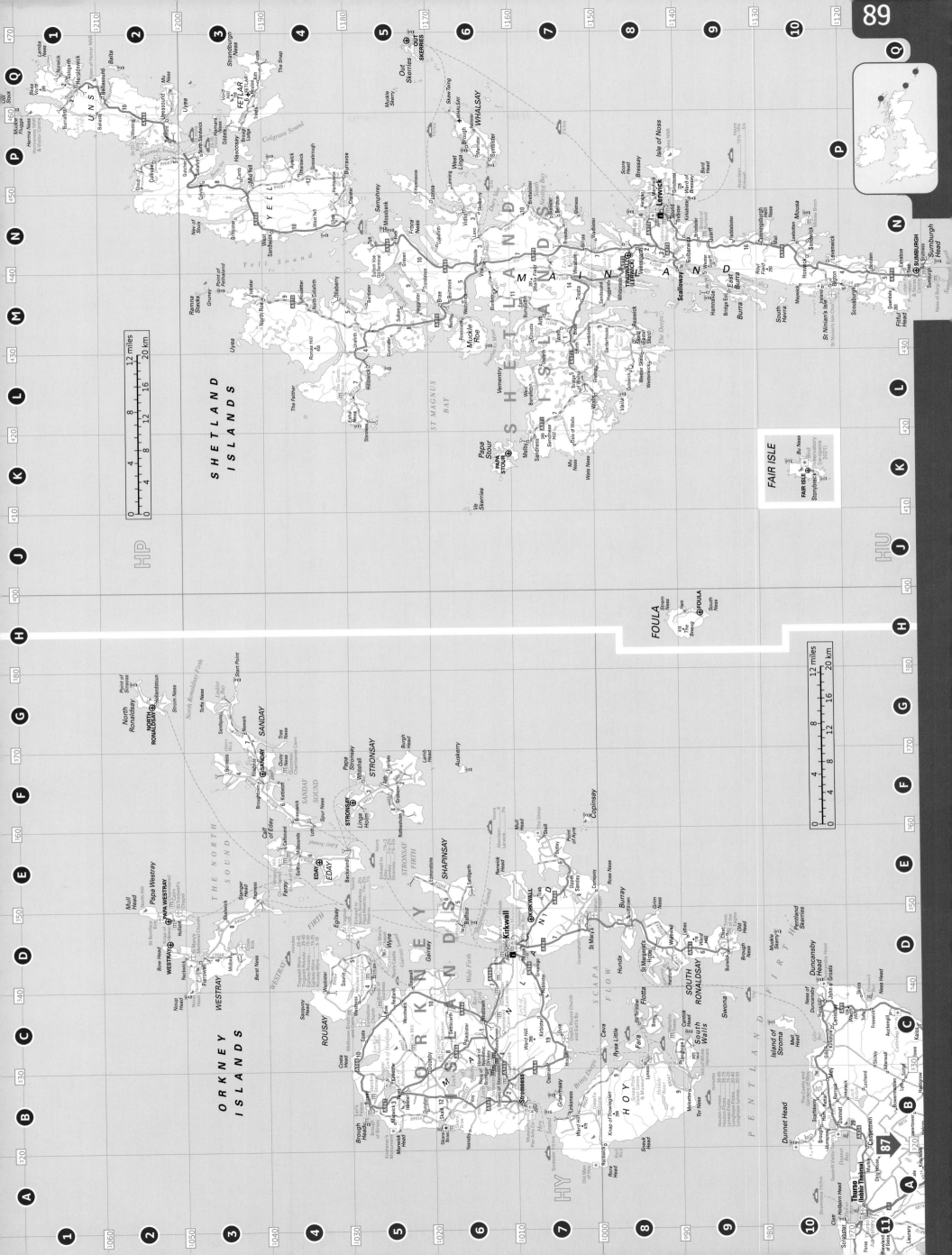

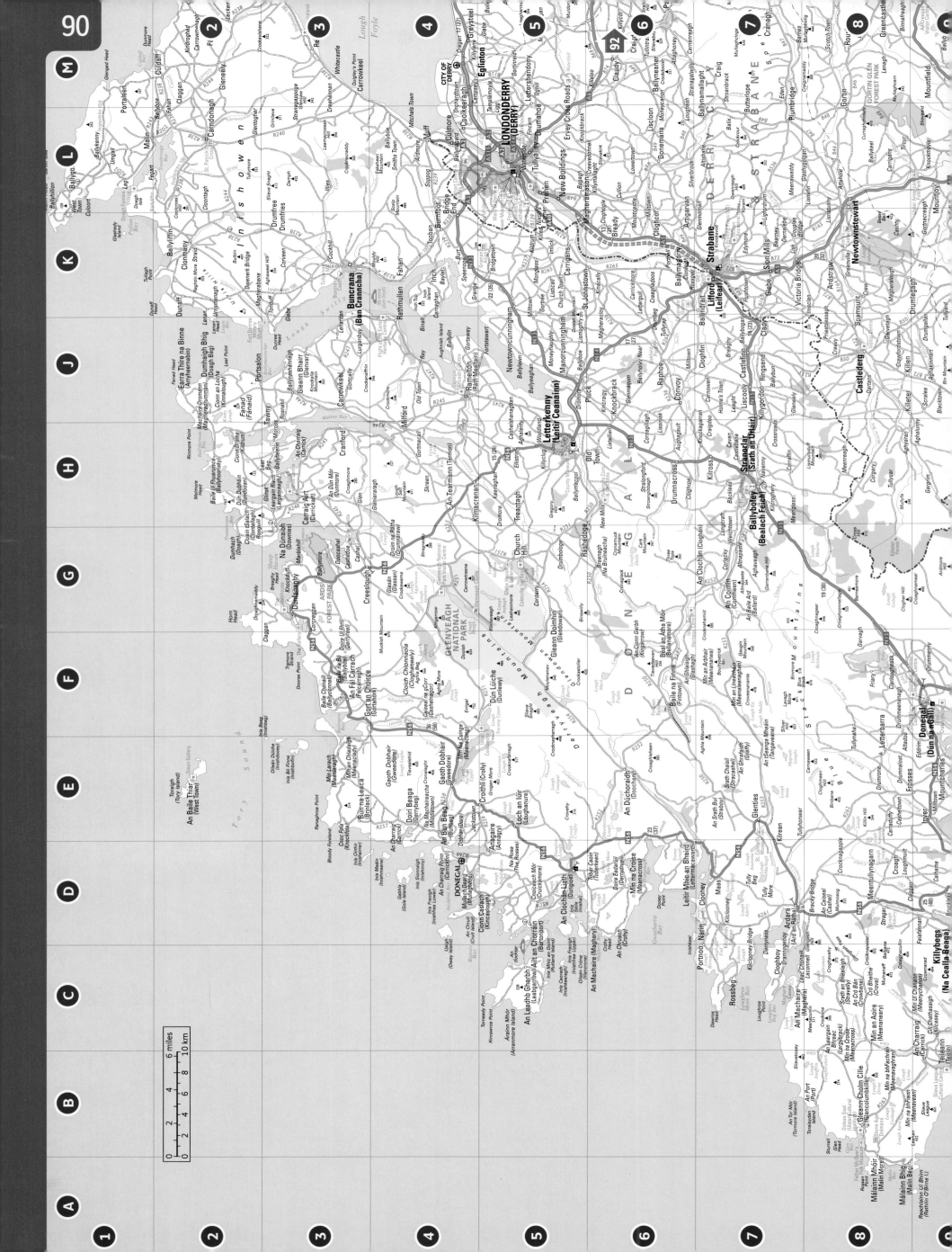

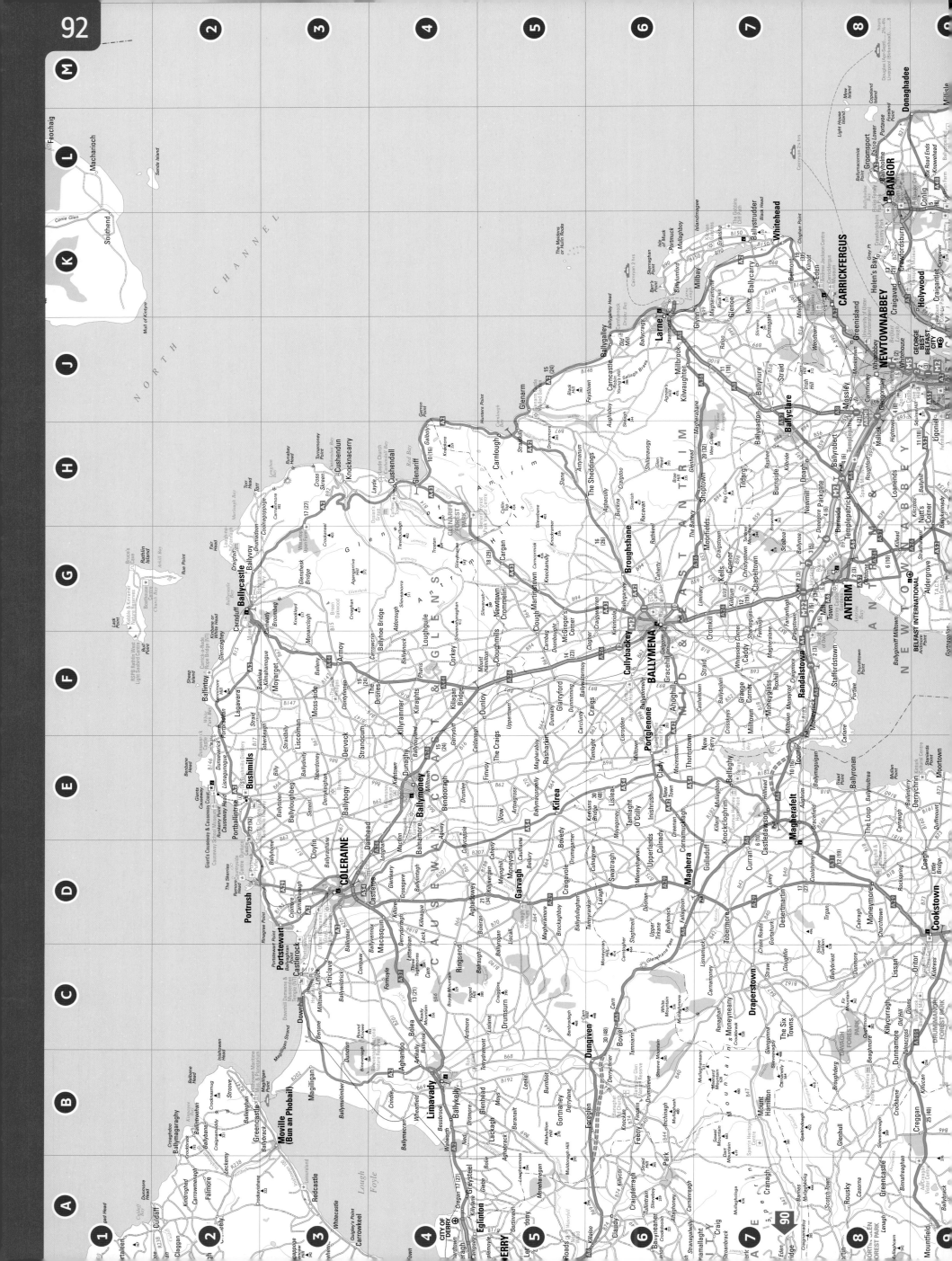

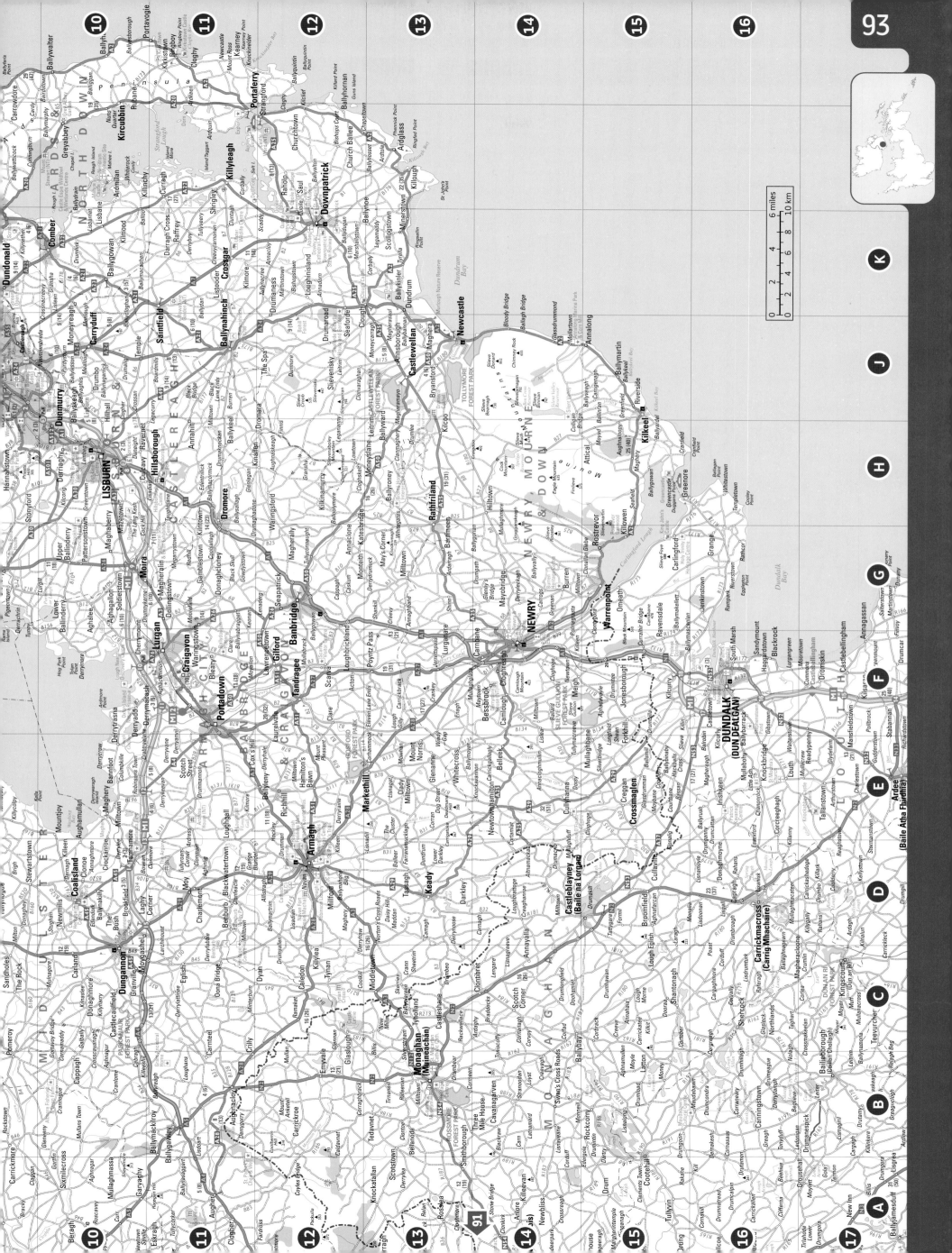

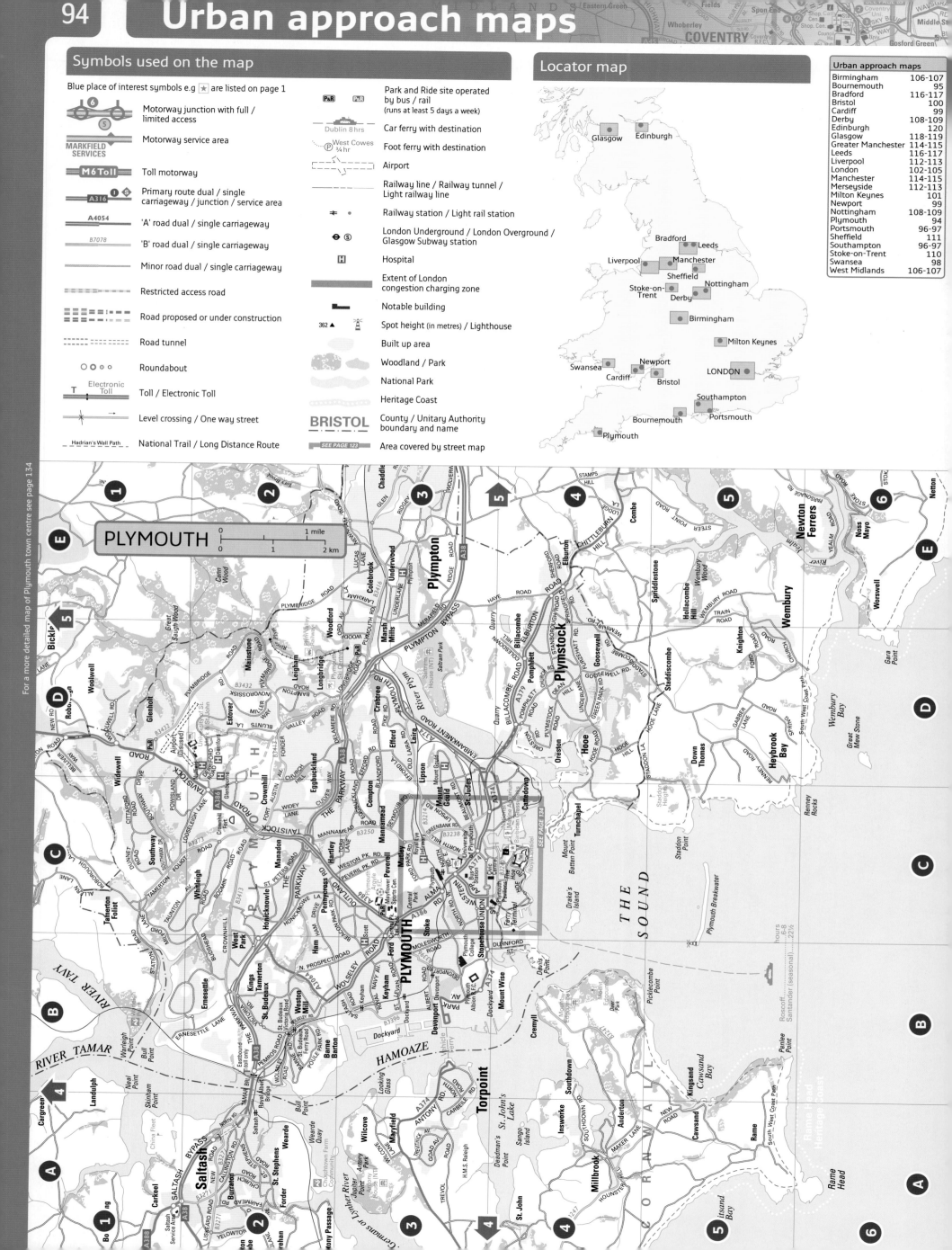

Symbols used on the map

Blue place of interest symbols e.g ★ are listed on page 1

- Motorway junction with full / limited access
- MARKFIELD SERVICES — Motorway service area
- M6 Toll — Toll motorway
- A316 — Primary route dual / single carriageway / junction / service area
- A4054 — 'A' road dual / single carriageway
- B7078 — 'B' road dual / single carriageway
- Minor road dual / single carriageway
- Restricted access road
- Road proposed or under construction
- Road tunnel
- Roundabout
- T — Toll / Electronic Toll
- Level crossing / One way street
- Hadrian's Wall Path — National Trail / Long Distance Route
- P&R / P&R — Park and Ride site operated by bus / rail (runs at least 5 days a week)
- Dublin 8 hrs — Car ferry with destination
- West Cowes ¼ hr — Foot ferry with destination
- Airport
- Railway line / Railway tunnel / Light railway line
- Railway station / Light rail station
- London Underground / London Overground / Glasgow Subway station
- H — Hospital
- Extent of London congestion charging zone
- Notable building
- 362 ▲ — Spot height (in metres) / Lighthouse
- Built up area
- Woodland / Park
- National Park
- Heritage Coast
- BRISTOL — County / Unitary Authority boundary and name
- SEE PAGE 123 — Area covered by street map

Locator map

Glasgow, Edinburgh, Bradford, Leeds, Liverpool, Manchester, Sheffield, Nottingham, Stoke-on-Trent, Derby, Birmingham, Milton Keynes, Swansea, Newport, Cardiff, Bristol, LONDON, Southampton, Bournemouth, Portsmouth, Plymouth

PLYMOUTH

For a more detailed map of Plymouth town centre see see page 134

For a more detailed map of Bournemouth town centre see page 123

BOURNEMOUTH

0 ———— 1 mile
0 —— 1 —— 2 km

POOLE BAY

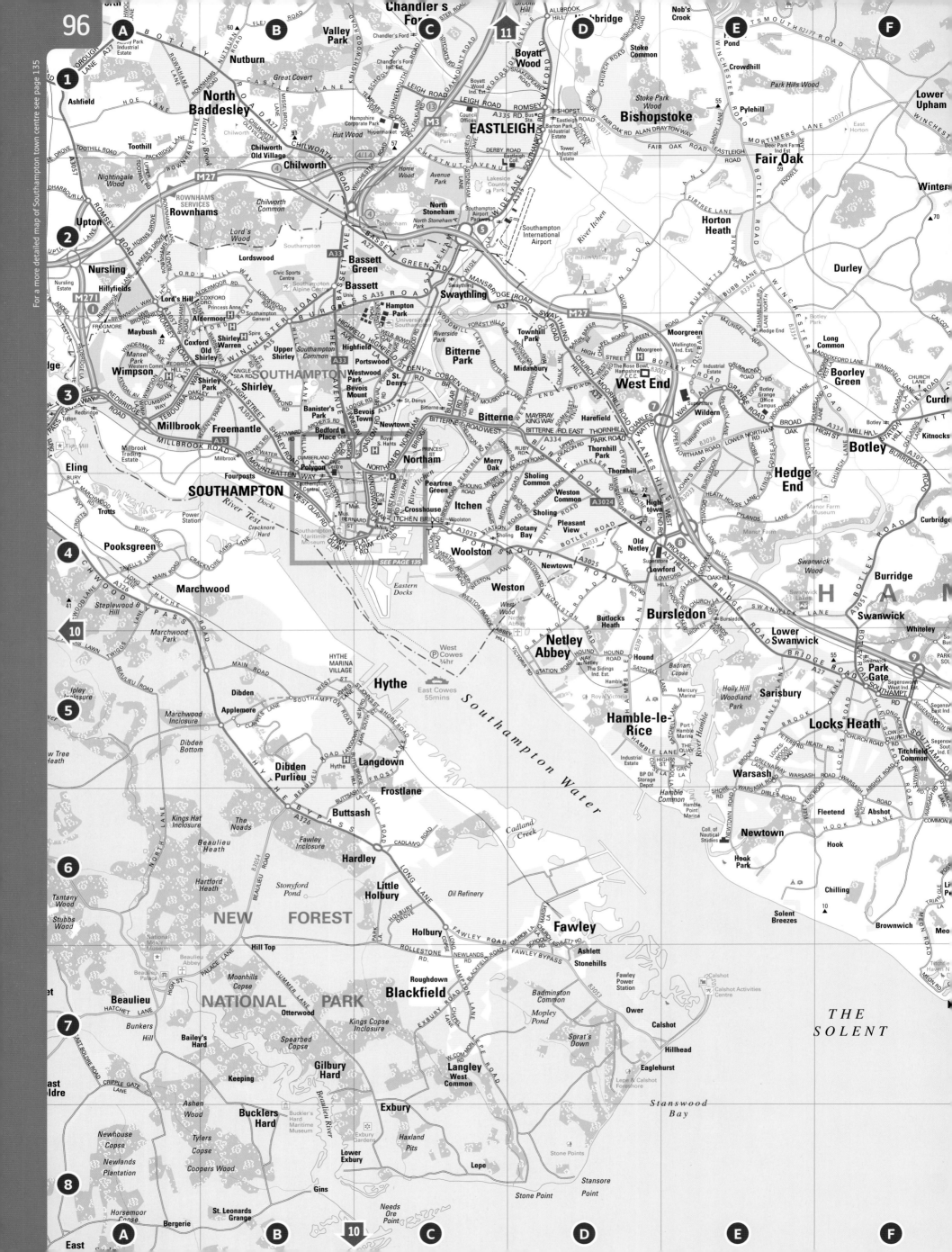

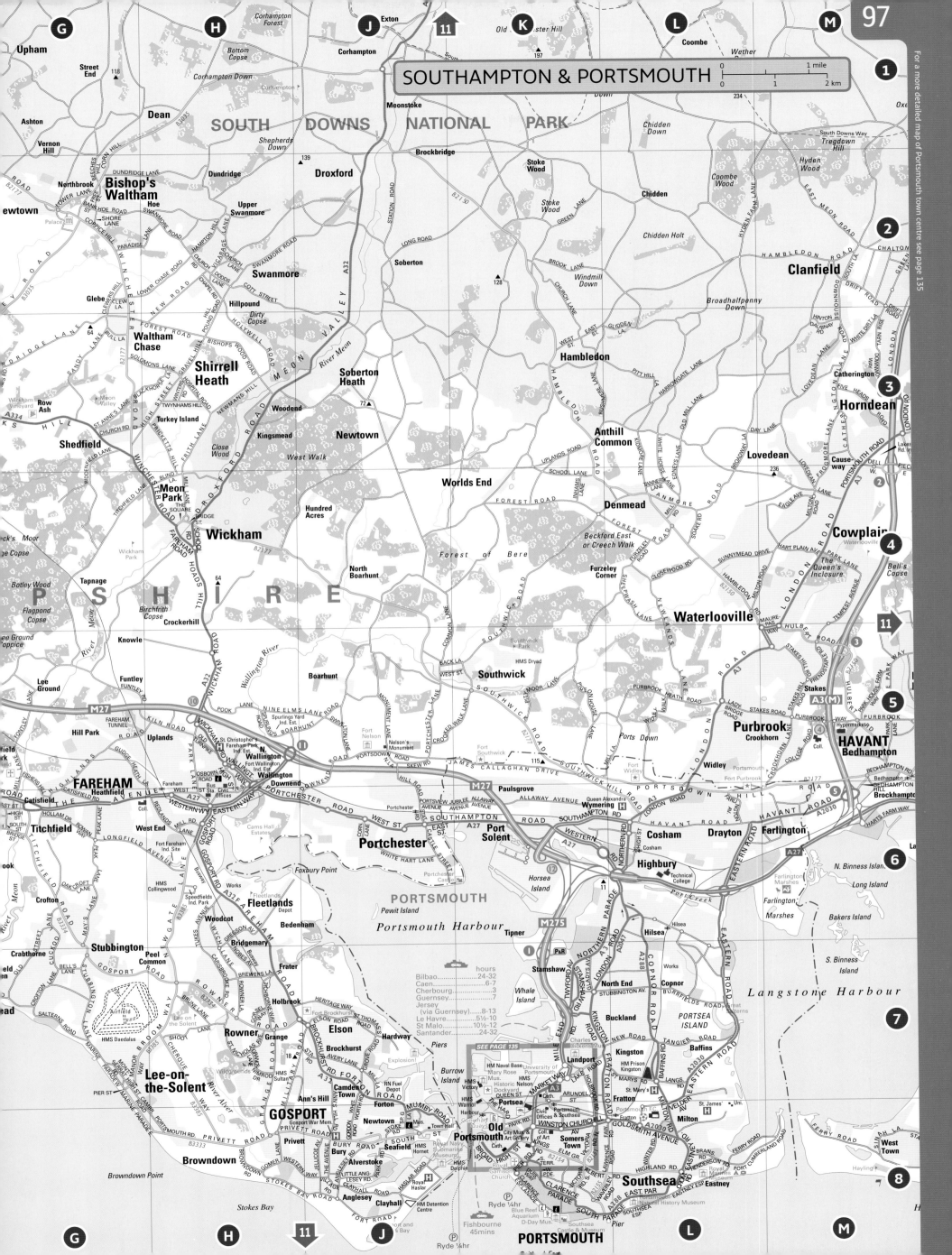

SWANSEA

0   1 mile
0   1   2 km

For a more detailed map of Swansea town centre see page 136

For a more detailed map of Cardiff town centre see page 124

CARDIFF & NEWPORT

0   1 mile
0 1
   2 km

BRISTOL CHANNEL

NEWPORT

CARDIFF

CAERPHILLY

RHONDDA
CYNON TAFF

VALE OF GLAMORGAN

BRISTOL

For a more detailed map of Bristol town centre see page 123

0 — 1 mile
0 — 1 — 2 km

GLOUCESTERSHIRE

SOUTH GLOUCESTERSHIRE

BATH & NORTH EAST SOMERSET

NORTH SOMERSET

Chipping Sodbury · Goose Green · Yate · Stover · Westerleigh · Rodford · Coalpit Heath · Frampton End · Frampton Cotterell · Iron Acton · England Cross · North Woods · Winterbourne · Winterbourne Down · Hick's Common · Watley's End · Whiteshill · Hambrook · Bromley Heath · Downend · Frenchay · Staple Hill · Mangotsfield · Vinny Green · Emersons Green · Lyde Green · Richmond · Pomphrey Hill · Blackhorse · Soundwell · New Cheltenham · Rodway Hill · Two Mile Hill · Hillfields · Fishponds · Kingswood · Mount Hill · Warmley · Goose Green · North Common · Webb's Heath · Bridgeyate · Wick · Beach · Siston · Abson · Doynton · Dyrham · Hinton · Pucklechurch · Parkfield · Shortwood · Holbrook Common · North Stoke · Upper Weston · Lansdown · Tadwick · Langridge · Swineford · Saltford · Keynsham · Somerdale · Oldland Common · Oldland · Longwell Green · Hanham Green · Hanham · Cadbury Heath · Barr's Court · Stone Hill · Conham · Brislington · Stockwood · Broom Hill · St. Anne's Park · Netham · Crew's Hole · Speedwell · Whitehall · Easton · Eastville · Stapleton · Broomhill · Clay Hill · Ridgeway · St. George · Summerhill · Whitehall · Lawrence Hill · Barton Hill · St. Philips · BRISTOL · Windmill Hill · Knowle · Lower Knowle · Totterdown · Filwood Park · Novers Park · Hengrove Park · Hengrove · Whitchurch · Hartcliffe · Withywood · Highridge · Bishopsworth · Headley Park · Bedminster Down · Bedminster · Ashton Gate · Ashton Vale · Bower Ashton · Long Ashton · Leigh Woods · Abbots Leigh · Failand · Lower Failand · Easton-in-Gordano · Pill · Ham Green · Shirehampton · Avonmouth · Cabot Park · Lawrence Weston · Kings Weston · Sea Mills · Coombe Dingle · Henbury · Sneyd Park · Stoke Bishop · Westbury-on-Trym · Redland · Cotham · Clifton · Hotwells · Montpelier · Ashley Down · Bishopston · Horfield · Henleaze · Golden Hill · Southmead · Brentry · Eastfield · Westbury Park · Lockleaze · Filton · Horfield · Harry Stoke · Little Stoke · Stoke Gifford · Great Stoke · Bradley Stoke · Patchway · Woodlands · Catbrain · Cribbs Causeway · Easter Compton · Compton Greenfield · Marsh Common · Berwick · Hallen · Chemical Works · Y's non

University of the West of England

River Avon · River Frome · Bristol & Clifton · River Boyd

Bristol International Airport · Cambridge Batch · Barrow Common · Barrow Gurney · Flax Bourton

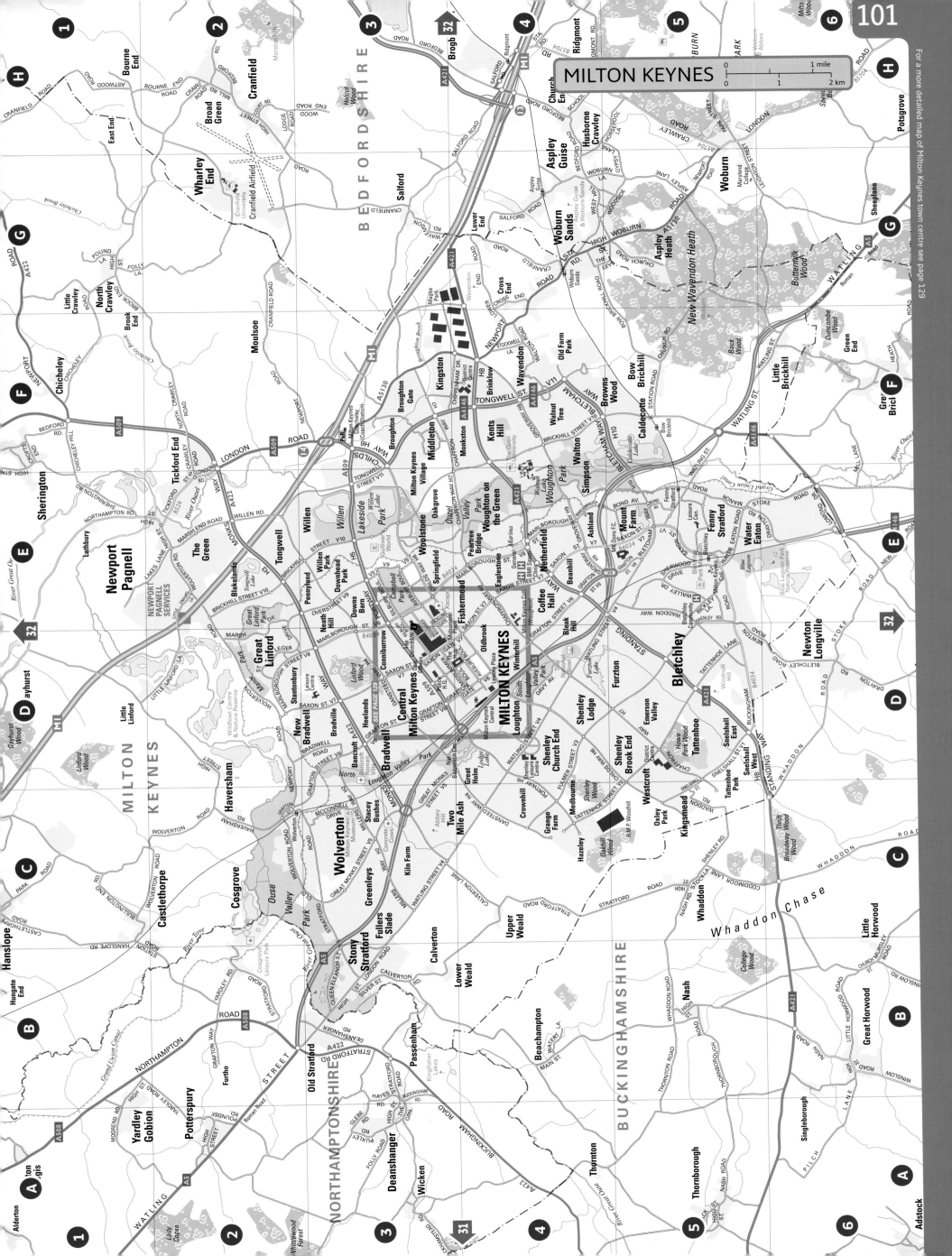

GREATER LONDON - WEST

For a more detailed map of Central London see page 132

0 — 1 mile — 2 km

For a more detailed map of Central London see page 132

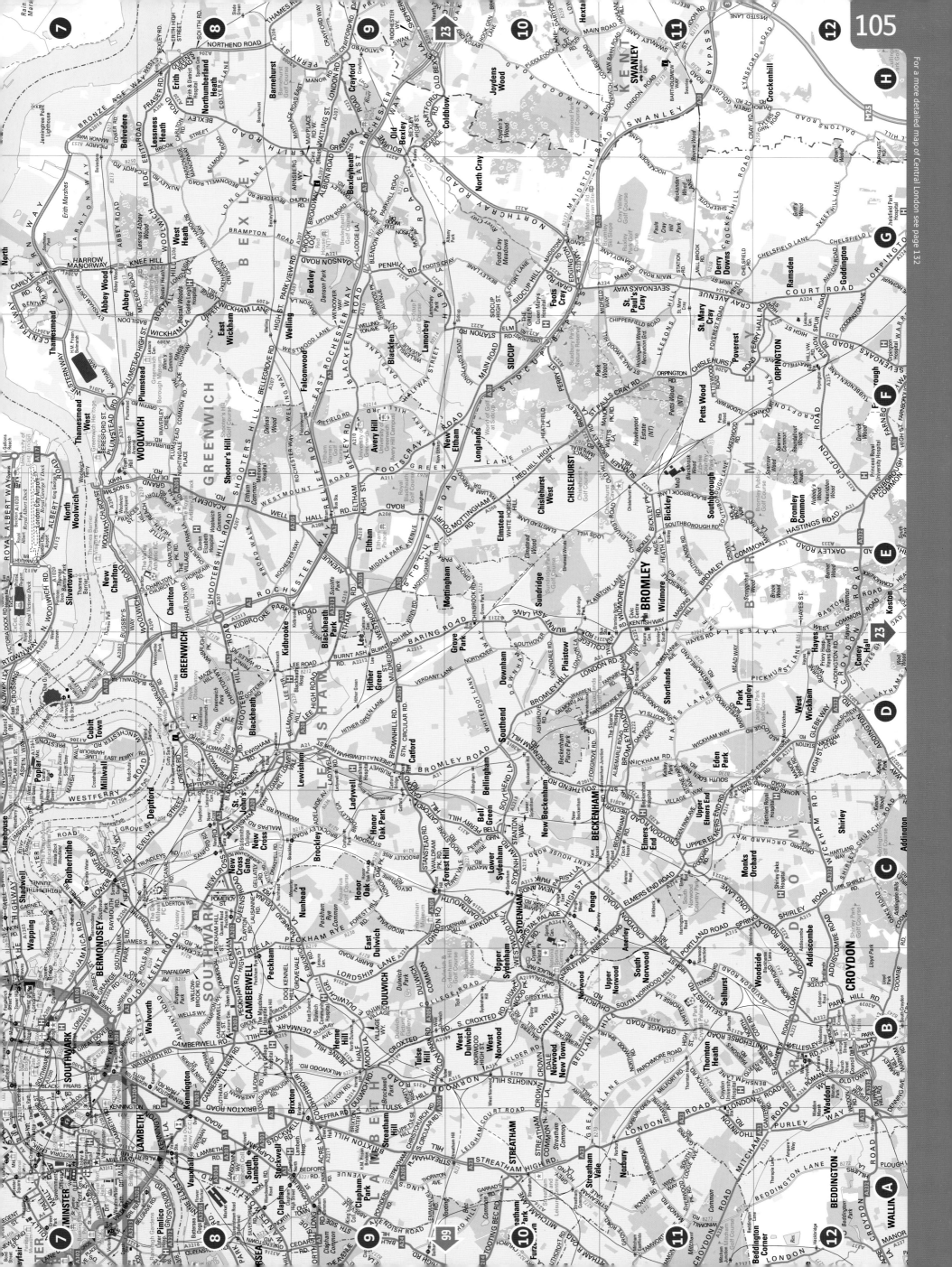

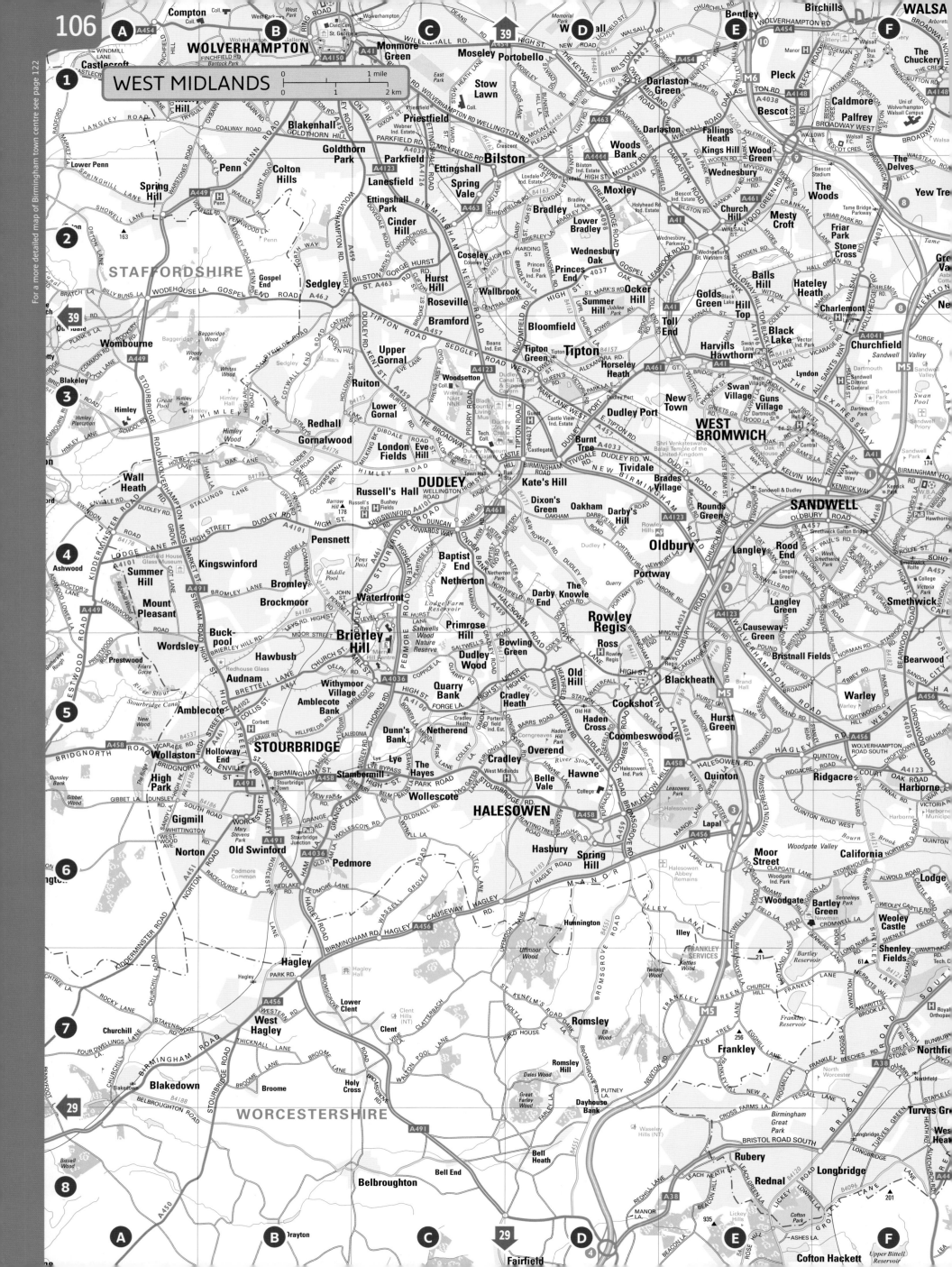

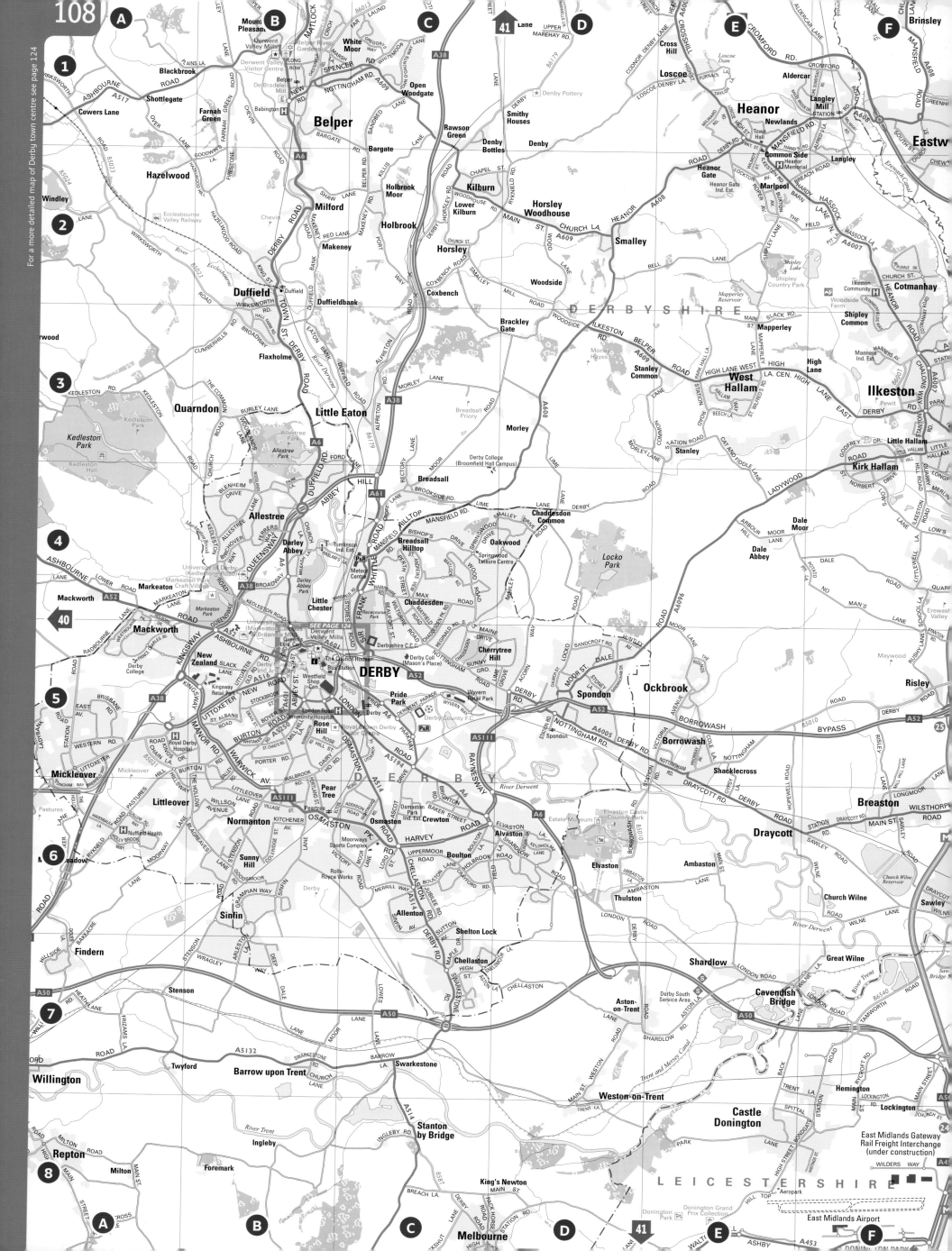

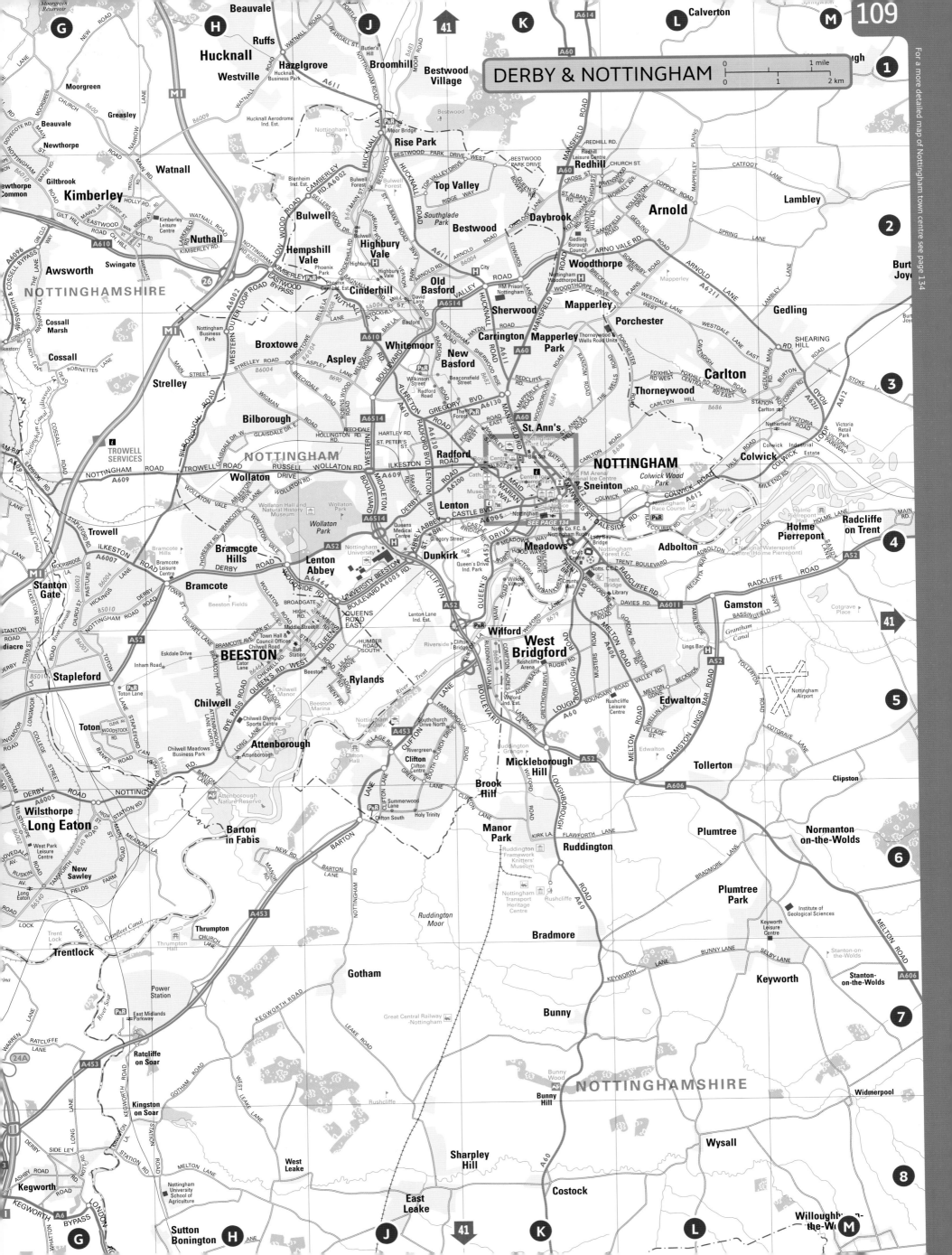

STOKE-ON-TRENT

For a more detailed map of Stoke-on-Trent town centre see page 136

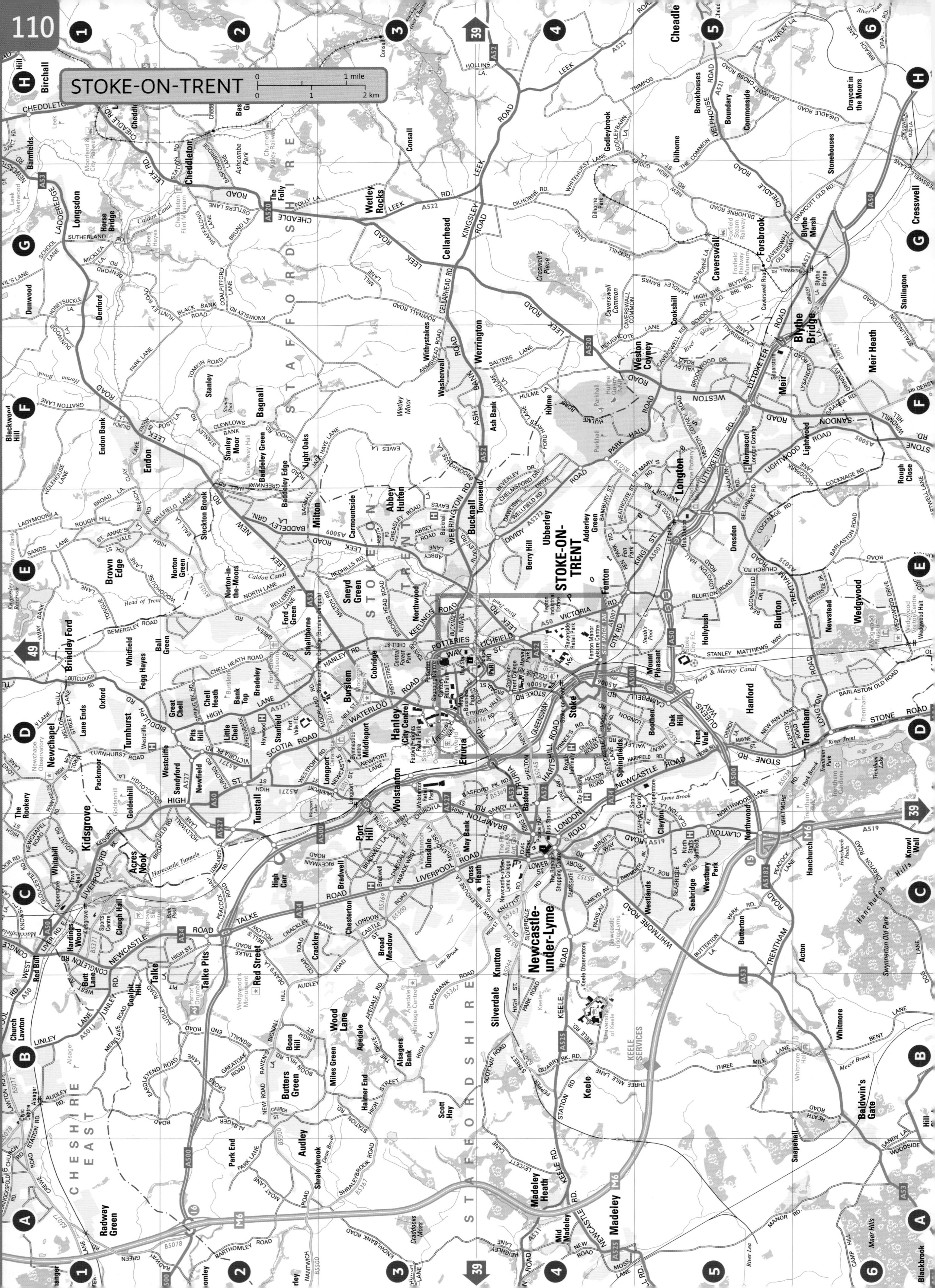

0 1 mile
0 1 2 km

STAFFORDSHIRE

CHESHIRE EAST

STOKE-ON-TRENT

Newcastle-under-Lyme

Cheadle

Blythe Bridge

Longton

Hanley (City Centre)

Burslem

Tunstall

Stoke

Fenton

Kidsgrove

Keele

Madeley

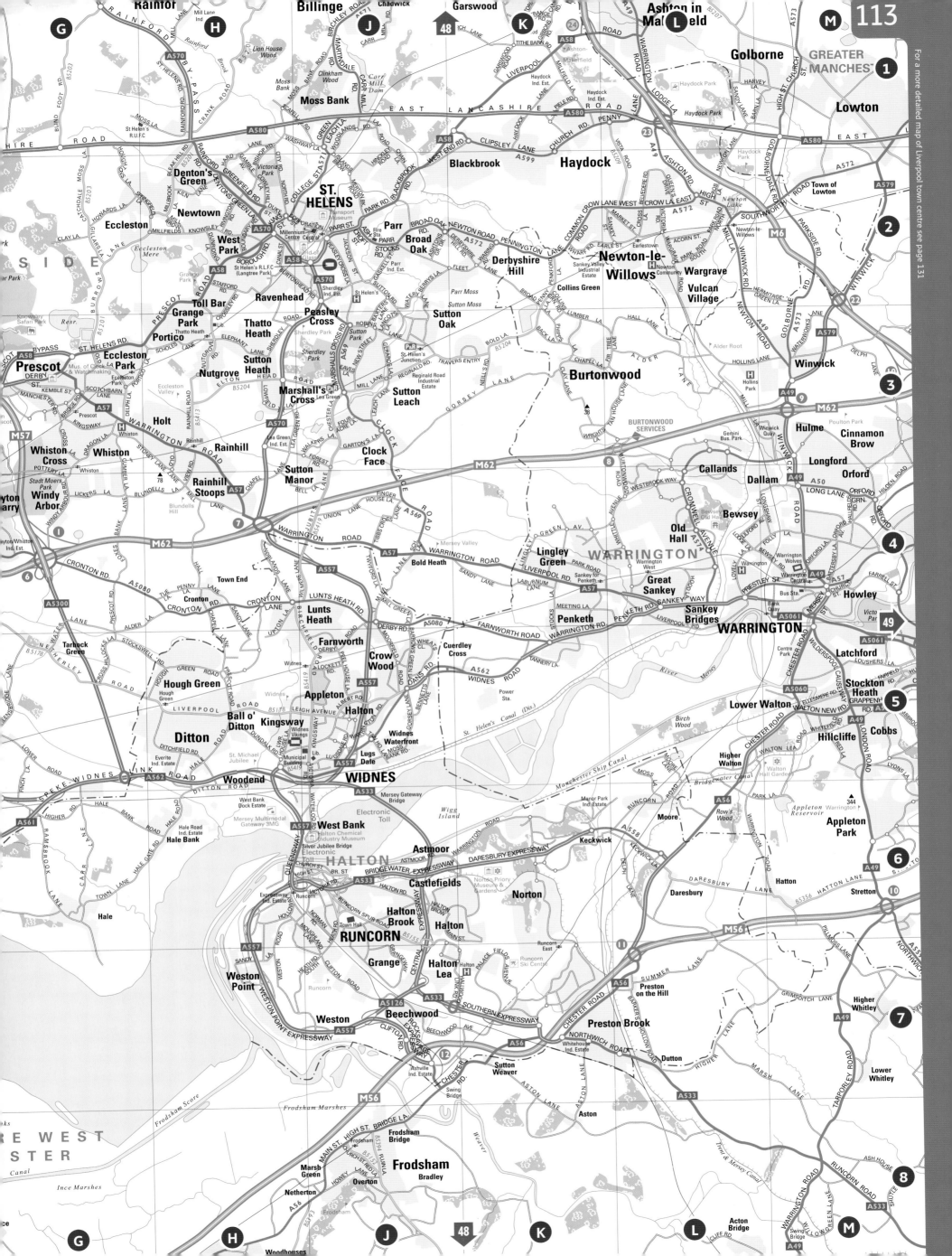

GREATER MANCHESTER

For a more detailed map of Manchester town centre see page 133

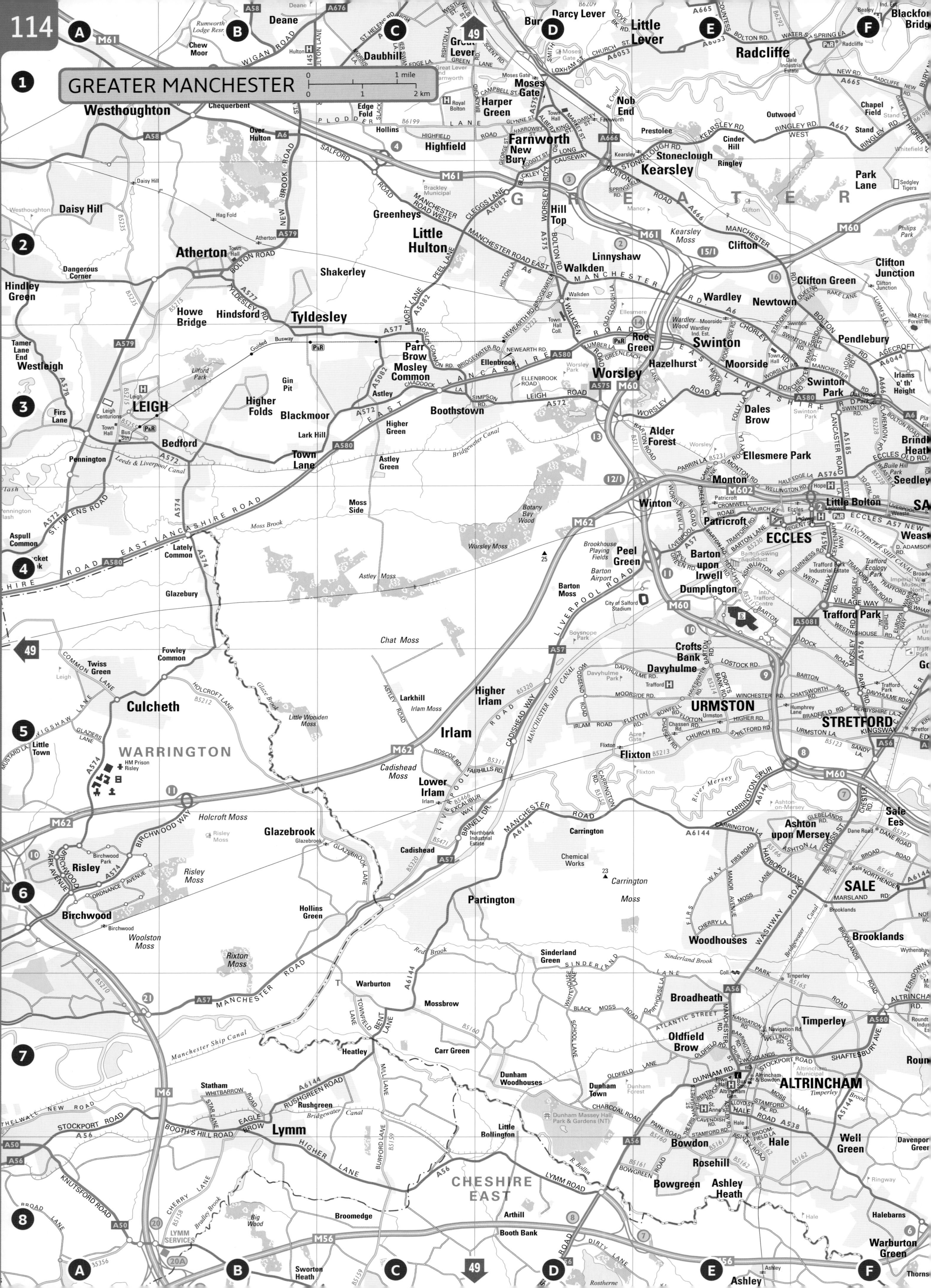

0 ___ 1 mile
0 ___ 1 ___ 2 km

A B C D E F

Westhoughton Deane Daubhill Darcy Lever Little Lever Blackford Bridge
Chew Moor Bury Radcliffe
Chequerbent Over Hulton Hollins Great Lever Moses Gate Chapel Field Stand
Highfield Harper Green Nob End Outwood Ringley Rd West Sedgley Tigers
Daisy Hill Hag Fold Highfield Farnworth New Bury Prestolee StonClough Cinder Hill Park Lane
Hindley Green Atherton Greenheys Hill Top Kearsley Ringley Clifton
Dangerous Corner Shakerley Little Hulton Walkden Linnyshaw Clifton Clifton Green Clifton Junction
Tamer Lane End Howe Bridge Tyldesley Walkden Wardley Newtown
Westleigh Hindsford Parr Brow Ellenbrook Roe Green Swinton Pendlebury
Mosley Common Worsley Hazelhurst Moorside Swinton Park Irlams o' th' Height
LEIGH Higher Folds Astley Boothstown Worsley Dales Brow Ellesmere Park Brindle Heath
Firs Lane Blackmoor Higher Green Alder Forest Seedley
Bedford Lark Hill Town Lane Astley Green Monton Eccles
Pennington Moss Side Winton Patricroft
Aspull Common Lately Common Barton upon Irwell
Glazebury Astley Moss Dumplington Trafford Park
Fowley Common Chat Moss Peel Green Crofts Bank Davyhulme
Twiss Green Larkhill Barton Moss Higher Irlam Davyhulme Urmston Stretford
Culcheth Irlam Moss Irlam Urmston Kingsway
WARRINGTON Little Town Cadishead Moss Lower Irlam Flixton
Risley Glazebrook Cadishead Carrington Ashton upon Mersey Sale
Birchwood Hollins Green Partington Carrington Moss Woodhouses Brooklands
Woolston Moss Rixton Moss Sinderland Green Broadheath Timperley
Warburton Mossbrow Carr Green Oldfield Brow ALTRINCHAM
Heatley Dunham Woodhouses Dunham Town Hale
Statham Rushgreen Lymm Little Bollington Bowdon Well Green
Broomedge Arthill Bowgreen Rosehill Ashley Heath
CHESHIRE EAST Booth Bank Bowgreen Halebarns
Sworton Heath Ashley Warburton Green

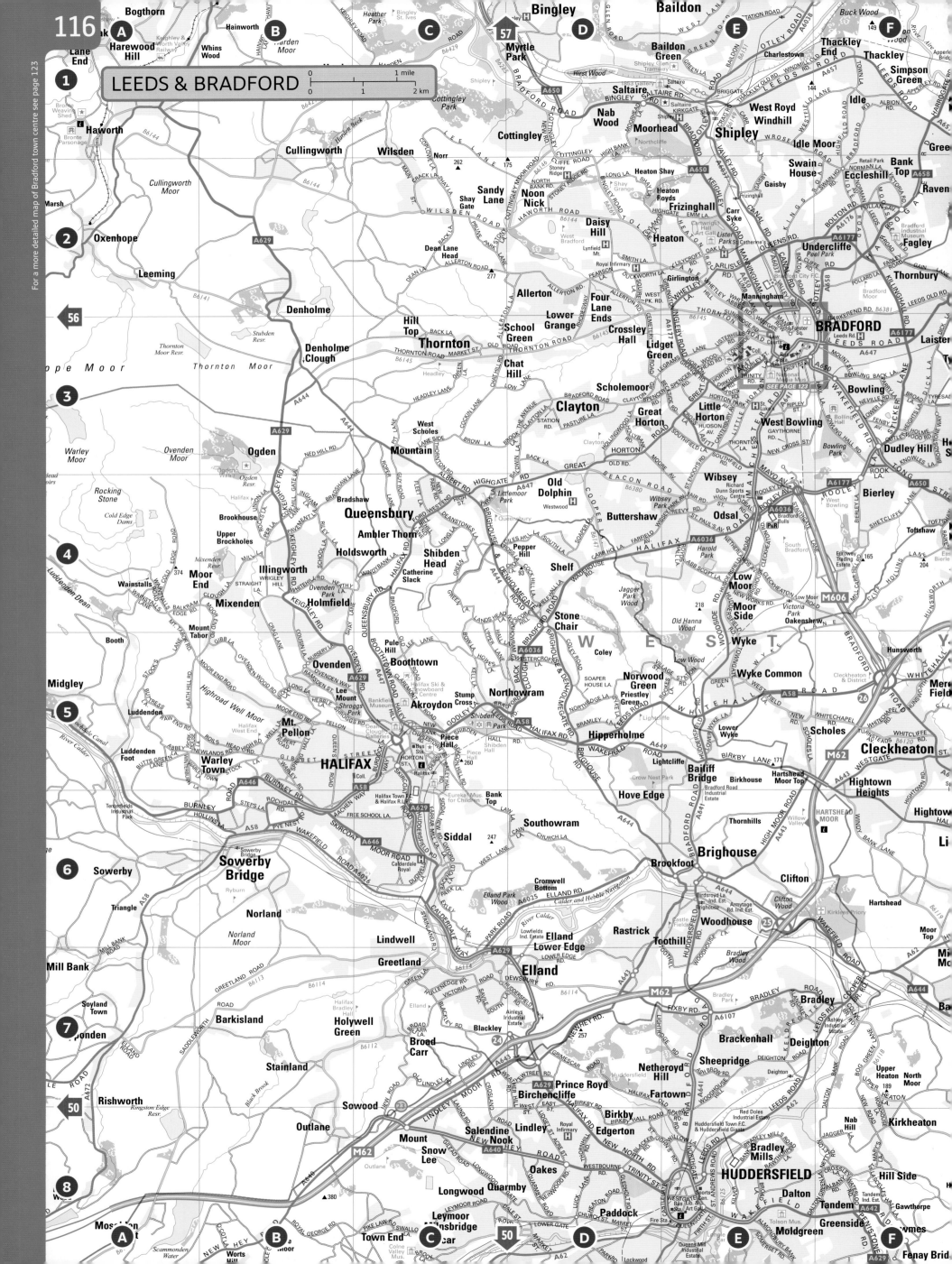

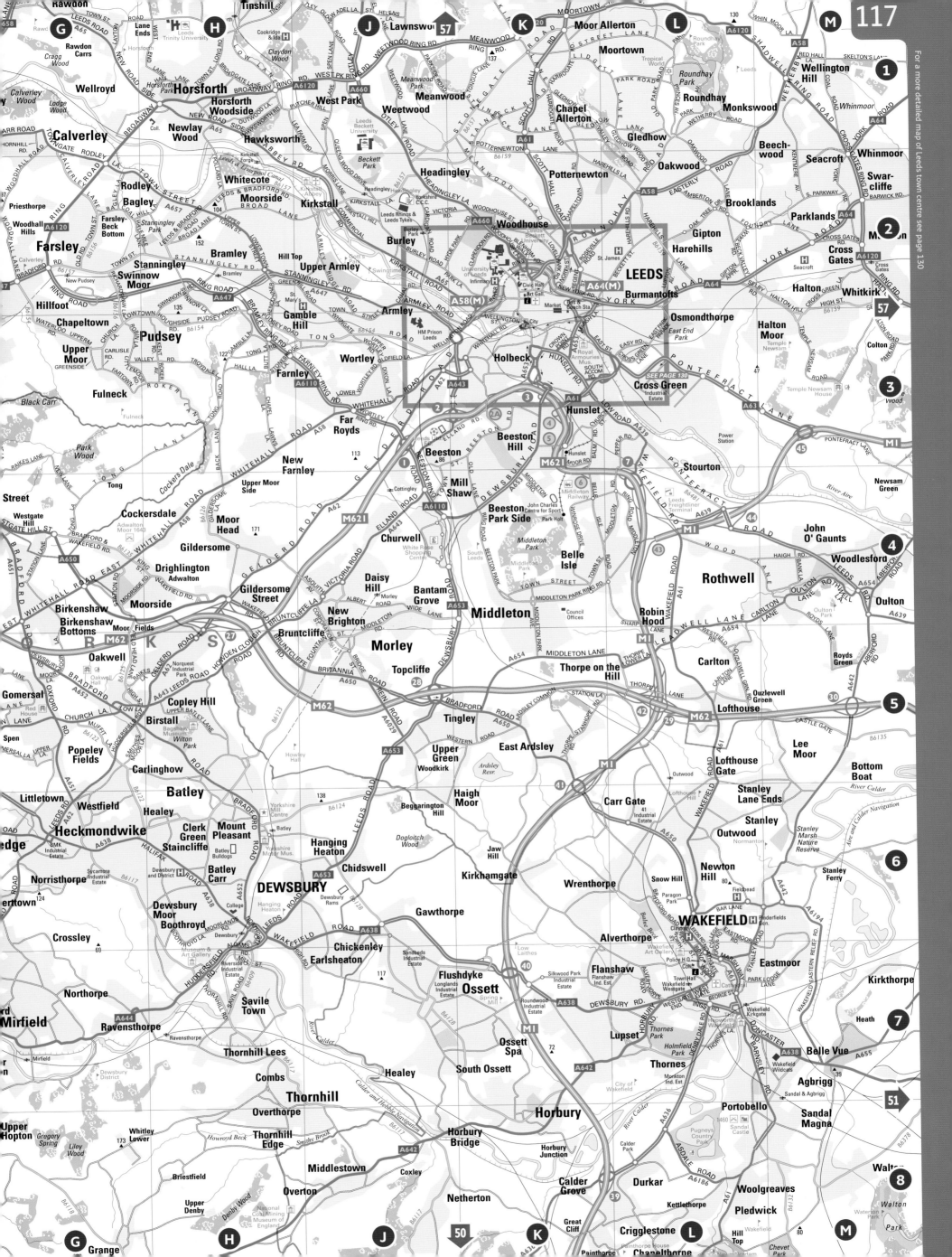

EDINBURGH

0 1 mile
0 1 2 km

For a more detailed map of Edinburgh town centre see page 126

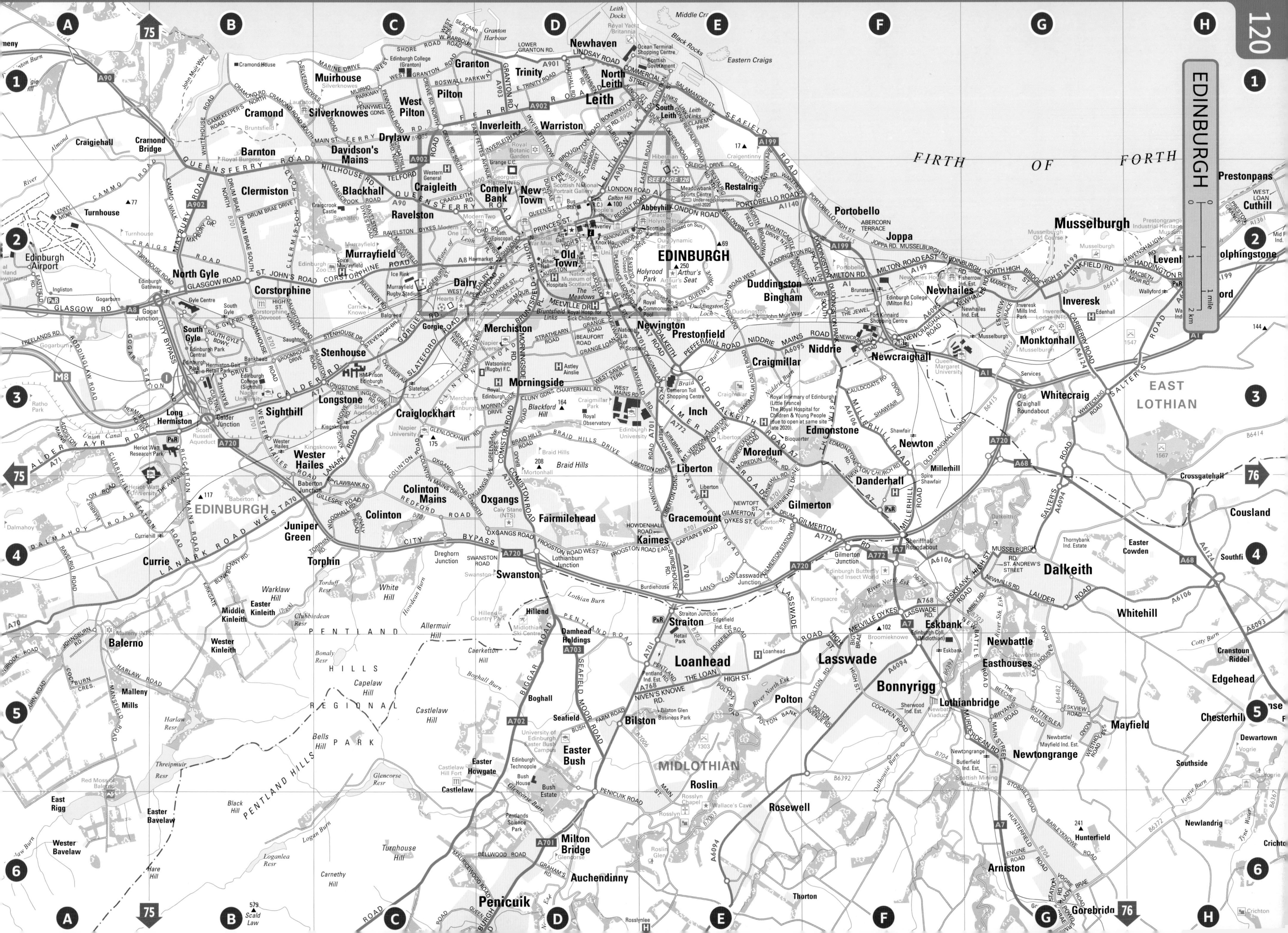

Symbols used on the map

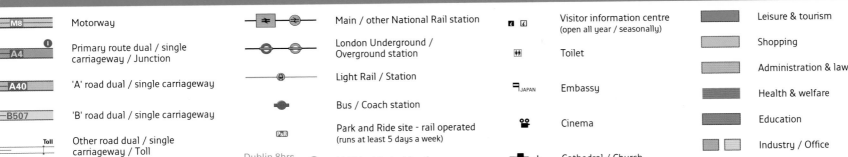

M8	Motorway		Main / other National Rail station		Visitor information centre (open all year / seasonally)
A4	Primary route dual / single carriageway / Junction		London Underground / Overground station		Toilet
A40	'A' road dual / single carriageway		Light Rail / Station		Embassy
B507	'B' road dual / single carriageway		Bus / Coach station		Cinema
Toll	Other road dual / single carriageway / Toll	P+R	Park and Ride site – rail operated (runs at least 5 days a week)		Cathedral / Church
	One way street / Orbital route	Dublin 8hrs	Vehicle / Pedestrian ferry		Mosque / Synagogue / Other place of worship
	Access restriction	P	Car park		Park / Garden / Sports ground
	Pedestrian street / Street market		Theatre		Cemetery
	Minor road / Track		Major hotel		Leisure & tourism
FB	Footpath / Footbridge		Public House		Shopping
	Road under construction		Police station		Administration & law
	Extent of London congestion charging zone	Lib	Library		Health & welfare
		PO	Post Office		Education
					Industry / Office
					Other notable building

Locator map

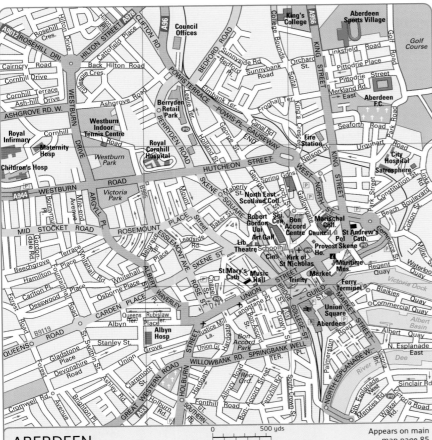

ABERDEEN

Appears on main map page 85

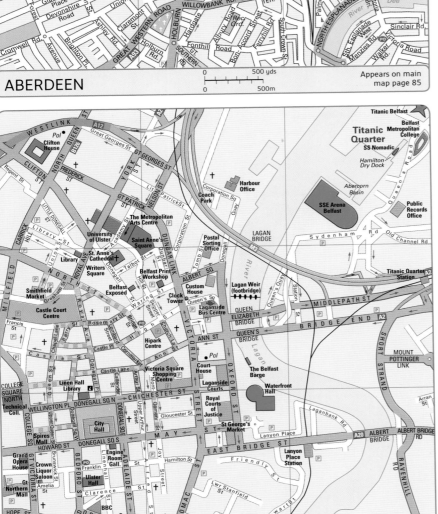

BELFAST

Appears on main map page 93

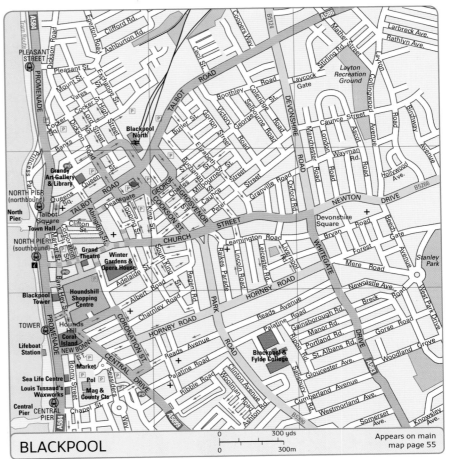

BLACKPOOL

Appears on main map page 55

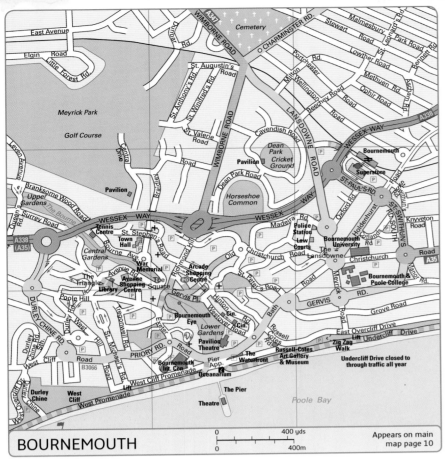
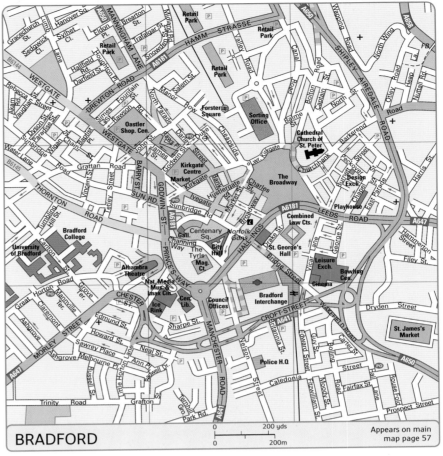

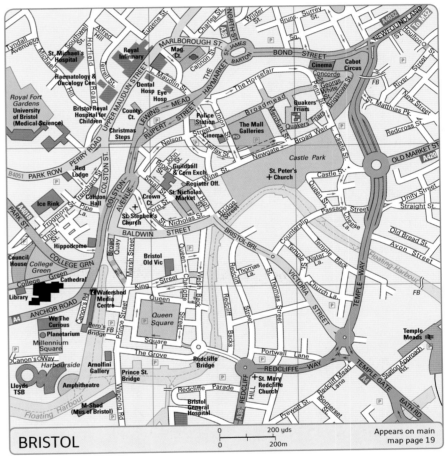
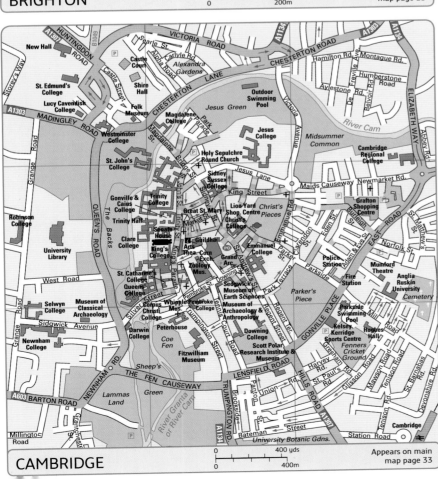
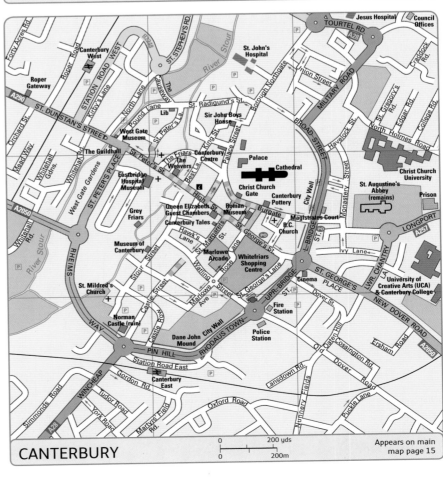

BOURNEMOUTH

Appears on main map page 10

BRADFORD

Appears on main map page 57

BRIGHTON

Appears on main map page 13

BRISTOL

Appears on main map page 19

CAMBRIDGE

Appears on main map page 33

CANTERBURY

Appears on main map page 15

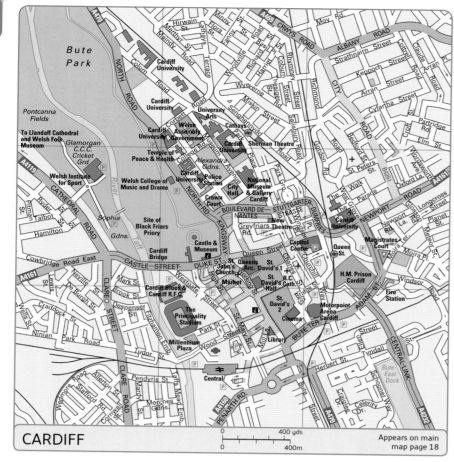

CARDIFF

Appears on main
map page 18

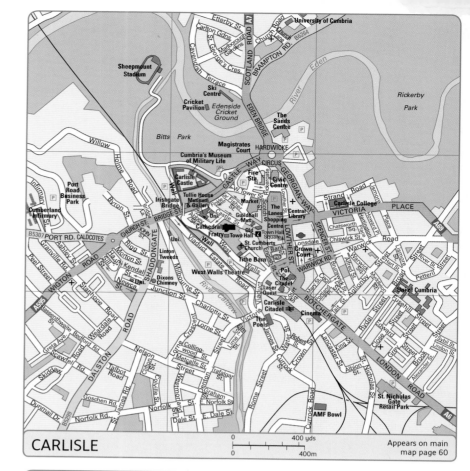

CARLISLE

Appears on main
map page 60

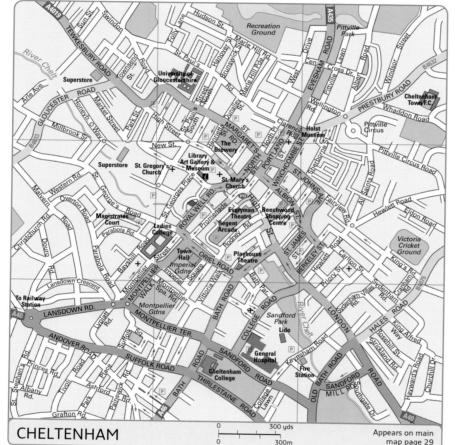

CHELTENHAM

Appears on main
map page 29

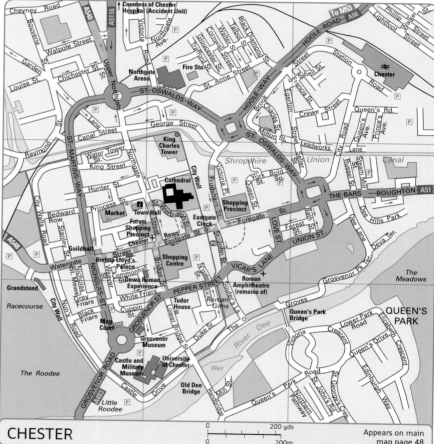

CHESTER

Appears on main
map page 48

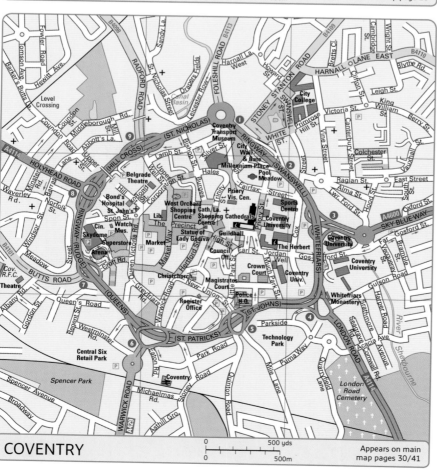

COVENTRY

Appears on main
map pages 30/41

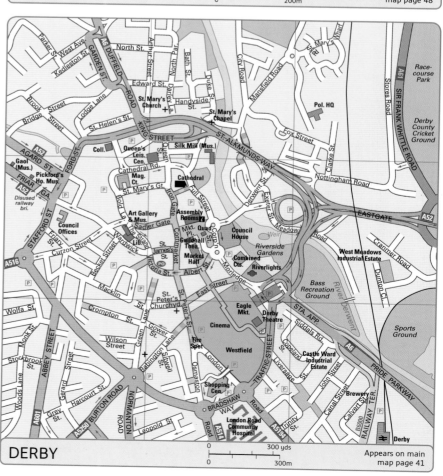

DERBY

Appears on main
map page 41

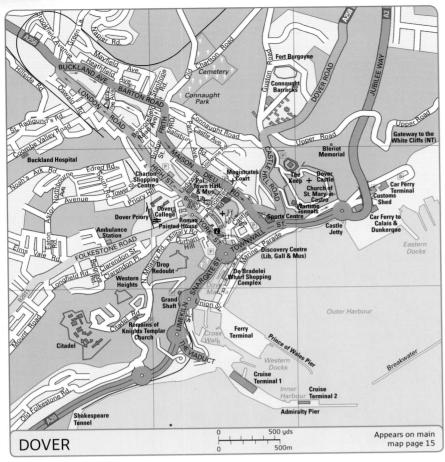

DOVER

500 yds
500m

Appears on main
map page 15

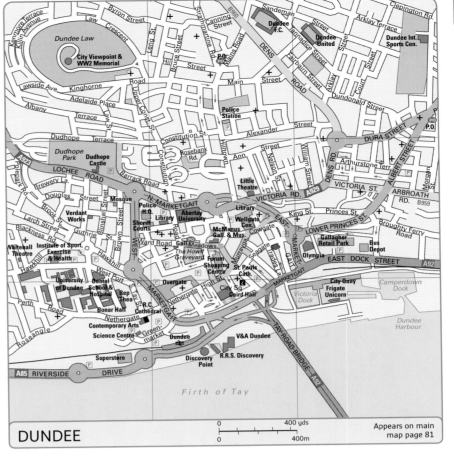

DUNDEE

400 yds
400m

Appears on main
map page 81

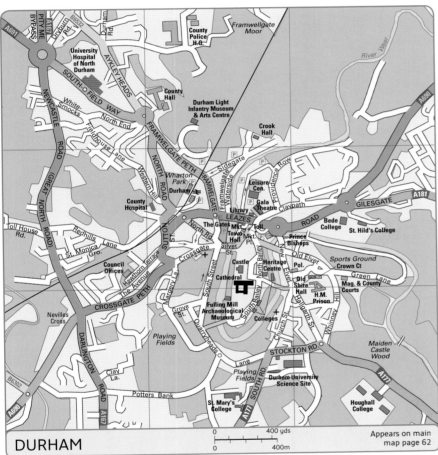

DURHAM

400 yds
400m

Appears on main
map page 62

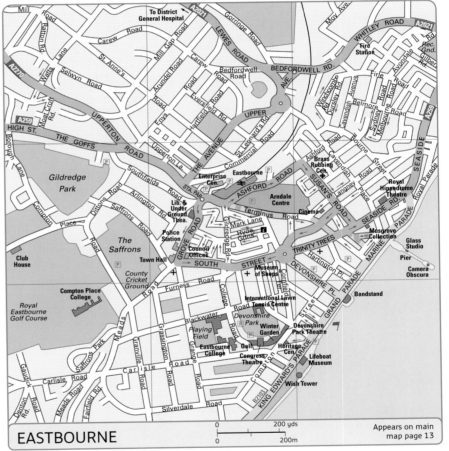

EASTBOURNE

200 yds
200m

Appears on main
map page 13

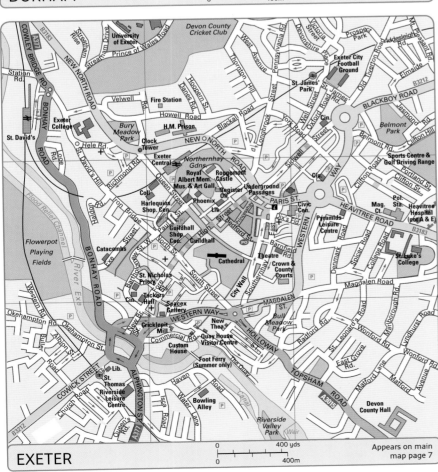

EXETER

400 yds
400m

Appears on main
map page 7

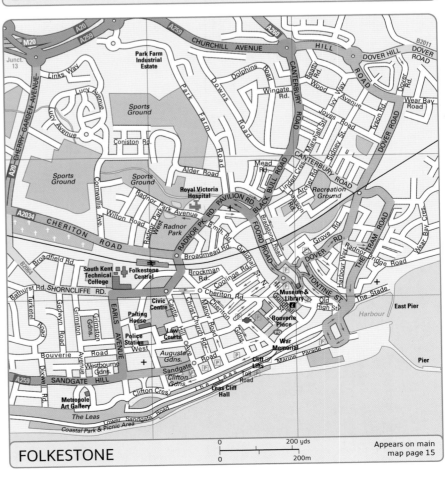

FOLKESTONE

200 yds
200m

Appears on main
map page 15

EDINBURGH

0   1/4 mile
0.25   0.5 km

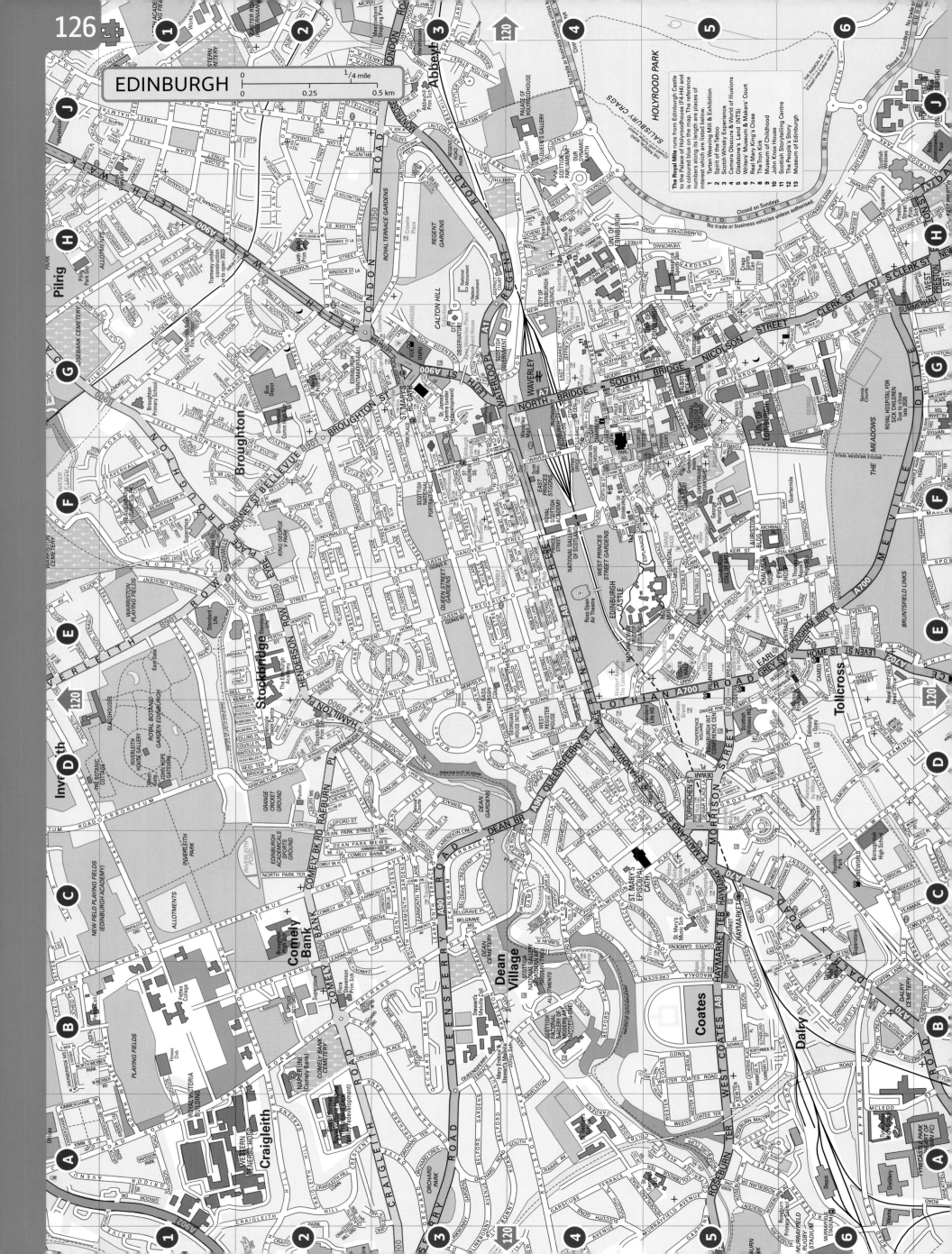

The Royal Mile runs from Edinburgh Castle to the Palace of Holyroodhouse (F4-H4) and is coloured blue on the map. The reference numbers along its length are the places of interest which are listed below.

1 Tartan Weaving Mill & Exhibition
2 Spirit of the Tattoo
3 Scotch Whisky Experience
4 Camera Obscura & World of Illusions
5 Gladstone's Land (NTS)
6 Writers' Museum & Makars' Court
7 Real Mary King's Close
8 The Tron Kirk
9 Museum of Childhood
10 John Knox House
11 Scottish Storytelling Centre
12 The People's Story
13 Museum of Edinburgh

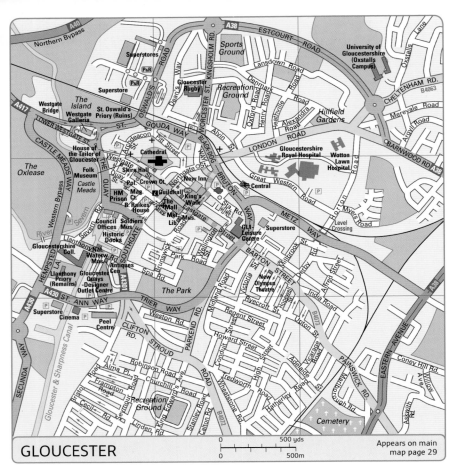

GLOUCESTER

0   500 yds
0   500m

Appears on main map page 29

GUILDFORD

0   200 yds
0   200m

Appears on main map page 22

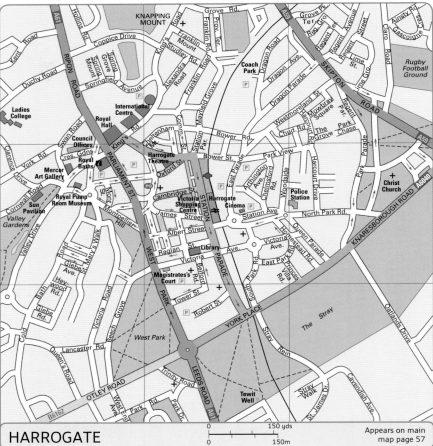

HARROGATE

0   150 yds
0   150m

Appears on main map page 57

HASTINGS

0   500 yds
0   500m

Appears on main map page 14

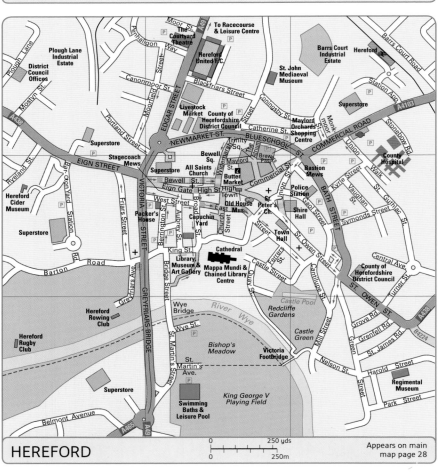

HEREFORD

0   250 yds
0   250m

Appears on main map page 28

HULL (KINGSTON UPON HULL)

0   300 yds
0   300m

Appears on main map page 59

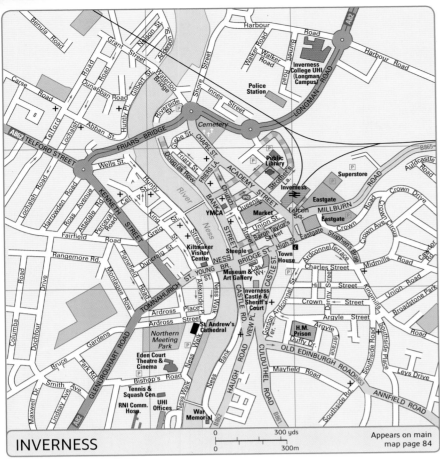

INVERNESS

300 yds
300m

Appears on main
map page 84

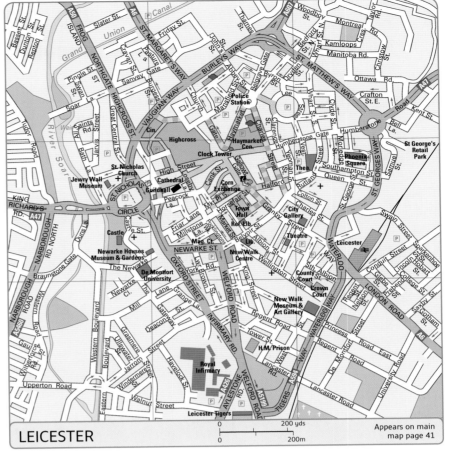

LEICESTER

200 yds
200m

Appears on main
map page 41

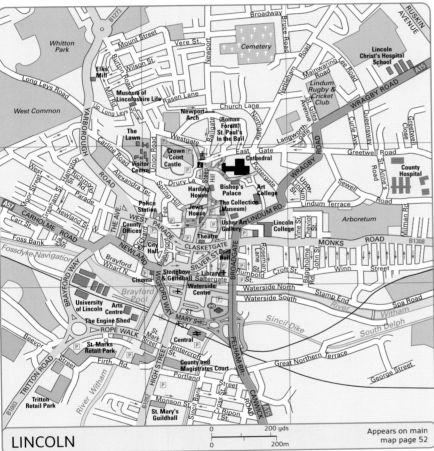

LINCOLN

200 yds
200m

Appears on main
map page 52

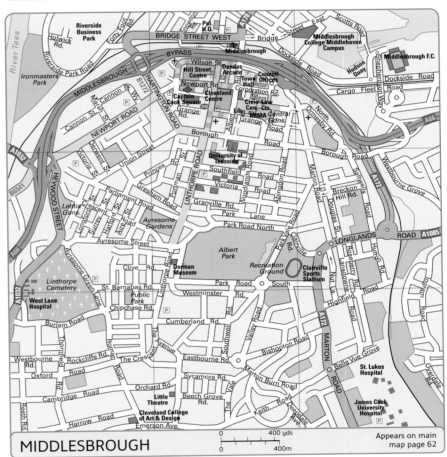

MIDDLESBROUGH

400 yds
400m

Appears on main
map page 62

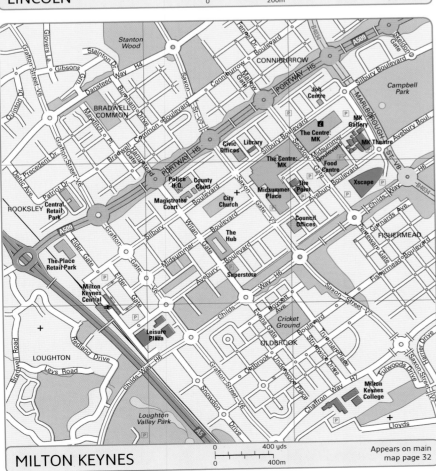

MILTON KEYNES

400 yds
400m

Appears on main
map page 32

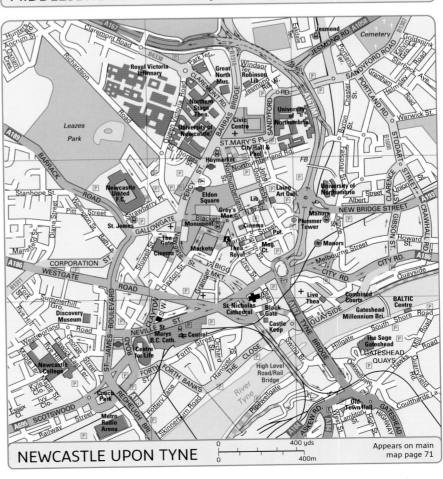

NEWCASTLE UPON TYNE

400 yds
400m

Appears on main
map page 71

CENTRAL LONDON

0   0.25   0.5 km   1/4 mile

MANCHESTER
0
0.25
1/4 mile
0.5 km

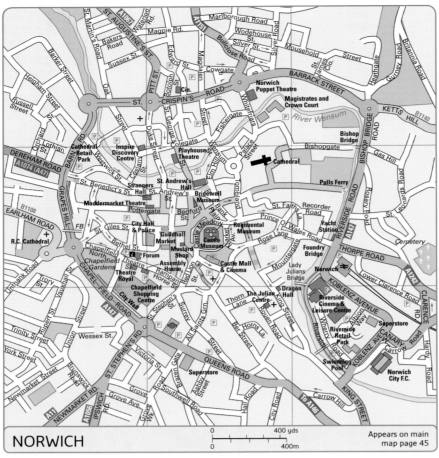

NORWICH

0 ____ 400 yds
0 ____ 400m

Appears on main
map page 45

NOTTINGHAM

0 ____ 400 yds
0 ____ 400m

Appears on main
map page 41

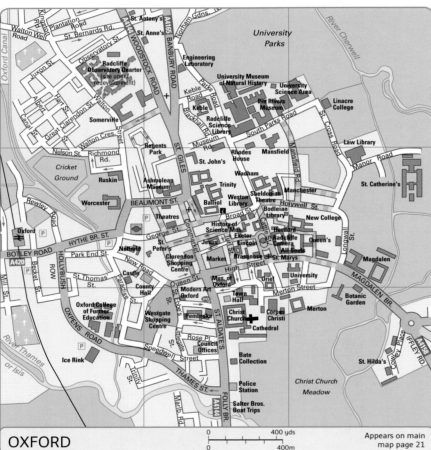

OXFORD

0 ____ 400 yds
0 ____ 400m

Appears on main
map page 21

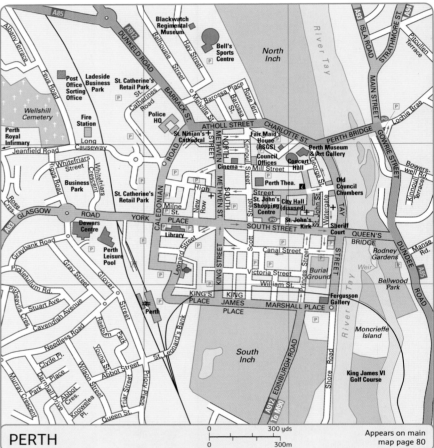

PERTH

0 ____ 300 yds
0 ____ 300m

Appears on main
map page 80

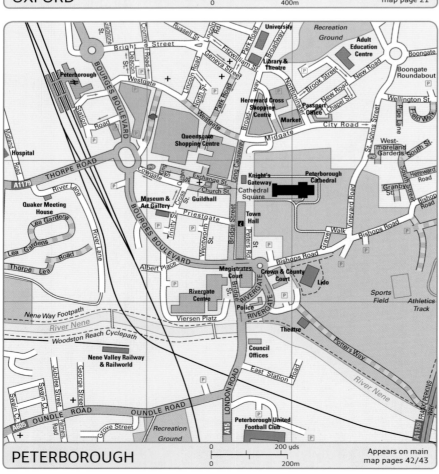

PETERBOROUGH

0 ____ 200 yds
0 ____ 200m

Appears on main
map pages 42/43

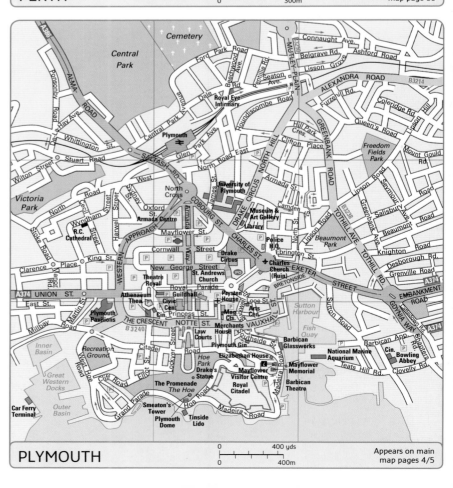

PLYMOUTH

0 ____ 400 yds
0 ____ 400m

Appears on main
map pages 4/5

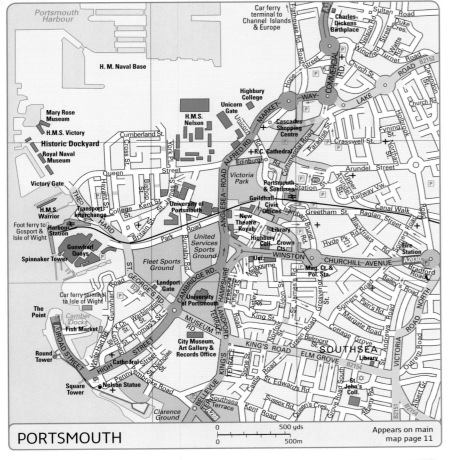

PORTSMOUTH

Appears on main map page 11

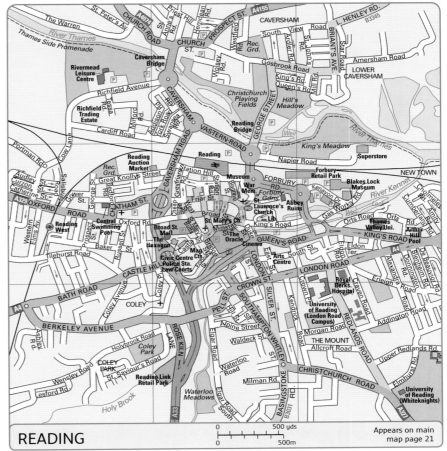

READING

Appears on main map page 21

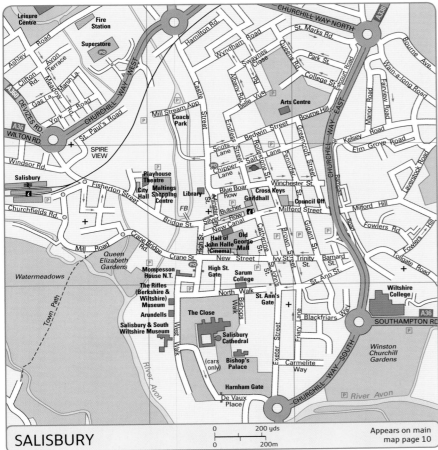

SALISBURY

Appears on main map page 10

SCARBOROUGH

Appears on main map page 59

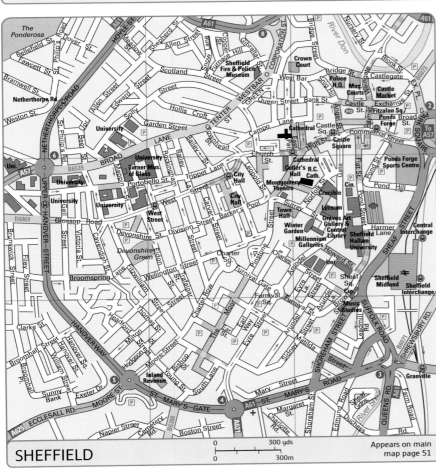

SHEFFIELD

Appears on main map page 51

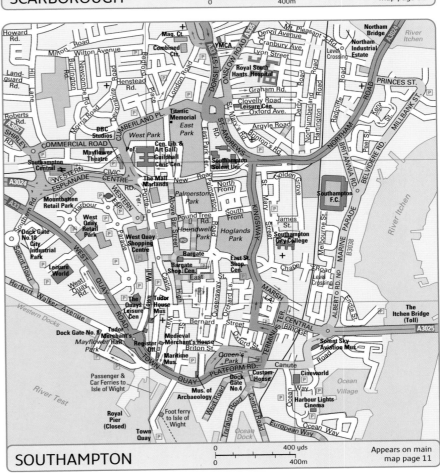

SOUTHAMPTON

Appears on main map page 11

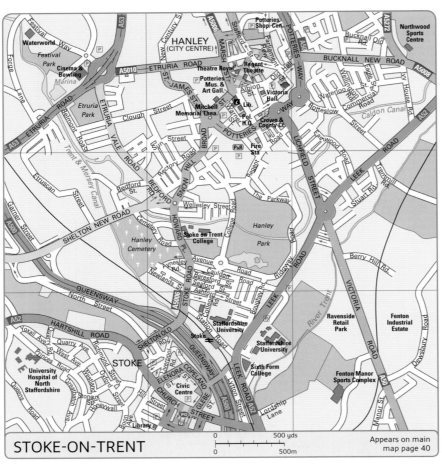

STOKE-ON-TRENT

Appears on main map page 40

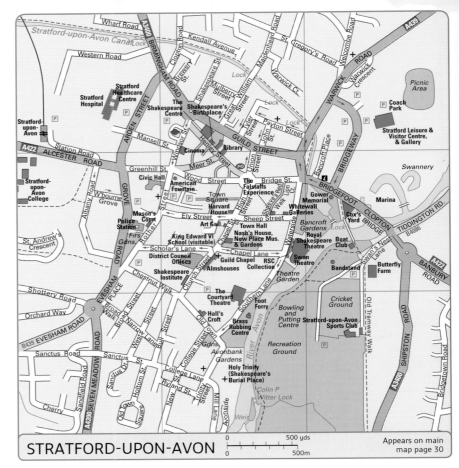

STRATFORD-UPON-AVON

Appears on main map page 30

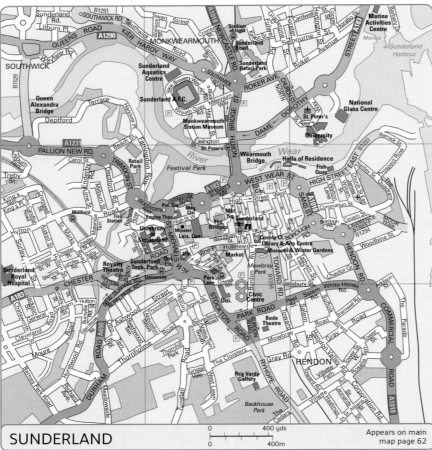

SUNDERLAND

Appears on main map page 62

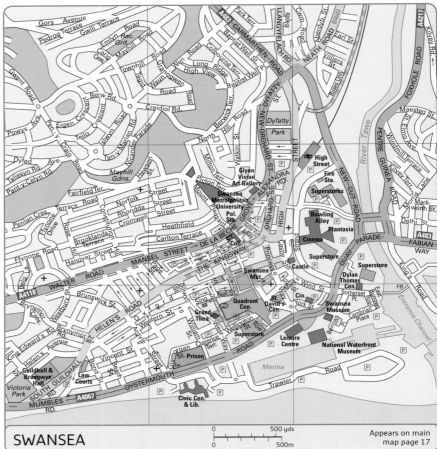

SWANSEA

Appears on main map page 17

SWINDON

Appears on main map page 20

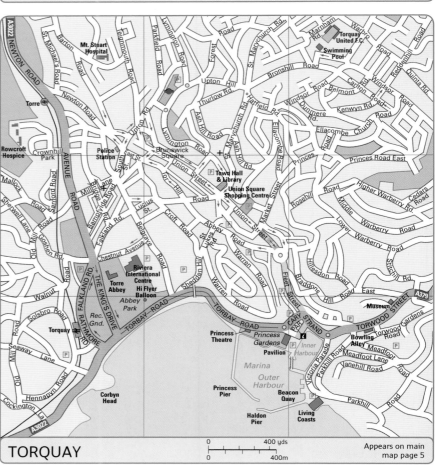

TORQUAY

Appears on main map page 5

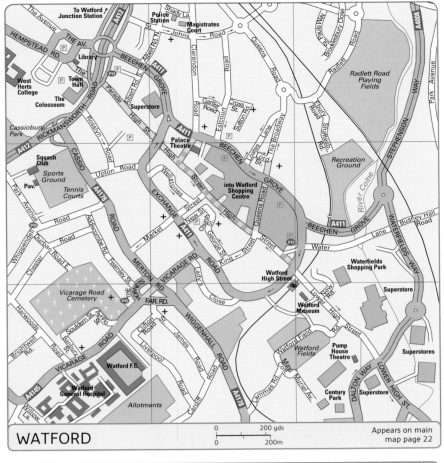

WATFORD

Appears on main map page 22

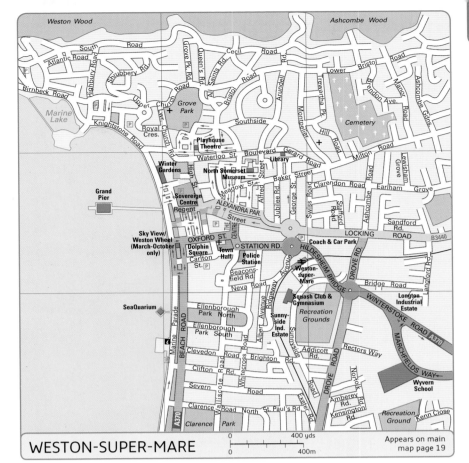

WESTON-SUPER-MARE

Appears on main map page 19

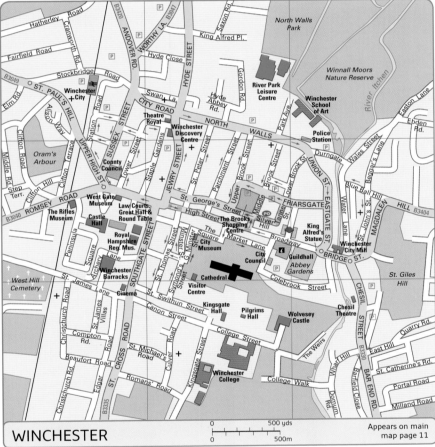

WINCHESTER

Appears on main map page 11

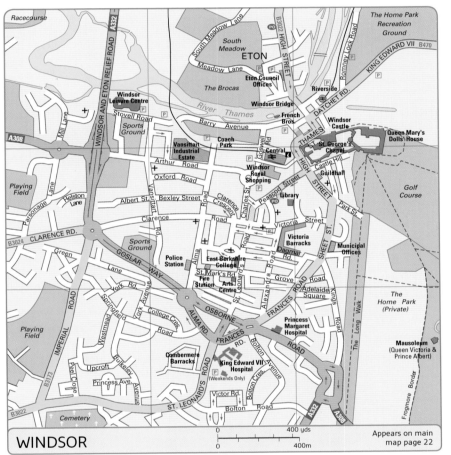

WINDSOR

Appears on main map page 22

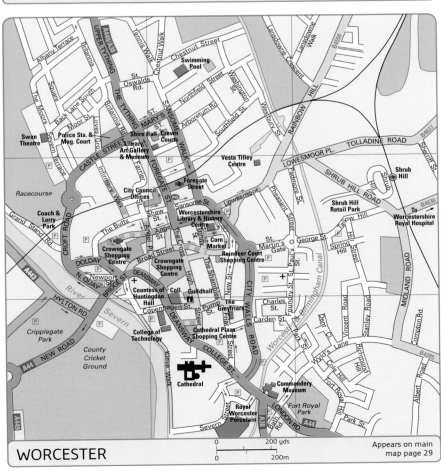

WORCESTER

Appears on main map page 29

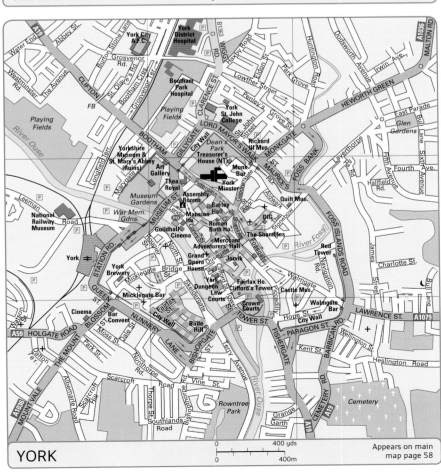

YORK

Appears on main map page 58

Using the index

Place, place of interest and World Heritage Site names are followed by a **page number** and a grid reference in black type. The feature can be found on the map somewhere within the grid square shown.

Where two or more places have the same name the abbreviated *county* or *unitary authority* names are shown to distinguish between them. A list of these abbreviated names appears below.

A selection of the most popular places of interest are shown within the index in blue type. Their postcode information is supplied after the county / unitary authority names to aid integration with satnav systems.

Sites with World Heritage Status are shown within the index in maroon type.

A&B	Argyll & Bute	Med	Medway
A&N	Antrim & Newtownabbey	Mersey	Merseyside
A&NDown	Ards & North Down	Middl	Middlesbrough
AB&C	Armagh City, Banbridge & Craigavon	Midlo	Midlothian
		Mon	Monmouthshire
Aber	Aberdeenshire	NM&D	Newry, Mourne & Down
B&H	Brighton & Hove	Na H-E. Siar	Na H-Eileanan Siar
B'burn	Blackburn with Darwen		(Western Isles)
B'pool	Blackpool	N'hants	Northamptonshire
BGwent	Blaenau Gwent	N'umb	Northumberland
Bed	Bedford	NAyr	North Ayrshire
BCP	Bournemouth, Christchurch & Poole	NELincs	North East Lincolnshire
		NLan	North Lanarkshire
BrackF	Bracknell Forest	NLincs	North Lincolnshire
Bucks	Buckinghamshire	NPT	Neath Port Talbot
CC&G	Causeway Coast & Glens	NSom	North Somerset
Caerp	Caerphilly	NYorks	North Yorkshire
Cambs	Cambridgeshire	Norf	Norfolk
Carmar	Carmarthenshire	Nott	Nottingham
CenBeds	Central Bedfordshire	Notts	Nottinghamshire
Cere	Ceredigion	Ork	Orkney
Chanl	Channel Islands	Oxon	Oxfordshire
ChesE	Cheshire East	P&K	Perth & Kinross
ChesW&C	Cheshire West & Chester	Pembs	Pembrokeshire
Corn	Cornwall	Peter	Peterborough
Cumb	Cumbria	Plym	Plymouth
D&G	Dumfries & Galloway	Ports	Portsmouth
D&S	Derry City & Strabane	R&C	Redcar & Cleveland
Darl	Darlington	RCT	Rhondda Cynon Taff
Denb	Denbighshire	Read	Reading
Derbys	Derbyshire	Renf	Renfrewshire
Dur	Durham	Rut	Rutland
EAyr	East Ayrshire	S'end	Southend-on-Sea
EDun	East Dunbartonshire	SAyr	South Ayrshire
ELoth	East Lothian	SGlos	South Gloucestershire
ERenf	East Renfrewshire	SLan	South Lanarkshire
ERid	East Riding of Yorkshire	SYorks	South Yorkshire
ESuss	East Sussex	ScBord	Scottish Borders
Edin	Edinburgh	Shet	Shetland
F&O	Fermanagh & Omagh	Shrop	Shropshire
Falk	Falkirk	Slo	Slough
Flints	Flintshire	Som	Somerset
Glas	Glasgow	Soton	Southampton
Glos	Gloucestershire	Staffs	Staffordshire
GtLon	Greater London	Stir	Stirling
GtMan	Greater Manchester	Stock	Stockton-on-Tees
Gwyn	Gwynedd	Stoke	Stoke-on-Trent
Hants	Hampshire	Suff	Suffolk
Hart	Hartlepool	Surr	Surrey
Here	Herefordshire	Swan	Swansea
Herts	Hertfordshire	Swin	Swindon
High	Highland	T&W	Tyne & Wear
Hull	Kingston upon Hull	Tel&W	Telford & Wrekin
Invcly	Inverclyde	Thur	Thurrock
IoA	Isle of Anglesey	VGlam	Vale of Glamorgan
IoM	Isle of Man	W&M	Windsor & Maidenhead
IoS	Isles of Scilly	W'ham	Wokingham
IoW	Isle of Wight	WBerks	West Berkshire
L&C	Lisburn & Castlereagh	WDun	West Dunbartonshire
Lancs	Lancashire	WLoth	West Lothian
Leic	Leicester	WMid	West Midlands
Leics	Leicestershire	WSuss	West Sussex
Lincs	Lincolnshire	WYorks	West Yorkshire
M&EAnt	Mid & East Antrim	Warks	Warwickshire
MK	Milton Keynes	Warr	Warrington
MTyd	Merthyr Tydfil	Wilts	Wiltshire
MUlst	Mid Ulster	Worcs	Worcestershire
		Wrex	Wrexham

1 Bath & North East Somerset
2 Blaenau Gwent
3 Bournemouth, Christchurch & Poole
4 Bracknell Forest
5 Bridgend
6 Bristol
7 Caerphilly
8 Cardiff
9 Clackmannanshire
10 Darlington
11 Dundee
12 East Dunbartonshire
13 East Renfrewshire
14 Glasgow
15 Halton
16 Hartlepool
17 Inverclyde
18 Luton
19 Merthyr Tydfil
20 Middlesbrough
21 Monmouthshire
22 Neath Port Talbot
23 Newport
24 North Lanarkshire
25 Plymouth
26 Portsmouth
27 Reading
28 Redcar And Cleveland
29 Renfrewshire
30 Rhondda Cynon Taff
31 Slough
32 South Gloucestershire
33 Southampton
34 Stockton-on-Tees
35 Telford & Wrekin
36 Torfaen
37 Vale Of Glamorgan
38 Warrington
39 West Dunbartonshire
40 Windsor & Maidenhead
41 Wokingham

Bohuntine 79 P2
Bojewyan 2 A5
Bokiddick 4 A4
Bolam Dur 62 B4
Bolam N'umb 71 F5
Bolam Lake Country Park N'umb NE20 0HE 71 F5
Bolberry 5 G7
Bold Heath 48 E4
Bolderwood 10 D4
Boldon 71 J7
Boldon Colliery 71 J7
Boldre 10 E5
Boldron 62 A5
Bole 51 K4
Bolea 92 C4
Bolehill 50 E7
Boleigh 2 B6
Bolenowe 2 D5
Boleran 92 D5
Boleside 76 C7
Bolgoed 17 K5
Bolham Devon 7 H4
Bolham Notts 51 K4
Bolham Water 7 K4
Bolise 90 M5
Bolingey 2 E3
Bollington 49 J5
Bolney 13 F4
Bolnhurst 32 D3
Bolsover 51 G5
Bolsterstone 50 E3
Bolstone 28 E5
Boltby 57 K1
Bolter End 22 A2
Bolton Cumb 61 H4
Bolton ELoth 76 D3
Bolton ERid 58 D4
Bolton GtMan 49 G2
Bolton N'umb 71 G2
Bolton Abbey 57 F4
Bolton Abbey Estate NYorks BD23 6EX 57 F4
Bolton Bridge 57 F4
Bolton by Bowland 56 C5
Bolton Houses 55 H6
Bolton Low Houses 60 D2
Bolton Museum & Art Gallery GtMan BL1 1SE 49 G2
Bolton Percy 58 B5
Bolton Priory NYorks BD23 6EX 57 F4
Bolton upon Dearne 51 G2
Bolton Wood Lane 60 D2
Boltonfellend 69 K7
Boltongate 60 D2
Bolton-le-Sands 55 H3
Bolton-on-Swale 62 C7
Bolventor 4 B3
Bombie 65 H6
Bomere Heath 38 D4
Bonar Bridge 84 A1
Bonawe (Bun Atha) 79 M7
Bonby 52 D1
Boncath 17 F2
Bonchester Bridge 70 A2
Bonchurch 11 G7
Bondleigh 6 E5
Bonds 55 H5
Bonehill 40 D5
Bo'ness 75 H2
Bonhill 74 B3
Boningale 40 A5
Bonjedward 70 B1
Bonkle 75 G5
Bonning Gate 61 F7
Bonnington Edin 75 K4
Bonnington Kent 15 F4
Bonnybridge 75 G2
Bonnykelly 85 N5
Bonnyrigg 76 B4
Bonsall 50 E7
Bont 28 C7
Bont Dolgadfan 37 H5
Bont Newydd 37 G3
Bontddu 37 F4
Bont-goch (Elerch) 37 F7
Bonthorpe 53 H5
Bont-newydd Conwy 47 J5
Bontnewydd Gwyn 46 C6
Bontuchel 47 J7
Bonvilston 18 D4
Bon-y-maen 17 K6
Boode 6 D2
Boohay 5 K5
Booker 22 B2
Booley 38 E3
Boorley Green 11 G3
Boosbeck 63 G5
Boose's Green 34 C5
Boot 60 C6
Boot Street 35 G4
Booth 57 F7
Booth Bank 50 C1
Booth Green 49 J4
Booth Wood 50 C1
Boothby Graffoe 52 C7
Boothby Pagnell 42 C2
Boothstown 49 G2
Boothville 31 J2
Bootle Cumb 54 E1
Bootle Mersey 48 C3
Booton 45 F3
Boots Green 49 G5
Booze 62 A6
Boquhan 74 D2
Boraston 29 F1
Bordeaux 3 J5
Borden Kent 24 E5
Borden WSuss 12 B4
Bordley 56 E3
Bordon 11 J1
Boreham Essex 24 D1
Boreham Wilts 20 B7
Boreham Street 13 K5
Borehamwood 22 E2
Boreland D&G 64 D4
Boreland D&G 69 G4
Boreley 29 H2
Boreraig 82 B5
Borgh Na H-E. Siar 88 A8
Borgh Na H-E. Siar 88 E9
Borghastan 88 G3
Borgue D&G 65 G6
Borgue High 87 P7
Borley 34 C4
Borley Green Essex 34 C4
Borley Green Suff 34 D2
Borness 65 G6
Bornisketaig 82 D3
Borough Green 23 K6
Boroughbridge 57 J3
Borras Head 48 C7
Borrowash 41 G2
Borrowby NYorks 57 K1
Borrowby NYorks 63 H5
Borrowdale 60 D5
Borstal 24 D5
Borth 37 F7
Borthwick 76 B5
Borthwickbrae 69 K2
Borthwickshiels 69 K2
Borth-y-Gest 36 E2
Borve High 82 E6
Borve (Borgh) Na H-E. Siar 88 K2
Borwick 55 J2
Borwick Rails 54 E2
Bosavern 2 A5
Bosbury 29 F4
Boscarne 4 A4
Boscastle 4 A1
Boscastle Pottery Corn PL35 0HE 4 B1
Boscombe BCP 10 C5
Boscombe Wilts 10 D1
Bosham 12 B6
Bosham Hoe 12 B6
Bosherston 16 C6
Bosley 49 J6
Bossall 58 D3
Bossiney 4 A2
Bossingham 15 G3
Bossington Hants 10 E1
Bossington Som 7 G1
Bostock Green 49 F6
Boston 43 G1
Boston Spa 57 K5
Boswarthan 2 B5
Boswinger 3 G4
Bosworth Battlefield Country Park Leics CV13 0AD 41 G5
Botallack 2 A5
Botanic Garden Oxon OX1 4AZ 134 Oxford
Botany Bay Lancs PR6 9AF 48 E1
Botany Bay 23 G2
Botcheston 41 G5
Botesdale 34 E1
Bothal 71 H5
Bothamsall 51 J5
Bothel 60 C3
Bothenhampton 8 D5
Bothwell 75 F5
Botley Bucks 22 C1
Botley Hants 11 G3
Botley Oxon 21 H1
Botloe's Green 29 G6
Botolph Claydon 31 J6
Botolphs 12 E6
Botolph's Bridge 15 G4
Bottacks 83 Q4
Bottesford Leics 42 B2
Bottesford NLincs 52 B2
Bottisham 33 J2
Bottlesford 20 E6
Bottom Boat 57 J7
Bottom of Hutton 55 H7
Bottom o'th'Moor 49 F1
Bottoms 56 E7
Botton Head 56 B3
Botusfleming 4 E4
Botwnnog 36 B2
Bough Beech 23 H7
Boughrood 28 A5
Boughspring 19 J2
Boughton Norf 44 B5
Boughton Notts 51 J6
Boughton N'hants 31 J2
Boughton Aluph 15 F3
Boughton Lees 15 F3
Boughton Malherbe 14 D3
Boughton Monchelsea 14 C2
Boughton Street 15 F2
Boulby 63 H5
Bouldnor 10 E6
Bouldon 38 E7
Boulge 35 G3
Boulmer 71 H2
Boulston 16 C4
Boultenstone Hotel 85 J9
Boultham 52 C6
Boundary Derbys 41 F4
Boundary Staffs 40 B1
Bourn 33 G3
Bourne 42 D3
Bourne End Bucks 22 B3
Bourne End CenBeds 32 C4
Bourne End Herts 22 D1
Bournebridge 23 J2
Bournemouth Airport 10 C5
Bournemouth International Centre BH2 5BH 123 Bournemouth
Bournheath 29 J1
Bournmoor 62 D1
Bournville 40 C7
Bourton Bucks 31 J5
Bourton Dorset 9 G1
Bourton NSom 19 G5
Bourton Oxon 21 F3
Bourton Shrop 38 E6
Bourton Wilts 20 D5
Bourton on Dunsmore 31 F1
Bourton-on-the-Hill 30 C5
Bourton-on-the-Water 30 C6
Boustead Hill 60 D1
Bouth 55 G1
Bouthwaite 57 G2
Bovean 93 D10
Boveney 22 C4
Boveridge 10 B3
Boverton 18 C5
Bovey Tracey 5 J3
Boviel 92 C6
Bovingdon 22 D1
Bovinger 23 J1
Bovington Camp 9 H6
Bow Cumb 60 E1
Bow Devon 5 J5
Bow Devon 7 F5
Bow Ork 89 C8
Bow Brickhill 32 C5
Bow Street Cere 37 F7
Bow Street Norf 44 E6
Bowbank 61 L4
Bowburn 62 D3
Bowcombe 11 F6
Bowd 7 K6
Bowden Devon 5 J6
Bowden ScBord 76 D7
Bowden Hill 20 C5
Bowdon 49 G4
Bower 70 C5
Bower Hinton 8 D3
Bower House Tye 34 D4
Bowerchalke 10 B2
Bowerhill 20 C5
Bowermadden 87 Q3
Bowers 40 A2
Bowers Gifford 24 D3
Bowershall 75 J1
Bowertower 87 Q3
Bowes 61 L5
Bowgreave 55 H5
Bowhousebog 75 G5
Bowithick 4 B2
Bowker's Green 48 D2
Bowland Bridge 55 H1
Bowley 28 E3
Bowley Town 28 E3
Bowlhead Green 12 C3
Bowling WDun 74 C3
Bowling WYorks 57 G6
Bowling Bank 38 C1
Bowlish 19 K7
Bowmanstead 60 E7
Bowmore 72 B4
Bowness-on-Solway 69 H7
Bowness-on-Windermere 60 F7
Bowood House & Gardens Wilts SN11 0LZ 20 C5
Bowscale 60 E3
Bowsden 77 H6
Bowside Lodge 87 L3
Bowston 61 F7
Bowthorpe 45 F5
Bowtrees 75 H2
Box Glos 20 B1
Box Wilts 20 B5
Box End 32 D4
Boxbush Glos 29 F6
Boxbush Glos 29 G7
Boxford Suff 34 D4
Boxford WBerks 21 H4
Boxgrove 12 C6
Boxley 14 C2
Boxmoor 22 D1
Box's Shop 6 A5
Boxted Essex 34 D5
Boxted Suff 34 C3
Boxted Cross 34 D5
Boxwell 20 B2
Boxworth 33 G2
Boxworth End 33 G2
Boyden Gate 25 J5
Boydston 74 C7
Boylestone 40 D2
Boyndie 85 L4
Boynton 59 H3
Boys Hill 9 F4
Boyton Corn 6 B6
Boyton Suff 35 H4
Boyton Wilts 9 J1
Boyton Cross 24 C1
Boyton End 34 B4
Bozeat 32 C3
Braaid 54 C6
Braal Castle 87 P3
Brabling Green 35 G2
Brabourne 15 F3
Brabourne Lees 15 F3
Bracadale 82 D7
Braceborough 42 D4
Bracebridge Heath 52 C6
Braceby 42 D2
Bracewell 56 D5
Brachla 83 R7
Brackenber 61 J5
Brackenbottom 56 D2
Brackenfield 51 F7
Bracklesham 12 B7
Brackley A&B 73 G2
Brackley N'hants 31 G5
Brackley Gate 41 F1
Brackley Hatch 31 H4
Bracknell 22 B5
Bracky 91 M9
Braco 80 D10
Bracon Ash 45 F6
Bracora 82 H11
Bracorina 82 H11
Bradbourne 50 E7
Bradbury 62 D4
Bradda 54 A6
Braddan 31 H4
Braddock 4 B4
Bradenham Bucks 22 B2
Bradenham Norf 44 D5
Bradenstoke 20 D4
Bradfield Devon 7 J5
Bradfield Essex 35 F5
Bradfield Norf 45 G2
Bradfield WBerks 21 K4
Bradfield Combust 34 C3
Bradfield Green 49 F7
Bradfield Heath 35 F6
Bradfield Southend (Southend) 21 J4
Bradfield St. Clare 34 D3
Bradfield St. George 34 D2
Bradford Corn 4 B3
Bradford Derbys 50 E6
Bradford Devon 6 C5
Bradford N'umb 71 G1
Bradford N'umb 77 K7
Bradford WYorks 57 G6
Bradford Abbas 8 E3
Bradford Cathedral Church of St. Peter WYorks BD1 4EH 123 Bradford
Bradford Leigh 20 B5
Bradford Peverell 9 F5
Bradford-on-Avon 20 B5
Bradford-on-Tone 7 K3
Bradgate Park Leics LE6 0HE 41 H4
Bradiford 6 D2
Brading 11 H6
Bradley ChesW&C 48 E5
Bradley Derbys 40 E1
Bradley Hants 21 K7
Bradley NELincs 53 F2
Bradley (Low Bradley) NYorks 57 F5
Bradley Staffs 40 A4
Bradley WMid 40 B6
Bradley Fold 49 G2
Bradley Green Warks 40 E5
Bradley Green Worcs 29 J2
Bradley in the Moors 40 C1
Bradley Mills 50 D1
Bradley Stoke 19 K3
Bradlingill 60 C4
Bradmore Notts 41 H2
Bradmore WMid 40 A6
Bradney 8 C1
Bradninch 7 J5
Bradnop 50 C7
Bradnor Green 28 B3
Bradpole 8 D5
Bradshaw GtMan 49 G1
Bradshaw WYorks 57 F6
Bradstone 6 B7
Bradwall Green 49 G6
Bradwell Derbys 50 D4
Bradwell Devon 6 C1
Bradwell Essex 34 C6
Bradwell MK 32 B5
Bradwell Norf 45 K5
Bradwell Grove 21 F1
Bradwell Waterside 25 F1
Bradwell-on-Sea 25 G1
Bradworthy 6 B4
Brae D&G 65 J3
Brae High 86 G9
Brae Shet 89 M6
Brae of Achnahaird 86 C8
Braeantra 83 R3
Braedownie 80 H3
Braegrum 80 F8
Braehead D&G 64 E5
Braehead Glas 74 D4
Braehead SLan 75 G7
Braehead SLan 75 H5
Braehead of Lunan 81 M5
Braeleny 80 B9
Braemar 84 F11
Braemore High 83 M3
Braemore High 87 N6
Braeswick 89 F4
Brafferton Darl 62 C4
Brafferton NYorks 57 K2
Brafield-on-the-Green 32 B3
Bragar 88 H3
Bragbury End 33 F6
Bragenham 32 C6
Braichmelyn 46 E6
Braides 55 H4
Braidley 57 F1
Braidwood 75 G6
Braigo 72 A4
Brailsford 40 E1
Brain's Green 19 K1
Braintree 34 B6
Braiseworth 35 F1
Braishfield 10 E2
Braithwaite Cumb 60 D4
Braithwaite SYorks 51 J1
Braithwaite WYorks 57 F5
Braithwell 51 H3
Bramber 12 E5
Brambletye 13 H3
Brambridge 11 F2
Bramcote Notts 41 H2
Bramcote Warks 41 G7
Bramdean 11 H2
Bramerton 45 G5
Bramfield Herts 33 F7
Bramfield Suff 35 H1
Bramford 35 F4
Bramhall 49 H4
Bramham 57 K5
Bramhope 57 H5
Bramley Hants 21 K6
Bramley Surr 22 D7
Bramley SYorks 51 G3
Bramley Corner 21 K6
Bramley Head 57 G4
Bramley Vale 51 G6
Bramling 15 H2
Brampford Speke 7 H6
Brampton Cambs 33 F1
Brampton Cumb 61 H4
Brampton Cumb 70 A7
Brampton Derbys 51 F5
Brampton Lincs 52 B5
Brampton Norf 45 G3
Brampton Suff 45 J7
Brampton SYorks 51 G2
Brampton Abbotts 29 F6
Brampton Ash 42 A7
Brampton Bryan 28 C1
Brampton en le Morthen 51 G4
Brampton Street 45 J7
Brampton Valley Way Country Park N'hants NN6 9DG 31 J1
Bramshall 40 C2
Bramshaw 10 D3
Bramshill 22 A5
Bramshott 12 B3
Bramwell 8 D2
Bran End 33 K6
Brancaster 44 B1
Brancaster Staithe 44 B1
Brancepeth 62 C3
Branchill 84 E5
Brand Green 29 G6
Brandelhow 60 D4
Branderburgh 84 G3
Brandesburton 59 H5
Brandeston 35 G2
Brandis Corner 6 C5
Brandiston 45 F3
Brandlingill 60 C4
Brandon Dur 62 C3
Brandon Lincs 42 C1
Brandon N'umb 71 F2
Brandon Suff 44 B7
Brandon Warks 31 F1
Brandon Bank 44 A7
Brandon Creek 44 A6
Brandon Park Suff IP27 0SU 44 B7
Brandon Parva 44 E5
Brandon to Bishop Auckland Walk Dur DH7 7RJ 62 C3
Brandsby 58 B2
Brandy Wharf 52 D3
Brane 2 B6
Branksome 10 B5
Branksome Park 10 B5
Bransbury 21 H7
Bransby 52 B5
Branscombe 7 K7
Bransford 29 G3
Bransford Bridge 29 H3
Bransgore 10 C5
Bransholme 59 H6
Branson's Cross 30 B1
Branston Leics 42 B3
Branston Lincs 52 D6
Branston Staffs 40 E3
Branston Booths 52 D6
Branston Water Park Staffs DE14 3EZ 40 E3
Brant Broughton 52 C7
Brantham 35 F5
Branthwaite Cumb 60 B4
Branthwaite Cumb 60 D3
Brantingham 59 F7
Branton N'umb 71 F2
Branton SYorks 51 J2
Brantwood 60 E7
Branxholm Bridgend 69 K2
Branxholme 69 K2
Branxton 77 G7
Brassey Green 48 E6
Brassington 50 E7
Brasted 23 H6
Brasted Chart 23 H6
Bratoft 53 H6
Brattleby 52 C4
Bratton Som 7 H1
Bratton Tel&W 39 F4
Bratton Wilts 20 C6
Bratton Clovelly 6 C6
Bratton Fleming 6 E2
Bratton Seymour 9 F2
Braughing 33 G6
Brauncewell 52 D7
Braunston N'hants 31 G2
Braunston Rut 42 B5
Braunstone 41 H5
Braunton 6 C2
Brawby 58 D2
Brawdy 16 B3
Brawith 63 F6
Brawl 87 L3
Brawlbin 87 N4
Bray 22 C4
Bray Shop 4 D3
Bray Wick 22 B4
Braybrooke 42 A7
Braydon Side 20 D3
Brayford 6 E2
Brayshaw 56 C4
Braythorn 57 H5
Brayton 58 C6
Braywoodside 22 B4
Brazacott 4 C1
Brea 2 D4
Breach Kent 15 G3
Breach Kent 24 E5
Breachwood Green 32 E6
Breaden Heath 38 D2
Breadsall 41 F2
Breadstone 20 A1
Bready 90 K6
Breage 2 D6
Bream 19 K1
Breamore 10 C3
Brean 19 F6
Breanais 88 E5
Brearton 57 J3
Breascleit 88 H4
Breaston 41 G2
Brechfa 17 J2
Brechin 81 M4
Brecklate 66 A2
Breckles 44 D6
Brecon (Aberhonddu) 27 K6
Brecon Beacons Int. Dark Sky Reserve Carmar/Powys 27 H7
Brecon Beacons Visitor Centre Powys LD3 8ER 27 J6
Breconside 68 D3
Bredbury 49 J3
Brede 14 D6
Bredenbury 29 F3
Bredfield 35 G3
Bredgar 24 E5
Bredhurst 24 D5
Bredon 29 J5
Bredon's Hardwick 29 J5
Bredon's Norton 29 J5
Bredwardine 28 C4
Breedon on the Hill 41 G3
Breibhig 88 K4
Breich 75 H4
Breightmet 49 G2
Breighton 58 D6
Breinton 28 D5
Breinton Common 28 D5
Bremhill 20 C4
Bremhill Wick 20 C4
Brenchley 23 K7
Brendon Devon 6 B4
Brendon Devon 6 B5
Brendon Devon 7 F1
Brenkley 71 H6
Brent Eleigh 34 D4
Brent Knoll 19 G6
Brent Pelham 33 H5
Brentford 22 E4
Brentingby 42 A4
Brentwood 23 J2
Brenzett 15 F5
Brenzett Green 15 F5
Breoch 65 H5
Brereton 40 C4
Brereton Green 49 G6
Brereton Heath 49 H6
Breretonhill 40 C4
Bressay 89 P8
Bressingham 44 E7
Bressingham Common 44 E7
Bressingham Steam Museum & Gardens Norf IP22 2AA 44 E7
Bretby 40 E3
Bretford 31 F1
Bretforton 30 B4
Bretherdale Head 61 G6
Bretherton 55 H7
Brettabister 89 N7
Brettenham Norf 44 D7
Brettenham Suff 34 D3
Bretton Derbys 50 D5
Bretton Flints 48 C6
Bretton Peter 42 E5
Brevig 88 A9
Brewlands Bridge 80 G4
Brewood 40 A5
Briantspuddle 9 H5
Brick End 33 J6
Brickendon 23 G1
Bricket Wood 22 E1
Brickfields Horse Country IoW PO33 3TH 11 G5
Brickkiln Green 34 B5
Bricklehampton 29 J4
Bride 54 D3
Bridekirk 60 C3
Bridell 16 E1
Bridestowe 6 D7
Brideswell 85 K7
Bridford 7 G7
Bridge Corn 2 D4
Bridge Kent 15 G2
Bridge End Cumb 55 F1
Bridge End Devon 5 G6
Bridge End Essex 33 K5
Bridge End Lincs 42 E2
Bridge End Shet 89 M9
Bridge Hewick 57 J2
Bridge of Alford 85 K9
Bridge of Allan 75 F1
Bridge of Avon 84 F7
Bridge of Awe (Drochaid Abha) 79 M7
Bridge of Balgie 80 A6
Bridge of Brown 84 F8
Bridge of Cally 80 G5
Bridge of Canny 85 L11
Bridge of Craigisla 80 H5
Bridge of Dee 65 H4
Bridge of Don 85 P10
Bridge of Dun 81 M5
Bridge of Dye 81 M2
Bridge of Earn 80 G9
Bridge of Ericht 80 A5
Bridge of Forss 87 N3
Bridge of Gaur 80 A5
Bridge of Orchy (Drochaid Urchaidh) 79 P7
Bridge of Tynet 84 H4
Bridge of Walls 89 L7
Bridge of Weir 74 B4
Bridge Reeve 6 E4
Bridge Sollers 28 D4
Bridge Street 34 C4
Bridge Trafford 48 D5
Bridgefoot Angus 81 J7
Bridgefoot Cambs 33 H4
Bridgefoot Cumb 60 B4
Bridgehampton 8 E2
Bridgehill 62 A1
Bridgemary 11 G4
Bridgend A&B 72 B4
Bridgend A&B 73 G1
Bridgend Aber 85 M6
Bridgend Angus 81 L4
Bridgend (Pen-y-bont ar Ogwr) Bridgend 18 C4
Bridgend Corn 4 B5
Bridgend Cumb 60 F5
Bridgend Moray 84 H7
Bridgend WLoth 75 J3
Bridgend of Lintrathen 80 H5
Bridgerule 6 A5
Bridges 38 C6
Bridgeton 74 E4
Bridgetown Corn 6 B7
Bridgetown Som 7 H2
Bridgewater Hall, Manchester GtMan M2 3WS 133 E5
Bridgeyate 19 K4
Bridgham 44 D7
Bridgnorth 39 G6
Bridgnorth Cliff Railway Shrop WV16 4AH 39 G6
Bridgtown 40 B5
Bridgwater 8 B1
Bridlington 59 H3
Bridport 8 D5
Bridstow 28 E6
Brierfield 56 D6
Brierley Glos 29 F7
Brierley Here 28 D3
Brierley SYorks 51 G1
Brierley Hill 40 B7
Brierton 62 E4
Briestfield 50 E1
Brig o'Turk 80 A10
Brigg 52 D2
Briggate 45 H3
Briggswath 63 J6
Brigh 93 D9
Brigham Cumb 60 B3
Brigham ERid 59 G4
Brighouse 57 G7
Brighstone 11 F6
Brightgate 50 E7
Brighthampton 21 G1
Brightholmlee 50 E3
Brightling 13 K4
Brightlingsea 34 E7
Brighton B&H 13 G6
Brighton Corn 3 G3
Brighton Centre, The B&H BN1 2GR 123 Brighton
Brighton Museum & Art Gallery B&H BN1 1EE 123 Brighton
Brighton City (Shoreham) Airport 12 E6
Brighton Pier B&H BN2 1TW 123 Brighton
Brightons 75 H3
Brightwalton 21 H4
Brightwalton Green 21 H4
Brightwell 35 G4
Brightwell Baldwin 21 K2
Brightwell Upperton 21 K2
Brightwell-cum-Sotwell 21 J2
Brignall 62 A5
Brigsley 53 F2
Brigsteer 55 H1
Brigstock 42 C7
Brill Bucks 31 H7
Brill Corn 2 E6
Brilley 28 B4
Brilley Mountain 28 B3
Brimaston 16 C3
Brimfield 28 E2
Brimington 51 G5
Brimington Common 51 G5
Brimley 5 J3
Brimpsfield 29 J7
Brimpton 21 J5
Brimscombe 20 B1
Brimstage 48 C4
Brindham 19 J7
Brindister 89 N9
Brindle 55 J7
Brindley Ford 49 H7
Brineton 40 A4
Bringhurst 42 B6
Brington 32 D1
Brinian 89 D5
Briningham 44 E2
Brinkhill 53 G5
Brinkley Cambs 33 K3
Brinkley Notts 51 K7
Brinklow 31 F1
Brinkworth 20 D3
Brinscall 56 B7
Brinsea 19 H5
Brinsley 41 G1
Brinsop 28 D4
Brinsworth 51 G3
Brinton 44 E2
Brisco 60 F1
Brisley 44 D3
Brislington 19 K4
Brissenden Green 14 E4
Bristol 19 J4
Bristol Airport 19 J5
Bristol Cathedral BS1 5TJ 123 Bristol
Bristol City Museum & Art Gallery Bristol BS8 1RL 100 C4
Bristol Zoo Bristol BS8 3HA 100 C4
Briston 44 E2
Britannia 56 D7
Britford 10 C2
Brithdir Caerp 18 E1
Brithdir Gwyn 37 G4
Brithem Bottom 7 J4
British Empire & Commonwealth Museum BS1 6QH 123 Bristol
British Library (St. Pancras) GtLon NW1 2DB 104 A6
British Museum GtLon WC1B 3DG 132 E1
Briton Ferry (Llansawel) 18 A2
Britwell 22 C3
Britwell Salome 21 K2
Brixham 5 K5
Brixton Devon 5 F5
Brixton GtLon 23 G4
Brixton Deverill 9 H1
Brixworth 31 J1
Brixworth Country Park N'hants NN6 9DG 31 J1
Brize Norton 21 F1
Broad Alley 29 H2
Broad Blunsdon 20 E2
Broad Campden 30 C5
Broad Carr 50 C1
Broad Chalke 10 B2
Broad Ford 14 C4
Broad Green Cambs 33 K3
Broad Green CenBeds 32 C4
Broad Green Essex 33 H5
Broad Green Essex 34 C6
Broad Green Mersey 48 D3
Broad Green Suff 34 E3
Broad Green Worcs 29 G3
Broad Haven 16 B4
Broad Hill 33 J1
Broad Hinton 20 E4
Broad Laying 21 H5
Broad Marston 30 C4
Broad Oak Carmar 17 J3
Broad Oak Cumb 60 C7
Broad Oak ESuss 13 K4
Broad Oak ESuss 14 D6
Broad Oak Here 28 D6
Broad Road 35 G1
Broad Street ESuss 14 D6
Broad Street Kent 14 D2
Broad Street Wilts 20 E6
Broad Street Green 24 E1
Broad Town 20 D4
Broadbottom 49 J3
Broadbridge 12 B6
Broadbridge Heath 12 E3
Broadclyst 7 H6
Broadfield Lancs 55 J7
Broadfield Lancs 56 C7
Broadford (An t-Ath Leathann) 82 G8
Broadford Airport 82 G8
Broadford Bridge 12 D4
Broadgate 54 E1
Broadhaugh 69 K3
Broadheath GtMan 49 G4
Broadheath Worcs 29 F2
Broadhembury 7 K5
Broadhempston 5 J4
Broadholme 52 B5
Broadland Row 14 D6
Broadlay 17 G5
Broadley Lancs 49 H1
Broadley Moray 84 H4
Broadley Common 23 H1
Broadmayne 9 G6
Broadmeadows 76 C7
Broadmere 21 K7
Broadmoor 16 D5
Broadnymett 7 F5
Broadoak Dorset 8 D5
Broadoak Glos 29 F7
Broadoak Kent 25 H5
Broadoak End 33 G7
Broad's Green 33 K7
Broadstairs 25 K5
Broadstone BCP 10 B5
Broadstone Shrop 38 E7
Broadstreet Common 19 G3
Broadwas 29 G3
Broadwater Herts 33 F6
Broadwater WSuss 12 E6
Broadwater Down 13 J3
Broadwaters 29 H1
Broadway Carmar 17 F4
Broadway Carmar 17 G5
Broadway Pembs 16 B4
Broadway Som 8 C3
Broadway Suff 35 H1
Broadway Worcs 30 C5
Broadwell Glos 30 D6
Broadwell Oxon 21 F1
Broadwell Warks 31 F2
Broadwell House 61 L1
Broadwey 9 F6
Broadwindsor 8 D4
Broadwood Kelly 6 E5
Broadwoodwidger 6 C7
Brobury 28 C4
Brocastle 18 C4
Brochel 82 F6
Brochloch 67 K4
Brockaghboy 92 D5
Brockamin 29 G3
Brockbridge 11 H3
Brockdish 35 G1
Brockenhurst 10 D4
Brockford Green 35 F2
Brockford Street 35 F2
Brockhall 31 H2
Brockham 22 E7
Brockhampton Glos 29 J6
Brockhampton Glos 30 B6
Brockhampton Here 28 E5
Brockhampton Here 29 F3
Brockhampton Green 9 G4
Brockholes Lancs PR5 0AG 55 J6
Brockholes 50 D1
Brockhurst Hants 11 G4
Brockhurst WSuss 13 H3
Brocklebank 60 E2
Brocklesby 52 E1
Brockley NSom 19 H5
Brockley Suff 34 C3
Brockley Green 34 B4
Brock's Green 21 J5
Brockton Shrop 38 C5
Brockton Shrop 38 C7
Brockton Shrop 38 E6
Brockton Shrop 39 G5
Brockton Tel&W 39 G4
Brockweir 19 J1
Brockwood Park 11 H2
Brockworth 29 H7
Brocolitia (Frontiers of the Roman Empire) N'umb 70 D6
Brocton 40 B4
Brodick 73 J7
Brodsworth 51 H2
Brogborough 32 C5
Brogden 56 D5
Brogyntyn 38 B2
Broken Cross ChesE 49 H5
Broken Cross ChesW&C 49 F5
Brokenborough 20 C3
Brokes 62 B7
Bromborough 48 C4
Brome 35 F1
Brome Street 35 F1
Bromeswell 35 H3
Bromfield Cumb 60 C2
Bromfield Shrop 28 D1
Bromham Bed 32 D3
Bromham Wilts 20 C5
Bromley GtLon 23 H5
Bromley SYorks 51 F3
Bromley Cross 49 G1
Bromley Green 14 E4
Brompton Med 24 D5
Brompton NYorks 59 F1
Brompton NYorks 62 D7
Brompton Shrop 38 E5
Brompton on Swale 62 C7
Brompton Ralph 7 J2
Brompton Regis 7 H2
Bromsash 29 F6
Bromsberrow 29 G5
Bromsberrow Heath 29 G5
Bromsgrove 29 J1
Bromstead Heath 40 A4
Bromyard 29 F3
Bromyard Downs 29 F3
Bronaber 37 G2
Brondesbury 23 F3
Brongest 17 G1
Bronington 38 D2
Bronllys 28 A5
Bronnant 27 F2
Brontë Weaving Shed WYorks BD22 8EP 116 A1
Bronwydd Arms 17 H3
Bronydd 28 B4
Bron-y-gaer 17 G4
Bronygarth 38 B2
Brook Carmar 17 F5
Brook Hants 10 D3
Brook Hants 10 E2
Brook IoW 10 E6
Brook Kent 15 F3
Brook Surr 12 C3
Brook Surr 22 D7
Brook Bottom 49 J2
Brook End Bed 32 D2
Brook End Herts 33 G6
Brook End MK 32 C4
Brook End Worcs 29 H4
Brook Hill 10 D3
Brook Street Essex 23 J2
Brook Street Kent 14 E4
Brook Street Suff 34 C4
Brook Street WSuss 13 G4
Brooke Norf 45 G6
Brooke Rut 42 B5
Brookeborough 91 K12
Brookend Glos 19 J2
Brookend Glos 19 K1
Brookfield Derbys 50 C3
Brookfield Mid Ulster 93 D10
Brookhampton 21 K2
Brookhouse ChesE 49 J5
Brookhouse Denb 47 J6
Brookhouse Lancs 55 J3
Brookhouse SYorks 51 H4
Brookhouse Green 49 H6
Brookhouses 40 B1
Brookland 14 E5
Brooklands D&G 65 J3
Brooklands Shrop 38 E1
Brooklands Museum Surr KT13 0QN 22 D5
Brookmans Park 23 F1
Brooks 38 A6
Brooks Green 12 E4
Brooksby 41 J4
Brookside Miniature Railway ChesE SK12 1BZ 115 L8
Brookthorpe 29 H7
Brookwood 22 C6
Broom CenBeds 32 E4
Broom Fife 81 J10
Broom Warks 30 B3
Broom Green 44 D3
Broom Hill Dorset 10 B4
Broom Hill Worcs 29 J1
Broombeg 92 G3
Broomcroft 38 E5
Broome Norf 45 H6
Broome Shrop 38 D7
Broome Worcs 29 J1
Broome Wood 71 G2
Broomedge 49 G4
Broomer's Corner 12 E4
Broomfield Essex 34 B7
Broomfield Kent 14 D2
Broomfield Kent 25 H5
Broomfield Som 8 B1
Broomfleet 58 E7
Broomhall Green 39 F1
Broomhaugh 71 F7
Broomhill Bristol 19 K4
Broomhill N'umb 71 H3
Broomielaw 62 A5
Broomley 71 F7
Broompark 62 C2
Broom's Green 29 G5
Brora 87 M9
Broseley 39 F5
Brotherlee 61 L3
Brothertoft 43 F1
Brotherton 57 K7
Brotton 63 G5
Broubster 87 N3
Brough Cumb 61 J5
Brough Derbys 50 D4
Brough ERid 59 F7
Brough High 87 Q2
Brough Notts 52 B7
Brough Shet 89 P6
Brough Lodge 89 P3
Brough Sowerby 61 J5
Broughall 38 E1
Brougham 61 G4
Brougham Hall Cumb CA10 2DE 61 G4
Broughderg 92 B8
Broughshane 92 G6
Broughton Bucks 32 B7
Broughton Cambs 33 F1
Broughton Flints 48 C6
Broughton Hants 10 E1
Broughton Lancs 55 J6
Broughton MK 32 B4
Broughton NLincs 52 C2
Broughton NYorks 56 E4
Broughton NYorks 58 D2
Broughton N'hants 32 B1
Broughton Oxon 31 F5
Broughton ScBord 75 K7
Broughton VGlam 18 C4
Broughton Astley 41 H6
Broughton Beck 55 F1
Broughton Gifford 20 B5
Broughton Green 29 J2
Broughton Hackett 29 J3
Broughton in Furness 55 F1
Broughton Mills 60 D7
Broughton Moor 60 B3
Broughton Poggs 21 F1
Broughtown 89 F3
Broughty Ferry 81 K7
Brown Candover 11 G1
Brown Edge Lancs 48 C1
Brown Edge Staffs 49 J7
Brown Heath 48 D6
Brown Lees 49 H7
Brown Street 34 E2
Brownber 61 J6
Browndown 11 G5
Brownheath 38 D3
Brownhills 40 C5
Brownieside 71 G1
Brownlow 49 H6
Brownlow Heath 49 H6
Brown's Bank 39 F1
Brownsea Island Dorset BH13 7EE 10 B6
Brownshill 20 B1
Brownshill Green 41 F7
Brownsover 31 G1
Brownston 5 G5
Browston Green 45 J5
Broxa 63 K7
Broxbourne 23 G1
Broxburn ELoth 76 E3
Broxburn WLoth 75 J3
Broxholme 52 C5
Broxted 33 J6
Broxton 48 D7
Broxwood 28 C3
Broyle Side 13 H5
Brue (Brù) 88 J3
Bruera 48 D6
Bruern 30 D6
Bruernish 88 B9
Bruichladdich 72 A4
Bruisyard 35 H2
Bruisyard Street 35 H2
Brumby 52 C1
Brund 50 D6
Brundall 45 H5
Brundish Norf 45 H6
Brundish Suff 35 G2
Brundish Street 35 G1
Brunstock 60 F1
Brunswick Village 71 H6
Bruntingthorpe 41 J6
Brunton Fife 81 J8
Brunton N'umb 71 H1
Brunton Wilts 21 F6
Brunton Turret (Frontiers of the Roman Empire) N'umb NE46 4EJ 70 E7
Bruscarnagh 91 M13
Brushfield 50 D5
Brushford Devon 6 E5
Brushford Som 7 H3
Bruton 9 F1
Bryansford 93 J13
Bryanston 9 H4
Bryant's Bottom 22 B2
Brydekirk 69 G6
Brymbo 48 B7
Brymor Ice Cream NYorks HG4 4PG 57 G1
Brympton 8 E3
Bryn Caerp 18 E2
Bryn Carmar 17 J5
Bryn ChesW&C 49 F5
Bryn GtMan 48 E2
Bryn NPT 18 B2
Bryn Shrop 38 B7
Bryn Bach Country Park BGwent NP22 3AY 18 E1
Bryn Bwbach 37 F2
Bryn Gates 48 E2
Bryn Pen-y-lan 38 C1
Brynamman 27 G7
Brynberian 16 E2
Bryncae 18 C3
Bryncethin 18 C3
Bryncir 36 D1
Bryncoch Bridgend 18 C3
Bryn-côch NPT 18 A2
Bryncroes 36 B2
Bryncrug 37 F5
Bryneglwys 38 A1
Brynford 47 K5
Bryngwran 46 B5
Bryngwyn Mon 19 G1
Bryngwyn Powys 28 A4
Bryn-henllan 16 D2
Brynhoffnant 26 C3
Bryning 55 H6
Brynithel 19 F1
Brynmawr BGwent 28 A7
Bryn-mawr Gwyn 36 B2
Brynmelyn 28 A1
Brynmenyn 18 C3
Brynna 18 C3
Brynnau Gwynion 18 C3
Brynog 26 E3
Bryn-penarth 38 A5
Brynrefail Gwyn 46 D6
Brynrefail IoA 46 C4
Brynsadler 18 D3
Brynsaithmarchog 47 J7
Brynsiencyn 46 C6
Bryn-teg IoA 46 C4
Brynteg Wrex 48 C7
Bryn-y-cochin 38 C2
Brynygwenin 28 C7
Bryn-y-maen 47 G5
Bubbenhall 30 E1
Bubnell 50 E5
Bubwith 58 D6
Buccleuch 69 J2
Buchan 65 H4
Buchanan Castle 74 C2
Buchanty 80 E8
Buchlyvie 74 D1
Buckabank 60 E2
Buckby Wharf 31 H2
Buckden Cambs 32 E2
Buckden NYorks 56 E2
Buckenham 45 H5
Buckerell 7 K5
Buckfast 5 H4
Buckfast Abbey Devon TQ11 0EE 5 H4
Buckfastleigh 5 H4
Buckhaven 76 B1
Buckholm 76 C7
Buckholt 28 E7
Buckhorn Weston 9 G2
Buckhurst Hill 23 H2
Buckie 85 J4
Buckingham 31 H5
Buckingham Palace GtLon SW1A 1AA 132 B5
Buckland Bucks 32 B7
Buckland Devon 5 G6
Buckland Glos 30 B5
Buckland Hants 10 E5
Buckland Here 28 E3
Buckland Herts 33 G5
Buckland Kent 15 J3
Buckland Oxon 21 G2
Buckland Surr 23 F6
Buckland Brewer 6 C3
Buckland Common 22 C1
Buckland Dinham 20 A6
Buckland Filleigh 6 C5
Buckland in the Moor 5 H3
Buckland Monachorum 4 E4
Buckland Newton 9 F4
Buckland Ripers 9 F6
Buckland St. Mary 8 B3
Buckland-tout-Saints 5 H6
Bucklebury 21 J4
Bucklers Hard 11 F5
Bucklesham 35 G4
Buckley (Bwcle) 48 B6
Buckley Green 30 C2
Bucklow Hill 49 G4
Buckman Corner 12 E4
Buckminster 42 B3
Buckna 92 H6
Bucknall 52 E6
Bucknell Oxon 31 G6
Bucknell Shrop 28 C1
Buckridge 29 G1
Buck's Cross 6 B3
Bucks Green 12 D3
Bucks Hill 22 D1
Bucks Horn Oak 22 B7
Buck's Mills 6 B3
Bucksburn 85 N10
Buckspool 16 C6
Buckton ERid 59 H2
Buckton Here 28 C1
Buckton N'umb 77 J7
Buckton Vale 49 J2
Buckworth 32 E1
Budbrooke 30 D2
Budby 51 J5
Bude 6 A5
Budge's Shop 4 D5
Budlake 7 H5
Budle 77 K7
Budleigh Salterton 7 J7
Budock Water 2 E5
Budore 92 H9
Budworth Heath 49 F5
Buerton 39 F1
Bugbrooke 31 H3
Buggan 91 G11
Buglawton 49 H6
Bugle 4 A5
Bugthorpe 58 D4
Building End 33 H5
Buildwas 39 F5
Builth Road 27 K3
Builth Wells (Llanfair-ym-Muallt) 27 K3
Bulby 42 D3
Bulcote 41 J1
Buldoo 87 M3
Bulford 20 E7
Bulford Camp 20 E7
Bulkeley 48 E7
Bulkington Warks 41 F7
Bulkington Wilts 20 C6
Bulkworthy 6 B4
Bull Bay (Porth Llechog) 46 C3
Bull Green 14 E4
Bullbridge 51 F7
Bullbrook 22 B5
Bullen's Green 23 F1
Bulley 29 G7
Bullington 52 D5
Bullpot Farm 56 B1
Bulls Cross 23 G2
Bull's Green Herts 33 F7
Bull's Green Norf 45 J6
Bullwood 73 K3
Bulmer Essex 34 C4
Bulmer NYorks 58 C3
Bulmer Tye 34 C5
Bulphan 24 C3
Bulstone 7 K7
Bulverhythe 14 C7
Bulwell 41 H1
Bulwick 42 C6
Bumble's Green 23 H1
Bun 91 K14
Bun Abhainn Eadarra 88 G7
Bunarkaig 79 N2
Bunbury 48 E7
Bunbury Heath 48 E7
Bunchrew 84 A6
Bundalloch 83 J8
Bunessan 78 E8
Bungay 45 H7
Bunker's Hill 53 F7
Bunlarie 73 F7
Bunmhullin 88 B7
Bunnahabhain 72 C3
Bunneil 91 L13
Bunny 41 H3
Buntait 83 P7
Buntingford 33 G6
Bunwell 45 F6
Bunwell Street 45 F6
Burbage Derbys 50 C5
Burbage Leics 41 G6
Burbage Wilts 21 F5
Burbage Common Leics LE10 3DD 41 G6
Burchett's Green 22 B3
Burcombe 10 B1
Burcot Oxon 21 J2
Burcot Worcs 29 J1
Burcott 32 B6
Burdale 58 E3
Burdocks 12 D4
Burdon 62 D1
Burdrop 30 E5
Bure Valley Railway Norf NR11 6BW 45 G3
Bures 34 D5
Bures Green 34 D5
Burfa 28 B2
Burford Oxon 30 D7
Burford Shrop 28 E2
Burg 78 F6
Burgate 34 E1
Burgates 11 J2
Burge End 32 E5
Burgess Hill 13 G5
Burgh 35 G3
Burgh by Sands 60 E1
Burgh Castle 45 J5
Burgh Heath 23 F6
Burgh le Marsh 53 H6
Burgh next Aylsham 45 G3
Burgh on Bain 53 F4
Burgh St. Margaret (Fleggburgh) 45 J4
Burgh St. Peter 45 J6
Burghclere 21 H5
Burghead 84 F4
Burghfield 21 K5
Burghfield Common 21 K5
Burghfield Hill 21 K5
Burghill 28 D4
Burghwallis 51 H1
Burham 24 D5
Buriton 11 J2
Burland 49 F7
Burlawn 3 G2
Burleigh 22 C5
Burlescombe 7 J4
Burleston 9 G5
Burley Hants 10 D4
Burley Rut 42 B4
Burley WYorks 57 H6
Burley Gate 28 E4
Burley in Wharfedale 57 G5
Burley Street 10 D4
Burley Woodhead 57 G5
Burleydam 39 F1
Burlingjobb 28 B3
Burlow 13 J5
Burlton 38 D3
Burmarsh 15 G4
Burmington 30 D5
Burn 58 B7
Burn Naze 55 G5
Burnage 49 H3
Burnaston 40 E2
Burnby 58 E5
Burncross 51 F3
Burndell 12 C6
Burnden 49 G2
Burnedge 49 J1
Burneside 61 G7
Burness 89 F3
Burneston 57 J1
Burnett 19 K5
Burnfoot CC&G 92 B5
Burnfoot ScBord 69 K2
Burnfoot ScBord 70 A2
Burnham Bucks 22 C3
Burnham NLincs 52 D1
Burnham Deepdale 44 C1
Burnham Green 33 F7
Burnham Market 44 C1
Burnham Norton 44 C1
Burnham Overy Staithe 44 C1
Burnham Overy Town 44 C1
Burnham Thorpe 44 C1
Burnham-on-Crouch 25 F2
Burnham-on-Sea 19 G7
Burnhaven 85 R6
Burnhead D&G 67 K5
Burnhead D&G 68 D4
Burnhervie 85 M9
Burnhill Green 39 G5
Burnhope 62 B2
Burnhouse 74 B5
Burniston 63 K7
Burnley 56 D6
Burnmouth 77 H4
Burnopfield 62 B1
Burn's Green 33 G6
Burns National Heritage Park SAyr KA7 4PQ 67 H2
Burnsall 57 F3
Burnside A&N 92 H7
Burnside A&N 92 G8
Burnside EAyr 67 K3
Burnside WLoth 75 J3
Burnstones 61 H1
Burnswark 69 G6
Burnt Hill 21 J4
Burnt Houses 62 B4
Burnt Oak 23 F2

Burnt Yates 57 H3
Burntcliff Top 49 J6
Burntisland 76 A2
Burnton EAyr 67 J2
Burnton EAyr 67 J3
Burntwood 40 C5
Burntwood Green 40 C5
Burnworthy 7 K4
Burpham Surr 22 D6
Burpham WSuss 12 D6
Burra 89 M9
Burradon N'umb 70 E3
Burradon T&W 71 H6
Burrafirth 89 Q1
Burras 2 D5
Burraton Corn 4 E4
Burraton Corn 4 E5
Burravoe Shet 89 M6
Burravoe Shet 89 P5
Burray 89 D8
Burrell Collection Glas G43 1AT 118 D5
Burrells 61 H5
Burrelton 80 H7
Burren L&C 93 J11
Burren NM&D 93 G14
Burridge Devon 8 C4
Burridge Hants 11 G3
Burrill 57 H1
Burringham 52 B2
Burrington Devon 6 E4
Burrington Here 28 D1
Burrington NSom 19 H6
Burrough Green 33 K3
Burrough on the Hill 42 A4
Burrow Som 7 H1
Burrow Som 8 D3
Burrow Bridge 8 C1
Burrowhill 22 C5
Burrows Cross 22 D7
Burry 17 H6
Burry Green 17 H6
Burry Port 17 H5
Burscough 48 D1
Burscough Bridge 48 D1
Bursea 58 E6
Burshill 59 G5
Bursledon 11 F4
Burslem 40 A1
Burstall 35 F4
Burstock 8 D4
Burston Norf 45 F7
Burston Staffs 40 B2
Burstow 23 G7
Burstwick 59 J7
Burtersett 56 D1
Burthorpe 34 B2
Burthwaite 60 F2
Burtle 19 H7
Burtle Hill 19 G7
Burton BCP 10 C5
Burton ChesW&C 48 C5
Burton ChesW&C 48 E6
Burton Lincs 52 C5
Burton N'umb 77 K7
Burton Pembs 16 C5
Burton Som 7 K1
Burton Wilts 9 H1
Burton Wilts 20 B4
Burton Agnes 59 H3
Burton Bradstock 8 D6
Burton Coggles 42 C3
Burton End 33 J6
Burton Ferry 16 C5
Burton Fleming 59 G2
Burton Green Warks 30 D1
Burton Green Wrex 48 C7
Burton Hastings 41 G7
Burton in Lonsdale 56 B2
Burton Joyce 41 J1
Burton Latimer 32 C1
Burton Lazars 42 A4
Burton Leonard 57 J3
Burton on the Wolds 41 H3
Burton Overy 41 J6
Burton Pedwardine 42 E1
Burton Pidsea 59 J6
Burton Salmon 57 K7
Burton Stather 52 B1
Burton upon Stather 52 B1
Burton upon Trent 40 E3
Burton-in-Kendal 55 J2
Burton's Green 34 C6
Burtonwood 48 E3
Burwardsley 48 E7
Burwarton 39 F7
Burwash 13 K4
Burwash Common 13 K4
Burwash Weald 13 K4
Burwell Cambs 33 J2
Burwell Lincs 53 G5
Burwen 46 C3
Burwick 89 D9
Bury Cambs 43 F7
Bury GtMan 49 H1
Bury Som 7 H3
Bury WSuss 12 D5
Bury End 30 B5
Bury Green 33 H6
Bury St. Edmunds 34 C2
Buryas Bridge 2 B6
Burythorpe 58 D3
Busbridge 22 C7
Busby 74 D5
Buscot 21 F2
Bush 6 A5
Bush Bank 28 D3
Bush Crathie 84 G11
Bush Green 45 G7
Bushbury 40 B5
Bushby 41 J5
Bushey 22 E2
Bushey Heath 22 E2
Bushley 29 H5
Bushley Green 29 H5
Bushmills 92 E2
Bushton 20 D4
Bushy Common 44 D4
Business Design Centre, Islington GtLon N1 0QH 104 B6
Busk 61 H2
Buslingthorpe 52 D4
Bussage 20 B1
Busta 89 M6
Butcher's Common 45 H3
Butcher's Cross 13 J4
Butcher's Pasture 33 K6
Butcombe 19 J5
Bute 73 J4
Bute Town 18 E1
Butleigh 8 E1
Butleigh Wootton 8 E1
Butler's Cross 22 B1
Butler's Hill 41 H1
Butlers Marston 30 E4
Butlersbank 38 E3
Butley 35 H3
Butley Abbey 35 H4
Butley Low Corner 35 H4
Butley Mills 35 H3
Butley Town 49 J5
Butt Green 49 F7
Butt Lane 49 H7
Butterburn 70 B6
Buttercrambe 58 D4
Butterknowle 62 B4
Butterleigh 7 H5
Butterley 51 G7
Butterlope 90 L7
Buttermere Cumb 60 C5
Buttermere Wilts 21 G5
Butters Green 49 H7
Buttershaw 57 G6
Butterstone 80 F6
Butterton Staffs 40 A1
Butterton Staffs 50 C7
Butterwick Dur 62 D4
Butterwick Lincs 43 G1
Butterwick NYorks 58 D2
Butterwick NYorks 59 F2
Buttington 38 B5
Buttonbridge 29 G1
Buttonoak 29 G1
Buttons' Green 34 D3
Butts 7 G7
Butt's Green Essex 24 D1
Butt's Green Hants 10 D2
Buttsash 11 F4
Buxhall 34 E3
Buxted 13 H4
Buxton Derbys 50 C5
Buxton Norf 45 G3
Buxton Heath 45 F3
Buxworth 50 C4
Bwlch 28 A6
Bwlch-clawdd 17 G2
Bwlch-derwin 36 D1
Bwlchgwyn 48 B7
Bwlch-llan 26 E3
Bwlchnewydd 17 G3
Bwlchtocyn 36 C3
Bwlch-y-cibau 38 A4
Bwlch-y-ddar 38 A3
Bwlchyfadfa 17 H1
Bwlch-y-ffridd 37 K6
Bwlch-y-groes 17 F2
Bwlchyllyn 46 D7
Bwlchymynydd 17 J6
Bwlch-y-sarnau 27 K1
Byers Green 62 C3
Byfield 31 G3
Byfleet 22 D5
Byford 28 C4
Bygrave 33 F5
Byker 71 H7
Byland Abbey 58 B2
Bylane End 4 C5
Bylchau 47 H6
Byley 49 G6
Bynea 17 J6
Byrness 70 C3
Bystock 7 J7
Bythorn 32 D1
Byton 28 C2
Bywell 71 F7
Byworth 12 C4

C

Cabourne 52 E2
Cabrach A&B 72 C4
Cabrach Moray 84 H8
Cabragh Mid Ulster 92 D8
Cabragh Mid Ulster 93 C10
Cabus 55 H5
Cackle Street ESuss 13 H4
Cackle Street ESuss 14 D6
Cacrabank 69 J2
Cadbury 7 H5
Cadbury Barton 6 E4
Cadbury Heath 19 K4
Cadbury World WMid B30 1JR 107 G7
Cadder 74 E3
Cadderlie 79 M7
Caddington 32 D7
Caddonfoot 76 C7
Caddy 92 F7
Cade Street 13 K4
Cadeby Leics 41 G5
Cadeby SYorks 51 H2
Cadeleigh 7 H5
Cader 47 J6
Cadgwith 2 E7
Cadishead 49 G3
Cadle 17 K6
Cadley Lancs 55 J6
Cadley Wilts 21 F5
Cadmore End 22 A2
Cadnam 10 D3
Cadney 52 D2
Cadole 48 B6
Cadover Bridge 5 F4
Cadoxton 18 E5
Cadoxton-Juxta-Neath 18 A2
Cadwell 32 E5
Cadwst 37 K2
Cady 91 H10
Cadzow 75 F5
Cae Ddafydd 37 F1
Caeathro 46 D6
Caehopkin 27 H7
Caenby 52 D4
Caenby Corner 52 C4
Caer Llan 19 H1
Caerau Bridgend 18 B2
Caerau Cardiff 18 E4
Caerdeon 37 F4
Caerfarchell 16 A3
Caergeiliog 46 B5
Caergwrle 48 C7
Caerhun 47 F5
Caer-Lan 27 H7
Caerleon 19 G2
Caernarfon 46 C6
Caernarfon Castle (Castles & Town Walls of King Edward in Gwynedd) Gwyn LL55 2AY 46 C6
Caerphilly 18 E3
Caersws 37 K6
Caerwedros 26 C3
Caerwent 19 H2
Caerwys 47 K5
Caethle Farm 37 F6
Caggan 84 C9
Caggle Street 28 C7
Caheny 92 D5
Caherty 92 G6
Caim 46 E4
Caio 17 K2
Cairisiadar 88 F4
Cairminis 88 F9
Cairnbaan 73 G1
Cairnbulg 85 Q4
Cairncross Angus 81 L3
Cairncross ScBord 77 G4
Cairncurran 74 B4
Cairndoon 64 D7
Cairndow 79 N9
Cairness 85 Q4
Cairneyhill 75 J2
Cairngorm Mountain High PH22 1RB 84 D10
Cairnie 85 J6
Cairnorrie 85 N6
Cairnryan 64 A4
Cairnsmore 64 E4
Caister-on-Sea 45 K4
Caistor 52 E2
Caistor St. Edmund 45 G5
Caistron 70 E3
Caithness Crystal Visitor Centre Norf PE30 4NE 44 A4
Cake Street 44 E6
Cakebole 29 H1
Calbourne 11 F6
Calceby 53 G5
Calcoed 47 K5
Calcot 21 K4
Calcott Kent 25 H5
Calcott Shrop 38 D4
Calcotts Green 29 G7
Calcutt 20 E2
Caldanagh 92 F4
Caldarvan 74 C2
Caldbeck 60 E3
Caldbergh 57 F1
Caldecote Cambs 33 G3
Caldecote Cambs 42 E7
Caldecote Herts 33 F5
Caldecote N'hants 31 H3
Caldecote Warks 41 F6
Caldecott N'hants 32 C2
Caldecott Oxon 21 H2
Caldecott Rut 42 B6
Calder Bridge 60 B6
Calder Grove 51 F1
Calder Vale 55 J5
Calderbank 75 F4
Calderbrook 49 J1
Caldercruix 75 G4
Calderglen 74 E5
Calderglen Country Park SLan G75 0QZ 119 H8
Caldermill 74 E6
Caldey Island 16 E6
Caldicot 19 H3
Caldwell Derbys 40 E4
Caldwell ERenf 74 C5
Caldwell NYorks 62 B5
Caldy 48 B4
Calebreck 60 E3
Caledon 93 C12
Caledrhydiau 26 D3
Calford Green 33 K4
Calfsound 89 E4
Calgary 78 E5
Califer 84 E5
California Falk 75 H3
California Norf 45 K4
California Suff 35 G4
California Country Park W'ham RG40 4HT 22 A5
Calke 41 F3
Calke Abbey Derbys DE73 7LE 41 F3
Calkill 90 L9
Callakille 82 G5
Callaly 71 F3
Callander 80 B10
Callanish (Calanais) 88 H4
Callaughton 39 F6
Callerton Lane End 71 G7
Calliburn 66 B1
Calligarry 82 G10
Callington 4 D4
Callingwood 40 D3
Callisterhall 69 H5
Callow 28 D5
Callow End 29 H4
Callow Hill Wilts 20 D3
Callow Hill Worcs 29 G1
Callow Hill Worcs 30 B2
Callows Grave 28 E2
Calmore 10 E3
Calmsden 20 D1
Calne 20 C4
Calow 51 G5
Calshot 11 F4
Calstock 4 E4
Calstone Wellington 20 D5
Calthorpe 45 F2
Calthwaite 61 F2
Calton NYorks 56 E4
Calton Staffs 50 D7
Calveley 48 E7
Calver 50 E5
Calver Hill 28 C4
Calverhall 39 F2
Calverleigh 7 H4
Calverley 57 H6
Calvert 31 H6
Calverton MK 31 J5
Calverton Notts 41 J1
Calvine 80 C4
Calvo 60 C1
Cam CC&G 92 C4
Cam Glos 20 A2
Camagh 93 D13
Camasnacroise 79 K5
Camastianavaig 82 F7
Camault Muir 83 R6
Camb 89 P3
Camber 14 E6
Camberley 22 B5
Camberwell 23 G4
Camblesforth 58 C7
Cambo 71 F5
Cambois 71 J5
Camborne 2 D5
Camborne & Redruth Mining District (Cornwall & West Devon Mining Landscape) Corn 2 D4
Cambourne 33 G3
Cambridge Cambs 33 H3
Cambridge Glos 20 A1
Cambridge American Military Cemetery & Memorial Cambs CB23 7PH 33 G3
Cambridge International Airport 33 H3
Cambridge University Botanic Garden Cambs CB2 1JF 33 H3
Cambus 75 G1
Cambusbarron 75 F1
Cambuskenneth 75 G1
Cambuslang 74 E4
Cambusnethan 75 G5
Camden Town 23 F3
Camel Hill 8 E2
Camel Trail Corn PL27 7AL 3 G1
Cameley 19 K6
Camelford 4 B2
Camelon 75 G2
Camelsdale 12 B3
Camer 24 C5
Cameron House 74 B2
Camer's Green 29 G5
Camerton B&NESom 19 K6
Camerton Cumb 60 B3
Camerton ERid 59 J7
Camghouran 80 A5
Camis Eskan 74 B2
Camlough 93 F14
Cammachmore 85 P11
Cammeringham 52 C4
Camore 84 B1
Camp Hill Pembs 16 E4
Camp Hill Warks 41 F6
Campbeltown (Ceann Loch Chille Chiarain) 66 B1
Campbeltown Airport 66 A1
Camperdown 71 H6
Camperdown Country Park Dundee DD2 4TF 81 J7
Camps 75 K4
Camps End 33 K4
Campsall 51 H1
Campsea Ashe 35 H3
Campsey 90 M4
Campton 32 E5
Camptown 70 B2
Camquhart 73 H2
Camrose 16 C3
Camserney 80 D6
Camstraddan House 74 B1
Camus-luinie 83 K8
Camusrory 83 J11
Camusteel 82 H6
Camusterrach 82 H6
Camusvrachan 80 B6
Canada 10 D3
Canaston Bridge 16 D4
Candlesby 53 H6
Candy Mill 75 J6
Cane End 21 K4
Canewdon 24 E2
Canfield End 33 J6
Canford Bottom 10 B4
Canford Cliffs 10 B6
Canford Heath 10 B5
Canford Magna 10 B5
Canham's Green 34 E2
Canisbay 87 R2
Canley 30 E1
Cann 9 H2
Cann Common 9 H2
Canna 82 C10
Cannard's Grave 19 K7
Cannich (Canaich) 83 P7
Canning Town 23 H3
Cannington 8 B1
Cannock 40 B5
Cannock Wood 40 C4
Cannon Hall Country Park SYorks S75 4AT 50 E2
Cannon Hall Farm SYorks S75 4AT 50 E2
Cannon Hill Park WMid B13 8RD 107 H6
Cannop 29 F7
Canon Bridge 28 D4
Canon Frome 29 F4
Canon Pyon 28 D4
Canonbie 69 J6
Canons Ashby 31 G3
Canon's Town 2 C5
Canterbury 15 G2
Canterbury Cathedral (Canterbury Cathedral, St Augustine's Abbey, & St Martin's Church) Kent CT1 2EH 15 G2
Canterbury Tales, The Kent CT1 2TG 123 Canterbury
Cantley Norf 45 H5
Cantley SYorks 51 J2
Cantlop 38 E5
Canton 18 E4
Cantraydoune 84 B6
Cantsfield 56 B2
Canvey Island 24 D3
Canwell Hall 40 D5
Canwick 52 C6
Canworthy Water 4 C1
Caol 79 N3
Caolas 78 B6
Caolasnacon 79 N4
Capel Kent 23 K7
Capel Surr 22 E7
Capel Bangor 37 F7
Capel Betws Lleucu 27 F3
Capel Carmel 36 A3
Capel Celyn 37 H1
Capel Coch 46 C4
Capel Curig 47 F7
Capel Cynon 17 G1
Capel Dewi Carmar 17 H3
Capel Dewi Cere 17 H1
Capel Dewi Cere 37 F7
Capel Garmon 47 G7
Capel Gwyn Carmar 17 H3
Capel Gwyn IoA 46 B5
Capel Gwynfe 27 G6
Capel Hendre 17 J4
Capel Isaac 17 J3
Capel Iwan 17 F2
Capel le Ferne 15 H4
Capel Llanilltern 18 D3
Capel Mawr 46 C5
Capel Parc 46 C4
Capel Seion 27 F1
Capel St. Andrew 35 H4
Capel St. Mary 34 E5
Capel St. Silin 26 E3
Capel Tygwydd 17 F1
Capeluchaf 36 D1
Capelulo 47 F5
Capel-y-ffin 28 B5
Capel-y-graig 46 D6
Capenhurst 48 C5
Capernwray 55 J2
Capheaton 71 F5
Caplaw 74 C5
Capon's Green 35 G2
Cappagh AB&C 93 G12
Cappagh Mid Ulster 93 B10
Cappercleuch 69 H1
Cappleigill 69 G3
Capstone 24 D5
Capton Devon 5 J5
Capton Som 7 J2
Caputh 80 F6
Car Colston 42 A1
Caradon Mining District (Cornwall & West Devon Mining Landscape) Corn 3 K1
Caradon Town 4 C3
Carbellow 68 B1
Carbeth 74 D3
Carbis Bay 2 C5
Carbost High 82 D7
Carbost High 82 E6
Carbrain 75 F3
Carbrooke 44 D5
Carburton 51 J5
Carclunty 92 F5
Carco 68 C2
Carcroft 51 H1
Cardenden 76 A1
Cardeston 38 C4
Cardew 60 E2
Cardiff (Caerdydd) 18 E4
Cardiff Airport 18 D5
Cardiff Bay Visitor Centre Cardiff CF10 4PA 99 C6
Cardiff Castle & Museum CF10 3RB 124 Cardiff
Cardiff Millennium Stadium CF10 1GE 124 Cardiff
Cardigan (Aberteifi) 16 E1
Cardinal's Green 33 K4
Cardington Bed 32 D4
Cardington Shrop 38 E6
Cardinham 4 B4
Cardonald 74 D4
Cardoness 65 F5
Cardow 84 F6
Cardrona 76 A7
Cardross 74 B3
Cardurnock 60 C1
Cardy 93 L9
Careby 42 D4
Careston 81 L5
Carew 16 D5
Carew Cheriton 16 D5
Carew Newton 16 D5
Carey 28 E5
Carfin 75 F5
Carfrae 76 D4
Carfraemill 76 D5
Cargan 92 G5
Cargate Green 45 H4
Cargen 65 K3
Cargenbridge 65 K3
Cargill 80 G7
Cargo 60 E1
Cargreen 4 E4
Carham 77 F7
Carhampton 7 J1
Carharrack 2 E4
Carie P&K 80 B5
Carie P&K 80 B7
Carines 2 E3
Carinish (Cairinis) 88 C2
Carisbrooke 11 F6
Carisbrooke Castle & Museum IoW PO30 1XY 11 F6
Cark 55 G2
Carkeel 4 E4
Carland 93 C10
Carland Cross 3 F3
Carlane 92 F8
Carlatton 61 G1
Carlby 42 D4
Carlecotes 50 D2
Carleen 2 D6
Carleton Cumb 60 F1
Carleton Cumb 61 G4
Carleton Lancs 55 G5
Carleton NYorks 56 E5
Carleton WYorks 57 K7
Carleton Fishery 67 F5
Carleton Forehoe 44 E5
Carleton Rode 44 E6
Carleton St. Peter 45 H5
Carlin How 63 H5
Carlisle 60 F1
Carlisle Cathedral Cumb CA3 8TZ 124 Carlisle
Carlisle Lake District Airport 69 K7
Carlisle Park, Morpeth N'umb NE61 1YD 71 G5
Carloggas 3 F2
Carlops 75 K5
Carloway (Càrlabhagh) 88 H3
Carlton Bed 32 C3
Carlton Cambs 33 K3
Carlton Leics 41 F5
Carlton Notts 41 J1
Carlton NYorks 57 F1
Carlton NYorks 58 C1
Carlton NYorks 58 C7
Carlton Stock 62 D4
Carlton Suff 35 H2
Carlton SYorks 51 F1
Carlton WYorks 57 J7
Carlton Colville 45 K6
Carlton Curlieu 41 J6
Carlton Green 33 K3
Carlton Husthwaite 57 K2
Carlton in Lindrick 51 H4
Carlton Miniott 57 J1
Carlton Scroop 42 C1
Carlton-in-Cleveland 63 F6
Carlton-le-Moorland 52 C7
Carlton-on-Trent 52 B6
Carluke 75 G5
Carlyon Bay 4 A5
Carmacoup 68 C1
Carmarthen (Caerfyrddin) 17 H3
Carmel Carmar 17 J4
Carmel Flints 47 K5
Carmel Gwyn 46 C7
Carmel IoA 46 B4
Carmichael 75 H7
Carmunnock 74 D5
Carmyle 74 E4
Carmyllie 81 L6
Carn A&B 72 A5
Carn CC&G 92 C6
Carn Brea Village 2 D4
Carnaby 59 H3
Carnach 83 L8
Carnagh 93 D14
Carnalbanagh 92 D3
Carnalea 91 L10
Carnamoney 92 C7
Carnanreagh 90 M6
Carnassarie 79 K10
Carnaugh 92 E8
Carnbane 93 F14
Carnbee 81 L10
Carnbeg 92 F5
Carnbo 80 F10
Carncastle 92 J6
Carnduff 92 F2
Carnduncan 72 A4
Carneatly 92 F3
Carnforth 55 H2
Carnhedryn 16 B3
Carnhell Green 2 D5
Carnkie Corn 2 D5
Carnkie Corn 2 E5
Carnlough 92 H5
Carnmoney 92 J8
Carnmore 72 B6
Carno 37 J6
Carnoch High 83 N5
Carnoch High 83 P7
Carnoch High 84 C6
Carnock 75 J2
Carnon Downs 3 F4
Carnoustie 81 L7
Carnteel 93 B11
Carntyne 74 E4
Carnwath 75 H6
Carnyorth 2 A5
Carol Green 30 D1
Carperby 57 F1
Carr 51 H3
Carr Hill 51 J3
Carr Houses 48 C2
Carr Shield 61 K2
Carr Vale 51 G5
Carradale 73 G7
Carrbridge 84 D8
Carrefour Selous 3 J7
Carreglefn 46 B4
Carreg-wen 17 F1
Carrhouse 51 K2
Carrick A&B 73 H2
Carrick F&O 91 J9
Carrick Castle 73 K1
Carrick-a-Rede Rope Bridge CC&G BT54 6LS 92 F2
Carrickbrack 93 F13
Carrickfergus 92 K8
Carrickfergus Castle M&EAnt BT38 7BG 92 K8
Carrickgallogly 93 E14
Carrickmore 93 B9
Carrickyheenan 91 L13
Carriden 75 J2
Carrigans 90 L8
Carrigenagh 93 J15
Carrine 66 A3
Carrington GtMan 49 G3
Carrington Lincs 53 G7
Carrington Midlo 76 B4
Carroch 68 B4
Carrog Conwy 37 G1
Carrog Denb 38 A1
Carrogs 93 G14
Carron A&B 73 H1
Carron Falk 75 G2
Carron Moray 84 G6
Carron Bridge 75 F2
Carronbridge 68 D4
Carronshore 75 G2
Carrow Hill 19 H2
Carrowcrin 92 F4
Carrowdore 93 L9
Carrutherstown 69 G6
Carruthmuir 74 B4
Carrville 62 D2
Carry 73 H4
Carryduff 93 J10
Carsaig 78 G8
Carscreugh 64 C4
Carse 73 F4
Carsegowan 64 E5
Carseriggan 64 D4
Carsethorn 65 K5
Carshalton 23 F5
Carshalton Beeches 23 F5
Carsie 80 G6
Carsington 50 E7
Carsington Water Derbys DE6 1ST 50 E7
Carsluith 64 E5
Carsphairn 67 K4
Carstairs 75 H6
Carstairs Junction 75 H6
Carswell Marsh 21 G2
Carter's Clay 10 E2
Carterton 21 F1
Carterway Heads 62 A1
Carthew 4 A5
Carthorpe 57 J1
Cartington 71 F3
Cartland 75 G6
Cartmel 55 G2
Cartmel Fell 55 H1
Cartworth 50 D2
Carway 17 H5
Cascades Adventure Pool Devon EX33 1NZ 6 C2
Cascob 28 B2
Cashel Farm 74 C1
Cashes Green 20 B1
Cashlie 79 R6
Cashmoor 9 J3
Cashty 90 K8
Caskum 93 G12
Casorna 90 M8
Cassencarie 64 E5
Cassington 31 F7
Cassop 62 D3
Castell 47 F6
Castell Gorfod 17 F3
Castell Howell 17 H1
Castellau 18 D3
Castell-y-bwch 19 F2
Casterton 56 B2
Castle Acre 44 C4
Castle Ashby 32 B3
Castle Bolton 62 A7
Castle Bromwich 40 D7
Castle Bytham 42 C4
Castle Caereinion 38 A5
Castle Camps 33 K4
Castle Carrock 61 G1
Castle Cary 9 F1
Castle Combe 20 B4
Castle Donington 41 G3
Castle Douglas 65 H4
Castle Drogo Devon EX6 6PB 7 F6
Castle Eaton 20 E2
Castle Eden 62 E3
Castle Eden Dene National Nature Reserve Dur SR8 1NJ 62 E3
Castle End 30 D1
Castle Frome 29 F4
Castle Gate 2 B5
Castle Goring 12 E6
Castle Green 22 C5
Castle Gresley 40 E4
Castle Heaton 77 H6
Castle Hedingham 34 B5
Castle Hill Kent 23 K7
Castle Hill Suff 35 F4
Castle Howard NYorks YO60 7DA 58 D3
Castle Kennedy 64 B5
Castle Levan 74 A3
Castle Madoc 27 K5
Castle Morris 16 C2
Castle O'er 69 H4
Castle Rising 44 A3
Castle Semple Water Country Park Renf PA12 4HJ 74 B5
Castlebay (Bàgh a'Chaisteil) 88 A9
Castlebythe 16 D3
Castlecary 75 F3
Castlecaulfield 93 C10
Castlecraig High 84 C4
Castlecraig ScBord 75 K6
Castledawson 92 E7
Castlederg 90 J8
Castlefairn 68 C5
Castleford 57 K7
Castlemartin 16 C6
Castlemilk D&G 69 G6
Castlemilk Glas 74 E5
Castlemorton 29 G5
Castlereagh 93 J9
Castlerigg 60 D4
Castlerock 92 C3
Castleside 62 A2
Castlesteads 70 A7
Castlethorpe 31 J4
Castleton A&B 73 G2
Castleton Derbys 50 D4
Castleton GtMan 49 H1
Castleton Newport 19 F3
Castleton NYorks 63 G6
Castleton ScBord 70 A4
Castletown Dorset 9 F7
Castletown High 87 P3
Castletown IoM 54 B7
Castletown T&W 62 D1
Castleweary 69 K3
Castlewellan 93 J13
Castlewigg 64 E6
Castley 57 H5
Caston 44 D6
Castor 42 E6
Castramont 65 F4
Caswell 17 J7
Cat & Fiddle Inn 50 C5
Catacol 73 H6
Catbrain 19 J3
Catbrook 19 J1
Catchall 2 B6
Catcleugh 70 C3
Catcliffe 51 G4
Catcott 8 C1
Caterham 23 G6
Catfield 45 H3
Catford 23 G4
Catforth 55 H6
Cathays 18 E4
Cathcart 74 D4
Cathedine 28 A6
Catherine-de-Barnes 40 D7
Catherington 11 H3
Catherston Leweston 8 C5
Catherton 29 F1
Cathkin 74 E5
Catisfield 11 G4
Catlodge 84 A11
Catlowdy 69 K6
Catmere End 33 H5
Catmore 21 H3
Caton Devon 5 H3
Caton Lancs 55 J3
Caton Green 55 J3
Cator Court 5 G3
Catrine 67 K1
Catsfield 14 C6
Catsfield Stream 14 C6
Catshaw 50 E2
Catshill 29 J1
Cattadale 72 B4
Cattal 57 K4
Cattawade 34 E5
Catterall 55 J5
Catterick 62 C7
Catterick Bridge 62 C7
Catterick Garrison 62 B7
Catterlen 61 F3
Catterline 81 P3
Catterton 58 B5
Catteshall 22 C7
Catthorpe 31 G1
Cattishall 34 C2
Cattistock 8 E4
Catton Norf 45 G4
Catton NYorks 57 J2
Catton N'umb 61 K1
Catton Hall 40 E4
Catwick 59 H5
Catworth 32 D1
Caudle Green 29 J7
Caudwell's Mill & Craft Centre Derbys DE4 2EB 50 E6
Caulcott CenBeds 32 D4
Caulcott Oxon 31 G6
Cauldhame Stir 74 E1
Cauldhame Stir 80 D10
Cauldon 40 C1
Caulhame 92 D5
Caulkerbush 65 K5
Caulside 69 K5
Caundle Marsh 9 F3
Caunsall 40 A7
Caunton 51 K6
Causeway End D&G 64 E4
Causeway End Essex 33 K7
Causeway End Lancs 48 D1
Causeway Head 92 E2
Causewayhead Cumb 60 C1
Causewayhead Stir 75 G1
Causey 62 C1
Causey Arch Picnic Area Dur NE16 5EG 62 C1
Causey Park 71 G4
Cautley 61 H7
Cavan 91 L10
Cavanacross 91 J12
Cavendish 34 C4
Cavendish Bridge 41 G3
Cavenham 34 B2
Cavens 65 K5
Cavers 70 A2
Caversfield 31 G6
Caversham 22 A4
Caverswall 40 B1
Cawdor 84 C5
Cawkeld 59 F4
Cawkwell 53 F4
Cawood 58 B6
Cawsand 4 E6
Cawston Norf 45 F3
Cawston Warks 31 F1
Cawthorn 58 D1
Cawthorne 50 E2
Cawthorpe 42 D3
Cawton 58 C2
Caxton 33 G3
Caxton Gibbet 33 F2
Caynham 28 E1
Caythorpe Lincs 42 C1
Caythorpe Notts 41 J1
Cayton 59 G1
CC2000 Pembs SA67 8DD 16 D4
Ceallan 88 C3
Ceann a' Bhàigh Na H-E. Siar 88 B2
Ceann a' Bhàigh Na H-E. Siar 88 F9
Cearsiadair 88 J6
Cedig 37 J3
Cefn (Pontcysyllte Aqueduct & Canal) Denb/Powys/Wrex 38 B1
Cefn Berain 47 H6
Cefn Canol 38 B2
Cefn Cantref 27 K6
Cefn Coch Denb 47 K7
Cefn Coch Powys 37 K5
Cefn Cribwr 18 B3
Cefn Cross 18 B3
Cefn Einion 38 B7
Cefn Hengoed 18 E2
Cefn Llwyd 37 F7
Cefn Rhigos 18 C1
Cefn-brith 47 H7
Cefn-caer-Ferch 36 D1
Cefn-coch 38 A3
Cefn-coed-y-cymmer 18 D1
Cefn-ddwysarn 37 J2
Cefndeuddwr 37 G3
Cefneithin 17 J4
Cefn-gorwydd 27 J4
Cefn-gwyn 38 A7
Cefn-mawr 38 B1
Cefnpennar 18 D1
Cefn-y-bedd 48 C7
Cefn-y-pant 16 E3
Ceidio 46 C4
Ceidio Fawr 36 B2
Ceint 46 C5
Cellan 17 K1
Cellarhead 40 B1
Cemaes 46 B3
Cemmaes 37 H5
Cemmaes Road (Glantwymyn) 37 H5
Cenarth 17 F1
Cennin 36 D1
Centre for Life T&W NE1 4EP 129 Newcastle upon Tyne
Ceramica Stoke ST6 3DS 110 D3
Ceres 81 K9
Cerist 37 J7
Cerne Abbas 9 F4
Cerney Wick 20 D2
Cerrigceinwen 46 C5
Cerrigydrudion 37 J1
Cessford 70 C1
Ceunant 46 D6
Chaceley 29 H5
Chacewater 2 E4
Chackmore 31 H5
Chacombe 31 F4
Chad Valley 40 C7
Chadderton 49 J2
Chadderton Fold 49 H2
Chaddesden 41 F2
Chaddesley Corbett 29 H1
Chaddleworth 21 H4
Chadlington 30 E6
Chadshunt 30 E3
Chadstone 32 B3
Chadwell Leics 42 A3
Chadwell Shrop 39 G4
Chadwell St. Mary 24 C4
Chadwick End 30 D1
Chaffcombe 8 C3
Chafford Hundred 24 C4
Chagford 7 F7
Chailey 13 G5
Chainhurst 14 C3
Chalbury 10 B4
Chalbury Common 10 B4
Chaldon 23 G6
Chaldon Herring (East Chaldon) 9 G6
Chale 11 F7
Chale Green 11 F6
Chalfont Common 22 D2
Chalfont St. Giles 22 C2
Chalfont St. Peter 22 D2
Chalford Glos 20 B1
Chalford Wilts 20 B7
Chalgrove 21 K2
Chalk 24 C4
Chalk End 33 K7
Challaborough 5 G6
Challacombe 6 E1
Challoch 64 D4
Challock 15 F2
Chalmington 8 E4
Chalton CenBeds 32 D6
Chalton Hants 11 J3
Chalvey 22 C4
Chalvington 13 J6
Champany 75 J3
Chancery 26 E1
Chandler's Cross 22 D2
Chandler's Ford 11 F2
Channel Islands 3 G7
Channel's End 32 E3
Chantry Som 20 A7
Chantry Suff 35 F4
Chapel 76 A1
Chapel Allerton Som 19 H6
Chapel Allerton WYorks 57 J6
Chapel Amble 3 G1
Chapel Brampton 31 J2
Chapel Chorlton 40 A2
Chapel Cleeve 7 J1
Chapel Cross 13 K4
Chapel End 32 D4
Chapel Green Warks 31 F2
Chapel Green Warks 40 E7
Chapel Haddlesey 58 B7
Chapel Hill Aber 85 Q7
Chapel Hill Lincs 53 F7
Chapel Hill Mon 19 J1
Chapel Hill NYorks 57 J5
Chapel Knapp 20 B5
Chapel Lawn 28 C1
Chapel Leigh 7 K3
Chapel Milton 50 C4
Chapel of Garioch 85 M8
Chapel Rossan 64 B6
Chapel Row Essex 24 D1
Chapel Row WBerks 21 J5
Chapel St. Leonards 53 J5
Chapel Stile 60 E6
Chapel Town 3 F3
Chapeldonan 67 F3
Chapelend Way 34 B5
Chapel-en-le-Frith 50 C4
Chapelgate 43 H3
Chapelhall 75 F4
Chapelhill P&K 80 F7
Chapelhill P&K 80 H8
Chapelknowe 69 J6
Chapel-le-Dale 56 C2
Chapelthorpe 51 F1
Chapelton Angus 81 M6
Chapelton Devon 6 D3
Chapelton SLan 74 E6
Chapeltown B'burn 49 G1
Chapeltown Cumb 69 K6
Chapeltown M&EAnt 92 G7
Chapeltown Moray 84 G8
Chapeltown NM&D 93 L12
Chapeltown SYorks 51 F3
Chapmans Well 6 B6
Chapmanslade 20 B7
Chapmore End 33 G7
Chappel 34 C6
Charaton 4 D4
Chard 8 C4
Chard Junction 8 C4
Chardleigh Green 8 C3
Chardstock 8 C4
Charfield 20 A2
Charing 14 E3
Charing Cross 10 C3
Charing Heath 14 E3
Charingworth 30 C5
Charlbury 30 E7
Charlcombe 20 A5
Charlecote 30 D3
Charlemont 93 D11
Charles 6 E2
Charles Tye 34 E3
Charlesfield 69 G7
Charleshill 22 B7
Charleston 81 J6
Charlestown Aberdeen 85 P10
Charlestown Corn 4 A5
Charlestown Derbys 50 C3
Charlestown Dorset 9 F7
Charlestown Fife 75 J2
Charlestown GtMan 49 H2
Charlestown High 83 J3
Charlestown High 84 A6
Charlestown WYorks 56 E7
Charlestown WYorks 57 G6
Charlestown (Cornwall & West Devon Mining Landscape) Corn 3 H3
Charlestown of Aberlour (Aberlour) 84 G6
Charlesworth 50 C3
Charlinch 8 B1
Charlotteville 22 D7
Charlton GtLon 23 H4
Charlton Hants 21 G7
Charlton Herts 32 E6
Charlton N'hants 31 G5
Charlton N'umb 70 D5
Charlton Oxon 21 H3
Charlton Som 8 B2
Charlton Som 19 K6
Charlton Som 19 K7
Charlton Tel&W 38 E4
Charlton Wilts 9 J2
Charlton Wilts 20 C3
Charlton Wilts 20 E6
Charlton Worcs 30 B4
Charlton WSuss 12 B5
Charlton Abbots 30 B6
Charlton Adam 8 E2
Charlton Down 9 F5
Charlton Horethorne 9 F2
Charlton Kings 29 J6
Charlton Mackrell 8 E2
Charlton Marshall 9 H4
Charlton Musgrove 9 G2
Charlton on the Hill 9 H4
Charlton-All-Saints 10 C2
Charlton-on-Otmoor 31 G7
Charltons 63 G5
Charlwood 23 F7
Charminster 9 F5
Charmouth 8 C5
Charndon 31 H6
Charney Bassett 21 G2
Charnock Richard 48 E1
Charsfield 35 G3
Chart Corner 14 C3
Chart Sutton 14 D3
Charter Alley 21 J6
Charterhouse 19 H6
Charterville Allotments 21 G1
Chartham 15 G2
Chartham Hatch 15 G2
Chartridge 22 C1
Chartwell Kent TN16 1PS 23 H6
Charvil 22 A4
Charwelton 31 G3
Chase End Street 29 G5
Chase Terrace 40 C5
Chasetown 40 C5
Chastleton 30 D6
Chasty 6 B5
Chatburn 56 C5
Chatcull 39 G2
Chatelherault Country Park SLan ML3 7UE 119 K8
Chatham 24 D5
Chatham Green 34 B7
Chatham Historic Dockyard Med ME4 4TZ 24 D5
Chathill 71 G1
Chatsworth Farmyard & Adventure Playground Derbys DE45 1PP 50 E5
Chatsworth House Derbys DE45 1PP 50 E5
Chattenden 24 D4
Chatteris 43 G7
Chattisham 34 E4
Chatto 70 C2
Chatton 71 F1
Chaul End 32 D6
Chavey Down 22 B5
Chawleigh 7 F4
Chawley 21 H1
Chawston 32 E3
Chawton 11 J1
Chazey Heath 21 K4
Cheadle GtMan 49 H4
Cheadle Staffs 40 C1
Cheadle Heath 49 H4
Cheadle Hulme 49 H4
Cheam 23 F5
Cheapside 22 C5
Chearsley 31 J7
Chebsey 40 A3
Checkendon 21 K3
Checkley ChesE 39 G1
Checkley Here 28 E5
Checkley Staffs 40 C2
Checkley Green 39 G1
Chedburgh 34 B3
Cheddar 19 H6
Cheddar Caves & Gorge Som BS27 3QF 19 H6
Cheddington 32 C7
Cheddleton 49 J7
Cheddon Fitzpaine 8 B2
Chedglow 20 C2
Chedgrave 45 H6
Chedington 8 D4
Chediston 35 H1
Chediston Green 35 H1
Chedworth 30 B7
Chedzoy 8 C1
Cheesden 49 H1
Cheeseman's Green 15 F4
Cheetham Hill 49 H2
Cheglinch 6 D1
Cheldon 7 F4
Chelford 49 H5
Chellaston 41 F2
Chells 33 F6
Chelmarsh 39 G7
Chelmondiston 35 G5
Chelmorton 50 D6
Chelmsford 24 D1
Chelmsford Cathedral Essex CM1 1TY 24 D1
Chelmsley Wood 40 D7
Chelsea 23 F4
Chelsfield 23 H5
Chelsham 23 G6
Chelston Heath 7 K3
Chelsworth 34 D4
Cheltenham 29 J6
Chelveston 32 C2
Chelvey 19 H5
Chelwood 19 K5
Chelwood Common 13 H4
Chelwood Gate 13 H4
Chelworth 20 C2
Cheney Longville 38 D7
Chenies 22 D2
Chepstow (Cas-gwent) 19 J2
Cherhill 20 D4
Cherington Glos 20 C2
Cherington Warks 30 D5
Cheriton Devon 7 F1
Cheriton Hants 11 G2
Cheriton Kent 15 G4
Cheriton Pembs 16 C6
Cheriton Swan 17 H6
Cheriton Bishop 7 F6
Cheriton Cross 7 F6
Cheriton Fitzpaine 7 G5
Cherrington 39 F3
Cherry Burton 59 F5
Cherry Green 33 J6
Cherry Hinton 33 H3
Cherry Willingham 52 D5
Cherrymount 93 F10
Chertsey 22 D5
Cheselbourne 9 G5
Chesham 22 C1
Chesham Bois 22 C1
Cheshire Farm Ice Cream, Tattenhall ChesW&C CH3 9NE 48 D7
Cheshunt 23 G1
Cheslyn Hay 40 B5
Chessington 22 E5
Chessington World of Adventures GtLon KT9 2NE 22 E5
Chestall 40 C4
Chester 48 D6
Chester Cathedral ChesW&C CH1 2HU 124 Chester
Chester Moor 62 C2
Chester Zoo ChesW&C CH2 1LH 48 D5
Chesterblade 19 K7
Chesterfield Derbys 51 F5
Chesterfield Staffs 40 D5
Chester-le-Street 62 C1
Chesters ScBord 70 B1
Chesters ScBord 70 B2
Chesters Roman Fort (Frontiers of the Roman Empire) N'umb NE46 4EU 70 E7
Chesterton Cambs 33 H2
Chesterton Cambs 42 E6
Chesterton Oxon 31 G6
Chesterton Shrop 39 G6
Chesterton Staffs 40 A1
Chesterton Warks 30 E3
Chesterton Green 30 E3
Chestfield 25 H5
Cheston 5 G5
Cheswardine 39 G3
Cheswick 77 J6
Cheswick Buildings 77 J6
Cheswick Green 30 C1
Chetnole 9 F4
Chettiscombe 7 H4
Chettisham 43 J7
Chettle 9 J3
Chetton 39 F6
Chetwode 31 H6
Chetwynd Aston 39 G4
Chetwynd Park 39 G3
Cheveley 33 K2
Chevening 23 H6
Cheverell's Green 32 D7
Chevin Forest Park WYorks LS21 3JL 57 H5
Chevington 34 B3
Chevithorne 7 H4
Chew Magna 19 J5
Chew Moor 49 F2
Chew Stoke 19 J5
Chewton Keynsham 19 K5
Chewton Mendip 19 J6
Chichacott 6 E6
Chicheley 32 C4
Chichester 12 B6
Chichester Cathedral WSuss PO19 1PX 12 B6
Chickerell 9 F6
Chickering 35 G1
Chicklade 9 J1
Chickney 33 J6
Chicksands 32 E5
Chidden 11 H3
Chidden Holt 11 H3
Chiddingfold 12 C3
Chiddingly 13 J5
Chiddingstone 23 H7
Chiddingstone Causeway 23 J7
Chiddingstone Hoath 23 H7
Chideock 8 D5
Chidham 11 J4
Chidswell 57 H7
Chieveley 21 H4
Chignall Smealy 33 K7
Chignall St. James 24 C1
Chigwell 23 H2
Chigwell Row 23 H2
Chilbolton 21 G7
Chilcomb 11 G2
Chilcombe 8 E5
Chilcompton 19 K6
Chilcote 40 E4
Child Okeford 9 H3
Childer Thornton 48 C5
Childerditch 24 C3
Childrey 21 G3
Child's Ercall 39 F3
Childs Hill 23 F3
Childswickham 30 B5
Childwall 48 D4
Childwick Green 32 E7
Chilfrome 8 E5
Chilgrove 12 B5
Chilham 15 F2
Chilhampton 10 B1
Chilla 6 C5
Chillaton 6 C7
Chillenden 15 H2
Chillerton 11 F6
Chillesford 35 H3
Chilley 5 H5
Chillingham 71 F1
Chillington Devon 5 H6
Chillington Som 8 C3
Chilmark 9 J1
Chilson Oxon 30 E7
Chilson Som 8 C4
Chilsworthy Corn 4 E3
Chilsworthy Devon 6 B5
Chilthorne Domer 8 E3
Chilton Bucks 31 H7
Chilton Devon 7 G5
Chilton Dur 62 C4
Chilton Oxon 21 H3
Chilton Suff 34 C4
Chilton Candover 11 G1
Chilton Cantelo 8 E2
Chilton Foliat 21 G4
Chilton Polden 8 C1
Chilton Street 34 B4
Chilton Trinity 8 B1
Chilvers Coton 41 F6
Chilwell 41 H2
Chilworth Hants 11 F3
Chilworth Surr 22 D7
Chimney 21 G1
Chimney Street 34 B4
Chineham 21 K6
Chingford 23 G2
Chinley 50 C4
Chinley Head 50 C4
Chinnor 22 A1
Chipchase Castle 70 D6
Chipley 7 K3
Chipnall 39 G2
Chippenham Cambs 33 K2
Chippenham Wilts 20 C4
Chipperfield 22 D1
Chipping Herts 33 G5
Chipping Lancs 56 B5
Chipping Campden 30 C5
Chipping Hill 34 C7
Chipping Norton 30 E6
Chipping Ongar 23 J1
Chipping Sodbury 20 A3
Chipping Warden 31 F4
Chipstable 7 J3
Chipstead Kent 23 H6
Chipstead Surr 23 F6
Chirbury 38 B6
Chirk (Pontcysyllte Aqueduct & Canal) Denb/Powys/Wrex 38 B2
Chirk (Y Waun) 38 B2
Chirk Green 38 B2
Chirmorrie 64 C3
Chirnside 77 G5
Chirnsidebridge 77 G5
Chirton T&W 71 J7
Chirton Wilts 20 D6
Chisbury 21 F5
Chiscan 66 A2
Chiselborough 8 D3
Chiseldon 20 E4
Chiserley 57 F7
Chislehampton 21 J2
Chislehurst 23 H4
Chislet 25 J5
Chiswell Green 22 E1
Chiswick 23 F4
Chiswick End 33 G4
Chisworth 49 J3
Chithurst 12 B4
Chittering 33 H2
Chitterne 20 C7
Chittlehamholt 6 E3
Chittlehampton 6 E3
Chittoe 20 C5
Chivelstone 5 H7

145

Gors 27 F1
Gorsedd 47 K5
Gorseinon 17 J6
Gorseybank 50 E7
Gorsgoch 26 D3
Gorslas 17 J4
Gorsley 29 F6
Gorsley Common 29 F6
Gorstage 49 F5
Gorstan 83 P4
Gorsty Hill 40 D3
Gortaclare 91 M10
Gortahurk 92 D7
Gortavoy Bridge 93 C10
Gortenorn 78 H4
Gortfin 91 M10
Gortin 90 L8
Gortinreid 90 M5
Gortmullan 91 J14
Gortnacreagh 90 L9
Gortnagallon 92 G9
Gortnahey 92 B5
Gortnalee 91 F11
Gorton 49 H3
Gortreagh 92 C9
Gosbeck 35 F3
Gosberton 43 F2
Gosberton Clough 42 E3
Goseley Dale 41 F3
Gosfield 34 B6
Gosford Here 28 E2
Gosford Oxon 31 G7
Gosforth Cumb 60 B6
Gosforth T&W 71 H7
Gosland Green 48 E7
Gosmore 32 E6
Gospel End 40 A6
Gosport 11 H5
Gossabrough 89 P4
Gossington 20 A1
Gossops Green 13 F3
Goswick 77 J6
Gotham 41 H2
Gotherington 29 J6
Gothers 3 G3
Gott 89 N8
Gotton 8 B2
Goudhurst 14 C4
Goulceby 53 F5
Gourdon 81 P3
Gourock 74 A3
Govan 74 D4
Goveton 51 K7
Goveton 5 H6
Govilon 28 B7
Gowdall 58 C7
Gowdystown 93 G11
Gowerton 17 J6
Gowkhall 75 J2
Gowkthrapple 75 F5
Gowthorpe 58 D4
Goxhill ERid 59 H5
Goxhill NLincs 59 H7
Goytre 18 A3
Gozzard's Ford 21 H2
Grabhair 88 J6
Graby 42 D3
Gracefield 92 E8
Gracehill 92 F6
Gradbach 49 J6
Grade 2 E7
Gradeley Green 48 E7
Graffham 12 C5
Grafham Cambs 32 E2
Grafham Surr 22 D7
Grafham Water Cambs PE28 0BH 32 E2
Grafton Here 28 D5
Grafton NYorks 57 K3
Grafton Oxon 21 F1
Grafton Shrop 38 D4
Grafton Worcs 28 E2
Grafton Worcs 29 J5
Grafton Flyford 29 J3
Grafton Regis 31 J4
Grafton Underwood 42 C7
Grafty Green 14 D3
Graianrhyd 48 B7
Graig Carmar 17 H5
Graig Conwy 47 G5
Graig Denb 47 J5
Graig-fechan 47 K7
Grain 24 E4
Grainel 72 A4
Grains Bar 49 J2
Grainsby 53 F3
Grainthorpe 53 G3
Graizelound 51 K3
Grampound 3 G4
Grampound Road 3 G3
Granborough 31 J6
Granby 42 A2
Grand Pier, Teignmouth Devon TQ14 8BB 5 K3
Grandborough 31 F2
Grandes Rocques 3 J5
Grandtully 80 E5
Grange Cumb 60 D5
Grange EAyr 74 C7
Grange High 83 P7
Grange Med 24 D5
Grange Mersey 48 B4
Grange Mid Ulster 93 D9
Grange Blundel 93 D11
Grange Corner 92 F7
Grange de Lings 52 C5
Grange Hill 23 H2
Grange Moor 50 E1
Grange of Lindores 80 H9
Grange Villa 62 C1
Grangee 93 L9
Grangemill 50 E7
Grangemouth 75 H3
Grange-over-Sands 55 H2
Grangeston 67 G4
Grangetown Cardiff 18 E4
Grangetown R&C 63 F4
Gransha AB&C 93 H12
Gransha L&C 93 K10
Gransha M&EAnt 92 K7
Gransmoor 59 H4
Granston 16 B2
Grantchester 33 H3
Grantham 42 C2
Grantley 57 H2
Granton 76 A3
Granton House 69 F3
Grantown-on-Spey 84 E8
Grantsfield 28 E2
Grantshouse 77 G4
Granville 93 C10
Grappenhall 49 F4
Grasby 52 D2
Grasmere 60 E6
Grass Green 34 B5
Grasscroft 49 J2
Grassendale 48 C4
Grassgarth 60 F7
Grassholme 61 L4
Grassington 57 F3
Grassmoor 51 G6
Grassthorpe 51 K6
Grateley 21 F7
Gratwich 40 C2
Gravel Hill 22 D2
Graveley Cambs 33 F2
Graveley Herts 33 F6
Gravelly Hill 40 D6
Gravels 38 C5
Graven 89 N5
Graveney 25 G5
Gravesend 24 C4
Grayingham 52 C3
Grayrigg 61 G7
Grays 24 C4
Grayshott 12 B3
Grayswood 12 C3
Grazeley 21 K5
Greasbrough 51 G3
Greasby 48 B4
Great Aberystwyth Camera Obscura Cere SY23 2DN 36 E7
Great Abington 33 J4
Great Addington 32 C1
Great Alne 30 C3
Great Altcar 48 C2
Great Amwell 33 G7
Great Asby 61 H5
Great Ashfield 34 D2
Great Ayton 63 F5
Great Baddow 24 D1
Great Bardfield 33 K5
Great Barford 32 E3
Great Barr 40 C6
Great Barrington 30 D7
Great Barrow 48 D6
Great Barton 34 C2
Great Barugh 58 D2
Great Bavington 70 E5
Great Bealings 35 G4
Great Bedwyn 21 F5
Great Bentley 35 F6
Great Bernera 88 G4
Great Billing 32 B2
Great Bircham 44 B2
Great Blakenham 35 F3
Great Bolas 39 F3
Great Bookham 22 E6
Great Bourton 31 F4
Great Bowden 42 A7
Great Bradley 33 K3
Great Braxted 34 C7
Great Bricett 34 E3
Great Brickhill 32 C5
Great Bridgeford 40 A3
Great Brington 31 H2
Great Bromley 34 E6
Great Broughton Cumb 60 B3
Great Broughton NYorks 63 F6
Great Buckland 24 C5
Great Budworth 49 F5
Great Burdon 62 D5
Great Burstead 24 C2
Great Busby 63 F6
Great Cambourne 33 G3
Great Canfield 33 J7
Great Canney 24 E1
Great Carlton 53 H4
Great Casterton 42 D5
Great Chalfield 20 B5
Great Chart 14 E3
Great Chatwell 39 G4
Great Chell 49 H7
Great Chesterford 33 J4
Great Cheverell 20 C6
Great Chishill 33 H5
Great Clacton 35 F7
Great Clifton 60 B4
Great Coates 53 F2
Great Comberton 29 J4
Great Corby 61 F1
Great Cornard 34 C4
Great Cowden 59 J5
Great Coxwell 21 F2
Great Crakehall 57 H1
Great Cransley 32 B1
Great Cressingham 44 C5
Great Crosby 48 C2
Great Crosthwaite 60 D4
Great Cubley 40 D2
Great Cumbrae 73 K5
Great Dalby 42 A4
Great Doddington 32 B2
Great Doward 28 E7
Great Dunham 44 C4
Great Dunmow 33 K6
Great Durnford 10 C1
Great Easton Essex 33 K6
Great Easton Leics 42 B6
Great Eccleston 55 H5
Great Edstone 58 D1
Great Ellingham 44 E6
Great Elm 20 A7
Great Eversden 33 G3
Great Fencote 62 C7
Great Finborough 34 E3
Great Fransham 44 C4
Great Gaddesden 32 D7
Great Gidding 42 E7
Great Givendale 58 E4
Great Glemham 35 H2
Great Glen 41 J6
Great Gonerby 42 B2
Great Gransden 33 F3
Great Green Cambs 33 F4
Great Green Norf 45 G7
Great Green Suff 34 D3
Great Green Suff 34 E1
Great Green Suff 35 F1
Great Habton 58 D2
Great Hale 42 E1
Great Hall Hants SO23 8UJ 137 Winchester
Great Hallingbury 33 J7
Great Hampden 22 B1
Great Harrowden 32 B1
Great Harwood 56 C6
Great Haseley 21 K1
Great Hatfield 59 H5
Great Haywood 40 C3
Great Heath 41 F7
Great Heck 58 B7
Great Henny 34 C5
Great Hinton 20 C6
Great Hockham 44 D6
Great Holland 35 G7
Great Horkesley 34 D5
Great Hormead 33 H5
Great Horton 57 G6
Great Horwood 31 J5
Great Houghton N'hants 31 J3
Great Houghton SYorks 51 G2
Great Hucklow 50 D5
Great Kelk 59 H4
Great Kimble 22 B1
Great Kingshill 22 B2
Great Langton 62 C7
Great Leighs 34 B7
Great Limber 52 E2
Great Linford 32 B4
Great Livermere 34 C1
Great Longstone 50 E5
Great Lumley 62 C2
Great Lyth 38 D5
Great Malvern 29 G4
Great Maplestead 34 C5
Great Marton 55 G6
Great Massingham 44 B3
Great Melton 45 F5
Great Milton 21 K1
Great Missenden 22 B1
Great Mitton 56 C6
Great Mongeham 15 J2
Great Moulton 45 F6
Great Munden 33 G6
Great Musgrave 61 J5
Great Ness 38 D4
Great Notley 34 B6
Great Nurcot 7 H2
Great Oak 19 G1
Great Oakley Essex 35 F6
Great Oakley N'hants 42 B7
Great Offley 32 E6
Great Orme Tramway Conwy LL30 2HG 47 F4
Great Ormside 61 J5
Great Orton 60 E1
Great Ouseburn 57 K3
Great Oxendon 42 A7
Great Oxney Green 24 C1
Great Palgrave 44 C4
Great Parndon 23 H1
Great Paxton 33 F2
Great Plumpton 55 G6
Great Plumstead 45 H5
Great Ponton 42 C2
Great Potheridge 6 D4
Great Preston 57 J7
Great Purston 31 G5
Great Raveley 43 F7
Great Rissington 30 C7
Great Rollright 30 E5
Great Ryburgh 44 D3
Great Ryle 71 F2
Great Ryton 38 D5
Great Saling 34 B6
Great Salkeld 61 G3
Great Sampford 33 K5
Great Sankey 48 E4
Great Saredon 40 B5
Great Saxham 34 B2
Great Shefford 21 G4
Great Shelford 33 H3
Great Smeaton 62 D6
Great Snoring 44 D2
Great Somerford 20 C3
Great St. Mary's Church Cambs CB2 3PQ 123 Cambridge
Great Stainton 62 D4
Great Stambridge 25 F2
Great Staughton 32 E2
Great Steeping 53 H6
Great Stonar 15 J2
Great Strickland 61 G4
Great Stukeley 33 F1
Great Sturton 53 F5
Great Sutton ChesW&C 48 C5
Great Sutton Shrop 38 E7
Great Swinburne 70 E6
Great Tew 30 E6
Great Tey 34 C6
Great Thorness 11 F5
Great Thurlow 33 K4
Great Torr 5 G6
Great Torrington 6 C4
Great Tosson 71 F3
Great Totham Essex 34 C7
Great Totham Essex 34 C7
Great Tows 53 F3
Great Urswick 55 F2
Great Wakering 25 F3
Great Waldingfield 34 D4
Great Walsingham 44 D2
Great Waltham 33 K7
Great Warley 23 J2
Great Washbourne 29 J5
Great Weeke 7 F7
Great Welnetham 34 C3
Great Wenham 34 E5
Great Whittington 71 F6
Great Wigborough 34 D7
Great Wilbraham 33 J3
Great Wilne 41 G2
Great Wishford 10 B1
Great Witcombe 29 J7
Great Witley 29 G2
Great Wolford 30 D5
Great Wratting 33 K4
Great Wymondley 33 F6
Great Wyrley 40 B5
Great Wytheford 38 E4
Great Yarmouth 45 K5
Great Yeldham 34 B5
Greatford 42 D4
Greatgate 40 C1
Greatham Hants 11 J1
Greatham Hart 62 E4
Greatham WSuss 12 D5
Greatness 23 J6
Greatstone-on-Sea 15 F5
Greatworth 31 G4
Green 47 J6
Green Cross 12 B3
Green End Bed 32 E3
Green End Bucks 32 C5
Green End Cambs 33 F1
Green End Cambs 33 G1
Green End Herts 33 G5
Green End Herts 33 G6
Green End Warks 40 E7
Green Hammerton 57 K4
Green Hill 20 D3
Green Lane 30 B2
Green Moor 50 E3
Green Ore 19 J6
Green Quarter 61 F6
Green Street ESuss 14 C6
Green Street Herts 22 E2
Green Street Herts 33 H6
Green Street Worcs 29 H4
Green Street WSuss 12 E4
Green Street Green GtLon 23 H5
Green Street Green Kent 23 J4
Green Tye 33 H7
Greenan 93 G14
Greencastle F&O 90 M8
Greencastle NM&D 93 H15
Greencroft 62 B2
Greendykes 71 F1
Greenend 30 E6
Greenfaulds 75 F3
Greenfield CenBeds 32 D5
Greenfield (Maes-Glas) Flints 47 K5
Greenfield GtMan 50 C2
Greenfield High 83 N10
Greenfield Lincs 53 H5
Greenfield NM&D 93 J15
Greenfield Oxon 22 A2
Greenford 22 E3
Greengairs 75 F3
Greengates 57 G6
Greengill 60 C3
Greenhalgh 55 H6
Greenham 21 H5
Greenhaugh 70 C5
Greenhead 70 B7
Greenheys 49 G2
Greenhill D&G 69 G6
Greenhill GtLon 22 E3
Greenhill SYorks 51 F4
Greenhithe 23 J4
Greenholm 74 D7
Greenholme 61 G6
Greenhow Hill 57 G3
Greenigo 89 D7
Greenisland 92 J8
Greenlands 22 A3
Greenlaw 77 F6
Greenloaning 80 D10
Greenmeadow 19 F2
Greenmoor Hill 21 K3
Greenmount 49 G1
Greenock 74 A3
Greenodd 55 G1
Greens Norton 31 H4
Greenside T&W 71 G7
Greenside WYorks 50 D1
Greenstead 34 E6
Greenstead Green 34 C6
Greensted 23 J1
Greensted Green 23 J1
Greenville 90 K8
Greenway Pembs 16 D2
Greenway Som 8 C2
Greenwell 61 G1
Greenwich 23 G4
Greenwood Forest Park, Y Felinheli Gwyn LL56 4QN 46 D6
Greet 30 B5
Greete 28 E1
Greetham Lincs 53 G5
Greetham Rut 42 C4
Greetland 57 F7
Gregson Lane 55 J7
Greinton 8 D1
Grenaby 54 B6
Grendon N'hants 32 B2
Grendon Warks 40 E6
Grendon Common 40 E6
Grendon Green 28 E3
Grendon Underwood 31 H6
Grenitote (Greinetobht) 88 C1
Grenofen 4 E3
Grenoside 51 F3
Greosabhagh 88 G8
Gresford 48 C7
Gresham 45 F2
Greshornish 82 D5
Gress (Griais) 88 K3
Gressenhall 44 D4
Gressingham 55 J3
Greta Bridge 62 A5
Gretna 69 J7
Gretna Green 69 J7
Gretton Glos 30 B5
Gretton N'hants 42 C6
Gretton Shrop 38 E6
Grewelthorpe 57 H2
Greyabbey 93 L10
Greygarth 57 G2
Greylake 8 C1
Greys Green 22 A3
Greysouthen 60 B4
Greystead 70 C5
Greysteel 90 M4
Greystoke 60 F3
Greystone 56 D5
Greystones 51 F4
Greywell 22 A6
Gribthorpe 58 D6
Gribton 68 E5
Griff 41 F7
Griffithstown 19 F2
Grigghall 61 F7
Grimeford Village 49 F1
Grimesthorpe 51 F3
Grimethorpe 51 G2
Griminish (Griminis) 88 B3
Grimister 89 N3
Grimley 29 H2
Grimmet 67 H2
Grimoldby 53 G4
Grimpo 38 C3
Grimsargh 55 J6
Grimsay (Griomsaigh) 88 C3
Grimsbury 31 F4
Grimsby 53 F2
Grimscote 31 H3
Grimscott 6 A5
Grimshader (Griomsiadar) 88 K5
Grimsthorpe 42 D3
Grimston ERid 59 J6
Grimston Leics 41 J3
Grimston Norf 44 B3
Grimstone 9 F5
Grimstone End 34 D2
Grindale 59 H2
Grindiscol 89 N9
Grindle 39 G5
Grindleford 50 E5
Grindleton 56 C5
Grindley 40 C3
Grindley Brook 38 E1
Grindlow 50 D5
Grindon N'umb 77 H6
Grindon Staffs 50 C7
Grindon Stock 62 D4
Grindon T&W 62 D1
Gringley on the Hill 51 K3
Grinsdale 60 E1
Grinshill 38 E3
Grinton 62 A7
Grisdale 61 J7
Gristhorpe 59 G1
Griston 44 D6
Gritley 89 E7
Grittenham 20 D3
Grittleton 20 B4
Grizebeck 55 F1
Grizedale 60 E7
Grizedale Forest Park Cumb LA22 0QJ 60 E7
Grobister 89 F5
Groby 41 H5
Groes 47 J6
Groes-faen 18 D3
Groesffordd 36 B2
Groesffordd Marli 47 J5
Groeslon Gwyn 46 C7
Groeslon Gwyn 46 D6
Groes-lwyd 38 B4
Groes-wen 18 E3
Grogport 73 G6
Groigearraidh 88 B5
Gromford 35 H3
Gronant 47 J4
Groombridge 13 J3
Groombridge Place Gardens Kent TN3 9QG 13 J3
Groomsport 92 L8
Grosmont Mon 28 D6
Grosmont NYorks 63 J6
Groton 34 D4
Groundistone Heights 69 K2
Grouville 3 K7
Grove Bucks 32 C6
Grove Dorset 9 F7
Grove Kent 25 J5
Grove Notts 51 K5
Grove Oxon 21 H2
Grove End 24 E5
Grove Green 14 C2
Grove Park 23 H4
Grove Town 57 K7
Grovehill 22 D1
Grovesend SGlos 19 K3
Grovesend Swan 17 J5
Gruids 86 H9
Gruline 78 G6
Grumbla 2 B6
Grundisburgh 35 G3
Gruting 89 L8
Grutness 89 N11
Gualachulain 79 N6
Guardbridge 81 K9
Guarlford 29 H4
Gubbergill 60 B7
Gubblecote 32 C7
Guernsey 3 J5
Guernsey Airport 3 H6
Guestling Green 14 D6
Guestling Thorn 14 D6
Guestwick 44 E3
Guestwick Green 44 E3
Guide 56 C7
Guide Post 71 H5
Guilden Down 38 C7
Guilden Morden 33 F4
Guilden Sutton 48 D6
Guildford 22 C7
Guildford House Gallery Surr GU1 3AJ 128 Guildford
Guildtown 80 G7
Guilsborough 31 H1
Guilsfield (Cegidfa) 38 B4
Guilthwaite 51 G4
Guisborough 63 G5
Guiseley 57 G5
Guist 44 E3
Guith 89 E4
Guiting Power 30 B6
Gulberwick 89 N9
Gulladuff 92 D7
Gullane 76 C2
Gullane Bents ELoth EH31 2AZ 76 C2
Gulval 2 B5
Gulworthy 4 E3
Gumfreston 16 E5
Gumley 41 J6
Gunby Lincs 42 C3
Gunby Lincs 53 H6
Gundleton 11 H1
Gunn 6 E2
Gunnersbury 22 E4
Gunnerside 61 L7
Gunnerton 70 E6
Gunness 52 B1
Gunnislake 4 E3
Gunnister 89 M5
Gunstone 40 A5
Gunter's Bridge 12 C4
Gunthorpe Norf 44 E2
Gunthorpe Notts 41 J1
Gunthorpe Rut 42 B5
Gunville 11 F6
Gunwalloe 2 D6
Gupworthy 7 H2
Gurnard 11 F5
Gurnett 49 J5
Gurney Slade 19 K7
Gurnos MTyd 18 D1
Gurnos Powys 18 A1
Gushmere 15 F2
Gussage All Saints 10 B3
Gussage St. Andrew 9 J3
Gussage St. Michael 9 J3
Guston 15 J3
Gutcher 89 P3
Guthram Gowt 42 E3
Guthrie 81 L5
Guyhirn 43 G5
Guy's Head 43 H3
Guy's Marsh 9 H2
Guyzance 71 H3
Gwaelod-y-garth 18 E3
Gwaenysgor 47 J4
Gwaithla 28 B3
Gwalchmai 46 B5
Gwastad 16 D3
Gwastadnant 46 E7
Gwaun-Cae-Gurwen 27 G7
Gwaynynog 47 J6
Gwbert 16 E1
Gweek 2 E6
Gwehelog 19 G1
Gwenddwr 27 K4
Gwendreath 2 E7
Gwennap 2 E4
Gwennap Mining District (Cornwall & West Devon Mining Landscape) Corn 2 E4
Gwenter 2 E7
Gwernaffield 48 B6
Gwernesney 19 H1
Gwernogle 17 J2
Gwernymynydd 48 B6
Gwern-y-Steeple 18 D4
Gwersyllt 48 C7
Gwespyr 47 K4
Gwinear 2 C5
Gwithian 2 C4
Gwredog 46 C4
Gwrhay 18 E2
Gwyddelwern 37 K1
Gwyddgrug 17 H2
Gwynfryn 48 B7
Gwystre 27 K2
Gwytherin 47 G6
Gyfelia 38 C1
Gyre 89 C7
Gyrn Goch 36 D1

H

Habberley 38 C5
Habin 12 B4
Habost (Tabost) 88 L1
Habrough 52 E1
Haccombe 5 J3
Hacconby 42 E3
Haceby 42 D2
Hacheston 35 H3
Hackbridge 23 F5
Hackenthorpe 51 G4
Hackford 44 E5
Hackforth 62 C7
Hackleton 32 B3
Hacklinge 15 J2
Hackness 63 K7
Hackney 23 G3
Hackthorn 52 C4
Hackthorpe 61 G4
Hacton 23 J3
Hadden 77 F7
Haddenham Bucks 22 A1
Haddenham Cambs 33 H1
Haddington ELoth 76 D3
Haddington Lincs 52 C6
Haddiscoe 45 J6
Haddo Country Park Aber AB41 7EQ 85 N7
Haddon 42 E6
Hade Edge 50 D2
Hademore 40 D5
Hadfield 50 C3
Hadham Cross 33 H7
Hadham Ford 33 H6
Hadleigh Essex 24 E3
Hadleigh Suff 34 E4
Hadleigh Castle Country Park Essex SS7 2PP 24 E3
Hadleigh Farm Essex SS7 2AP 24 E3
Hadleigh Heath 34 D4
Hadley Tel&W 39 F4
Hadley Worcs 29 H2
Hadley End 40 D3
Hadley Wood 23 F2
Hadlow 23 K7
Hadlow Down 13 J4
Hadnall 38 E3
Hadrian's Wall (Frontiers of the Roman Empire) Cumb/N'umb 69 K7 & 71 F7
Hadspen 9 F1
Hadstock 33 J4
Hadston 71 H4
Hadzor 29 J2
Haffenden Quarter 14 D3
Hafod Bridge 17 K2
Hafod-Dinbych 47 G7
Hafodunos 47 G6
Hafodyrynys 19 F2
Haggate 56 D6
Haggbeck 69 K6
Haggersta 89 M8
Haggerston GtLon 23 G3
Haggerston N'umb 77 J6
Haggrister 89 M5
Haggs 75 F3
Hagley Here 28 E4
Hagley Worcs 40 B7
Hagnaby Lincs 53 G6
Hagnaby Lincs 53 H5
Hague Bar 49 J4
Hagworthingham 53 G6
Haigh 49 F2
Haigh Hall Country Park GtMan WN2 1PE 48 E2
Haighton Green 55 J6
Hail Weston 32 E2
Haile 60 B6
Hailes 30 B5
Hailey Herts 33 G7
Hailey Oxon 21 J3
Hailey Oxon 30 E7
Hailsham 13 J6
Hainault 23 H2
Hainault Forest Country Park Essex IG7 4QN 104 G2
Haine 25 K5
Hainford 45 G4
Hainton 52 E4
Haisthorpe 59 H3
Hakin 16 B5
Halam 51 J7
Halbeath 75 K2
Halberton 7 J4
Halcro 87 Q3
Hale Cumb 55 J2
Hale GtMan 49 G4
Hale Halton 48 D4
Hale Hants 10 C3
Hale Surr 22 B7
Hale Bank 48 D4
Hale Barns 49 G4
Hale Nook 55 G5
Hale Street 23 K7
Hales Norf 45 H6
Hales Staffs 39 G2
Hales Green 40 D1
Hales Place 15 G2
Halesgate 43 G3
Halesowen 40 B7
Halesworth 35 H1
Halewood 48 D4
Half Way Inn 7 J6
Halford Devon 5 J3
Halford Shrop 38 D7
Halford Warks 30 D4
Halfpenny 55 J1
Halfpenny Green 40 A6
Halfway Carmar 17 J5
Halfway Carmar 17 K2
Halfway Powys 27 H5
Halfway SYorks 51 G4
Halfway WBerks 21 H5
Halfway Bridge 12 C4
Halfway House 38 C4
Halfway Houses Kent 25 F4
Halfway Houses Lincs 52 B6
Halghton Mill 38 D1
Halifax 57 F7
Halistra 82 C5
Halket 74 C5
Halkirk 87 P4
Halkyn 48 B5
Hall 74 C5
Hall Cross 55 H7
Hall Dunnerdale 60 D7
Hall Green ChesE 49 H7
Hall Green Lancs 55 H7
Hall Green WMid 40 D7
Hall Grove 33 F7
Hall of the Forest 38 B7
Halland 13 J5
Hallaton 42 A6
Hallatrow 19 K6
Hallbankgate 61 G1
Hallen 19 J3
Hallfield Gate 51 F7
Hallglen 75 G3
Hallin 82 C5
Halling 24 D5
Hallington Lincs 53 G4
Hallington N'umb 70 E6
Halliwell 49 F1
Halloughton 51 J7
Hallow 29 H3
Hallow Heath 29 H3
Hallrule 70 A2
Halls 76 E3
Halls Green Essex 23 H1
Hall's Green Herts 33 F6
Hallsands 5 J7
Hallthwaites 54 E1
Hallwood Green 29 F5
Hallworthy 4 B2
Hallyne 75 K6
Halmer End 39 G1
Halmond's Frome 29 F4
Halmore 19 K1
Halmyre Mains 75 K6
Halnaker 12 C6
Halsall 48 C1
Halse N'hants 31 G4
Halse Som 7 K3
Halsetown 2 C5
Halsham 59 J7
Halsinger 6 D2
Halstead Essex 34 C5
Halstead Kent 23 H5
Halstead Leics 42 A5
Halstock 8 E4
Halsway 7 K2
Haltemprice Farm 59 G6
Haltham 53 F6
Haltoft End 43 G1
Halton Bucks 32 B7
Halton Halton 48 E4
Halton Lancs 55 J3
Halton N'umb 70 E7
Halton Wrex 38 C2
Halton East 57 F4
Halton Gill 56 D2
Halton Green 55 J3
Halton Holegate 53 H6
Halton Lea Gate 61 H1
Halton Park 55 J3
Halton West 56 D4
Haltwhistle 70 C7
Halvergate 45 J5
Halwell 5 H5
Halwill 6 C6
Halwill Junction 6 C6
Ham Devon 8 B4
Ham Glos 19 K2
Ham Glos 29 J6
Ham GtLon 22 E4
Ham High 87 Q2
Ham Kent 15 J2
Ham Plym 4 E5
Ham Shet 89 H9
Ham Som 8 B2
Ham Som 8 B3
Ham Wilts 21 G5
Ham Common 9 H2
Ham Green Here 29 G4
Ham Green Kent 14 D5
Ham Green Kent 24 E5
Ham Green NSom 19 J4
Ham Green Worcs 30 B2
Ham Hill 24 C5
Ham Hill Country Park Som TA14 6RW 8 D3
Ham Street 8 E1
Hambleden 22 A3
Hambledon Hants 11 H3
Hambledon Surr 12 C3
Hamble-le-Rice 11 F4
Hambleton Lancs 55 G5
Hambleton NYorks 58 B6
Hambridge 8 C2
Hambrook SGlos 19 K4
Hambrook WSuss 11 J4
Hameringham 53 G6
Hamerton 32 E1
Hamilton 75 F5
Hamilton's Bawn 93 E12
Hamlet Devon 7 K6
Hamlet Dorset 8 E4
Hammer 12 B3
Hammerpot 12 D6
Hammersmith 23 F4
Hammersmith Apollo GtLon W6 9QH 103 F8
Hammerwich 40 C5
Hammerwood 13 H3
Hammond Street 23 G1
Hammoon 9 H3
Hamnavoe Shet 89 M9
Hamnavoe Shet 89 N4
Hamnavoe Shet 89 N5
Hamnish Clifford 28 E3
Hamp 8 B1
Hampden Park 13 K6
Hampden Park Stadium Glas G42 9BA 118 E6
Hamperden End 33 J5
Hampnett 30 C7
Hampole 51 H2
Hampreston 10 B5
Hampstead 23 F3
Hampstead Norreys 21 J4
Hampsthwaite 57 H4
Hampton Devon 8 B5
Hampton GtLon 22 E5
Hampton Kent 25 H5
Hampton Peter 42 E6
Hampton Shrop 39 G7
Hampton Swin 20 E2
Hampton Worcs 30 B4
Hampton Bishop 28 E5
Hampton Court Palace & Garden GtLon KT8 9AU 103 D11
Hampton Fields 20 B2
Hampton Heath 38 D1
Hampton in Arden 40 E7
Hampton Loade 39 G7
Hampton Lovett 29 H2
Hampton Lucy 30 D3
Hampton on the Hill 30 D2
Hampton Poyle 31 G7
Hampton Wick 22 E5
Hamptworth 10 D3
Hamsey 13 H5
Hamstall Ridware 40 D4
Hamstead 10 E5
Hamstead Marshall 21 H5
Hamsteels 62 B2
Hamsterley Dur 62 B1
Hamsterley Dur 62 B3
Hamsterley Forest Dur DL13 3NL 62 A4
Hamstreet 15 F4
Hamworthy 9 J5
Hanbury Staffs 40 D3
Hanbury Worcs 29 J2
Hanbury Woodend 40 D3
Hanby 42 D2
Hanchurch 40 A1
Handa Island 86 D5
Handale 63 H5
Handbridge 48 D6
Handcross 13 F3
Handforth 49 H4
Handley ChesW&C 48 D7
Handley Derbys 51 F6
Handley Green 24 C1
Handsacre 40 C4
Handside 33 F7
Handsworth SYorks 51 G4
Handsworth WMid 40 C6
Handwoodbank 38 D4
Handy Cross 22 B2
Hanford Dorset 9 H3
Hanford Stoke 40 A1
Hanging Bridge 40 D1
Hanging Houghton 31 J1
Hanging Langford 10 B1
Hangingshaw 69 G5
Hanham 19 K4
Hankelow 39 F1
Hankerton 20 C2
Hankham 13 K6
Hanley 40 A1
Hanley Castle 29 H4
Hanley Child 29 F2
Hanley Swan 29 H4
Hanley William 29 F2
Hanlith 56 E3
Hanmer 38 D2
Hannah 53 H5
Hannahstown 93 H9
Hannington Hants 21 J6
Hannington N'hants 32 B1
Hannington Swin 20 E2
Hannington Wick 20 E2
Hanslope 32 B4
Hanthorpe 42 D3
Hanwell GtLon 22 E3
Hanwell Oxon 31 F4
Hanwood 38 D5
Hanworth GtLon 22 E4
Hanworth Norf 45 F2
Happisburgh 45 H2
Happisburgh Common 45 H3
Hapsford 48 D5
Hapton Lancs 56 C6
Hapton Norf 45 F6
Harberton 5 H5
Harbertonford 5 H5
Harbledown 15 G2
Harborne 40 C7
Harborough Magna 31 F1
Harbottle 70 E3
Harbour Park Amusements, Littlehampton WSuss BN17 5LL 12 D6
Harbourneford 5 H4
Harbridge 10 C3
Harbridge Green 10 C3
Harburn 75 J4
Harbury 30 E3
Harby Leics 42 A2
Harby Notts 52 B5
Harcombe 7 K6
Harcombe Bottom 8 C5
Harden WMid 40 C5
Harden WYorks 57 F6
Hardendale 61 G5
Hardenhuish 20 C4
Hardgate Aber 85 M10
Hardgate NYorks 57 H3
Hardham 12 D5
Hardhorn 55 G6
Hardingham 44 E5
Hardingstone 31 J3
Hardington 20 A6
Hardington Mandeville 8 E3
Hardington Marsh 8 E4
Hardington Moor 8 E3
Hardley 11 F4
Hardley Street 45 H5
Hardmead 32 C4
Hardraw 61 K7
Hardstoft 51 G6
Hardway Hants 11 H4
Hardway Som 9 G1
Hardwick Bucks 32 B7
Hardwick Cambs 33 G3
Hardwick Lincs 52 B5
Hardwick Norf 45 G6
Hardwick N'hants 32 B2
Hardwick Oxon 21 G1
Hardwick Oxon 31 G6
Hardwick SYorks 51 G4
Hardwick WMid 40 C6
Hardwick Hall Derbys S44 5QJ 51 G6
Hardwick Hall Country Park, Sedgefield Dur TS21 2EH 62 D4
Hardwick Village 51 J5
Hardwicke Glos 29 G7
Hardwicke Glos 29 J6
Hardwicke Here 28 B4
Hardy's Green 34 D6
Hare Green 34 E6
Hare Hatch 22 B4
Hare Street Herts 33 G6
Hare Street Herts 33 G6
Hareby 53 G6
Harecroft 57 F6
Hareden 56 B4
Harefield 22 D2
Harehill 40 D2
Harehills 57 J6
Harehope 71 F1
Harelaw 75 H6
Hareplain 14 D4
Harescough 61 H2
Harescombe 29 H7
Haresfield 29 H7
Hareshaw NLan 75 G4
Hareshaw SLan 74 E6
Harestock 11 F1
Harewood 57 J5
Harewood End 28 E6
Harewood House WYorks LS17 9LG 57 J5
Harford Devon 5 G5
Harford Devon 7 G6
Hargate 45 F6
Hargatewall 50 D5
Hargrave ChesW&C 48 D6
Hargrave N'hants 32 D1
Hargrave Suff 34 B3
Hargrave Green 34 B3
Harker 69 J7
Harkstead 35 F5
Harlaston 40 E4
Harlaxton 42 B2
Harle Syke 56 D6
Harlech 36 E2
Harlech Castle (Castles & Town Walls of King Edward in Gwynedd) Gwyn LL46 2YH 36 E2
Harlequin 41 J2
Harlescott 38 E4
Harlesden 23 F3
Harleston Devon 5 H6
Harleston Norf 45 G7
Harleston Suff 34 E2
Harlestone 31 J2
Harley Shrop 38 E5
Harley SYorks 51 F3
Harleyholm 75 H7
Harlington CenBeds 32 D5
Harlington GtLon 22 D4
Harlosh 82 C6
Harlow 23 H1
Harlow Hill 71 F7
Harlthorpe 58 D6
Harlton 33 G3
Harlyn 3 F1
Harman's Cross 9 J6
Harmby 57 G1
Harmer Green 33 F7
Harmer Hill 38 D3
Harmondsworth 22 D4
Harmston 52 C6
Harnage 38 E5
Harnham 10 C2
Harnhill 20 D1
Harold Hill 23 J2
Harold Park 23 J2
Harold Wood 23 J2
Haroldston West 16 B4
Haroldswick 89 Q1
Harome 58 C1
Harpenden 32 E7
Harpford 7 J6
Harpham 59 G3
Harpley Norf 44 B3
Harpley Worcs 29 F2
Harpole 31 H2
Harprigg 56 B1
Harpsden 22 A3
Harpswell 52 C4
Harpur Hill 50 C5
Harpurhey 49 H2
Harracott 6 D3
Harrietfield 80 E8
Harrietsham 14 D2
Harringay 23 G3
Harrington Cumb 60 A4
Harrington Lincs 53 G5
Harrington N'hants 31 J1
Harringworth 42 C6
Harris 82 D11
Harris Green 45 G6
Harris Museum & Art Gallery, Preston Lancs PR1 2PP 55 J7
Harriseahead 49 H7
Harriston 60 C2
Harrogate 57 J4
Harrogate International Centre NYorks HG1 5LA 128 Harrogate
Harrold 32 C3
Harrold-Odell Country Park Bed MK43 7DS 32 C3
Harrop Fold 56 C5
Harrow 22 E3
Harrow Green 34 C3
Harrow Museum GtLon HA2 6PX 102 C4
Harrow on the Hill 22 E3
Harrow Weald 22 E2
Harrowbarrow 4 E3
Harrowden 32 D4
Harrowgate Hill 62 C5
Harry Stoke 19 K4
Harston Cambs 33 H3
Harston Leics 42 B2
Harswell 58 E5
Hart 62 E3
Hartburn 71 F5
Hartest 34 C3
Hartfield 13 H3
Hartford Cambs 33 F1
Hartford ChesW&C 49 F5
Hartford Som 7 H3
Hartford End 33 K7
Hartfordbridge 22 A6
Hartforth 62 B6
Hartgrove 9 H3
Harthill ChesW&C 48 E7
Harthill NLan 75 H4
Harthill SYorks 51 G4
Hartington 50 D6
Hartington Hall 71 F5
Hartland 6 A3
Hartland Quay 6 A3
Hartlebury 29 H1
Hartlepool 63 F3
Hartlepool's Maritime Experience Hart TS24 0XZ 63 F3
Hartley Cumb 61 J6
Hartley Kent 14 C4
Hartley Kent 24 C5
Hartley N'umb 71 J6
Hartley Green 40 B3
Hartley Mauditt 11 J1
Hartley Wespall 21 K6
Hartley Wintney 22 A6
Hartlington 57 F3
Hartlip 24 E5
Hartoft End 63 H7
Harton NYorks 58 D3
Harton Shrop 38 D7
Harton T&W 71 J7
Hartpury 29 H6
Hartrigge 70 B1
Hartshead 57 G7
Hartshill 41 F6
Hartsholme Country Park Lincs LN6 0EY 52 C6
Hartshorne 41 F3
Hartsop 60 F5
Hartwell Bucks 31 J7
Hartwell ESuss 13 H3
Hartwell N'hants 31 J3
Hartwith 57 H3
Hartwood 75 G5
Harvel 24 C5
Harvington Worcs 29 H1
Harvington Worcs 30 B4
Harwell Notts 51 J3
Harwell Oxon 21 H3
Harwich 35 G5
Harwood Dur 61 K3
Harwood GtMan 49 G1
Harwood N'umb 71 F4
Harwood Dale 63 K7
Harwood on Teviot 69 K3
Harworth 51 J3
Hasbury 40 B7
Hascombe 22 D7
Haselbech 31 J1
Haselbury Plucknett 8 D3
Haseley 30 D2
Haseley Knob 30 D1
Haselor 30 C3
Hasfield 29 H6
Hasguard 16 B5
Haskayne 48 C2
Hasketon 35 G3
Hasland 51 F6
Hasland Green 51 F6
Haslemere 12 C3
Haslingden 56 C7
Haslingden Grane 56 C7
Haslingfield 33 H3
Haslington 49 G7
Hassall 49 G7
Hassall Green 49 G7
Hassell Street 15 F3
Hassendean 70 A1
Hassingham 45 H5
Hassocks 13 G5
Hassop 50 E5
Hasthorpe 53 H6
Hastigrow 87 Q3
Hastingleigh 15 F3
Hastings ESuss 14 D7
Hastings Som 8 C3
Hastings Fishermen's Museum ESuss TN34 3DW 128 Hastings
Hastingwood 23 H1
Hastoe 22 C1
Haswell 62 D2
Haswell Plough 62 D2
Hatch CenBeds 32 E4
Hatch Hants 21 K6
Hatch Beauchamp 8 C2
Hatch End 22 E2
Hatch Green 8 C3
Hatching Green 32 E7
Hatchmere 48 E5
Hatcliffe 53 F2
Hatfield Here 28 E3
Hatfield Herts 23 F1
Hatfield SYorks 51 J2
Hatfield Broad Oak 33 J7
Hatfield Heath 33 J7
Hatfield House Herts AL9 5NF 23 F1
Hatfield Peverel 34 B7
Hatfield Woodhouse 51 J2
Hatford 21 G2
Hatherden 21 G6
Hatherleigh 6 D5
Hathern 41 G3
Hatherop 20 E1
Hathersage 50 E4
Hathersage Booths 50 E4
Hathershaw 49 J2
Hatherton ChesE 39 F1
Hatherton Staffs 40 B4
Hatley St. George 33 F3
Hatt 4 D4
Hattingley 11 H1
Hatton Aber 85 Q7
Hatton Derbys 40 E3
Hatton GtLon 22 E4
Hatton Lincs 52 E5
Hatton Shrop 38 D6
Hatton Warks 30 D2
Hatton Warr 48 E4
Hatton Country World Warks CV35 8XA 30 D2
Hatton Heath 48 D6
Hatton of Fintray 85 N9
Haugh 53 H5
Haugh Head 71 F1
Haugh of Glass 85 J7
Haugh of Urr 65 J4
Haugham 53 G4
Haughhead 74 E3
Haughley 34 E2
Haughley Green 34 E2
Haughley New Street 34 E2
Haughton ChesE 48 E7
Haughton Notts 51 J5
Haughton Powys 38 C4
Haughton Shrop 38 C3
Haughton Shrop 38 E4
Haughton Shrop 39 F6
Haughton Staffs 40 A3
Haughton Green 49 J3
Haughton Le Skerne 62 D5
Haultwick 33 G6
Haunton 40 E4
Hauxton 33 H3
Havannah 49 H6
Havant 11 J4
Haven 28 D3
Havenstreet 11 G5
Havercroft 51 F1
Haverfordwest (Hwlffordd) 16 C4
Haverhill 33 K4
Haverigg 54 E2
Havering Park 23 H2
Havering-atte-Bower 23 J2
Haversham 32 B4
Haverthwaite 55 G1
Haverton Hill 62 E4
Haviker Street 14 C3
Havyat 8 E1
Hawarden (Penarlâg) 48 C6
Hawbridge 29 J4
Hawbush Green 34 B6
Hawcoat 55 F2
Hawes 56 D1
Hawe's Green 45 G6
Hawick 70 A2
Hawkchurch 8 C4
Hawkedon 34 B3
Hawkenbury Kent 13 J3
Hawkenbury Kent 14 D3
Hawkeridge 20 B6
Hawkerland 7 J7
Hawkes End 40 E7
Hawkesbury 20 A3
Hawkesbury Upton 20 A3
Hawkhill 71 H2
Hawkhurst 14 C4
Hawkinge 15 H3
Hawkley 11 J2
Hawkridge 7 G2
Hawkshead 60 E7
Hawkshead Hill 60 E7
Hawksheads 55 H3
Hawksland 75 G6
Hawkswick 56 E2
Hawksworth Notts 42 A1
Hawksworth WYorks 57 G5
Hawksworth WYorks 57 H6
Hawkwell Essex 24 E2
Hawkwell N'umb 71 F6
Hawley Hants 22 B6
Hawley Kent 23 J4
Hawley's Corner 23 H6
Hawling 30 B6
Hawnby 58 B1
Haworth 57 F6
Hawstead 34 C3
Hawstead Green 34 C3
Hawthorn Dur 62 E2
Hawthorn Hants 11 H1
Hawthorn RCT 18 D3
Hawthorn Wilts 20 B5
Hawthorn Hill BrackF 22 B4
Hawthorn Hill Lincs 53 F7
Hawthorpe 42 D3
Hawton 51 K7
Haxby 58 C4
Haxey 51 K2
Haxted 23 H7
Haxton 20 E7
Hay Green 43 J4
Hay Mills 40 D7
Hay Street 33 G6
Haydock 48 E3
Haydon Dorset 9 F3
Haydon Swin 20 E3
Haydon Bridge 70 D7
Haydon Wick 20 E3
Hayes GtLon 22 D3
Hayes GtLon 23 H5
Hayes End 22 D3
Hayfield Derbys 50 C4
Hayfield Fife 76 A1
Haygrove 8 B1
Hayhillock 81 L6
Hayle 2 C5
Hayling Island 11 J4
Haymoor Green 49 F7
Hayne 7 G6
Haynes 32 E4
Haynes Church End 32 D4
Haynes West End 32 D4
Hay-on-Wye (Y Gelli Gandryll) 28 B4
Hayscastle 16 B3
Hayscastle Cross 16 C3
Hayton Cumb 60 C2
Hayton Cumb 61 G1
Hayton ERid 58 E5
Hayton Notts 51 K4
Hayton's Bent 38 E7
Haytor Vale 5 H3
Haytown 6 B4
Hayward Gallery GtLon SE1 8XZ 132 F4
Haywards Heath 13 G4
Haywood Oaks 51 J7
Hazel End 33 H6
Hazel Grove 49 J4
Hazel Street 13 K3
Hazelbank 75 G6
Hazelbury Bryan 9 G4
Hazeleigh 24 E1
Hazeley 22 A6
Hazelhurst 49 G1
Hazelside 68 D1
Hazelslack 55 H2
Hazelslade 40 C4
Hazelwood Derbys 41 F1
Hazelwood GtLon 23 H5
Hazlefield 65 H6
Hazlehead Aberdeen 85 N10
Hazlehead SYorks 50 D2
Hazlemere 22 B2
Hazlerigg 71 H6
Hazleton 30 B7
Hazon 71 G3
Heacham 44 A2
Head Bridge 6 E4
Headbourne Worthy 11 F1
Headcorn 14 D3

Headingley **57** H6
Headington **21** J1
Headlam **62** B5
Headless Cross **30** B2
Headley *Hants* **12** B3
Headley *Hants* **21** J5
Headley *Surr* **23** F6
Headley Down **12** B3
Headley Heath **30** B1
Headon **51** K5
Heads Nook **61** F1
Heady Hill **49** H1
Heage **51** F7
Healaugh *NYorks* **58** B5
Healaugh *NYorks* **62** A7
Heald Green **49** H4
Heale *Devon* **6** E1
Heale *Som* **8** C2
Healey *Lancs* **49** H1
Healey *NYorks* **57** G1
Healey *N'umb* **62** A1
Healey *WYorks* **57** H7
Healeyfield **62** A2
Healey's Cornish Cyder Farm *Corn* TR4 9LW **2** E3
Healing **53** F1
Heamoor **2** B5
Heaning **60** F7
Heanor **41** G1
Heanton Punchardon **6** D2
Heanton Satchville **6** D4
Heap Bridge **49** H1
Heapey **56** B7
Heapham **52** B4
Hearn **12** B3
Heart of Neolithic Orkney *Ork* **89** C6
Heart of the Country Centre *Staffs* WS14 9QR **40** D5
Hearthstane **69** G1
Heasley Mill **7** F2
Heast **82** G9
Heath *Cardiff* **18** E3
Heath *Derbys* **51** G6
Heath *WYorks* **51** F1
Heath & Reach **32** C6
Heath End *Derbys* **41** F3
Heath End *Hants* **21** H5
Heath End *Hants* **21** J5
Heath End *Surr* **22** B7
Heath Hayes **40** C4
Heath Hill **39** G4
Heath House **19** H7
Heath Town **40** B6
Heathbrook **39** F3
Heathcote *Derbys* **50** D6
Heathcote *Shrop* **39** F3
Heathencote **31** J4
Heather **41** F4
Heatherton Activity Park *Pembs* SA70 8RJ **16** D5
Heathfield *Devon* **5** J3
Heathfield *ESuss* **13** J4
Heathfield *NYorks* **57** G3
Heathfield *Som* **7** K3
Heathrow Airport **22** D4
Heathton **40** A6
Heatley **49** G4
Heaton *Lancs* **55** H3
Heaton *Staffs* **49** J6
Heaton *T&W* **71** H7
Heaton *WYorks* **57** G6
Heaton Moor **49** H3
Heaton Park *GtMan* M25 2SW **115** G2
Heaton's Bridge **48** D1
Heaverham **23** J6
Heaviley **49** J4
Heavitree **7** H6
Hebburn **71** J7
Hebden **57** F3
Hebden Bridge **56** E7
Hebden Green **49** F6
Hebing End **33** G6
Hebron *Carmar* **16** E3
Hebron *N'umb* **71** G5
Heck **69** F5
Heckfield **22** A5
Heckfield Green **35** F1
Heckfordbridge **34** D6
Heckingham **45** H6
Heckington **42** E1
Heckmondwike **57** H7
Heddington **20** C5
Heddon-on-the-Wall **71** G7
Hedenham **45** H6
Hedge End **11** F3
Hedgerley **22** C3
Hedging **8** C2
Hedley on the Hill **62** A1
Hednesford **40** C4
Hedon **59** H7
Hedsor **22** C3
Heeley **51** F4
Heighington *Darl* **62** C4
Heighington *Lincs* **52** D6
Heightington **29** G1
Heights of Brae **83** R4
Heilam **86** G4
Heisker Islands (Monach Islands) **88** A2
Heithat **69** G5
Heiton **77** F7
Hele *Devon* **5** H3
Hele *Devon* **6** B6
Hele *Devon* **6** D1
Hele *Devon* **7** H5
Hele *Som* **7** K3
Hele *Torbay* **5** K4
Hele Bridge **6** D5
Hele Lane **7** F4
Helebridge **6** A5
Helen's Bay **92** K8
Helensburgh **74** A2
Helford **2** E6
Helhoughton **44** C3
Helions Bumpstead **33** K4
Hell Corner **21** G5
Hellaby **51** H3
Helland *Corn* **4** A3
Helland *Som* **8** C2
Hellandbridge **4** A3
Hellesdon **45** G4
Hellidon **31** G3
Hellifield **56** D4
Hellingly **13** J5
Hellington **45** H5
Helmdon **31** G4
Helmingham **35** F3
Helmington Row **62** B3
Helmsdale **87** N8
Helmshore **56** C7
Helmsley **58** C1
Helperby **57** K3
Helperthorpe **59** F2
Helpringham **42** E1
Helpston **42** E5
Helsby **48** D5
Helsey **53** J5
Helston **2** D6
Helstone **4** A2
Helton **61** G4
Helwith **62** A6
Helwith Bridge **56** D3
Hem **38** B5
Hemborough Post **5** J5
Hemel Hempstead **22** D1
Hemerdon **5** F5
Hemingbrough **58** C6
Hemingby **53** F5
Hemingfield **51** F2
Hemingford Abbots **33** F1
Hemingford Grey **33** F1
Hemingstone **35** F3
Hemington *Leics* **41** G3
Hemington *N'hants* **42** D7
Hemington *Som* **20** A6
Hemley **35** G4
Hemlington **62** E5
Hemp Green **35** H2
Hempholme **59** G4
Hempnall **45** G6
Hempnall Green **45** G6
Hempstead *Essex* **33** K5
Hempstead *Med* **24** D5
Hempstead *Norf* **45** F2
Hempstead *Norf* **45** J3
Hempsted **29** H7
Hempton *Norf* **44** D3
Hempton *Oxon* **31** F5
Hemsby **45** J4
Hemswell **52** C3
Hemswell Cliff **52** C4
Hemsworth **51** G1
Hemyock **7** K4
Henbury *Bristol* **19** J4
Henbury *ChesE* **49** H5
Henderland **65** J3
Hendersyde Park **77** F7
Hendham **5** H5
Hendon *GtLon* **23** F3
Hendon *T&W* **62** D1
Hendraburnick **4** B2
Hendre *Bridgend* **18** C3
Hendre *Gwyn* **36** C2
Hendreforgan **18** C3
Hendy **17** J5
Heneglwys **46** C5
Henfield *SGlos* **19** K4
Henfield *WSuss* **13** F5
Henford **6** B6
Henghurst **14** E4
Hengoed *Caerp* **18** E2
Hengoed *Powys* **28** B3
Hengoed *Shrop* **38** B2
Hengrave **34** C2
Henham **33** J6
Heniarth **38** A5
Henlade **8** B2
Henley *Dorset* **9** F4
Henley *Shrop* **28** E1
Henley *Som* **8** D1
Henley *Som* **8** D4
Henley *Suff* **35** F3
Henley *WSuss* **12** B4
Henley Corner **8** D1
Henley Park **22** C6
Henley-in-Arden **30** C2
Henley-on-Thames **22** A3
Henley's Down **14** C6
Henllan *Carmar* **17** G1
Henllan *Denb* **47** J6
Henllan Amgoed **16** E3
Henllys **19** F2
Henlow **32** E5
Hennock **7** G7
Henny Street **34** C5
Henryd **47** F5
Henry's Moat **16** D3
Hensall **58** B7
Henshaw **70** C7
Hensingham **60** A5
Henstead **45** J7
Hensting **11** F2
Henstridge **9** G3
Henstridge Ash **9** G3
Henstridge Bowden **9** F2
Henstridge Marsh **9** G2
Henton *Oxon* **22** A1
Henton *Som* **19** H7
Henwood **4** C3
Heogan **89** N8
Heol Senni **27** J6
Heolgerrig **18** D1
Heol-y-Cyw **18** C3
Hepburn **71** F1
Hepburn Bell **71** F1
Hepple **70** E3
Hepscott **71** H5
Hepthorne Lane **51** G6
Heptonstall **56** E7
Hepworth *Suff* **34** D1
Hepworth *WYorks* **50** D2
Hepworth South Common **34** D1
Herbrandston **16** B5
Hereford **28** E4
Hereford Cathedral *Here* HR1 2NG **128** Hereford
Heriot **76** B5
Heritage Motor Centre, Gaydon *Warks* CV35 0BJ **30** E3
Herm **3** K5
Hermiston **75** K3
Hermitage *D&G* **65** H4
Hermitage *Dorset* **9** F4
Hermitage *ScBord* **70** A4
Hermitage *WBerks* **21** J4
Hermitage *WSuss* **11** J4
Hermitage Green **49** F3
Hermon *Carmar* **17** G2
Hermon *IoA* **46** B6
Hermon *Pembs* **17** F2
Herne **25** H5
Herne Bay **25** H5
Herne Common **25** H5
Herne Pound **23** K6
Herner **6** D3
Hernhill **25** G5
Herodsfoot **4** C4
Herongate **24** C2
Heron's Ghyll **13** H4
Heronsgate **22** D2
Herriard **21** K7
Herringfleet **45** J6
Herring's Green **32** D4
Herringswell **34** B2
Herringthorpe **51** G3
Hersden **25** H5
Hersham *Corn* **6** A5
Hersham *Surr* **22** E5
Herstmonceux **13** K5
Herston **89** D8
Hertford **33** G7
Hertford Heath **33** G7
Hertingfordbury **33** G7
Hesket Newmarket **60** E3
Hesketh Bank **55** H7
Hesketh Lane **56** B5
Heskin Green **48** E1
Hesleden **62** E3
Hesleyside **70** D5
Heslington **58** C4
Hessay **58** B4
Hessenford **4** D5
Hessett **34** D2
Hessle **59** G7
Hest Bank **55** H3
Hester's Way **29** J6
Hestley Green **35** F2
Heston **22** E4
Heswall **48** B4
Hethe **31** G6
Hethelpit Cross **29** G6
Hetherington **70** D6
Hethersett **45** F5
Hethersgill **69** K7
Hethpool **70** D1
Hett **62** C3
Hetton **56** E4
Hetton-le-Hole **62** D2
Heugh **71** F6
Heugh-head **84** H9
Heveningham **35** H1
Hever **23** H7
Hever Castle & Gardens *Kent* TN8 7NG **23** H7
Heversham **55** H1
Hevingham **45** F3
Hewas Water **3** G4
Hewell Grange **30** B2
Hewell Lane **30** B2
Hewelsfield **19** J1
Hewelsfield Common **19** J1
Hewish *NSom* **19** H5
Hewish *Som* **8** D4
Hewood **8** C4
Heworth **58** C4
Hewton **6** D6
Hexham **70** E7
Hexham Abbey *N'umb* NE46 3NB **70** E7
Hextable **23** J4
Hexthorpe **51** H2
Hexton **32** E5
Hexworthy **5** G3
Hey **56** D5
Hey Houses **55** G7
Heybridge *Essex* **24** C2
Heybridge *Essex* **24** E1
Heybridge Basin **24** E1
Heybrook Bay **4** E6
Heydon *Cambs* **33** H4
Heydon *Norf* **45** F3
Heydour **42** D2
Heyop **28** B1
Heysham **55** H3
Heyshaw **57** G3
Heyshott **12** B5
Heyside **49** J2
Heytesbury **20** C7
Heythrop **30** E6
Heywood *GtMan* **49** H1
Heywood *Wilts* **20** B6
Hibaldstow **52** C2
Hibb's Green **34** C3
Hickleton **51** G2
Hickling *Norf* **45** J3
Hickling *Notts* **41** J3
Hickling Green **45** J3
Hickling Heath **45** J3
Hickstead **13** F4
Hidcote Bartrim **30** C4
Hidcote Boyce **30** C4
Hidcote Manor Garden *Glos* GL55 6LR **30** C4
High Ackworth **51** G1
High Angerton **71** F5
High Bankhill **61** G2
High Beach **23** H2
High Bentham **56** B3
High Bickington **6** D3
High Birkwith **56** C2
High Blantyre **74** E5
High Bonnybridge **75** G3
High Borgue **65** G5
High Bradfield **50** E3
High Bradley **57** F5
High Bransholme **59** H6
High Bray **6** E2
High Bridge **60** E2
High Brooms **23** J7
High Bullen **6** D3
High Burton **57** H1
High Buston **71** H3
High Callerton **71** G6
High Casterton **56** B2
High Catton **58** D4
High Close **62** B5
High Cogges **21** G1
High Common **45** F7
High Coniscliffe **62** C5
High Crompton **49** J2
High Cross *Hants* **11** J2
High Cross *Herts* **33** G7
High Cross *WSuss* **13** F5
High Easter **33** K7
High Ellington **57** G1
High Entercommon **62** D6
High Ercall **38** E4
High Etherley **62** B4
High Ferry **43** G1
High Flatts **50** E2
High Garrett **34** B6
High Gate **56** E7
High Grange **62** B3
High Green *Norf* **44** D4
High Green *Norf* **44** D5
High Green *Norf* **45** F5
High Green *Suff* **34** C2
High Green *SYorks* **51** F3
High Green *Worcs* **29** H4
High Halden **14** D4
High Halstow **24** D4
High Ham **8** D1
High Harrington **60** B4
High Harrogate **57** J4
High Hatton **39** F3
High Hauxley **71** H3
High Hawsker **63** K6
High Heath *Shrop* **39** F3
High Heath *WMid* **40** C5
High Hesket **61** F2
High Hesleden **62** E3
High Hoyland **50** E1
High Hunsley **59** F6
High Hurstwood **13** H4
High Hutton **58** D3
High Ibry **60** D3
High Kelling **44** E2
High Kilburn **58** B2
High Kingthorpe **58** E1
High Knipe **61** G5
High Lane *Derbys* **41** G1
High Lane *GtMan* **49** J4
High Lane *Worcs* **29** F2
High Laver **23** J1
High Legh **49** G4
High Leven **62** E5
High Littleton **19** K6
High Lodge Forest Centre *Suff* IP27 0AF **44** C7
High Lorton **60** C4
High Marishes **58** E2
High Marnham **52** B5
High Melton **51** H2
High Moor **51** G4
High Moorland Visitor Centre, Princetown *Devon* PL20 6QF **5** F3
High Newton **55** H1
High Newton-by-the-Sea **71** H1
High Nibthwaite **60** D7
High Offley **39** G3
High Ongar **23** J1
High Onn **40** A4
High Park Corner **34** E6
High Roding **33** K7
High Shaw **61** K7
High Spen **71** G7
High Stoop **62** B2
High Street *Corn* **3** G3
High Street *Kent* **14** C4
High Street *Suff* **34** C4
High Street *Suff* **35** J1
High Street *Suff* **35** J3
High Street *Suff* **45** H7
High Street Green **34** E3
High Throston **62** E3
High Town **40** B4
High Toynton **53** F6
High Trewhitt **71** F3
High Wham **62** B4
High Wigsell **14** C5
High Woods Country Park *Essex* CO4 5JR **34** E6
High Woolaston **19** J2
High Worsall **62** D6
High Wray **60** E7
High Wych **33** H7
High Wycombe **22** B2
Higham *Derbys* **51** F7
Higham *Kent* **24** D4
Higham *Lancs* **56** D6
Higham *Suff* **34** B2
Higham *Suff* **34** E5
Higham *SYorks* **51** F2
Higham Dykes **71** G6
Higham Ferrers **32** C2
Higham Gobian **32** E5
Higham on the Hill **41** F6
Higham Wood **23** K7
Highampton **6** C5
Highams Park **23** G2
Highbridge *Hants* **11** F2
Highbridge *Som* **19** G7
Highbrook **13** G3
Highburton **50** D1
Highbury **19** K7
Highclere **21** H5
Highcliffe **10** D5
Higher Alham **19** K7
Higher Ansty **9** G4
Higher Ashton **7** G7
Higher Ballam **55** G6
Higher Bentham (High Bentham) **56** B3
Higher Blackley **49** H2
Higher Brixham **5** K5
Higher Cheriton **7** K5
Higher Combe **7** H2
Higher Folds **49** F2
Higher Gabwell **5** K4
Higher Green **49** G3
Higher Halstock Leigh **8** E4
Higher Kingcombe **8** E5
Higher Kinnerton **48** C6
Higher Muddiford **6** D2
Higher Nyland **9** G2
Higher Prestacott **6** B6
Higher Standen **56** C5
Higher Tale **7** J5
Higher Thrushgill **56** B3
Higher Town *Corn* **4** A4
Higher Town *IoS* **2** C1
Higher Walreddon **4** E3
Higher Walton *Lancs* **55** J7
Higher Walton *Warr* **48** E4
Higher Wambrook **8** B4
Higher Whatcombe **9** H4
Higher Wheelton **56** B7
Higher Whiteleigh **4** C1
Higher Whitley **49** F4
Higher Wincham **49** F5
Higher Woodhill **49** G1
Higher Woodsford **9** G6
Higher Wraxall **8** E4
Higher Wych **38** D1
Highfield *ERid* **58** D6
Highfield *NAyr* **74** B5
Highfield *Oxon* **31** G6
Highfield *SYorks* **51** F4
Highfield *T&W* **62** B1
Highfields *Cambs* **33** G3
Highfields *N'umb* **77** H5
Highgate *ESuss* **13** H3
Highgate *GtLon* **23** F3
Highgreen Manor **70** D4
Highlane *ChesE* **49** H6
Highlane *Derbys* **51** G4
Highlaws **60** C2
Highleadon **29** G6
Highleigh *Devon* **7** H3
Highleigh *WSuss* **12** B7
Highley **39** G7
Highmead **17** J1
Highmoor Cross **21** K3
Highmoor Hill **19** H3
Highnam **29** G7
Highstead **25** J5
Highsted **25** F5
Highstreet **25** G5
Highstreet Green *Essex* **34** B5
Highstreet Green *Surr* **12** C3
Hightae **69** F6
Highter's Heath **30** B1
Hightown *A&N* **92** J8
Hightown *Hants* **10** C4
Hightown *Mersey* **48** B2
Hightown Green **34** D3
Highway **20** D4
Highweek **5** J3
Highwood **29** F2
Highwood Hill **23** F2
Highworth **21** F2
Hilborough **44** C5
Hilcote **51** G7
Hilcott **20** E6
Hilden Park **23** J7
Hildenborough **23** J7
Hildersham **33** J4
Hilderstone **40** B2
Hilderthorpe **59** H3
Hilfield **9** F4
Hilgay **44** A6
Hill *SGlos* **19** K2
Hill *Warks* **31** F2
Hill *Worcs* **29** J4
Hill Brow **11** J2
Hill Chorlton **39** G2
Hill Common **45** J3
Hill Cottages **63** H7
Hill Croome **29** H4
Hill Deverill **20** B7
Hill Dyke **43** G1
Hill End *Dur* **62** A3
Hill End *Fife* **75** J1
Hill End *Glos* **29** H5
Hill End *GtLon* **22** D2
Hill End *NYorks* **57** F4
Hill Green **33** H5
Hill Head **11** G4
Hill Houses **29** F1
Hill Mountain **16** C5
Hill of Beath **75** K1
Hill of Fearn **84** C3
Hill Ridware **40** C4
Hill Row **33** H1
Hill Side **50** D1
Hill Street **10** E3
Hill Top *Hants* **11** F4
Hill Top *SYorks* **50** E4
Hill Top *SYorks* **51** G3
Hill View **9** J5
Hill Wootton **30** E2
Hillam **58** B7
Hillbeck **61** J5
Hillberry **54** C6
Hillborough **25** J5
Hillbutts **9** J4
Hillclifflane **40** E1
Hillend *Fife* **75** K2
Hillend *Midlo* **76** A4
Hillend *NLan* **75** G4
Hillend *Swan* **17** H6
Hillend Green **29** G6
Hillersland **28** E7
Hillesden **31** H6
Hillesley **20** A3
Hillfarrance **7** K3
Hillfoot End **32** E5
Hillhall **93** H10
Hillhead *Devon* **5** K5
Hillhead *Mid Ulster* **92** E7
Hillhead *SAyr* **67** J1
Hilliard's Cross **40** D4
Hillingdon **22** D3
Hillington *Glas* **74** D4
Hillington *Norf* **44** B3
Hillmorton **31** G1
Hillockhead **84** H10
Hillowton **65** H4
Hillpound **11** G3
Hill's End **32** C5
Hills Town **51** G6
Hillsborough *L&C* **93** H11
Hillsborough *SYorks* **51** F3
Hillsborough Castle *L&C* BT26 6AG **93** H11
Hillsford Bridge **7** F1
Hillside *Aber* **85** P11
Hillside *Angus* **81** N4
Hillside *Shet* **89** N6
Hillside *Worcs* **29** G2
Hillswick **89** L5
Hilltown **93** H14
Hillway **11** H6
Hillyfields **10** E3
Hilmarton **20** D4
Hilperton **20** B6
Hilsea **11** H4
Hilston **59** J6
Hilton *Cambs* **33** F2
Hilton *Cumb* **61** J4
Hilton *Derbys* **40** E2
Hilton *Dorset* **9** G4
Hilton *Dur* **62** B4
Hilton *Shrop* **39** G6
Hilton *Staffs* **40** C5
Hilton *Stock* **62** E5
Hilton of Cadboll **84** C3
Himbleton **29** J3
Himley **40** A6
Himley Hall & Park *WMid* DY3 4DF **106** A3
Hincaster **55** J1
Hinchley Wood **22** E5
Hinckley **41** G6
Hinderclay **34** E1
Hinderton **48** C5
Hinderwell **63** H5
Hindford **38** C2
Hindhead **12** B3
Hindley *GtMan* **49** F2
Hindley *N'umb* **62** A1
Hindley Green **49** F2
Hindlip **29** H3
Hindolveston **44** E3
Hindon *Som* **7** H1
Hindon *Wilts* **9** J1
Hindringham **44** D2
Hingham **44** E5
Hinksford **40** A7
Hinstock **39** F3
Hintlesham **34** E4
Hinton *Glos* **19** K1
Hinton *Hants* **10** D5
Hinton *Here* **28** C5
Hinton *N'hants* **31** G3
Hinton *SGlos* **20** A4
Hinton *Shrop* **38** D5
Hinton Admiral **10** D5
Hinton Ampner **11** G2
Hinton Blewett **19** J6
Hinton Charterhouse **20** A6
Hinton Martell **10** B4
Hinton on the Green **30** B4
Hinton Parva *Dorset* **9** J4
Hinton Parva *Swin* **21** F3
Hinton St. George **8** D3
Hinton St. Mary **9** G3
Hinton Waldrist **21** G2
Hinton-in-the-Hedges **31** G5
Hints *Shrop* **29** F1
Hints *Staffs* **40** D5
Hinwick **32** C2
Hinxhill **15** F3
Hinxton **33** H4
Hinxworth **33** F4
Hipperholme **57** G7
Hipsburn **71** H2
Hipswell **62** B7
Hirnant **37** K3
Hirst **71** H5
Hirst Courtney **58** C7
Hirwaen **47** K6
Hirwaun **18** C1
Hiscott **6** D3
Histon **33** H2
Hitcham *Bucks* **22** C3
Hitcham *Suff* **34** D3
Hitchin **32** E6
Hither Green **23** G4
Hittisleigh **7** F6
Hittisleigh Barton **7** F6
Hive **58** E6
Hixon **40** C3
H.M.S. Belfast *GtLon* SE1 2JH **105** B7
H.M.S. Victory PO1 3PX **135** Portsmouth
H.M.S. Warrior PO1 3QX **135** Portsmouth
Hoaden **15** H2
Hoaldalbert **28** C6
Hoar Cross **40** D3
Hoar Park Craft Centre *Warks* CV10 0QU **40** E6
Hoarwithy **28** E6
Hoath **25** J5
Hobarris **28** C1
Hobbister **89** C7
Hobbles Green **34** B3
Hobbs Cross **23** H2
Hobbs Lots Bridge **43** G5
Hobkirk **70** A2
Hobland Hall **45** K5
Hobson **62** B1
Hoby **41** J4
Hockerill **33** H6
Hockering **44** E4
Hockerton **51** K7
Hockley *AB&C* **93** E12
Hockley *Essex* **24** E2
Hockley Heath **30** C1
Hockliffe **32** C6
Hockwold cum Wilton **44** B7
Hockworthy **7** J4
Hoddesdon **23** G1
Hoddlesden **56** C7
Hodgehill **49** H6
Hodgeston **16** D6
Hodnet **39** F3
Hodnetheath **39** F3
Hodsoll Street **24** C5
Hodson **20** E3
Hodthorpe **51** H5
Hoe **44** D4
Hoe Gate **11** H3
Hoff **61** H5
Hoffleet Stow **43** F2
Hoggard's Green **34** C3
Hoggeston **32** B6
Hoggrill's End **40** E6
Hogha Gearraidh **88** B1
Hoghton **56** B7
Hognaston **50** E7
Hogsthorpe **53** J5
Holbeach **43** G3
Holbeach Bank **43** G3
Holbeach Clough **43** G3
Holbeach Drove **43** G4
Holbeach Hurn **43** G3
Holbeach St. Johns **43** G4
Holbeach St. Marks **43** G2
Holbeach St. Matthew **43** H2
Holbeck **51** H5
Holbeck Woodhouse **51** H5
Holberrow Green **30** B3
Holbeton **5** G5
Holborough **24** D5
Holbrook *Derbys* **41** F1
Holbrook *Suff* **35** F5
Holbrooks **41** F7
Holburn **77** J7
Holbury **11** F4
Holcombe *Devon* **5** K3
Holcombe *GtMan* **49** G1
Holcombe *Som* **19** K7
Holcombe Burnell Barton **7** G6
Holcombe Rogus **7** J4
Holcot **31** J2
Holden **56** C5
Holden Gate **56** D7
Holdenby **31** H2
Holdenhurst **10** C5
Holder's Green **33** K6
Holders Hill **23** F3
Holdgate **38** E7
Holdingham **42** D1
Holditch **8** C4
Hole **7** K4
Hole Park **14** D4
Holehouse **50** C3
Hole-in-the-Wall **29** F6
Holford **7** K1
Holgate **58** B4
Holker **55** G2
Holkham **44** C1
Hollacombe *Devon* **6** B5
Hollacombe *Devon* **7** G5
Hollacombe Town **6** E4
Holland *Ork* **89** D2
Holland *Surr* **23** H6
Holland Fen **43** F1
Holland-on-Sea **35** F7
Hollandstoun **89** G2
Hollee **69** H7
Hollesley **35** H4
Hollicombe **5** K4
Hollingbourne **14** D2
Hollingbury **13** G6
Hollingrove **13** K4
Hollington *Derbys* **40** E2
Hollington *ESuss* **14** C6
Hollington *Staffs* **40** C2
Hollingworth **50** C3
Hollins **51** F5
Hollins Green **49** F3
Hollins Lane **55** H4
Hollinsclough **50** C6
Hollinwood *GtMan* **49** J2
Hollinwood *Shrop* **38** E2
Hollocombe **6** E4
Hollow Meadows **50** E4
Holloway **51** F7
Hollowell **31** H1
Holly Bush **38** D1
Holly End **43** H5
Holly Green **22** A1
Hollybush *Caerp* **18** E1
Hollybush *EAyr* **67** H2
Hollybush *Worcs* **29** G5
Hollyhurst **38** E1
Hollym **59** K7
Hollywater **12** B3
Hollywood **30** B1
Holm **69** H4
Holm of Drumlanrig **68** D4
Holmbridge **50** D2
Holmbury St. Mary **22** E7
Holmbush **13** F3
Holme *Cambs* **42** E7
Holme *Cumb* **55** J2
Holme *NLincs* **52** C2
Holme *Notts* **52** B7
Holme *NYorks* **57** J1
Holme *WYorks* **50** D2
Holme Chapel **56** D7
Holme Hale **44** C5
Holme Lacy **28** E5
Holme Marsh **28** C3
Holme next the Sea **44** B1
Holme on the Wolds **59** F5
Holme Pierrepont **41** J2
Holme St. Cuthbert **60** C2
Holme-on-Spalding-Moor **58** E6
Holmer **28** E4
Holmer Green **22** C2
Holmes **48** D1
Holmes Chapel **49** G6
Holme's Hill **13** J5
Holmesfield **51** F5
Holmeswood **48** D1
Holmewood **51** G6
Holmfield **57** F7
Holmfirth **50** D2
Holmhead *D&G* **68** C5
Holmhead *EAyr* **67** K1
Holmpton **59** K7
Holmrook **60** B6
Holmside **62** C2
Holmsleigh Green **8** B4
Holmston **67** H1
Holmwrangle **61** G2
Holne **5** H4
Holnest **9** F4
Holnicote **7** H1
Holsworthy **6** B5
Holsworthy Beacon **6** B5
Holt *Dorset* **10** B4
Holt *Norf* **44** E2
Holt *Wilts* **20** B5
Holt *Worcs* **29** H2
Holt *Wrex* **48** D7
Holt End *Hants* **11** H1
Holt End *Worcs* **30** B2
Holt Fleet **29** H2
Holt Heath *Dorset* **10** B4
Holt Heath *Worcs* **29** H2
Holt Wood **10** B4
Holtby **58** C4
Holton *Oxon* **21** K1
Holton *Som* **9** F2
Holton *Suff* **35** J1
Holton cum Beckering **52** E4
Holton Heath **9** J5
Holton le Clay **53** F2
Holton le Moor **52** D3
Holton St. Mary **34** E5
Holtspur **22** C3
Holtye **13** H3
Holtye Common **13** H3
Holway **8** B2
Holwell *Dorset* **9** F3
Holwell *Herts* **32** E5
Holwell *Leics* **42** A3
Holwell *Oxon* **21** F1
Holwell *Som* **20** A7
Holwick **61** L4
Holworth **9** G6
Holy Cross **29** J1
Holy Island *IoA* **46** A5
Holy Island (Lindisfarne) *N'umb* **77** K6
Holy Trinity Church *Warks* CV37 6BG **136** Stratford-upon-Avon
Holy Trinity Church, Skipton *NYorks* BD23 1NJ **56** E4
Holybourne **22** A7
Holyfield **23** G1
Holyhead (Caergybi) **46** A4
Holymoorside **51** F6
Holyport **22** B4
Holystone **70** E3
Holytown **75** F4
Holywell *Cambs* **33** G1
Holywell *Corn* **2** E3
Holywell *Dorset* **8** E4
Holywell *ESuss* **13** K7
Holywell *F&O* **91** G13
Holywell (Treffynnon) *Flints* **47** K5
Holywell *N'umb* **71** J6
Holywell Bay Fun Park *Corn* TR8 5PW **2** E3
Holywell Green **50** C1
Holywell Lake **7** K3
Holywell Row **34** B1
Holywood *A&NDown* **92** K9
Holywood *D&G* **68** E5
Hom Green **28** E6
Homer **39** F5
Homersfield **45** G7
Homington **10** C2
Honey Hill **25** H5
Honey Street **20** E5
Honey Tye **34** D5
Honeyborough **16** C5
Honeybourne **30** C4
Honeychurch **6** E5
Honicknowle **4** E5
Honiley **30** D1
Honing **45** H3
Honingham **45** F4
Honington *Lincs* **42** C1
Honington *Suff* **34** D1
Honington *Warks* **30** D4
Honiton **7** K5
Honkley **48** C7
Honley **50** D1
Hoo *Med* **24** D4
Hoo *Suff* **35** G3
Hoo Green **49** G4
Hoo Meavy **5** F4
Hood Green **51** F2
Hood Hill **51** F3
Hooe *ESuss* **13** K6
Hooe *Plym* **5** F5
Hooe Common **13** K5
Hook *Cambs* **43** H6
Hook *ERid* **58** D7
Hook *GtLon* **22** E5
Hook *Hants* **11** G4
Hook *Hants* **22** A6
Hook *Pembs* **16** C4
Hook *Wilts* **20** D3
Hook Green *Kent* **13** K3
Hook Green *Kent* **23** J4
Hook Green *Kent* **24** C4
Hook Green *Kent* **24** C5
Hook Norton **30** E5
Hook-a-Gate **38** D5
Hooke **8** E4
Hookgate **39** G2
Hookway **7** G6
Hookwood **23** F7
Hoole **48** D6
Hooley **23** F6
Hoop **19** J1
Hooton **48** C5
Hooton Levitt **51** H3
Hooton Pagnell **51** G2
Hooton Roberts **51** G3
Hop Farm, The *Kent* TN12 6PY **23** K7
Hop Pocket, The *Here* WR6 5BT **29** F4
Hop Pole **42** E4
Hopcrofts Holt **31** F6
Hope *Derbys* **50** D4
Hope *Devon* **5** G7
Hope *Flints* **48** C7
Hope *Powys* **38** B5
Hope *Shrop* **38** C5
Hope *Staffs* **50** D7
Hope Bagot **28** E1
Hope Bowdler **38** D6
Hope End Green **33** J6
Hope Mansell **29** F7
Hope under Dinmore **28** E3
Hopehouse **69** H2
Hopeman **84** F4
Hope's Green **24** D3
Hopesay **38** C7
Hopkinstown **18** D2
Hopley's Green **28** C3
Hopperton **57** K4
Hopsford **41** G7
Hopstone **39** G6
Hopton *Derbys* **50** E7
Hopton *Norf* **45** K6
Hopton *Shrop* **38** C3
Hopton *Shrop* **38** E3
Hopton *Staffs* **40** B3
Hopton *Suff* **34** D1
Hopton Cangeford **38** E7
Hopton Castle **28** C1
Hopton Wafers **29** F1
Hoptonheath **28** C1
Hopwas **40** D5
Hopwood **30** B1
Horam **13** J5
Horbling **42** E2
Horbury **50** E1
Horden **62** E2
Horderley **38** D7
Hordle **10** D5
Hordley **38** C2
Horeb *Carmar* **17** H5
Horeb *Cere* **17** G1
Horeb *Flints* **48** B7
Horfield **19** J4
Horham **35** G1
Horkesley Heath **34** D6
Horkstow **52** C1
Horley *Oxon* **31** F4
Horley *Surr* **23** F7
Horn Hill **22** D2
Hornblotton **8** E1
Hornblotton Green **8** E1
Hornby *Lancs* **55** J3
Hornby *NYorks* **62** C7
Hornby *NYorks* **62** D6
Horncastle **53** F6
Hornchurch **23** J3
Horncliffe **77** H6
Horndean *Hants* **11** J3
Horndean *ScBord* **77** H6
Horndon **6** D7
Horndon on the Hill **24** C3
Horne **23** G7
Horne Row **24** D1
Horner **7** G1
Horniman Museum *GtLon* SE23 3PQ **105** C9
Horning **45** H4
Horninghold **42** B6
Horninglow **40** E3
Horningsea **33** H2
Horningsham **20** B7
Horningtoft **44** D3
Horningtops **4** C4
Horns Cross *Devon* **6** B3
Horns Cross *ESuss* **14** D5
Horns Green **23** H6
Hornsbury **8** C3
Hornsby **61** G2
Hornsby Gate **61** G1
Hornsea **59** J5
Hornsea Freeport *ERid* HU18 1UT **59** J5
Hornsey **23** G3
Hornton **30** E4
Horrabridge **5** F4
Horridge **5** H3
Horringer **34** C2
Horrocks Fold **49** G1
Horse Bridge **49** J7
Horsebridge *Devon* **4** E3
Horsebridge *Hants* **10** E1
Horsebrook **40** A4
Horsecastle **19** H5
Horsehay **39** F5
Horseheath **33** K4
Horsehouse **57** F1
Horsell **22** C6
Horseman's Green **38** D1
Horsenden **22** A1
Horseshoe Green **23** H7
Horseway **43** H7
Horsey **45** J3
Horsey Corner **45** J3
Horsford **45** F4
Horsforth **57** H6
Horsham *Worcs* **29** G3
Horsham *WSuss* **12** E3
Horsham St. Faith **45** G4
Horsington *Lincs* **52** E6
Horsington *Som* **9** G2
Horsington Marsh **9** G2
Horsley *Derbys* **41** F1
Horsley *Glos* **20** B2
Horsley *N'umb* **70** D4
Horsley *N'umb* **71** F7
Horsley Cross **35** F6
Horsley Woodhouse **41** F1
Horsleycross Street **35** F6
Horsleygate **51** F5
Horsleyhill **70** A2
Horsmonden **23** K7
Horspath **21** J1
Horstead **45** G4
Horsted Keynes **13** G4
Horton *Bucks* **32** C7
Horton *Dorset* **10** B4
Horton *Lancs* **56** D4
Horton *N'hants* **32** B3
Horton *SGlos* **20** A3
Horton *Shrop* **38** D3
Horton *Som* **8** C3
Horton *Staffs* **49** J7
Horton *Swan* **17** H7
Horton *Tel&W* **39** F4
Horton *Wilts* **20** D5
Horton *W&M* **22** D4
Horton Cross **8** C3
Horton Grange **71** H6
Horton Green **38** D1
Horton Heath **11** F3
Horton in Ribblesdale **56** D2
Horton Inn **10** B4
Horton Kirby **23** J5
Horton Park Farm *Surr* KT19 8PT **22** E5
Horton-cum-Studley **31** H7
Horwich **49** F1
Horwich End **50** C4
Horwood **6** D3
Hoscar **48** D1
Hose **42** A3
Hoses **60** D7
Hosh **80** D8
Hosta **88** B1
Hoswick **89** N10
Hotham **58** E6
Hothfield **14** E3
Hoton **41** H3
Houbie **89** Q3
Houdston **67** F4
Hough **49** G7
Hough Green **48** D4
Hougham **42** B1
Hough-on-the-Hill **42** C1
Houghton *Cambs* **33** F1
Houghton *Cumb* **60** F1
Houghton *Devon* **5** G6
Houghton *Hants* **10** E1
Houghton *Pembs* **16** C5
Houghton *WSuss* **12** D5
Houghton Bank **62** C4
Houghton Conquest **32** D4
Houghton le Spring **62** D2
Houghton on the Hill **41** J5
Houghton Regis **32** D6
Houghton St. Giles **44** D2
Houghton-le-Side **62** C4
Houlsyke **63** H6
Hound **11** F4
Hound Green **22** A6
Houndslow **76** E6
Houndsmoor **7** K3
Houndwood **77** G4
Hounsdown **10** E3
Hounslow **22** E4
House of Marbles & Teign Valley Glass *Devon* TQ13 9DS **5** J3
Houses Hill **50** D1
Housesteads Roman Fort (Frontiers of the Roman Empire) *N'umb* NE47 6NN **70** C7
Housetter **89** M4
Housham Tye **33** J7
Houston **74** C4
Houstry **87** P6
Houton **89** C7
Hove **13** F6
Hove Edge **57** G7
Hoveringham **41** J1
Hoveton **45** H4
Hovingham **58** C2
How **61** G1
How Caple **29** F5
How End **32** D4
How Green **23** H7
How Man **60** A5
Howbrook **51** F3
Howden **58** D7
Howden Clough **57** H7
Howden-le-Wear **62** B3
Howe *Cumb* **55** H1
Howe *High* **87** R3
Howe *Norf* **45** G6
Howe *NYorks* **57** J1
Howe Green **24** D1
Howe Street *Essex* **33** K5
Howe Street *Essex* **33** K7
Howegreen **24** E1
Howell **42** E1
Howey **27** K3
Howgate *Cumb* **60** A4
Howgate *Midlo* **76** A5
Howgill *Lancs* **56** D5
Howgill *NYorks* **57** F4
Howick **71** H2
Howle **39** F3
Howle Hill **29** F6
Howlett End **33** J5
Howletts Wild Animal Park *Kent* CT4 5EL **15** G2
Howley **8** B4
Howmore (Tobha Mòr) **88** B5
Hownam **70** C2
Hownam Mains **70** C1
Howpasley **69** J3
Howsham *NLincs* **52** D2
Howsham *NYorks* **58** D3
Howt Green **24** E5
Howtel **77** G7
Howton **28** D6
Howwood **74** C4
Hoxne **35** F1
Hoy **89** B8
Hoylake **48** B4
Hoyland **51** F2
Hoylandswaine **50** E2
Hoyle **12** C5
Hubberholme **56** E2
Hubberston **16** B5
Hubbert's Bridge **43** F1
Huby *NYorks* **57** H5
Huby *NYorks* **58** B3
Hucclecote **29** H7
Hucking **14** D2
Hucknall **41** H1
Huddersfield **50** D1
Huddington **29** J3
Huddlesford **40** D5
Hudnall **32** D7
Hudscott **6** E3
Hudswell **62** B7
Huggate **58** E4
Hugglescote **41** G4
Hugh Town **2** C1
Hughenden Valley **22** B2
Hughley **38** E6
Hugmore **48** C7
Hugus **2** E4
Huish *Devon* **6** D4
Huish *Wilts* **20** E5
Huish Champflower **7** J3
Huish Episcopi **8** D2
Huisinis **88** E6
Hulcote **32** C5
Hulcott **32** B7
Hull **59** H7
Hulland **40** E1
Hulland Ward **40** E1
Hullavington **20** B3
Hullbridge **24** E2
Hulme **40** B1
Hulme End **50** D7
Hulme Walfield **49** H6
Hulver Street **45** J7
Hulverstone **10** E6
Humber *Devon* **5** J3
Humber *Here* **28** E3
Humber Bridge Country Park *ERid* HU13 0LN **59** G7
Humberside Airport **52** D1
Humberston **53** G2
Humberstone **41** J5
Humberton **57** K3
Humbie **76** C4
Humbleton *Dur* **62** A5
Humbleton *ERid* **59** J6
Humbleton *N'umb* **70** E1
Humby **42** D2
Hume **77** F6
Humehall **77** F6
Hummer **8** E3
Humshaugh **70** E6
Huna **87** R2
Huncoat **56** C6
Huncote **41** H6
Hundalee **70** B2
Hundall **51** F5
Hunderthwaite **61** L4
Hundleby **53** G6
Hundleton **16** C5
Hundon **34** B4
Hundred Acres **11** G3
Hundred End **55** H7
Hundred House **28** A3
Hungarton **41** J5
Hungate End **31** J4
Hungerford *Hants* **10** C3
Hungerford *Newbury* **21** G4
Hungerford *Shrop* **38** E7
Hungerford *WBerks* **21** G5
Hungerton **42** B3
Hunmanby **59** G2
Hunningham **30** E2
Hunningham Hill **30** E2
Hunny Hill **11** F6
Hunsdon **33** H7
Hunsingore **57** K4
Hunslet **57** J6
Hunsonby **61** G3
Hunspow **87** Q2
Hunstanton **44** A1
Hunstanworth **61** L2
Hunston *ESuss* **12** B6
Hunston *Suff* **34** D2
Hunston Green **34** D2
Hunt End **30** B2
Hunt House **63** J7
Huntercombe End **21** K3
Hunters Forstal **25** H5
Hunter's Inn **6** E1
Hunter's Quay **73** K3
Hunterston **73** K5
Huntford **70** B3
Huntham **8** C2
Huntingdon **33** F1
Huntingfield **35** H1
Huntingford **9** H1
Huntington *Here* **28** B3
Huntington *Here* **28** D4
Huntington *Staffs* **40** B4
Huntington *Tel&W* **39** F5
Huntington *York* **58** C4
Huntingtower **80** F8
Huntley **29** G7
Huntly **85** K7
Huntlywood **76** E6
Hunton *Hants* **21** H7
Hunton *Kent* **14** C3
Hunton *NYorks* **62** B7
Hunton Bridge **22** D1
Hunt's Cross **48** D4
Huntscott **7** H1
Huntsham **7** J3
Huntshaw **6** D3
Huntshaw Cross **6** D3
Huntshaw Water **6** D3
Huntspill **19** G7
Huntworth **8** C1
Hunwick **62** B3
Hunworth **44** E2
Hurcott *Som* **8** C3
Hurcott *Som* **8** E2
Hurdley **38** B6
Hurdsfield **49** J5
Hurley *Warks* **40** E6
Hurley *W&M* **22** B3
Hurley Bottom **22** B3
Hurlford **74** C7
Hurlston Green **48** C1
Hurn **10** C5
Hursley **11** F2
Hurst *NYorks* **62** A6
Hurst *W'ham* **22** A4
Hurst Green *Essex* **34** E7
Hurst Green *ESuss* **14** C5
Hurst Green *Lancs* **56** B6
Hurst Green *Surr* **23** G6
Hurst Wickham **13** F5
Hurstbourne Priors **21** H7
Hurstbourne Tarrant **21** G6
Hurstpierpoint **13** F5
Hurstwood **56** D6
Hurtmore **22** C7
Hurworth-on-Tees **62** D5
Hury **61** L4
Husbands Bosworth **41** J7
Husborne Crawley **32** C5
Husthwaite **58** B2
Hutcherleigh **5** H5
Huthwaite **51** G7
Huttoft **53** J5
Hutton *Cumb* **60** F4
Hutton *Essex* **24** C2
Hutton *Lancs* **55** H7
Hutton *NSom* **19** G6
Hutton *ScBord* **77** H5
Hutton Bonville **62** D6
Hutton Buscel **59** F1
Hutton Conyers **57** J2
Hutton Cranswick **59** G4
Hutton End **60** F3
Hutton Hang **57** G1
Hutton Henry **62** E3
Hutton Magna **62** B5
Hutton Mount **24** C2
Hutton Mulgrave **63** J6
Hutton Roof *Cumb* **55** J2
Hutton Roof *Cumb* **60** E3
Hutton Rudby **62** E6
Hutton Sessay **57** K2
Hutton Wandesley **58** B4
Hutton-le-Hole **63** H7
Huxham **7** H6
Huxham Green **8** E1
Huxley **48** E6
Huyton **48** D3
Hycemoor **54** D1
Hyde *Glos* **20** B1
Hyde *GtMan* **49** J3
Hyde End *WBerks* **21** J5
Hyde End *W'ham* **22** A5
Hyde Heath **22** C1
Hyde Lea **40** B4
Hydestile **22** C7
Hylands Park *Essex* CM2 8WQ **24** C1
Hyndford Bridge **75** H6
Hyndlee **70** A3
Hynish **78** A7
Hyssington **38** C6
Hythe *Hants* **11** F4
Hythe *Kent* **15** G4
Hythe End **22** D4
Hyton **54** D1

I

Iarsiadar **88** G4
Ibberton **9** G4
Ible **50** E7
Ibsley **10** C4
Ibstock **41** G4
Ibstone **22** A2
Ibthorpe **21** G6
Ibworth **21** J6
Icelton **19** G5
Ickburgh **44** C6
Ickenham **22** D3
Ickford **21** K1
Ickham **15** H2
Ickleford **32** E5
Icklesham **14** D6
Ickleton **33** H4
Icklingham **34** B1
Ickwell Green **32** E4
Icomb **30** D6
Idbury **30** D6
Iddesleigh **6** D5
Ide **7** H6
Ide Hill **23** H6
Ideford **5** J3
Iden **14** E5
Iden Green *Kent* **14** C4
Iden Green *Kent* **14** D4
Idle **57** G6
Idless **3** F4
Idlicote **30** D4
Idmiston **10** C1
Idridgehay **40** E1
Idridgehay Green **40** E1
Idrigil **82** D4
Idstone **21** F3
Iffley **21** J1
Ifield **13** F3
Ifieldwood **13** F3
Ifold **12** D3
Iford *BCP* **10** C5
Iford *ESuss* **13** H6
Ifton **19** H3
Ifton Heath **38** C2
Ightfield **38** E2
Ightham **23** J6
Iltham Mote *Kent* TN15 0NT **23** J6
Iken **35** J3
Ilam **50** D7
Ilchester **8** E2
Ilderton **71** F1
Ilford **23** H3
Ilfracombe **6** D1
Ilkeston **41** G1
Ilketshall St. Andrew **45** H7
Ilketshall St. Lawrence **45** H7
Ilketshall St. Margaret **45** H7
Ilkley **57** G5
Illey **40** B7
Illidge Green **49** G6
Illington **44** D7
Illingworth **57** F7
Illogan **2** D4
Illston on the Hill **42** A6
Ilmer **22** A1
Ilmington **30** D4
Ilminster **8** C3
Ilsington *Devon* **5** H3
Ilsington *Dorset* **9** G5
Ilston **17** J6
Ilton *NYorks* **57** G2
Ilton *Som* **8** C3
Imachar **73** G6
Imber **20** C7
Imeroo **91** K11
Immingham **52** E1
Immingham Dock **53** F1
Imperial War Museum North *GtMan* M17 1TZ **114** F4
Imperial War Museum, Duxford *Cambs* CB22 4QR **33** H4
Imperial War Museum, London *GtLon* SE1 6HZ **132** G6
Impington **33** H2

Inc - Lan

Ince 48 D5
Ince Blundell 48 C2
Ince-in-Makerfield 48 E2
Inch Kenneth 78 F7
Inchbare 81 M4
Inchberry 84 H5
Inchbraoch 81 N5
Inchgrundle 81 K3
Inchinagh 92 B6
Inchinnan 74 C4
Inchlaggan 83 M10
Inchmarnock 73 J5
Inchnacardoch Hotel 83 P9
Inchnadamph 86 E7
Inchree 79 M4
Inchrory 84 F10
Inchture 80 H8
Indian Queens 3 G3
Inerval 72 B6
Ingatestone 24 C2
Ingbirchworth 50 E2
Ingerthorpe 57 H3
Ingestre 40 B3
Ingham Lincs 52 C4
Ingham Norf 45 H3
Ingham Suff 34 C1
Ingham Corner 45 H3
Ingleborough 43 H4
Ingleby Derbys 41 F3
Ingleby Lincs 52 B5
Ingleby Arncliffe 62 E6
Ingleby Barwick 62 E5
Ingleby Cross 62 E6
Ingleby Greenhow 63 F6
Ingleigh Green 6 E5
Inglesbatch 20 A5
Inglesham 21 F2
Ingleton Dur 62 B4
Ingleton NYorks 56 B2
Inglewhite 55 J6
Ingliston 75 K3
Ingmire Hall 61 H7
Ingoe 71 F6
Ingoldisthorpe 44 A2
Ingoldmells 53 J6
Ingoldsby 42 D2
Ingon 30 D3
Ingram 71 F2
Ingrave 24 C2
Ingrow 57 F6
Ings 60 F7
Ingst 19 J3
Ingworth 45 F3
Inhurst 21 J5
Inisclan 90 J8
Inishrush 92 E6
Injebreck 54 C5
Inkberrow 30 B3
Inkersall 51 G5
Inkersall Green 51 G5
Inkpen 21 G5
Inkstack 87 Q2
Inmarsh 20 C5
Innellan 73 K4
Innerhadden 80 B5
Innerleithen 76 B7
Innerleven 81 J10
Innermessan 64 A4
Innerwick ELoth 77 F3
Innerwick P&K 80 A6
Innsworth 29 H6
Insch 85 L8
Insh 84 C10
Inskip 55 H6
Instow 6 C2
Intake 51 H2
Intech, Winchester Hants SO21 1HX 11 G2
International Centre, The, Telford Tel&W TF3 4JH 39 G5
Intwood 45 F5
Inver Aber 84 G11
Inver High 84 C2
Inver Mallie 79 N2
Inverailort 79 J2
Inveralligin 83 J5
Inverallochy 85 Q4
Inveraray (Inbhir Aora) 79 M10
Inverarish 82 F7
Inverarity 81 K6
Inverarnan (Inbhir Àirnein) 79 Q9
Inverasdale 83 J2
Inverbeg 74 B1
Inverbervie 81 P3
Inverbroom 83 M2
Invercassley 86 G9
Inverchaolain 73 J3
Invercharnan 79 N6
Inverchoran 83 N5
Invercreran 79 M6
Inverdruie 84 D9
Inveresk 76 B3
Inverey 80 F2
Inverfarigaig 83 R8
Invergarry (Inbhir Garadh) 83 P10
Invergeldie 80 C8
Invergloy 79 P2
Invergordon 84 B4
Invergowrie 81 J7
Inverharroch Farm 84 H7
Inverie 82 H10
Inverinan 79 L9
Inverinate 83 K8
Inverkeilor 81 M6
Inverkeithing 75 K2
Inverkeithny 85 L6
Inverkip 74 A4
Inverkirkaig 86 C8
Inverlael 83 M2
Inverlauren 74 B2
Inverlochlarig 79 R9
Inverlussa 72 E2
Invermore 92 J6
Invermoriston (Inbhir Moireasdan) 83 Q9
Invernaver 87 K3
Inverneil 73 G2
Inverness (Inbhir Nis) 84 A6
Inverness Airport 84 B5
Invernoaden 73 K1
Inveroran Hotel (Inbhir Orain) 79 P6
Inverroy 79 P2
Inversnaid Hotel 79 Q10
Inverugie 85 R6
Inveruglas (Inbhir Dhubhghlais) 79 Q10
Inverurie 85 M8
Invervar 80 B6
Invervegain 73 J3
Inwardleigh 6 D6
Inworth 34 C7
Iochdar (Eochar) 88 B4
Iona 78 D8
Iping 12 B4
Ipplepen 5 J4
Ipsden 21 K3
Ipstones 40 C1
Ipswich 35 F4
Irby 48 B4
Irby Hill 48 B4
Irby in the Marsh 53 H6
Irby upon Humber 52 E2
Irchester 32 C2
Irchester Country Park N'hants NN29 7DL 32 C2
Ireby Cumb 60 D3
Ireby Lancs 56 B2
Ireland 89 M10
Ireland's Cross 39 G1
Ireleth 55 F2
Ireshopeburn 61 K3
Irish Hill 92 J8
Irlam 49 G3
Irnham 42 D3
Iron Acton 19 K3
Iron Cross 30 B3
Ironbridge 39 F5
Ironbridge Gorge Tel&W TF8 7DQ 39 F5
Irons Bottom 23 F7
Ironville 51 G7
Irstead 45 H3
Irthington 69 K7
Irthlingborough 32 C1
Irton 59 G1
Irvine 74 B7
Irvinestown 91 J11
Isauld 87 M3
Isbister Ork 89 B5
Isbister Shet 89 M3
Isbister Shet 89 P6
Isfield 13 H5
Isham 32 B1
Isington 22 A7
Island of Stroma 87 R2
Islawr-dref 37 F4
Islay 72 A4
Islay Airport 72 B5
Islay House 72 B4
Isle Abbotts 8 C2
Isle Brewers 8 C2
Isle of Bute Discovery Centre A&B PA20 0AH 73 J4
Isle of Lewis (Eilean Leodhais) 88 J3
Isle of Man 54 C5
Isle of Man Airport 54 B7
Isle of May 76 E1
Isle of Noss 89 P8
Isle of Sheppey 25 F4
Isle of Walney 54 E3
Isle of Whithorn 64 E7
Isle of Wight 11 F6
Isle of Wight (Sandown Airport) 11 G6
Isle of Wight Pearl IoW PO30 4DD 11 F6
Isle of Wight Zoo IoW PO36 8QB 11 H6
Isleham 33 K1
Isleornsay (Eilean Iarmain) 82 G9
Isles of Scilly (Scilly Isles) 2 C1
Isleworth 22 E4
Isley Walton 41 G3
Islibhig 88 E5
Islip N'hants 32 C1
Islip Oxon 31 G7
Isombridge 39 F4
Istead Rise 24 C5
Itchen 11 F3
Itchen Abbas 11 G1
Itchen Stoke 11 G1
Itchen Valley Country Park Hants SO30 3HQ 96 D2
Itchingfield 12 E4
Itchington 19 K3
Itteringham 45 F2
Itton Devon 6 E6
Itton Mon 19 H2
Itton Common 19 H2
Ivegill 60 F2
Ivelet 61 L7
Iver 22 D3
Iver Heath 22 D3
Iveston 62 B1
Ivetsey Bank 40 A4
Ivinghoe 32 C7
Ivinghoe Aston 32 C7
Ivington 28 D3
Ivington Green 28 D3
Ivy Hatch 23 J6
Ivy Todd 44 C5
Ivybridge 5 G5
Ivychurch 15 F5
Iwade 25 F5
Iwerne Courtney (Shroton) 9 H3
Iwerne Minster 9 H3
Ixworth 34 D1
Ixworth Thorpe 34 D1

J

Jack Hill 57 G4
Jackfield 39 F5
Jacksdale 51 G7
Jackton 74 D5
Jacobstow 4 B1
Jacobstowe 6 D5
Jacobswell 22 C6
James Hamilton Heritage Park SLan G74 5LB 119 G7
James Pringle Weavers of Inverness High IV2 4RB 84 A6
Jameston 16 D6
Jamestown D&G 69 J4
Jamestown WDun 74 B2
Janefield 84 B5
Janetstown 87 R4
Janus Stones F&O BT93 8AA 91 G10
Jarrow 71 J7
Jarvis Brook 13 J3
Jasper's Green 34 B6
Jawcraig 75 G3
Jayes Park 22 E7
Jaywick 35 F7
Jealott's Hill 22 B4
Jeater Houses 62 E7
Jedburgh 70 B1
Jeffreyston 16 D5
Jemimaville 84 B4
Jephson Gardens Warks CV32 4ER 30 E2
Jericho 49 H1
Jerrettspass 93 F13
Jersay 75 G4
Jersey 3 J7
Jersey Airport 3 J7
Jersey Marine 18 A2
Jerviswood 75 G6
Jesmond 71 H7
Jevington 13 J6
Jinney Ring Craft Centre, The Worcs B60 4BU 29 J2
Jockey End 32 D7
Jodrell Bank 49 G5
Jodrell Bank Observatory ChesE SK11 9DL 49 G5
John Muir Country Park ELoth EH42 1UW 76 E3
John o' Groats 87 R2
Johnby 60 F3
John's Cross 14 C5
Johnshaven 81 N4
Johnson Street 45 H4
Johnston 16 C4
Johnstone 74 C4
Johnstone Castle 74 C4
Johnstonebridge 69 F4
Johnstons Cashmere Visitor Centre Moray IV30 4AF 84 G4
Johnstown Carmar 17 G4
Johnstown Wrex 38 C1
Jonesborough 93 F15
Joppa 67 J2
Jordans 22 C2
Jordanston 16 C2
Jorvik YO1 9WT 137 York
Jorvik Glass NYorks YO60 7DA 58 D3
Joy's Green 29 F7
Jumpers Common 10 C5
Juniper Green 75 K4
Juniper Hill 31 G5
Jura 72 D2
Jura House 72 C4
Jurby East 54 C4
Jurby West 54 C4

K

Kaber 61 J5
Kaimes 76 A4
Kames A&B 73 H3
Kames EAyr 68 B1
Katesbridge 93 H12
Kea 3 F4
Keadby 52 B1
Keady 93 D13
Keal Cotes 53 G6
Kearney 93 M11
Kearsley 49 G2
Kearstwick 56 B2
Kearton 62 A7
Keasden 56 C3
Keckwick 48 E4
Keddington 53 G4
Keddington Corner 53 G4
Kedington 34 B4
Kedleston 41 F1
Keelby 52 E1
Keele 40 A1
Keeley Green 32 D4
Keelham 57 F6
Keenaghan 91 F11
Keenans Bridge 92 E6
Keenthorne 8 B1
Keeran 91 L10
Keeres Green 33 J7
Keeston 16 B4
Keevil 20 C6
Kegworth 41 G3
Kehelland 2 D4
Keighley 57 F5
Keighley & Worth Valley Railway WYorks BD22 8NJ 57 F5
Keil 66 A3
Keilhill 85 M5
Keillmore 72 E2
Keills 72 C4
Keils 72 D4
Keinton Mandeville 8 E1
Keir House 75 F1
Keir Mill 68 D4
Keisby 42 D3
Keisley 61 J4
Keiss 87 R3
Keith 85 J5
Kelbrook 56 E5
Kelby 42 D1
Keld Cumb 61 G5
Keld NYorks 61 K6
Keldholme 58 D1
Keldy Castle 63 H7
Kelfield NLincs 52 B2
Kelfield NYorks 58 B6
Kelham 51 K7
Kella 54 C4
Kellacott 6 C7
Kellan 78 G6
Kellas Angus 81 K7
Kellas Moray 84 F5
Kellaton 5 H7
Kellaways 20 C4
Kelleth 61 H6
Kelleythorpe 59 G4
Kelling 44 E1
Kellington 58 B7
Kelloe 62 D3
Kelloholm 68 C2
Kelly Corn 4 A3
Kelly Devon 6 B7
Kelly Bray 4 D3
Kells 92 G7
Kelmarsh 31 J1
Kelmscott 21 F2
Kelsale 35 H2
Kelsall 48 E6
Kelsay 72 A5
Kelshall 33 G5
Kelsick 60 D1
Kelso 77 F7
Kelstedge 51 F6
Kelstern 53 F3
Kelston 20 A5
Kelton 65 K3
Kelton Hill (Rhonehouse) 65 H5
Kelty 75 K1
Kelvedon 34 C7
Kelvedon Hatch 23 J2
Kelvin Hall Glas G3 8AW 127 A2
Kelvingrove Art Gallery & Museum Glas G3 8AG 127 B2
Kelvinside 74 D4
Kelynack 2 A6
Kemacott 6 E1
Kemback 81 K9
Kemberton 39 G5
Kemble 20 C2
Kemerton 29 J5
Kemeys Commander 19 G1
Kemeys Inferior 19 G2
Kemnay 85 M9
Kemp Town 13 G6
Kempe's Corner 15 F3
Kempley 29 F6
Kempley Green 29 F6
Kemps Green 30 C1
Kempsey 29 H4
Kempsford 20 E2
Kempshott 21 J7
Kempston 32 D4
Kempston Hardwick 32 D4
Kempston West End 32 C4
Kempton 38 C7
Kemsing 23 J6
Kemsley 25 F5
Kenardington 14 E4
Kenchester 28 D4
Kencot 21 F1
Kendal 61 G7
Kenderchurch 28 D6
Kendleshire 19 K4
Kenfig 18 A3
Kenfig Hill 18 B3
Kenidjack 2 A5
Kenilworth 30 D1
Kenilworth Castle Warks CV8 1NE 30 D1
Kenknock 79 R7
Kenley GtLon 23 G5
Kenley Shrop 38 E5
Kenmore High 82 H5
Kenmore P&K 80 C6
Kenn Devon 7 H7
Kenn NSom 19 H5
Kennacraig 73 G4
Kennall Vale (Cornwall & West Devon Mining Landscape) Corn 2 E5
Kennards House 4 C2
Kennavay 88 H8
Kenneggy Downs 2 C6
Kennerleigh 7 G5
Kennet 75 H1
Kennethmont 85 K8
Kennett 33 K2
Kennford 7 H7
Kenninghall 44 E7
Kennington Kent 15 F3
Kennington Oxon 21 J1
Kennoway 81 J10
Kenny 8 C3
Kennyhill 33 K1
Kennythorpe 58 D3
Kenovay 78 A6
Kensaleyre 82 E5
Kensington 23 F3
Kensington Palace GtLon W8 4PX 103 G7
Kenstone 38 E3
Kensworth 32 D7
Kent & East Sussex Railway Kent TN30 6HE 14 D5
Kent Street ESuss 14 C6
Kent Street Kent 23 K6
Kentallen (Ceann an t-Sàilein) 79 M5
Kentchurch 28 D6
Kentford 34 B2
Kentisbeare 7 J5
Kentisbury 6 E1
Kentisbury Ford 6 E1
Kentish Town 23 F3
Kentmere 61 F6
Kenton Devon 7 H7
Kenton Suff 35 F2
Kenton T&W 71 H7
Kenton Corner 35 G2
Kentra 78 H4
Kents Bank 55 G2
Kent's Green 29 G6
Kent's Oak 10 E2
Kenwick 38 D2
Kenwood House GtLon NW3 7JR 102 H4
Kenwyn 3 F4
Kenyon 49 F3
Keoldale 86 F3
Keonan 93 G11
Keose (Ceòs) 88 J5
Keppoch A&B 74 B3
Keppoch High 83 J8
Keprigan 66 A2
Kepwick 62 E7
Keresley 41 F7
Kernborough 5 H6
Kerrera 79 K8
Kerridge 49 J5
Kerris 2 B6
Kerry (Ceri) 38 A6
Kerrycroy 73 K4
Kerry's Gate 28 C5
Kerrysdale 83 J3
Kersall 51 K6
Kersey 34 E4
Kersey Vale 34 E4
Kershopefoot 69 K5
Kerswell 7 J5
Kerswell Green 29 H4
Kerthen Wood 2 C5
Kesgrave 35 G4
Kesh 91 H10
Kessingland 45 K7
Kessingland Beach 45 K7
Kestle 3 G4
Kestle Mill 3 F3
Keston 23 H5
Keswick Cumb 60 D4
Keswick Norf 45 G5
Keswick Norf 45 H2
Ketley Bank 39 F4
Ketsby 53 G5
Kettering 32 B1
Ketteringham 45 F5
Kettins 80 H7
Kettle Corner 14 C2
Kettlebaston 34 D3
Kettlebrook 40 E5
Kettleburgh 35 G2
Kettlehill 81 J10
Kettleholm 69 G6
Kettleness 63 J5
Kettleshulme 49 J5
Kettlesing 57 H4
Kettlesing Bottom 57 H4
Kettlesing Head 57 H4
Kettlestone 44 D2
Kettlethorpe 52 B5
Kettletoft 89 F4
Kettlewell 56 E2
Ketton 42 C5
Kevingtown 23 H5
Kew 22 E4
Kewstoke 19 G5
Kexbrough 51 F2
Kexby Lincs 52 B4
Kexby York 58 D4
Key Green 49 H6
Keyham 41 J5
Keyhaven 10 E5
Keyingham 59 J7
Keymer 13 G5
Keynsham 19 K5
Key's Toft 53 H7
Keysoe 32 D2
Keysoe Row 32 D2
Keyston 32 D1
Keyworth 41 J2
Kibblesworth 62 C1
Kibworth Beauchamp 41 J6
Kibworth Harcourt 41 J6
Kidbrooke 23 H4
Kiddemore Green 40 A5
Kidderminster 29 H1
Kiddington 31 F6
Kidlington 31 F7
Kidmore End 21 K4
Kidnal 38 D1
Kidsdale 64 E7
Kidsgrove 49 H7
Kidstones 56 E1
Kidstown 92 E4
Kidwelly (Cydweli) 17 H5
Kielder 70 B4
Kielder Forest N'umb NE48 1ER 70 B4
Kielder Water N'umb NE48 1BX 70 C5
Kilbarchan 74 C4
Kilberry 73 F4
Kilbirnie 74 B5
Kilbride A&B 73 J4
Kilbride A&B 79 K8
Kilbride A&N 92 H7
Kilbride Farm 73 H4
Kilbridemore 73 J1
Kilburn Derbys 41 F1
Kilburn GtLon 23 F3
Kilburn NYorks 58 B2
Kilby 41 J6
Kilchattan Bay 73 K5
Kilchenzie 66 A1
Kilcheran 79 K7
Kilchiaran 72 A4
Kilchoan A&B 79 J9
Kilchoan High 78 F4
Kilchoman 72 A4
Kilchrenan (Cill Chrèanain) 79 M8
Kilchrist 66 A2
Kilclief 93 L12
Kilconquhar 81 K10
Kilcoo 93 H13
Kilcorig 93 H10
Kilcot 29 F6
Kilcoy 83 R5
Kilcreggan 74 A2
Kilcross 92 H9
Kildale 63 G6
Kildary 84 B3
Kildavie 66 B2
Kildonan 66 E1
Kildonan Lodge 87 M7
Kildonnan 78 F2
Kildrochet House 64 A5
Kildress 92 C9
Kildrum 92 G7
Kildrummy 85 J9
Kildwick 57 F5
Kilfinan 73 H3
Kilfinnan 83 N11
Kilgetty 16 E5
Kilgwrrwg Common 19 H2
Kilham ERid 59 G3
Kilham N'umb 77 G7
Kilkeel 93 J15
Kilkenneth 78 A6
Kilkenny 30 B7
Kilkerran A&B 66 B2
Kilkerran SAyr 67 H3
Kilkhampton 6 A4
Kilkinamurry 93 H12
Killadeas 91 J11
Killagan Bridge 92 F4
Killaloo 90 M6
Killamarsh 51 G4
Killarbran 91 L12
Killard 92 E7
Killay 17 K6
Killead 92 G8
Killeague 92 D4
Killean 72 E6
Killearn 74 D2
Killeen AB&C 93 E12
Killeen Mid Ulster 93 D10
Killeen NM&D 93 F14
Killeeshil 93 B11
Killellan 66 A2
Killen D&S 90 J8
Killen High 84 A5
Killerby 62 B4
Killerton Devon EX5 3LE 7 J5
Killerton 7 H5
Killeter 90 J8
Killichonan 80 A5
Killiechonate 79 P2
Killiechronan 78 G6
Killiecrankie 80 E4
Killilan 83 K7
Killimster 87 R4
Killin 80 A7
Killinallan 72 B3
Killinchy 93 L10
Killinghall 57 H4
Killington Cumb 56 B1
Killington Devon 6 E1
Killingworth 71 H6
Killochyett 76 C6
Killough 93 L13
Killowen 93 G15
Killucan 92 E8
Killundine 78 G6
Killure 92 D4
Killyclogher 91 L9
Killycolp 93 D9
Killycolpy 93 E9
Killycor 90 M6
Killycurragh 92 C8
Killyharry 93 C10
Killykergan 92 D5
Killylane 90 M4
Killylea 93 C12
Killyleagh 93 L11
Killymallaght 90 L6
Killynether 93 K9
Killyrammer 92 E4
Kilmacolm 74 B4
Kilmahamogue 92 F3
Kilmahog 80 B10
Kilmalieu 79 K5
Kilmaluag 82 E3
Kilmany 81 J8
Kilmarie 82 F9
Kilmarnock 74 C7
Kilmartin 73 G1
Kilmaurs 74 C6
Kilmelford 79 K9
Kilmeny 72 B4
Kilmersdon 19 K6
Kilmeston 11 G2
Kilmichael 66 A1
Kilmichael Glassary 73 G1
Kilmichael of Inverlussa 73 F2
Kilmington Devon 8 B5
Kilmington Wilts 9 G1
Kilmington Common 9 G1
Kilmood 93 K10
Kilmorack 83 Q6
Kilmore (A' Chille Mhòr) A&B 79 K8
Kilmore AB&C 93 E11
Kilmore High 82 G10
Kilmore NM&D 93 K11
Kilmory A&B 73 F2
Kilmory A&B 73 F3
Kilmory High 78 G3
Kilmory High 82 D10
Kilmory NAyr 66 D1
Kilmuir High 84 A6
Kilmuir High 84 B3
Kilmun 73 K2
Kiln Green Here 29 F7
Kiln Green W'ham 22 B4
Kiln Pit Hill 62 A1
Kilnave 72 A3
Kilncadzow 75 G6
Kilndown 14 C4
Kilnhurst 51 G3
Kilninian 78 F6
Kilninver 79 K8
Kilnsea 53 H1
Kilnsey 56 E3
Kilnwick 59 F5
Kilnwick Percy 58 E4
Kiloran 72 B1
Kilpatrick 66 D1
Kilpeck 28 D5
Kilphedir 87 M8
Kilpin 58 D7
Kilpin Pike 58 D7
Kilraghts 92 F4
Kilrea 92 E5
Kilrenny 81 L10
Kilroot 92 K8
Kilsally 93 D9
Kilsby 31 G1
Kilskeery 91 J11
Kilspindie 80 H8
Kilstay 64 B7
Kilsyth 75 F3
Kiltarlity 83 R6
Kilton Notts 51 H5
Kilton R&C 63 G5
Kilton Som 7 K1
Kilton Thorpe 63 G5
Kiltyrie 80 B7
Kilvaxter 82 D4
Kilve 7 K1
Kilverstone 44 C7
Kilvington 42 B1
Kilwaughter 92 J6
Kilwinning 74 B6
Kimberley Norf 44 E5
Kimberley Notts 41 H1
Kimberworth 51 G3
Kimble Wick 22 B1
Kimblesworth 62 C2
Kimbolton Cambs 32 D2
Kimbolton Here 28 E2
Kimbridge 10 E2
Kimcote 41 H7
Kimmeridge 9 J7
Kimmerston 77 H7
Kimpton Hants 21 F7
Kimpton Herts 32 E7
Kinakelly 91 K14
Kinallen 93 H12
Kinawley 91 J13
Kinbrace 87 L6
Kinbuck 80 C10
Kincaple 81 K9
Kincardine Fife 75 H2
Kincardine High 84 A2
Kincardine O'Neil 85 K11
Kinclaven 80 G7
Kincorth 85 P10
Kincraig 84 C10
Kindallachan 80 E5
Kineton Glos 30 B6
Kineton Warks 30 E3
Kineton Green 40 D7
Kinfauns 80 G8
King Sterndale 50 C5
Kingarth 73 J5
Kingcoed 19 H1
Kingerby 52 D3
Kingham 30 D6
Kingholm Quay 65 K3
Kinghorn 76 A2
Kinglassie 76 A1
Kingoodie 81 J8
King's Acre 28 D4
King's Bank 14 D5
King's Bromley 40 D4
Kings Caple 28 E6
King's Cliffe 42 D6
King's College Chapel, Cambridge Cambs CB2 1ST 33 H3
King's Coughton 30 B3
King's Green 29 G5
King's Heath 40 C7
King's Hill Kent 23 K6
King's Hill Warks 30 E1
King's Hill WMid 40 B6
Kings Langley 22 D1
King's Lynn 44 A3
King's Meaburn 61 H4
Kings Mills 3 H5
King's Moss 48 E2
Kings Muir 76 A7
King's Newnham 31 F1
King's Newton 41 F3
King's Norton Leics 41 J5
King's Norton WMid 30 B1
Kings Nympton 6 E4
King's Pyon 28 D3
Kings Ripton 33 F1
King's Somborne 10 E1
King's Stag 9 G3
King's Stanley 20 B1
King's Sutton 31 F5
King's Tamerton 4 E5
King's Walden 32 E6
Kings Worthy 11 F1
Kingsand 4 E5
Kingsbarns 81 L9
Kingsbridge Devon 5 H6
Kingsbridge Som 7 H2
Kingsburgh 82 D5
Kingsbury GtLon 22 E3
Kingsbury Warks 40 E6
Kingsbury Episcopi 8 D2
Kingsbury Water Park Warks B76 0DY 40 E6
Kingscavil 75 J3
Kingsclere 21 J6
Kingscote 20 B2
Kingscott 6 D4
Kingscross 66 E1
Kingsdon 8 E2
Kingsdown Kent 15 J3
Kingsdown Swin 20 E3
Kingsdown Wilts 20 B5
Kingseat 75 K1
Kingsey 22 A1
Kingsfold Pembs 16 C6
Kingsfold WSuss 12 E3
Kingsford Aberdeen 85 N10
Kingsford EAyr 74 C6
Kingsford Worcs 40 A7
Kingsgate 25 K4
Kingshall Street 34 D2
Kingsheanton 6 D2
Kingshouse 80 A8
Kingshouse Hotel 79 P5
Kingshurst 40 D7
Kingskerswell 5 J4
Kingskettle 81 J10
Kingsland Here 28 D2
Kingsland IoA 46 A4
Kingsley ChesW&C 48 E5
Kingsley Hants 11 J1
Kingsley Staffs 40 C1
Kingsley Green 12 B3
Kingsley Holt 40 C1
Kingslow 39 G6
Kingsmill 92 D9
Kingsmoor 23 H1
Kingsmuir Angus 81 K6
Kingsmuir Fife 81 L10
Kingsnorth 15 F4
Kingsnorth Power Station 24 E4
Kingstanding 40 C6
Kingsteignton 5 J3
Kingsthorne 28 D5
Kingsthorpe 31 J2
Kingston Cambs 33 G3
Kingston Corn 4 D3
Kingston Devon 5 G6
Kingston Devon 7 J7
Kingston Dorset 9 G4
Kingston Dorset 9 J7
Kingston ELoth 76 D2
Kingston GtMan 49 J3
Kingston Hants 10 C4
Kingston IoW 11 F6
Kingston Kent 15 G2
Kingston MK 32 C5
Kingston Moray 84 H4
Kingston WSuss 12 D6
Kingston Bagpuize 21 H2
Kingston Blount 22 A2
Kingston by Sea 13 F6
Kingston Deverill 9 H1
Kingston Gorse 12 D6
Kingston Lacy Dorset BH21 4EA 95 A2
Kingston Lisle 21 G3
Kingston Maurward 9 G5
Kingston near Lewes 13 G6
Kingston on Soar 41 H3
Kingston Russell 8 E5
Kingston Seymour 19 H5
Kingston St. Mary 8 B2
Kingston Stert 22 A1
Kingston upon Hull 59 H7
Kingston upon Thames 22 E5
Kingston Warren 21 G3
Kingstone Here 28 D5
Kingstone Here 29 F6
Kingstone Som 8 C3
Kingstone Staffs 40 C3
Kingstone Winslow 21 F3
Kingstown 60 E1
Kingswear 5 J5
Kingswell 74 D6
Kingswinford 40 A7
Kingswood Bucks 31 H7
Kingswood Glos 20 A2
Kingswood Here 28 B3
Kingswood Kent 14 D2
Kingswood Powys 38 B5
Kingswood SGlos 19 K4
Kingswood Som 7 K2
Kingswood Surr 23 F6
Kingswood Warks 30 C1
Kingthorpe 52 E5
Kington Here 28 B3
Kington Worcs 29 J3
Kington Langley 20 C4
Kington Magna 9 G2
Kington St. Michael 20 C4
Kingussie 84 B10
Kingweston 8 E1
Kinharvie 65 K4
Kinkell 74 E3
Kinlet 39 G7
Kinloch High 82 E11
Kinloch High 86 F6
Kinloch P&K 80 G6
Kinloch Hourn (Ceann Loch Shubhairne) 83 K10
Kinloch Laggan 80 A2
Kinloch Rannoch 80 B5
Kinlochard 79 R10
Kinlochbervie 86 E4
Kinlocheil 79 L3
Kinlochewe 83 L4
Kinlochleven (Ceann Loch Liobhann) 79 N4
Kinlochmoidart 79 J3
Kinlochmore 79 N4
Kinloss 84 E4
Kinmel Bay (Bae Cinmel) 47 H4
Kinmuck 85 N9
Kinnaber 81 N4
Kinnadie 85 P6
Kinnaird 80 H8
Kinneff 81 P3
Kinnelhead 69 F3
Kinnerley 38 C3
Kinnersley Here 28 C4
Kinnersley Worcs 29 H4
Kinnerton 28 B2
Kinnerton Green 48 C6
Kinnesswood 80 G10
Kinninvie 62 A4
Kinnoull 80 G8
Kinross 80 G10
Kinrossie 80 G7
Kinsbourne Green 32 E7
Kinsham Here 28 C2
Kinsham Worcs 29 J5
Kinsley 51 G1
Kinson 10 B5
Kintbury 21 G5
Kintessack 84 D4
Kintillo 80 G9
Kintocher 85 K10
Kinton Here 28 D1
Kinton Shrop 38 C4
Kintore 85 M9
Kintour 72 C5
Kintra A&B 72 B6
Kintra A&B 78 E8
Kinuachdrachd 73 F1
Kinveachy 84 D9
Kinver 40 A7
Kinwarton 30 C3
Kiplaw Croft 85 Q7
Kippax 57 K6
Kippen 74 E1
Kippford (Scaur) 65 J5
Kipping's Cross 23 K7
Kippington 23 J6
Kirbister 89 C7
Kirbuster 89 B5
Kirby Bedon 45 G5
Kirby Bellars 42 A4
Kirby Cane 45 H6
Kirby Corner 30 D1
Kirby Cross 35 G6
Kirby Fields 41 H5
Kirby Green 45 H6
Kirby Grindalythe 59 F3
Kirby Hill NYorks 57 J3
Kirby Hill NYorks 62 B6
Kirby Knowle 57 K1
Kirby le Soken 35 G6
Kirby Misperton 58 D2
Kirby Muxloe 41 H5
Kirby Row 45 H6
Kirby Sigston 62 E7
Kirby Underdale 58 E4
Kirby Wiske 57 J1
Kircubbin 93 L10
Kirdford 12 D4
Kirk 87 Q4
Kirk Bramwith 51 J1
Kirk Deighton 57 J4
Kirk Ella 59 G7
Kirk Hallam 41 G1
Kirk Hammerton 57 K4
Kirk Ireton 50 E7
Kirk Langley 40 E2
Kirk Merrington 62 C3
Kirk Michael 54 C4
Kirk of Shotts 75 G4
Kirk Sandall 51 J2
Kirk Smeaton 51 H1
Kirk Yetholm 70 D1
Kirkabister 89 N9
Kirkandrews 65 G6
Kirkandrews-upon-Eden 60 E1
Kirkbampton 60 E1
Kirkbean 65 K5
Kirkbride 60 D1
Kirkbuddo 81 L6
Kirkburn ERid 59 F4
Kirkburn ScBord 76 A7
Kirkburton 50 D1
Kirkby Lincs 52 D3
Kirkby Mersey 48 D3
Kirkby NYorks 63 F6
Kirkby Fleetham 62 C7
Kirkby Green 52 D7
Kirkby in Ashfield 51 G7
Kirkby la Thorpe 42 D1
Kirkby Lonsdale 56 B2
Kirkby Malham 56 D3
Kirkby Mallory 41 G5
Kirkby Malzeard 57 H2
Kirkby on Bain 53 F6
Kirkby Overblow 57 J5
Kirkby Stephen 61 J6
Kirkby Thore 61 H4
Kirkby Underwood 42 D3
Kirkby Wharfe 58 B5
Kirkby Woodhouse 51 G7
Kirkby-in-Furness 55 F1
Kirkbymoorside 58 C1
Kirkcaldy 76 A1
Kirkcambeck 70 A7
Kirkcolm 64 A4
Kirkconnel 68 C2
Kirkconnell 65 K4
Kirkcowan 64 D4
Kirkcudbright 65 G5
Kirkdale House 65 F5
Kirkdean 75 K6
Kirkfieldbank 75 G6
Kirkgunzeon 65 J4
Kirkham Lancs 55 H6
Kirkham NYorks 58 D3
Kirkhamgate 57 J7
Kirkharle 71 F5
Kirkhaugh 61 H2
Kirkheaton N'umb 71 F6
Kirkheaton WYorks 50 D1
Kirkhill 83 R6
Kirkhope 69 J1
Kirkibost (Circebost) 88 G4
Kirkinner 64 E5
Kirkinriola 92 G6
Kirkintilloch 74 E3
Kirkistown 93 M11
Kirkland Cumb 60 B5
Kirkland Cumb 61 H3
Kirkland D&G 68 C2
Kirkland D&G 68 D4
Kirkland D&G 69 F5
Kirkland of Longcastle 64 D6
Kirkleatham 63 F4
Kirklevington 62 E5
Kirkley 45 K6
Kirklington Notts 51 J7
Kirklington NYorks 57 J1
Kirklinton 69 K7
Kirkliston 75 K3
Kirkmaiden 64 B7
Kirkmichael P&K 80 F4
Kirkmichael SAyr 67 H3
Kirkmuirhill 75 F6
Kirknewton N'umb 77 H7
Kirknewton WLoth 75 K4
Kirkney 85 K7
Kirkoswald Cumb 61 G2
Kirkoswald SAyr 67 G3
Kirkpatrick Durham 65 H3
Kirkpatrick-Fleming 69 H6
Kirksanton 54 E1
Kirkstall 57 H6
Kirkstead 52 E6
Kirkstile 69 K4
Kirkstyle 87 R2
Kirkthorpe 57 J7
Kirkton Aber 85 L5
Kirkton Aber 85 L8
Kirkton Angus 81 K6
Kirkton D&G 68 E5
Kirkton High 83 J8
Kirkton High 84 B1
Kirkton ScBord 70 A2
Kirkton Manor 76 A7
Kirkton of Auchterhouse 81 J7
Kirkton of Bourtie 85 N8
Kirkton of Craig 81 N5
Kirkton of Culsalmond 85 L7
Kirkton of Durris 85 M11
Kirkton of Glenbuchat 84 H9
Kirkton of Glenisla 80 H4
Kirkton of Kingoldrum 81 J5
Kirkton of Kinnettles 81 K6
Kirkton of Lethendy 80 G6
Kirkton of Logie Buchan 85 P8
Kirkton of Maryculter 85 N11
Kirkton of Menmuir 81 L4
Kirkton of Rayne 85 L7
Kirkton of Skene 85 N10
Kirkton of Tealing 81 K7
Kirktonhill 74 B3
Kirktown 85 Q5
Kirktown of Alvah 85 L4
Kirktown of Deskford 85 K4
Kirktown of Fetteresso 81 P2
Kirktown of Slains 85 Q8
Kirkwall 89 D6
Kirkwall Airport 89 D7
Kirkwhelpington 70 E5
Kirmington 52 E1
Kirmond le Mire 52 E3
Kirn 73 K3
Kirriemuir 81 J5
Kirstead Green 45 G6
Kirtlebridge 69 H6
Kirtleton 69 H6
Kirtling 33 K3
Kirtling Green 33 K3
Kirtlington 31 G7
Kirtomy 87 K3
Kirton Lincs 43 G2
Kirton Notts 51 J6
Kirton Suff 35 G5
Kirton End 43 F1
Kirton Holme 43 F1
Kirton in Lindsey 52 C3
Kiscadale 66 E1
Kislingbury 31 H3
Kismeldon Bridge 6 B4
Kit Hill Country Park Corn PL17 8AX 4 D3
Kites Hardwick 31 F2
Kitley 5 F5
Kittisford 7 J3
Kittisford Barton 7 J3
Kittle 17 J7
Kitt's End 23 F2
Kitt's Green 40 D7
Kitwood 11 H1
Kivernoll 28 D5
Kiveton Park 51 G4
Klibreck 86 H6
Knaith 52 B4
Knaith Park 52 B4
Knap Corner 9 H2
Knaphill 22 C6
Knaplock 7 G2
Knapp P&K 80 H7
Knapp Som 8 C2
Knapthorpe 51 K7
Knaptoft 41 J7
Knapton Norf 45 H2
Knapton York 58 B4
Knapton Green 28 D3
Knapwell 33 G2
Knaresborough 57 J4
Knarsdale 61 H1
Knayton 57 K1
Knebworth 33 F6
Knebworth House Herts SG3 6PY 33 F6
Knedlington 58 D7
Kneesall 51 K6
Kneesworth 33 G4
Kneeton 42 A1
Knelston 17 H7
Knenhall 40 B2
Knettishall 44 D7
Knettishall Heath Country Park Suff IP22 2TQ 44 D7
Knightacott 6 E2
Knightcote 31 F3
Knightley 40 A3
Knightley Dale 40 A3
Knighton BCP 10 B5
Knighton Devon 5 F6
Knighton Dorset 9 F3
Knighton Leic 41 H5
Knighton (Tref-y-clawdd) Powys 28 B1
Knighton Som 7 K1
Knighton Staffs 39 G1
Knighton Staffs 39 G3
Knighton Wilts 21 F4
Knighton on Teme 29 F1
Knightswood 74 D4
Knightwick 29 G3
Knill 28 B2
Knipton 42 B2
Knitsley 62 B2
Kniveton 50 E7
Knock A&B 78 G7
Knock Cumb 61 H4
Knock Moray 85 K5
Knockalava 73 H1
Knockally 87 P7
Knockaloe Moar 54 B5
Knockan CC&G 92 B6
Knockan High 86 E8
Knockandhu 84 G8
Knockanorane 91 L13
Knockanully 92 G5
Knockarevan 91 K14
Knockarthur 87 K9
Knockavannon 93 E14
Knockbain 84 A5
Knockban 83 N4
Knockbrack 90 L5
Knockbrex 65 F6
Knockcloghrim 92 D7
Knockdee 87 P3
Knockdow 73 K3
Knockdown 20 B3
Knockenkelly 66 E1
Knockentiber 74 B7
Knockgray 67 K4
Knockholt 23 H6
Knockholt Pound 23 H6
Knockin 38 C3
Knockinelder 93 M11
Knockinlaw 74 C7
Knockintorran (Cnoc an Torrain) 88 B2
Knocklearn 65 H3
Knockmany Passage Grave MUlst BT76 0XJ 91 M11
Knockmill 23 J5
Knockmoyle 90 L9
Knocknacarry 92 H3
Knocknaha 66 A2
Knocknain 66 D7
Knocknalling 67 K5
Knocknashangan 91 F12
Knockrome 72 D3
Knocks 91 K13
Knocksharry 54 B5
Knockville 64 D3
Knodishall 35 J2
Knodishall Common 35 J2
Knodishall Green 35 J2
Knole 8 D2
Knolls Green 49 H5
Knolton 38 C2
Knook 20 C7
Knossington 42 B5
Knott End-on-Sea 55 G5
Knotting 32 D2
Knotting Green 32 D2
Knottingley 58 B7
Knotts 56 C4
Knotty Green 22 C2
Knowbury 28 E1
Knowe 64 D3
Knowehead 92 L9
Knowesgate 70 E5
Knoweside 67 G2
Knowetownhead 70 A2
Knowl Green 34 B4
Knowl Hill 22 B4
Knowl Wall 40 A2
Knowle Bristol 19 K4
Knowle Devon 6 C2
Knowle Devon 7 F5
Knowle Devon 7 J7
Knowle Shrop 28 E1
Knowle Som 7 H1
Knowle WMid 30 C1
Knowle Cross 7 J6
Knowle Green 56 B6
Knowle Hall 19 G7
Knowle St. Giles 8 C3
Knowlton Dorset 10 B3
Knowlton Kent 15 H2
Knowsley 48 D3
Knowsley Safari Park Mersey L34 4AN 113 G3
Knowstone 7 G3
Knucklas (Cnwclas) 28 B1
Knutsford 49 G5
Knypersley 49 H7
Kuggar 2 E7
Kyle of Lochalsh (Caol Loch Aillse) 82 H8
Kyleakin (Caol Acain) 82 H8
Kylerhea (Ceol Reatha) 82 H8
Kyles Scalpay (Caolas Scalpaigh) 88 H8
Kylesku 86 E6
Kylesmorar 83 J11
Kylestrome 86 E6
Kynaston 38 C3
Kynnersley 39 F4
Kyre Park 29 F2

L

Labost 88 H3
Lacasaigh 88 J5
Lace Market Centre NG1 1HF 134 Nottingham
Laceby 53 F2
Lacey Green 22 B1
Lach Dennis 49 G5
Lack 91 J10
Lackagh 92 B5
Lackalee (Leac a' Li) 88 G8
Lackford 34 B1
Lacock 20 C5
Ladbroke 31 F3
Laddingford 23 K7
Lade Bank 53 G7
Ladies Hill 55 H5
Ladock 3 F3
Lady Hall 54 E1
Lady Lever Art Gallery Mersey CH62 5EQ 112 B6
Ladybank 81 J9
Ladycross 6 B7
Ladykirk 77 G6
Ladysford 85 P4
Ladywood 29 H2
Lagavara 92 F2
Lagavulin 72 C6
Lagg A&B 72 D3
Lagg NAyr 66 D1
Lagg SAyr 67 G2
Laggan A&B 72 A5
Laggan (An Lagan) High 83 N11
Laggan High 84 A11
Laggan Moray 84 H7
Lagganulva 78 F6
Laghy Corner 93 D10
Lagrae 68 C2
Laide 83 K1
Laig 78 F2
Laight 68 B2
Laindon 24 C3
Laing Art Gallery T&W NE1 8AG 129 Newcastle upon Tyne
Lairg 86 H9
Lairigmor 79 N4
Laisterdyke 57 G6
Laithes 61 F3
Lake Devon 5 F4
Lake Devon 6 D2
Lake IoW 11 G6
Lake Wilts 10 C1
Lake District Visitor Centre at Brockhole Cumb LA23 1LJ 60 E6
Lakenham 45 G5
Lakenheath 44 B7
Lakes Aquarium Cumb LA12 8AS 55 G1
Lakes End 43 J6
Lakeside Cumb 55 G1
Lakeside Thur 23 J4
Lakeside & Haverthwaite Railway Cumb LA12 8AL 55 G1
Laleham 22 D5
Laleston 18 B4
Lamancha 76 A5
Lamarsh 34 C5
Lamas 45 G3
Lamb Corner 34 E5
Lamb Roe 56 C6
Lambden 77 F6
Lamberhurst 13 K3
Lamberhurst Quarter 13 K3
Lamberton 77 H5
Lambfell Moar 54 B5
Lambley Notts 41 J1
Lambley N'umb 61 H1
Lambourn 21 G4
Lambourn Woodlands 21 G4
Lambourne End 23 H2
Lambs Green 13 F3
Lambston 16 C4
Lambton 62 C1
Lamellion 4 C4
Lamerton 4 E3
Lamesley 62 C1
Lamington 75 H7
Lamlash 73 J7
Lamloch 67 K4
Lamonby 60 F3
Lamorna 2 B6
Lamorran 3 F4
Lampert 70 B6
Lampeter (Llanbedr Pont Steffan) 17 J1
Lampeter Velfrey 16 E4
Lamphey 16 D5
Lamplugh 60 B4
Lamport 31 J1
Lamyatt 9 F1
Lana Devon 6 B5
Lana Devon 6 B6
Lanark 75 G6
Lanarth 2 E6
Lancaster 55 H3
Lancaster Leisure Park Lancs LA1 3LA 55 H3
Lancaster Priory Lancs LA1 1YZ 55 H3
Lanchester 62 B2
Lancing 12 E6
Landbeach 33 H2
Landcross 6 C3
Landerberry 85 M10
Landewednack 2 E7
Landford 10 D3
Landican 48 B4
Landimore 17 H6
Landkey 6 D2
Landmoth 62 E7
Landore 17 K6
Landrake 4 D4
Land's End Corn TR19 7AA 2 A6
Land's End Airport 2 A6
Landscove 5 H4
Landshipping 16 D4
Landulph 4 E4
Landwade 33 K2
Landywood 40 B5
Lane Bottom 56 D6
Lane End Bucks 22 B2
Lane End Cumb 60 C7
Lane End Derbys 51 G6
Lane End Dorset 9 H5
Lane End Hants 11 G2
Lane End Here 29 F7
Lane End Kent 23 J4
Lane End Wilts 20 B7
Lane Ends Derbys 40 E2
Lane Ends GtMan 49 J3
Lane Ends Lancs 56 C6
Lane Ends NYorks 56 E5
Lane Green 40 A5
Lane Head Dur 62 A4
Lane Head Dur 62 B5
Lane Head GtMan 49 F3
Lane Head WYorks 50 D2
Lane Heads 55 H6
Lane Side 56 C7
Laneast 4 C2
Lane-end 4 A4
Laneham 52 B5
Lanehead Dur 61 K2
Lanehead N'umb 70 C5
Lanesend 16 D5
Lanesfield 40 B6

och Sgioport 88 C5
ochailort (Ceann Loch Ailleart) 79 J2
ochaline (Loch Àlainn) 78 H6
ochans 64 A5
ochbriggs 68 E5
ochawe (Loch Obha) 79 N8
ochboisdale (Loch Baghasdail) 88 B7
ochbuie 78 H8
ochcarron (Loch Carrann) 83 J6
ochdhu Hotel 87 N5
ochdon 79 J7
ochearnhead (Ceann Loch Èireann) 80 A8
ochee 81 J7
ochend (Ceann Loch) High 83 R7
ochend High 87 Q3
ocheport 88 C2
ochfoot 65 K3
ochgair 73 H1
ochgarthside 83 R9
ochgelly 75 K1
ochgilphead (Ceann Loch Gilb) 73 G2
ochgoilhead 79 P10
ochgoyn 74 D6
ochhill EAyr 67 K1
ochhill Moray 84 G4
ochinch Castle 64 B4
ochinver (Loch an Inbhir) 86 C7
ochlea 74 C7
ochmaben 69 F5
ochmaddy 88 D2
ochore 75 K1
ochore Meadows Country Park Fife KY5 8BA 75 K1
ochportain 88 D1
ochranza 73 H5
ochside Aber 81 N4
ochside High 86 G4
ochside High 87 L6
ochton 67 G5
ochuisge 79 J5
ochurr 68 C5
ochussie 83 Q5
ochwinnoch 74 B5
ockengate 4 A4
ockerbie 69 G5
ockeridge 20 E5
ockerley 10 D2
ocking 19 G6
ockington ERid 59 F5
ockington Leics 41 G3
ockleywood 39 F3
ocks Heath 11 G4
ocksbottom 23 H5
ocksgreen 11 F5
ockton 58 E1
ocomotion: The National Railway Museum at Shildon Dur DL4 1PQ 62 C4
oddington Leics 42 A5
oddington N'hants 32 B1
oddiswell 5 H6
oddon 45 H6
ode 33 J2
oders 8 D5
odsworth 12 C4
ofthouse NYorks 57 G2
ofthouse WYorks 57 J7
oftus 63 H5
ogan D&G 64 A6
ogan EAyr 67 K1
oganlea 75 H4
oggerheads 39 G2
oggerheads Country Park Denb CH7 5LH 47 K6
ogie Coldstone 85 J10
ogierait 80 E5
ogin 16 E3
olworth 33 G2
onbain 82 G5
ondesborough 58 E5
ondon 23 G3
ondon Apprentice 4 A6
ondon Ashford Airport 15 F5
ondon Beach 14 D4
ondon Biggin Hill Airport 23 H5
ondon City Airport 23 H3
ondon Colney 22 E1
ondon Eye GtLon SE1 7PB 132 F5
ondon Gatwick Airport 23 F7
ondon Heathrow Airport 22 D4
ondon Luton Airport 32 E6
ondon Minstead 10 D3
ondon Motor Museum GtLon UB3 4SB 103 B7
ondon Oxford Airport 31 F7
ondon Southend Airport 24 E3
ondon Stansted Airport 33 J6
ondon Transport Museum GtLon WC2E 7BB 132 E3
ondonderry (Derry) D&S 90 L5
ondonderry NYorks 57 H1
ondonthorpe 42 C2
ondubh 83 J2
ong Ashton 19 J4
ong Bank 29 G1
ong Bennington 42 B1
ong Bredy 8 E5
ong Buckby 31 H2
ong Clawson 42 A3
ong Compton Staffs 40 A3
ong Compton Warks 30 D5
ong Crendon 21 K1
ong Crichel 9 J3
ong Dean 20 B4
ong Downs 2 E5
ong Drax 58 C7
ong Duckmanton 51 G5
ong Eaton 41 G2
ong Gill 56 C4
ong Green ChesW&C 48 D5
ong Green Essex 34 D6
ong Green Worcs 29 H5
ong Hanborough 31 F7
ong Itchington 31 F2
ong Lane 39 F4
ong Lawford 31 F1
ong Load 8 D2
ong Marston Herts 32 B7
ong Marston NYorks 58 B4
ong Marston Warks 30 C4
ong Marton 61 H4
Long Meadowend 38 D7
Long Melford 34 C4
Long Newnton 20 C2
Long Preston 56 D4
Long Riston 59 H5
Long Stratton 45 F6
Long Street 31 J4
Long Sutton Hants 22 A7
Long Sutton Lincs 43 H3
Long Sutton Som 8 D2
Long Thurlow 34 E2
Long Whatton 41 G3
Long Wittenham 21 J2
Longbenton 71 H7
Longborough 30 C6
Longbridge Plym 5 F5
Longbridge Warks 30 D2
Longbridge WMid 30 B1
Longbridge Deverill 20 B7
Longburgh 60 E1
Longburton 9 F3
Longcliffe 50 E7
Longcombe 5 J5
Longcot 21 F2
Longcroft 75 F3
Longcross Devon 4 E3
Longcross Surr 22 C5
Longden 38 D5
Longdon Staffs 40 C4
Longdon Worcs 29 H5
Longdon Green 40 C4
Longdon upon Tern 39 F4
Longdown 7 G6
Longfield Kent 24 C5
Longfield NM&D 93 F15
Longfield Hill 24 C5
Longfleet 10 B5
Longford Derbys 40 E2
Longford Glos 29 H6
Longford GtLon 22 D4
Longford Shrop 39 F2
Longford Tel&W 39 G4
Longford WMid 41 F7
Longforgan 81 J8
Longformacus 76 E5
Longframlington 71 G3
Longham Dorset 10 B5
Longham Norf 44 D4
Longhirst 71 H5
Longhope Glos 29 F7
Longhope Ork 89 C8
Longhorsley 71 G4
Longhoughton 71 H2
Longlands Cumb 60 D3
Longlands GtLon 23 H4
Longlane Derbys 40 E2
Longlane WBerks 21 H4
Longleat House Wilts BA12 7NW 20 B7
Longleat Safari Park Wilts BA12 7NW 20 B7
Longlevens 29 H7
Longley 50 D2
Longley Green 29 G3
Longmanhill 85 M4
Longmoor Camp 11 J1
Longmorn 84 G5
Longnewton ScBord 70 A1
Longnewton Stock 62 D5
Longney 29 G7
Longniddry 76 C3
Longniddry Bents ELoth EH32 0PX 76 C3
Longnor Shrop 38 D5
Longnor Staffs 50 C6
Longparish 21 H7
Longridge Lancs 56 B6
Longridge Staffs 40 B4
Longridge WLoth 75 H4
Longridge End 29 H6
Longridge Towers 77 H5
Longriggend 75 G3
Longrock 2 C5
Longsdon 49 J7
Longshaw 48 E2
Longside 85 Q6
Longslow 39 F2
Longsowerby 60 E1
Longstanton 33 H2
Longstock 10 E1
Longstone 2 C5
Longstowe 33 G3
Longstreet 20 E6
Longthorpe 42 E6
Longton Lancs 55 H7
Longton Stoke 40 B1
Longtown Cumb 69 J7
Longtown Here 28 C6
Longville in the Dale 38 E6
Longwell Green 19 K4
Longwick 22 A1
Longwitton 71 F5
Longworth 21 G2
Longyester 76 D4
Lonmay 85 Q5
Looe 4 C5
Look Out Discovery Park, Bracknell BrackF RG12 7QW 22 B5
Loose 14 C2
Loosebeare 7 F5
Loosegate 43 G3
Loosley Row 22 B1
Lopcombe Corner 10 D1
Lopen 8 D3
Loppington 38 D3
Lorbottle 71 F3
Lorbottle Hall 71 F3
Lordington 11 J4
Lord's Cricket Ground & Museum GtLon NW8 8QN 102 G6
Lord's Hill 10 E3
Lorn 74 B2
Loscoe 41 G1
Loscombe 8 D5
Losgaintir (Luskentyre) 88 F8
Lossiemouth 84 G3
Lossit 72 A5
Lost Gardens of Heligan Corn PL26 6EN 3 G4
Lostock Gralam 49 F5
Lostock Green 49 F5
Lostock Junction 49 F2
Lostwithiel 4 B5
Loth 89 F4
Lothbeg 87 M8
Lothersdale 56 E5
Lotherton Hall Estate WYorks LS25 3EB 57 K6
Lothmore 87 M8
Loudwater 22 C2
Lough Gilly 93 F13
Loughan 92 D4
Loughans 93 B11
Loughash 90 M6
Loughborough 41 H4
Loughbrickland 93 G12
Loughgall 93 E11
Loughguile 92 F4
Loughinisland 93 K12
Loughmacrory 90 M9
Loughor 17 J6
Loughton Essex 23 H2
Loughton MK 32 B5
Loughton Shrop 39 F7
Louis Tussaud's Waxworks FY1 5AA 121 Blackpool
Lound Lincs 42 D4
Lound Notts 51 J4
Lound Suff 45 K6
Lount 41 F4
Louth 53 G4
Love Clough 56 D7
Lovedean 11 H3
Lover 10 D3
Loversall 51 H3
Loves Green 24 C1
Lovesome Hill 62 D7
Loveston 16 D5
Lovington 8 E1
Low Ackworth 51 G1
Low Angerton 71 F5
Low Ballevain 66 A1
Low Barlay 65 F5
Low Barlings 52 D5
Low Bentham (Lower Bentham) 56 B3
Low Bolton 62 A7
Low Bradfield 50 E3
Low Bradley (Bradley) 57 F5
Low Braithwaite 60 F2
Low Brunton 70 E6
Low Burnham 51 K2
Low Burton 57 H1
Low Buston 71 H3
Low Catton 58 D4
Low Coniscliffe 62 C5
Low Craighead 67 G3
Low Dinsdale 62 D5
Low Ellington 57 H1
Low Entercommon 62 D6
Low Etherley 62 B4
Low Fell 62 C1
Low Gate 70 E7
Low Grantley 57 H2
Low Green 34 C2
Low Habberley 29 H1
Low Ham 8 D2
Low Hawsker 63 K6
Low Haygarth 61 H7
Low Hesket 61 F2
Low Hesleyhurst 71 F4
Low Hutton 58 D3
Low Kingthorpe 58 E1
Low Laithe 57 G3
Low Langton 52 E5
Low Leighton 50 C4
Low Lorton 60 C4
Low Marishes 58 E2
Low Marnham 52 B6
Low Middleton 77 K7
Low Mill 63 G7
Low Moor Lancs 56 C5
Low Moor WYorks 57 G7
Low Moorsley 62 D2
Low Moresby 60 A4
Low Newton-by-the-Sea 71 H1
Low Row Cumb 70 A7
Low Row NYorks 61 L7
Low Stillaig 73 H4
Low Street 44 E5
Low Tharston 45 F6
Low Torry 75 J2
Low Town 71 G3
Low Toynton 53 F5
Low Wood 55 G1
Low Worsall 62 D6
Lowbands 29 G5
Lowdham 41 J1
Lowe 38 E2
Lowe Hill 49 J7
Lower Aisholt 8 B1
Lower Apperley 29 H6
Lower Arncott 31 H7
Lower Ashtead 22 E6
Lower Ashton 7 G7
Lower Assendon 22 A3
Lower Auchalick 73 H3
Lower Ballam 55 G6
Lower Ballinderry 93 G10
Lower Barewood 28 C3
Lower Bartle 55 H6
Lower Bayble (Pabail Iarach) 88 L4
Lower Beeding 13 F4
Lower Benefield 42 C7
Lower Bentham (Low Bentham) 56 B3
Lower Bentley 29 J2
Lower Berry Hill 28 E7
Lower Birchwood 51 G7
Lower Boddington 31 F3
Lower Boscaswell 2 A5
Lower Bourne 22 B7
Lower Brailes 30 E5
Lower Breakish 82 G8
Lower Bredbury 49 J3
Lower Broadheath 29 H3
Lower Brynamman 27 G7
Lower Bullingham 28 E5
Lower Bullington 21 H7
Lower Burgate 10 C3
Lower Burrow 8 D2
Lower Burton 28 D3
Lower Caldecote 32 E4
Lower Cam 20 A1
Lower Cambourne 33 G3
Lower Chapel 27 K5
Lower Cheriton 7 K5
Lower Chicksgrove 9 J1
Lower Chute 21 G6
Lower Clent 40 B7
Lower Creedy 7 G5
Lower Cumberworth 50 E2
Lower Darkley 93 D13
Lower Darwen 56 B7
Lower Dean 32 D2
Lower Diabaig 82 H4
Lower Dicker 13 J5
Lower Dinchope 38 D7
Lower Down 38 C7
Lower Drift 2 B6
Lower Dunsforth 57 K3
Lower Earley 22 A4
Lower Edmonton 23 G2
Lower Elkstone 50 C7
Lower End Bucks 21 K1
Lower End MK 32 C5
Lower End N'hants 32 B2
Lower Everleigh 20 E6
Lower Eythorne 15 H3
Lower Failand 19 J4
Lower Farringdon 11 J1
Lower Fittleworth 12 D5
Lower Foxdale 54 B6
Lower Freystrop 16 C4
Lower Froyle 22 A7
Lower Gabwell 5 K4
Lower Gledfield 83 R1
Lower Godney 19 H7
Lower Gravenhurst 32 E5
Lower Green Essex 33 H5
Lower Green Herts 32 E5
Lower Green Kent 23 K7
Lower Green Norf 44 D2
Lower Green Staffs 40 B5
Lower Green Bank 55 J4
Lower Halstock Leigh 8 E4
Lower Halstow 24 E5
Lower Hardres 15 G2
Lower Harpton 28 B2
Lower Hartshay 51 F7
Lower Hartwell 31 J7
Lower Hawthwaite 55 F1
Lower Haysden 23 J7
Lower Hayton 38 E7
Lower Heath 49 H6
Lower Hergest 28 B3
Lower Heyford 31 F6
Lower Higham 24 D4
Lower Holbrook 35 F5
Lower Hopton 50 E1
Lower Hordley 38 C3
Lower Horncroft 12 D5
Lower Horsebridge 13 J5
Lower Houses 50 D1
Lower Howsell 29 G4
Lower Kersal 49 H2
Lower Kilchattan 72 B1
Lower Kilcott 20 A3
Lower Killeyan 72 A6
Lower Kingcombe 8 E5
Lower Kingswood 23 F6
Lower Kinnerton 48 C6
Lower Langford 19 H5
Lower Largo 81 K10
Lower Leigh 40 C2
Lower Lemington 30 D5
Lower Lovacott 6 D3
Lower Loxhore 6 E2
Lower Lydbrook 28 E7
Lower Lye 28 D2
Lower Machen 19 F3
Lower Maes-coed 28 C5
Lower Mannington 10 B4
Lower Middleton Cheney 31 G4
Lower Milton 19 J7
Lower Moor 29 J4
Lower Morton 19 K2
Lower Nash 16 D5
Lower Nazeing 23 G1
Lower Netchwood 39 F6
Lower Nyland 9 G2
Lower Oddington 30 D6
Lower Penarth 18 E4
Lower Penn 40 A6
Lower Pennington 10 E5
Lower Peover 49 G5
Lower Pollicott 31 J7
Lower Quinton 30 C4
Lower Race 19 F1
Lower Rainham 24 E5
Lower Roadwater 7 J2
Lower Sapey 29 F2
Lower Seagry 20 C3
Lower Shelton 32 C4
Lower Shiplake 22 A4
Lower Shuckburgh 31 F2
Lower Slaughter 30 C6
Lower Soothill 57 H7
Lower Stanton St. Quintin 20 C3
Lower Stoke 24 E4
Lower Stondon 32 E5
Lower Stone 19 K2
Lower Stonnall 40 C5
Lower Stow Bedon 44 D6
Lower Street Dorset 9 H5
Lower Street ESuss 14 C6
Lower Street Norf 45 F2
Lower Street Norf 45 G2
Lower Street Suff 35 F3
Lower Stretton 49 F4
Lower Sundon 32 D6
Lower Swanwick 11 F4
Lower Swell 30 C6
Lower Tadmarton 31 F5
Lower Tale 7 J5
Lower Tean 40 C2
Lower Thurlton 45 J6
Lower Thurnham 55 H4
Lower Town Corn 2 D6
Lower Town Devon 5 H3
Lower Town IoS 2 C1
Lower Town Pembs 16 C2
Lower Trebullett 4 D3
Lower Tysoe 30 E4
Lower Upcott 7 G7
Lower Upham 11 G3
Lower Upnor 24 D4
Lower Vexford 7 K2
Lower Wallop 38 C5
Lower Walton 49 F4
Lower Waterhay 20 D2
Lower Weald 31 J5
Lower Wear 7 H7
Lower Weare 19 H6
Lower Welson 28 B3
Lower Whatley 20 A7
Lower Whitley 49 F5
Lower Wick 29 H3
Lower Wield 21 K7
Lower Winchendon (Nether Winchendon) 31 J7
Lower Withington 49 H6
Lower Woodend 22 B3
Lower Woodford 10 C1
Lower Wyche 29 G4
Lowerhouse 56 D6
Lowertown 90 L6
Lowesby 42 A5
Lowestoft 45 K6
Loweswater 60 C4
Lowfield Heath 23 F7
Lowgill Cumb 61 H7
Lowgill Lancs 56 B3
Lowick Cumb 55 F1
Lowick N'hants 42 C7
Lowick N'umb 77 J7
Lowick Bridge 55 F1
Lowick Green 55 F1
Lowry, The GtMan M50 3AZ 114 F4
Lowsonford 30 C2
Lowther 61 G4
Lowthorpe 59 G3
Lowton Devon 6 E5
Lowton GtMan 49 F3
Lowton Som 7 K4
Lowton Common 49 F3
Lowtown 93 H12
Loxbeare 7 H4
Loxhill 12 D3
Loxhore 6 E2
Loxley 30 D3
Loxley Green 40 C2
Loxton 19 G6
Loxwood 12 D3
Lubcroy 86 F9
Lubenham 42 A7
Lubmore 83 L5
Luccombe 7 H1
Luccombe Village 11 G6
Lucker 77 K7
Luckett 4 D3
Luckington 20 B3
Luckwell Bridge 7 H2
Lucton 28 D2
Lucy Cross 62 C5
Ludag 88 B7
Ludborough 53 F3
Ludbrook 5 G5
Ludchurch 16 E4
Luddenden 57 F7
Luddenden Foot 57 F7
Luddenham Court 25 F5
Luddesdown 24 C5
Luddington NLincs 52 B1
Luddington Warks 30 C3
Luddington in the Brook 42 E7
Ludford Lincs 52 E4
Ludford Shrop 28 E1
Ludgershall Bucks 31 H7
Ludgershall Wilts 21 F6
Ludgvan 2 C5
Ludham 45 H4
Ludlow 28 E1
Ludney 53 G3
Ludstock 29 F5
Ludstone 40 A6
Ludwell 9 J2
Ludworth 62 D2
Luffincott 6 B6
Luffness 76 C2
Lufton 8 E3
Lugar 67 K1
Luggate 76 D3
Luggate Burn 76 E3
Luggiebank 75 F3
Lugton 74 C5
Lugwardine 28 E4
Luib 82 F8
Luing 79 J9
Lulham 28 D4
Lullington Derbys 40 E4
Lullington Som 20 A6
Lulsgate Bottom 19 J5
Lulsley 29 G3
Lulworth Camp 9 H6
Lulworth Cove & Heritage Centre Dorset BH20 5RQ 9 H7
Lumb Lancs 56 D7
Lumb WYorks 57 F7
Lumbutts 56 E7
Lumby 57 K6
Lumphanan 85 K10
Lumphinnans 75 K1
Lumsdaine 77 G4
Lumsdale 51 F6
Lunan 81 M5
Lunanhead 81 K5
Luncarty 80 F8
Lund ERid 59 F5
Lund NYorks 58 C6
Lunderston Bay Invcly PA16 0DN 74 A3
Lundin Links 81 K10
Lundwood 51 F2
Lundy 6 A1
Luney 92 D7
Lunga 79 K10
Lunna 89 N6
Lunning 89 P6
Lunnon 17 J7
Lunsford's Cross 14 C6
Lunt 48 C2
Luntley 28 C3
Luppitt 7 K5
Lupset 51 F1
Lupton 55 J1
Lurgan 93 F11
Lurgashall 12 C4
Lurgill 93 G9
Lusby 53 G6
Luss 74 B1
Lussagiven 72 E2
Lusta 82 C5
Lustleigh 7 F7
Luston 28 D2
Luthermuir 81 M4
Luthrie 81 J9
Luton Devon 5 K3
Luton Devon 7 J5
Luton Luton 32 D6
Luton Med 24 D5
Luton Airport 32 E6
Lutterworth 41 H7
Lutton Devon 5 F5
Lutton Dorset 9 J6
Lutton Lincs 43 H3
Lutton N'hants 42 E7
Luxborough 7 H2
Luxulyan 4 A5
Lybster 87 Q6
Lydacott 6 C5
Lydbury North 38 C7
Lydcott 6 E2
Lydd 15 F5
Lydden 15 H3
Lyddington 42 B6
Lydd-on-Sea 15 F5
Lyde Green 19 K4
Lydeard St. Lawrence 7 K2
Lydford 6 D7
Lydford-on-Fosse 8 E1
Lydgate GtMan 49 J1
Lydgate GtMan 49 J2
Lydgate WYorks 56 E7
Lydham 38 C6
Lydiard Millicent 20 D3
Lydiard Tregoze 20 E3
Lydiate 48 C2
Lydlinch 9 G3
Lydney 19 K1
Lydstep 16 D6
Lye 40 B7
Lye Cross 19 H5
Lye Green Bucks 22 C1
Lye Green ESuss 13 J3
Lye Green Warks 30 C2
Lye's Green 20 B7
Lyford 21 G2
Lymbridge Green 15 G3
Lyme Regis 8 C5
Lyminge 15 G3
Lymington 10 E5
Lyminster 12 D6
Lymm 49 F4
Lymore 10 D5
Lympne 15 G4
Lympsham 19 G6
Lympstone 7 H7
Lynaberack 84 B11
Lynch 7 G1
Lynch Green 45 F5
Lynchat 84 B10
Lyndhurst 10 D4
Lyndon 42 C5
Lyne ScBord 76 A6
Lyne Surr 22 D5
Lyne Down 29 F5
Lyne of Gorthleck 83 R8
Lyne of Skene 85 M9
Lyne Station 76 A6
Lyneal 38 D2
Lyneham Oxon 30 D6
Lyneham Wilts 20 D4
Lyneholmeford 70 A6
Lynemore 84 E8
Lynemouth 71 H4
Lyness 89 C8
Lynford 44 C6
Lyng 44 E4
Lyngate 45 H3
Lynmouth 7 F1
Lynn 39 G4
Lynsted 25 F5
Lynstone 6 A5
Lynton 7 F1
Lynton & Lynmouth Cliff Railway Devon EX35 6EP 7 F1
Lyon's Gate 9 F4
Lyonshall 28 C3
Lyrabus 72 A4
Lytchett Matravers 9 J5
Lytchett Minster 9 J5
Lyth 87 Q3
Lytham 55 G7
Lytham St. Anne's 55 G7
Lythe 63 J5
Lythe Hill 12 C3
Lythes 89 D9

M

Mabe Burnthouse 2 E5
Mabie 65 K3
Mablethorpe 53 J4
Macclesfield 49 J5
Macclesfield Forest 49 J5
Macduff 85 M4
Macfinn 92 D4
Machan 75 F5
Machany 80 D9
Macharioch 66 B3
Machen 19 F3
Machrie A&B 72 A4
Machrie A&B 72 B6
Machrie NAyr 73 G7
Machrihanish 66 A1
Machrins 72 B1
Machynlleth 37 G5
Mackan 91 J13
Mackerye End 32 E7
Mackworth 41 F2
Macmerry 76 C3
Macosquin 92 D4
Madame Tussauds GtLon NW1 5LR 102 H6
Maddan 93 D13
Madderty 80 E8
Maddiston 75 H3
Madehurst 12 C5
Madeley Staffs 39 G1
Madeley Tel&W 39 G5
Madeley Heath 39 G1
Maders 4 D3
Madford 7 K4
Madingley 33 G2
Madjeston 9 H2
Madley 28 D5
Madresfield 29 H4
Madron 2 B5
Maenaddwyn 46 C4
Maenclochog 16 D3
Maendy Cardiff 18 E4
Maendy VGlam 18 D4
Maenporth 2 E6
Maentwrog 37 F1
Maen-y-groes 26 C3
Maer Corn 6 A5
Maer Staffs 39 G2
Maerdy Carmar 17 K3
Maerdy Carmar 17 K3
Maerdy Conwy 37 K1
Maerdy RCT 18 C2
Maesbrook 38 B3
Maesbury Marsh 38 C3
Maes-glas 19 F3
Maesgwynne 17 F3
Maeshafn 48 B6
Maeshowe (Heart of Neolithic Orkney) Ork KW16 3LB 89 C6
Maesllyn 17 G1
Maesmynis 27 K4
Maesteg 18 B2
Maes-Treylow 28 B2
Maesybont 17 J4
Maesycrugiau 17 H1
Maesycwmmer 18 E2
Magdalen Laver 23 J1
Maggieknockater 84 H6
Maggots End 33 H6
Maghaberry 93 G10
Magham Down 13 K5
Maghera Mid Ulster 92 D6
Maghera NM&D 93 J13
Magherabane 92 H7
Magheraboy 92 F5
Magherafelt 92 D7
Magheralane 92 F7
Magheralin 93 G11
Magherally 93 G12
Magheralough D&S 90 K8
Magheralough F&O 91 K11
Magheramason 90 K5
Magheramayo 93 H13
Magheramore 92 D5
Magheramorne 92 K7
Magherasaul 93 J13
Magheraveely 91 L14
Maghery AB&C 93 E10
Maghery AB&C 93 D12
Maghery NM&D 93 H15
Maghull 48 C2
Magilligan 92 B3
Magna Centre, Rotherham SYorks S60 1DX 111 D2
Magna Park 41 H7
Magonragh 91 K12
Magor 19 H3
Magpie Green 34 E1
Maguiresbridge 91 K13
Maiden Bradley 9 G1
Maiden Head 19 J5
Maiden Law 62 B2
Maiden Newton 8 E5
Maiden Wells 16 C6
Maidencombe 5 K4
Maidenhayne 8 B5
Maidenhead 22 B3
Maidens 67 G3
Maiden's Green 22 B4
Maidensgrove 22 A3
Maidenwell Corn 4 B3
Maidenwell Lincs 53 G5
Maidford 31 H3
Maids' Moreton 31 J5
Maidstone 14 C2
Maidwell 31 J1
Mail 89 N10
Maindee 19 G3
Maine 90 M9
Mainland Ork 89 B6
Mainland Shet 89 M7
Mains of Tig 67 F5
Mains of Watten 87 Q4
Mainsforth 62 D3
Mainsriddle 65 K5
Mainstone 38 B7
Maisemore 29 H6
Maizestown 92 E6
Major's Green 30 C1
Makendon 70 D3
Makeney 41 F1
Makerstoun 76 E7
Malborough 5 H7
Malden Rushett 22 E5
Maldon 24 E1
Malham 56 E3
Malin Bridge 51 F4
Mallaig (Malaig) 82 G11
Mallaigvaig 82 G11
Malleny Mills 75 K4
Malletsheugh 74 D5
Mallows Green 33 H6
Malltraeth 46 C6
Mallusk 92 H8
Mallwyd 37 H4
Malmesbury 20 C3
Malmsmead 7 F1
Malpas ChesW&C 38 D1
Malpas Corn 3 F4
Malpas Newport 19 G2
Maltby Lincs 53 G4
Maltby Stock 62 E5
Maltby SYorks 51 H3
Maltby le Marsh 53 H4
Malting End 34 B3
Malting Green 34 D7
Maltman's Hill 14 D3
Malton 58 D2
Malvern Link 29 G4
Malvern Wells 29 G4
Mambeg 74 A2
Mamble 29 F1
Mamhead 7 H7
Mamhilad 19 G1
Manaccan 2 E6
Manadon 4 E5
Manafon 38 A5
Manaton 7 F7
Manby 53 G4
Mancetter 41 F6
Manchester 49 H3
Manchester Airport 49 H4
Manchester Apollo GtMan M12 6AP 133 H6
Manchester Art Gallery GtMan M2 3JL 133 E4
Manchester Central GtMan M2 3GX 133 D5
Manchester Craft & Design Centre GtMan M4 5JD 133 F3
Manchester Museum GtMan M13 9PL 115 H4
Manchester United Museum & Stadium Tour Centre GtMan M16 0RA 115 G4
Mancot Royal 48 C6
Mandally (Manndalaidh) 83 N10
Manea 43 H7
Maneight 67 K3
Manfield 62 C5
Mangarstadh 88 F4
Mangerton 8 D5
Mangotsfield 19 K4
Mangrove Green 32 E6
Mankinholes 56 E7
Manley 48 E5
Manmoel 18 E1
Manningford Abbots 20 E6
Manningford Bohune 20 E6
Manningford Bruce 20 E6
Manningham 57 G6
Mannings Amusement Park Suff IP11 2DW 35 G5
Mannings Heath 13 F4
Mannington 10 B4
Manningtree 35 F5
Manor Farm Country Park Hants SO30 2ER 96 E4
Manor Park 22 C3
Manorbier 16 D6
Manorbier Newton 16 D5
Manordeifi 17 F1
Manordeilo 17 K3
Manorowen 16 C2
Mansell Gamage 28 C4
Mansell Lacy 28 D4
Mansergh 56 B1
Mansfield 51 H6
Mansfield Woodhouse 51 H6
Manson Green 44 E5
Mansriggs 55 F1
Manston Dorset 9 H3
Manston Kent 25 K5
Manston WYorks 57 J6
Manswood 9 J4
Manthorpe Lincs 42 C2
Manthorpe Lincs 42 D4
Manton NLincs 52 C2
Manton Notts 51 H5
Manton Rut 42 B5
Manton Wilts 20 E5
Manuden 33 H6
Manwood Green 33 J7
Maperton 9 F2
Maple Cross 22 D2
Maplebeck 51 K6
Mapledurham 21 K4
Mapledurwell 21 K6
Maplehurst 12 E4
Maplescombe 23 J5
Mapleton 40 D1
Mapperley Derbys 41 G1
Mapperley Notts 41 H1
Mapperton Dorset 8 E5
Mapperton Dorset 9 J5
Mappleborough Green 30 B2
Mappleton 59 J5
Mapplewell 51 F2
Mappowder 9 G4
Mar Lodge 84 E11
Màraig (Maaruig) 88 H7
Marazion 2 C5
Marbury 38 E1
Marbury Country Park ChesW&C CW9 6AT 49 F5
March 43 H6
Marcham 21 H2
Marchamley 38 E3
Marchamley Wood 38 E2
Marchington 40 D2
Marchington Woodlands 40 D3
Marchwiel 38 C1
Marchwood 10 E3
Marcross 18 C5
Marden Here 28 E4
Marden Kent 14 C3
Marden T&W 71 J6
Marden Wilts 20 D6
Marden Ash 23 J1
Marden Beech 14 C3
Marden Thorn 14 C3
Marden's Hill 13 H3
Mardon 77 H7
Mardy 28 C7
Mare Green 8 C2
Marefield 42 A5
Mareham le Fen 53 F6
Mareham on the Hill 53 F6
Maresfield 13 H4
Marfleet 59 H6
Marford 48 C7
Margam 18 A3
Margam Country Park NPT SA13 2TJ 18 B3
Margaret Marsh 9 H3
Margaret Roding 33 J7
Margaretting 24 C1
Margaretting Tye 24 C1
Margate 25 K4
Marganaheglish 73 J7
Margreig 65 J3
Margrove Park 63 G5
Marham 44 B5
Marhamchurch 6 A5
Marholm 42 E5
Marian Cwm 47 J5
Mariandyrys 46 E4
Marian-glas 46 D4
Mariansleigh 7 F3
Marine Town 25 F4
Marishader 82 E4
Maristow House 4 E4
Maritime Greenwich GtLon SE10 9NF 105 D8
Mark 19 G7
Mark Causeway 19 G7
Mark Cross 13 J3
Markbeech 23 H7
Markby 53 H5
Markdhu 64 B3
Markeaton 41 F2
Markeaton Park Craft Village Derby DE22 3BG 108 B4
Market Bosworth 41 G5
Market Bosworth Country Park Leics CV13 0LP 41 G5
Market Deeping 42 E4
Market Drayton 39 F2
Market Harborough 42 A7
Market Lavington 20 D6
Market Overton 42 B4
Market Rasen 52 E4
Market Stainton 53 F5
Market Street 45 G3
Market Warsop 51 H6
Market Weighton 58 E5
Market Weston 34 D1
Markethill 93 E13
Markfield 41 G4
Markham 18 E1
Markham Moor 51 K5
Markinch 80 H10
Markington 57 H3
Marks Gate 23 H2
Marks Tey 34 D6
Marksbury 19 K5
Markwell 4 D5
Markyate 32 D7
Marl Bank 29 G4
Marland 49 H1
Marlborough 20 E5
Marlbrook 29 J1
Marlcliff 30 B3
Marldon 5 J4
Marle Green 13 J5
Marlesford 35 H3
Marley Green 38 E1
Marley Hill 62 C1
Marlingford 45 F5
Marloes 16 A5
Marlow Bucks 22 B3
Marlow Here 28 D1
Marlpit Hill 23 H7
Marlpool 41 G1
Marnhull 9 G3
Marnoch 85 K5
Marple 49 J4
Marple Bridge 49 J4
Marr 51 H2
Marrel 87 N8
Marrick 62 A7
Marrister 89 P6
Marros 17 F5
Marsden T&W 71 J7
Marsden WYorks 50 C1
Marsett 56 E1
Marsh 8 B3
Marsh Baldon 21 J2
Marsh Benham 21 H5
Marsh Farm Country Park Essex CM3 5WP 24 E2
Marsh Gibbon 31 H6
Marsh Green Devon 7 J6
Marsh Green GtMan 48 E2
Marsh Green Kent 23 H7
Marsh Green Tel&W 39 F4
Marsh Lane 51 G5
Marsh Street 7 H1
Marshall Meadows 77 H5
Marshallstown 93 K12
Marshalsea 8 C4
Marshalswick 22 E1
Marsham 45 F3
Marshaw 55 J4
Marshborough 15 J2
Marshbrook 38 D7
Marshchapel 53 G3
Marshfield Newport 19 F3
Marshfield SGlos 20 A4
Marshgate 4 B1
Marshland St. James 43 J5
Marshside 48 C1
Marshwood 8 C5
Marske 62 B6
Marske-by-the-Sea 63 G4
Marsland Green 49 F3
Marston ChesW&C 49 F5
Marston Here 28 C3
Marston Lincs 42 B1
Marston Oxon 21 J1
Marston Staffs 40 A4
Marston Staffs 40 B3
Marston Warks 40 E6
Marston Wilts 20 C6
Marston Doles 31 F3
Marston Green 40 D7
Marston Magna 8 E2
Marston Meysey 20 E2
Marston Montgomery 40 D2
Marston Moretaine 32 C4
Marston on Dove 40 E3
Marston St. Lawrence 31 G4
Marston Stannett 28 E3
Marston Trussell 41 J7
Marston Vale Millennium Country Park CenBeds MK43 0PR 32 D4
Marstow 28 E7
Marsworth 32 C7
Marten 21 F5
Marthall 49 G5
Martham 45 J4
Martin Hants 10 B3
Martin Lincs 52 E7
Martin Lincs 53 F6
Martin Drove End 10 B2
Martin Hussingtree 29 H2
Martin Mere Lancs L40 0TA 48 D1
Martinhoe 6 E1
Martinscroft 49 F4
Martinstown Dorset 9 F6
Martinstown M&EAnt 92 G5
Martinstown NM&D 93 K12
Martlesham 35 G4
Martlesham Heath 35 G4
Martletwy 16 D4
Martley 29 G2
Martock 8 D3
Marton ChesE 49 H6
Marton Cumb 55 F2
Marton ERid 59 H6
Marton ERid 59 J3
Marton Lincs 52 B4
Marton Middl 63 F5
Marton NYorks 57 K3
Marton NYorks 58 D1
Marton Shrop 38 B5
Marton Shrop 38 D3
Marton Warks 31 F2
Marton Abbey 58 B3
Marton-in-the-Forest 58 B3
Marton-le-Moor 57 J2
Martyr Worthy 11 G1
Martyr's Green 22 D6
Marwell Zoo Hants SO21 1JH 96 E1
Marwick 89 B5
Marwood 6 D2
Mary Rose PO1 3LX 135 Portsmouth
Mary Tavy 5 F3
Marybank (An Lagaidh) High 83 Q5
Marybank Na H-E. Siar 88 K4
Maryburgh (Baile Mairi) 83 R5
Maryfield Corn 4 E5
Maryfield Shet 89 N8
Marygold 77 G5
Maryhill Aber 85 N6
Maryhill Glas 74 D4
Marykirk 81 M4
Marylebone GtLon 23 F3
Marylebone GtMan 48 E2
Marypark 84 F7
Maryport Cumb 60 B3
Maryport D&G 64 B7
Marystow 6 C7
Marywell Aber 85 K11
Marywell Angus 81 M6
Masham 57 H1
Mashbury 33 K7
Masongill 56 B2
Mastin Moor 51 G5
Mastrick 85 P10
Matchborough 30 B2
Matching 33 J7
Matching Green 33 J7
Matching Tye 33 J7
Matfen 71 F6
Matfield 23 K7
Mathern 19 J2
Mathon 29 G4
Mathry 16 B2
Matlaske 45 F2
Matlock 51 F6
Matlock Bank 51 F6
Matlock Bath 50 E7
Matson 29 H7
Matterdale End 60 E4
Mattersey 51 J4
Mattersey Thorpe 51 J4
Mattingley 22 A6
Mattishall 44 E4
Mattishall Burgh 44 E4
Mauchline 67 J1
Maud 85 P6
Maufant 3 K7
Maugersbury 30 C6
Maughold 54 D4
Maulden 32 D5
Maulds Meaburn 61 H5
Maunby 57 J1
Maund Bryan 28 E3
Maundown 7 J3
Mautby 45 J4
Mavesyn Ridware 40 C4
Mavis Enderby 53 G6
Maw Green 49 G7
Mawbray 60 B2
Mawdesley 48 D1
Mawdlam 18 B3
Mawgan 2 E6
Mawgan Porth 3 F2
Mawla 2 E4
Mawnan 2 E6
Mawnan Smith 2 E6
Mawsley 32 B1
Mawthorpe 53 H5
Maxey 42 E5
Maxstoke 40 E7
Maxted Street 15 G3
Maxton Kent 15 J3
Maxton ScBord 76 E7
Maxwellheugh 77 F7
Maxwelltown 65 K3
Maxworthy 4 C1
May Hill 29 G6
Mayals 17 K6
Maybole 67 H3
Maybury 22 D6
Mayfair 23 F3
Mayfield ESuss 13 J4
Mayfield Midlo 76 B4
Mayfield Staffs 40 D1
Mayford 22 C6
Mayland 25 F1
Maylandsea 25 F1
Maynard's Green 13 J5
Mayobridge 93 G14
Mayoghill 92 D5
Maypole IoS 2 C1
Maypole Kent 25 H5
Maypole Mon 28 D7
Maypole Green Essex 34 D6
Maypole Green Norf 45 J6
Maypole Green Suff 34 D3
Maypole Green Suff 35 G2
May's Corner 93 G13
May's Green NSom 19 G5
Mays Green Oxon 22 A3
Maytown 93 F14
Maywick 89 M10
Mazetown 93 H10
McGregor's Corner 92 G5
McInroy's Point 74 A3
Mead 6 A4
Mead End 10 B2
Meadgate 19 K6
Meadle 22 B1
Meadow Green 29 G3
Meadowhall 51 F3
Meadowmill 76 C3
Meadowtown 38 C5
Meadwell 6 C7
Meaford 40 A2
Meal Bank 61 G7
Mealough 93 J10
Meals 53 H3
Mealsgate 60 D2
Meanley 56 C5
Meanwood 57 H6
Mearbeck 56 D3
Meare 19 H7
Meare Green 8 B2
Mearns 74 D5
Mears Ashby 32 B2
Measham 41 F4
Meathop 55 H1
Meavag 88 G8
Meavy 5 F4
Medbourne 42 B6
Meddon 6 A4
Meden Vale 51 H6
Medlar 55 H6
Medmenham 22 B3
Medomsley 62 B1
Medstead 11 H1
Meenawaddy 90 L7
Meentullyclogh 91 H9
Meer Common 28 C3
Meer End 30 D1
Meerbrook 49 J6
Meesden 33 H5
Meeson 39 F3
Meeth 6 D5
Meeting House Hill 45 H3
Megarrystown 93 G11
Meggethead 69 G1
Meidrim 17 F3
Meifod Denb 47 J7
Meifod Powys 38 A4
Meigh 93 F14
Meigle 80 H6
Meikle Earnock 75 F5
Meikle Grenach 73 J4
Meikle Kilmory 73 J4
Meikle Rahane 74 A2
Meikle Wartle 85 M7
Meikleour 80 G7
Meikleyard 74 D7
Meinciau 17 H4
Meir 40 B1
Meirheath 40 B1
Melbost 88 K4
Melbost Borve (Mealabost) 88 K2
Melbourn 33 G4
Melbourne Derbys 41 F3
Melbourne ERid 58 D5
Melbury 6 B4
Melbury Abbas 9 H3
Melbury Bubb 8 E4
Melbury Osmond 8 E4
Melbury Sampford 8 E4
Melby 89 K7
Melchbourne 32 D2
Melcombe Bingham 9 G4
Melcombe Regis 9 F6
Meldon Devon 6 D6
Meldon N'umb 71 G5
Meldreth 33 G4
Meledor 3 G3
Melfort 79 K9
Melgarve 83 Q11
Meliden (Gallt Melyd) 47 J4
Melincourt 18 B1
Melin-y-coed 47 G6
Melin-y-ddol 37 K5
Melin-y-grug 37 K5
Melin-y-Wig 37 K1
Melkinthorpe 61 G4
Melkridge 70 C7
Melksham 20 C5
Melksham Forest 20 C5
Melldalloch 73 H3
Melling Lancs 55 J2
Melling Mersey 48 C2
Melling Mount 48 D2
Mellis 34 E1
Mellon Charles 83 J1
Mellon Udrigle 83 J1
Mellor GtMan 49 J4
Mellor Lancs 56 B6
Mellor Brook 56 B6
Mells 20 A7
Melmerby Cumb 61 H3
Melmerby NYorks 57 F1
Melmerby NYorks 57 J2
Melplash 8 D5
Melrose Aber 85 M4
Melrose ScBord 76 D7
Melsetter 89 B9
Melsonby 62 B6
Meltham 50 C1
Melton ERid 59 F7
Melton Suff 35 G3
Melton Constable 44 E2
Melton Mowbray 42 A4
Melton Ross 52 D1
Meltonby 58 D4
Melvaig 82 H2
Melverley 38 C4
Melverley Green 38 C4
Melvich 87 L3
Membury 8 B4
Memsie 85 P4
Memus 81 K5
Menabilly 4 A5
Menai Bridge (Porthaethwy) 46 D5
Mendham 45 G7
Mendlesham 35 F2
Mendlesham Green 34 E2
Menethorpe 58 D3
Menheniot 4 C4
Menithwood 29 G2
Mennock 68 D3
Menston 57 G5
Menstrie 75 G1
Mentmore 32 C7
Meoble 79 J2
Meole Brace 38 D4
Meon 11 G4
Meonstoke 11 H3
Meopham 24 C5
Meopham Green 24 C5
Mepal 43 H7
Meppershall 32 E5
Merbach 28 C4
Mercaston 40 E1
Mere ChesE 49 G4
Mere Wilts 9 H1
Mere Brow 48 D1
Mere Green 40 D6
Mere Heath 49 F5
Mereclough 56 D6
Mereside 55 G6
Meretown 39 G3
Mereworth 23 K6
Meriden 40 E7
Merkadale 82 D7
Merkland 65 H3
Merley 10 B5
Merlin's Bridge 16 C4
Merridge 8 B1
Merrifield 5 J6
Merrington 38 D3
Merrion 16 C6
Merriott 8 D3
Merrivale 5 F3
Merrow 22 D6
Merry Hill Herts 22 E2
Merry Hill WMid 40 A6
Merry Hill WMid 40 B7
Merrymeet 4 C4
Mersea Island 34 E7
Mersey Ferries Mersey CH44 6QY 131 A4
Merseyside Maritime Museum Mersey L3 4AQ 131 B5
Mersham 15 F4
Merstham 23 F6
Merston 12 B6
Merstone 11 G6
Merther 3 F4
Merthyr 17 G3
Merthyr Cynog 27 J5
Merthyr Dyfan 18 E5
Merthyr Mawr 18 B4
Merthyr Tydfil 18 D1
Merthyr Vale 18 D2
Merton Devon 6 D4
Merton Norf 44 D6
Merton Oxon 31 G7
Mervinslaw 70 B2
Meshaw 7 F4
Messing 34 D7
Messingham 52 B2
Metcombe 7 J6
Metfield 45 G7
Metherell 4 E4
Metheringham 52 D6
Methil 76 B1
Methlem 36 A2
Methley 57 J7
Methley Junction 57 J7
Methlick 85 N7

ewbridge NYorks 58 E1
ewbridge Oxon 21 H1
ewbridge Pembs 16 C2
ewbridge Wrex 38 B1
ewbridge Green 29 H5
ewbridge on Wye 27 K3
ewbridge-on-Usk 19 G2
ewbrough 70 D7
ewbuildings 7 F5
ewburgh Aber 85 P8
ewburgh Fife 80 H9
ewburgh Lancs 48 D1
ewburgh ScBord 69 J1
ewburn 71 G7
ewbury Som 19 K6
ewbury WBerks 21 H5
ewbury Wilts 20 B7
ewbury Park 23 H3
ewby Cumb 61 G4
ewby Lancs 56 D5
ewby NYorks 56 C3
ewby NYorks 59 G1
ewby NYorks 63 F5
ewby Bridge 55 G1
ewby Cote 56 C2
ewby Cross 60 E1
ewby East 61 F1
ewby Hall NYorks HG4 5AE 57 J3
ewby West 60 E1
ewby Wiske 57 J1
ewcastle A&NDown 93 M11
ewcastle Mon 28 D7
ewcastle NM&D 93 J13
ewcastle Shrop 38 B7
ewcastle Bridgend 18 B4
ewcastle Emlyn (Castell Newydd Emlyn) 17 G1
ewcastle International Airport 71 G6
ewcastle upon Tyne 71 H7
ewcastleton 69 K5
ewcastle-under-Lyme 40 A1
ewchapel Pembs 17 F2
ewchapel Staffs 49 H7
ewchapel Surr 23 G7
ewchurch Carmar 17 G3
ewchurch IoW 11 G6
ewchurch Kent 15 F4
ewchurch Lancs 56 D6
ewchurch Lancs 56 D7
ewchurch Mon 19 H2
ewchurch Powys 28 B3
ewchurch Staffs 40 D3
ewcott 8 B4
ewcraighall 76 B3
ewdigate 22 E7
ewell Green 22 B4
ewenden 14 D5
ewent 29 G6
ewerne 19 K1
ewfield Dur 62 C1
ewfield Dur 62 C3
ewfound 21 J6
ewgale 16 B3
ewgate 44 E1
ewgate Street 23 G1
ewhall ChesE 39 F1
ewhall Derbys 40 E3
ewham 71 G1
ewham Hall 71 G1
ewhaven 13 H6
ewhey 49 J1
ewholm 63 J5
ewhouse 75 F4
ewick 13 H4
ewingreen 15 G4
ewington Edin 76 A3
ewington Kent 15 G4
ewington Kent 24 E5
ewington Notts 51 J3
ewington Oxon 21 K2
ewington Bagpath 20 B2
ewland Cumb 55 G2
ewland Glos 19 J1
ewland Hull 59 G6
ewland NYorks 58 C7
ewland Oxon 30 E7
ewland Worcs 29 G4
ewlandrig 76 B4
ewlands Cumb 60 E3
ewlands Essex 24 E3
ewlands N'umb 62 A1
ewlands ScBord 70 A4
ewland's Corner 22 D7
ewlands of Geise 87 N3
ewlyn 2 B6
ewmachar 85 N9
ewmains 75 G5
ewman's End 33 J7
ewman's Green 34 C4
ewmarket Na H-E. Siar 88 K4
ewmarket Suff 33 K2
ewmill Aber 81 N2
ewmill A&N 92 H8
ewmill Moray 85 J5
ewmill ScBord 69 K2
ewmillerdam 51 F1
ewmillerdam Country Park WYorks WF2 6QP 117 L8
ewmills 93 D10
ewmiln 80 G7
ewmilns 74 D7
ewney Green 24 C1
ewnham Glos 29 F7
ewnham Hants 22 A6
ewnham Herts 33 F5
ewnham Kent 14 E2
ewnham N'hants 31 G3
ewnham Bridge 29 F2
ewnham Paddox 41 G7
ewport Corn 6 B7
ewport Devon 6 D2
ewport ERid 58 E6
ewport Essex 33 J5
ewport Glos 19 K2
ewport High 87 P7
ewport IoW 11 G6
ewport (Casnewydd) Newport 19 G3
ewport Norf 45 K4
ewport (Trefdraeth) Pembs 16 D2
ewport Som 8 C2
ewport Tel&W 39 G4
ewport Pagnell 32 B4
ewport-on-Tay 81 K8
ewpound Common 12 D4
ewquay 3 F2
ewquay Zoo Corn TR7 2LZ 3 F2
ewry 93 F14
ewsbank 49 H6
ewseat 85 M7
ewsells 33 G5
ewsham Lancs 55 J6
ewsham NYorks 57 J1
ewsham NYorks 62 B5
ewsham N'umb 71 H6
ewsholme ERid 58 D7
ewsholme Lancs 56 D4
ewsome 50 D1
ewstead Notts 51 H7
ewstead N'umb 71 G1
Newstead ScBord 76 D7
Newstead Abbey Notts NG15 8NA 51 H7
Newthorpe Notts 41 G1
Newthorpe NYorks 57 K6
Newtoft 52 D4
Newton A&B 73 J1
Newton Bridgend 18 B4
Newton Cambs 33 H4
Newton Cambs 43 H4
Newton Cardiff 19 F4
Newton ChesW&C 48 E5
Newton ChesW&C 48 E7
Newton Cumb 55 F2
Newton Derbys 51 G7
Newton D&G 69 G4
Newton GtMan 49 J3
Newton Here 28 C2
Newton Here 28 C5
Newton Here 28 E3
Newton High 83 R5
Newton High 84 B4
Newton High 84 B6
Newton Lancs 55 G6
Newton Lancs 55 J2
Newton Lincs 42 D2
Newton NAyr 73 H5
Newton Norf 44 C4
Newton Notts 41 J1
Newton N'hants 42 B7
Newton N'umb 70 E3
Newton N'umb 71 F7
Newton Pembs 16 B3
Newton Pembs 16 C5
Newton ScBord 70 B1
Newton SGlos 19 K2
Newton Shrop 38 D2
Newton SLan 75 H7
Newton Som 7 K2
Newton Staffs 40 C3
Newton Suff 34 D4
Newton Swan 17 K7
Newton Warks 31 G1
Newton Wilts 10 D2
Newton WLoth 75 J3
Newton WYorks 57 K7
Newton Abbot 5 J3
Newton Arlosh 60 D1
Newton Aycliffe 62 C4
Newton Bewley 62 E4
Newton Blossomville 32 C3
Newton Bromswold 32 C2
Newton Burgoland 41 F5
Newton by Toft 52 D4
Newton Ferrers 5 F6
Newton Flotman 45 G6
Newton Green 19 J2
Newton Harcourt 41 J6
Newton Kyme 57 K5
Newton Longville 32 B5
Newton Mearns 74 D5
Newton Morrell NYorks 62 C6
Newton Morrell Oxon 31 H6
Newton Mountain 16 C5
Newton Mulgrave 63 H5
Newton of Leys 84 A7
Newton on the Hill 38 D3
Newton on Trent 52 B5
Newton Poppleford 7 J7
Newton Purcell 31 H5
Newton Regis 40 E5
Newton Reigny 61 F3
Newton St. Cyres 7 G6
Newton St. Faith 45 G4
Newton St. Loe 20 A5
Newton St. Petrock 6 C4
Newton Stacey 21 H7
Newton Stewart 64 E4
Newton Tony 21 F7
Newton Tracey 6 D3
Newton under Roseberry 63 F5
Newton Underwood 71 G5
Newton upon Derwent 58 D5
Newton Valence 11 J1
Newton with Scales 55 H6
Newtonairds 68 D5
Newtongrange 76 B4
Newtonhill 85 P11
Newton-in-the-Isle 43 H4
Newton-le-Willows Mersey 48 E3
Newton-le-Willows NYorks 57 H1
Newtonmore (Baile Ùr an t-Slèibh) 84 B11
Newton-on-Ouse 58 B4
Newton-on-Rawcliffe 63 J7
Newton-on-the-Moor 71 G3
Newtown Bucks 22 C1
Newtown ChesW&C 48 E7
Newtown Corn 2 C6
Newtown Corn 4 C3
Newtown Cumb 70 A7
Newtown Derbys 49 J4
Newtown Devon 7 F3
Newtown Devon 7 J6
Newtown Dorset 8 D4
Newtown Glos 19 K1
Newtown GtMan 48 E2
Newtown GtMan 49 G2
Newtown Hants 10 D3
Newtown Hants 10 E2
Newtown Hants 11 G3
Newtown Hants 11 H3
Newtown Hants 21 H5
Newtown Here 28 D3
Newtown Here 29 F4
Newtown High 83 P10
Newtown IoM 54 C6
Newtown IoW 11 F5
Newtown NM&D 93 F14
Newtown N'umb 71 F1
Newtown N'umb 71 F3
Newtown Oxon 22 A3
Newtown (Y Drenewydd) Powys 38 A6
Newtown RCT 18 D2
Newtown Shrop 38 D2
Newtown Som 8 B1
Newtown Som 8 B3
Newtown Staffs 40 B5
Newtown Staffs 49 J6
Newtown Staffs 50 C6
Newtown Wilts 9 J2
Newtown Wilts 21 G5
Newtown Crommelin 92 G5
Newtown Linford 41 H5
Newtown St. Boswells 76 D7
Newtown Saville 91 M11
Newtown Unthank 41 G5
Newtownabbey 92 J8
Newtownards 93 K9
Newtownbreda 93 J9
Newtownbutler 91 L14
Newtownhamilton 93 E14
Newtown-in-St-Martin 2 E6
Newtownstewart 90 L8
Newtyle 80 H6
Newyears Green 22 D3
Neyland 16 C5
Nibley Glos 19 K1
Nibley SGlos 19 K3
Nibley Green 20 A2
Nicholashayne 7 K4
Nicholaston 17 J7
Nidd 57 J3
Nigg Aberdeen 85 P10
Nigg High 84 C3
Nightcott 7 G3
Nilig 47 J7
Nilston Rigg 70 D7
Nimlet 20 A4
Nine Ashes 23 J1
Nine Elms 20 E3
Nine Mile Burn 75 K5
Ninebanks 61 J1
Ninemile Bar (Crocketford) 65 J3
Nineveh 29 F2
Ninfield 14 C6
Ningwood 11 F6
Nisbet 70 B1
Niton 11 G7
Nitshill 74 D4
Nixon's Corner 90 L5
Nizels 23 J6
No Man's Heath ChesW&C 38 E1
No Man's Heath Warks 40 E5
No Man's Land 4 C5
Noah's Ark 23 J6
Noak Hill 23 J2
Noblehill 65 K3
Noblethorpe 50 E2
Nobottle 31 H2
Nocton 52 D6
Noddsdale 74 A4
Nogdam End 45 H5
Noke 31 G7
Nolton 16 B4
Nolton Haven 16 B4
Nomansland Devon 7 G4
Nomansland Wilts 10 D3
Noneley 38 D3
Nonington 15 H2
Nook Cumb 55 J1
Nook Cumb 69 K6
Norbreck 55 G5
Norbury ChesE 38 E1
Norbury Derbys 40 D1
Norbury GtLon 23 G4
Norbury Shrop 38 C6
Norbury Staffs 39 G3
Norbury Common 38 E1
Norbury Junction 39 G3
Norchard 16 D6
Norcott Brook 49 F4
Nordelph 43 J5
Norden Dorset 9 J6
Norden GtMan 49 H1
Nordley 39 F6
Norfolk Lavender, Heacham Norf PE31 7JE 44 A2
Norham 77 H6
Norland Town 57 F7
Norley 48 E5
Norleywood 10 E5
Norlington 13 H5
Norman Cross 42 E6
Normanby NLincs 52 B1
Normanby NYorks 58 D1
Normanby R&C 63 F5
Normanby by Stow 52 B4
Normanby Hall Country Park NLincs DN15 9HU 52 B1
Normanby le Wold 52 E3
Normanby-by-Spital 52 D4
Normandy 22 C6
Norman's Bay 13 K6
Norman's Green 7 J5
Normanston 45 K6
Normanton Derby 41 F2
Normanton Leics 42 B1
Normanton Lincs 42 C1
Normanton Notts 51 K7
Normanton Rut 42 C5
Normanton WYorks 57 J7
Normanton le Heath 41 F4
Normanton on Soar 41 H3
Normanton on Trent 51 K6
Normanton-on-the-Wolds 41 J2
Normoss 55 G6
Norrington Common 20 B5
Norris Green 4 E4
Norris Hill 41 F4
Norristhorpe 57 H7
North Acton 23 F3
North Anston 51 H4
North Ascot 22 C5
North Aston 31 F6
North Baddesley 10 E3
North Ballachulish (Baile a' Chaolais a Tuath) 79 M4
North Balloch 67 H4
North Barrow 9 F2
North Barsham 44 D2
North Bay Miniature Railway NYorks YO12 6PF 59 G1
North Benfleet 24 D3
North Bersted 12 C6
North Berwick 76 D2
North Boarhunt 11 H3
North Boisdale 88 B7
North Bovey 7 F7
North Bradley 20 B6
North Brentor 6 C7
North Brewham 9 G1
North Bridge 12 C3
North Buckland 6 C1
North Burlingham 45 H4
North Cadbury 9 F2
North Cairn 66 D6
North Camp 22 B6
North Carlton Lincs 52 C5
North Carlton Notts 51 H4
North Cave 58 E6
North Cerney 20 D1
North Chailey 13 G4
North Charford 10 C3
North Charlton 71 G1
North Cheriton 9 F2
North Chideock 8 D5
North Cliffe 58 E6
North Clifton 52 B5
North Cockerington 53 G3
North Coker 8 E3
North Collafirth 89 M4
North Common SGlos 19 K4
North Common Suff 34 D1
North Connel 79 L7
North Coombe 7 G5
North Cornelly 18 B3
North Corner 19 K3
North Cotes 53 G2
North Cove 45 J7
North Cowton 62 C6
North Crawley 32 C4
North Cray 23 H4
North Creake 44 C2
North Curry 8 C2
North Dalton 59 F4
North Deighton 57 J4
North Dell (Dail Bho Thuath) 88 K1
North Duffield 58 C6
North Elkington 53 F3
North Elmham 44 D3
North Elmsall 51 G1
North End Bucks 32 B6
North End Dorset 9 H2
North End ERid 59 H4
North End ERid 59 H5
North End ERid 59 J6
North End Essex 33 K7
North End Hants 10 C3
North End Hants 11 G2
North End Leics 41 H4
North End Norf 44 E6
North End NSom 19 H5
North End N'umb 71 G3
North End Ports 11 H4
North End WSuss 12 C6
North End WSuss 12 E5
North Erradale 82 H2
North Fambridge 24 E2
North Ferriby 59 F7
North Frodingham 59 H4
North Gorley 10 C3
North Green Norf 45 G7
North Green Suff 35 H1
North Green Suff 35 H2
North Green Suff 35 H2
North Grimston 58 E3
North Halling 24 D5
North Harby 52 B5
North Hayling 11 J4
North Hazelrigg 77 J7
North Heasley 7 F2
North Heath WBerks 21 H4
North Heath WSuss 12 D4
North Hill 4 C3
North Hillingdon 22 D3
North Hinksey 21 H1
North Holmwood 22 E7
North Houghton 10 E1
North Huish 5 H5
North Hykeham 52 C6
North Johnston 16 C4
North Kelsey 52 D2
North Kessock 84 A6
North Killingholme 52 E1
North Kilvington 57 K1
North Kilworth 41 J7
North Kingston 10 C4
North Kyme 52 E7
North Lancing 12 E6
North Lee 22 B1
North Lees 57 J2
North Leigh 30 E7
North Leverton with Habblesthorpe 51 K4
North Littleton 30 B4
North Lopham 44 E7
North Luffenham 42 C5
North Marden 12 B5
North Marston 31 J6
North Middleton Midlo 76 B5
North Middleton N'umb 71 F1
North Molton 7 F3
North Moreton 21 J3
North Mundham 12 B6
North Muskham 51 K7
North Newbald 59 F6
North Newington 31 F5
North Newnton 20 E6
North Newton 8 B1
North Nibley 20 A2
North Norfolk Railway Norf NR26 8RA 45 F1
North Oakley 21 J6
North Ockendon 23 J3
North Ormesby 63 F5
North Ormsby 53 F3
North Otterington 57 J1
North Owersby 52 D3
North Perrott 8 D4
North Petherton 8 B1
North Petherwin 4 C2
North Pickenham 44 C5
North Piddle 29 J3
North Plain 69 G7
North Pool 5 H6
North Poorton 8 E5
North Quarme 7 H2
North Queensferry 75 K2
North Radworthy 7 F2
North Rauceby 42 D1
North Reston 53 G4
North Riding Forest Park NYorks YO18 7LT 63 J7
North Rigton 57 H5
North Rode 49 H6
North Roe 89 M4
North Ronaldsay 89 G2
North Ronaldsay Airfield 89 G2
North Runcton 44 A4
North Sandwick 89 P3
North Scale 54 E3
North Scarle 52 B6
North Seaton 71 H5
North Shields 71 J7
North Shoebury 25 F3
North Side 43 F6
North Skelton 63 G5
North Somercotes 53 H3
North Stainley 57 H2
North Stainmore 61 K5
North Stifford 24 C3
North Stoke B&NESom 20 A5
North Stoke Oxon 21 K3
North Stoke WSuss 12 D5
North Stoneham 11 F3
North Street Hants 11 H1
North Street Kent 15 F2
North Street Med 24 E4
North Street WBerks 21 K4
North Sunderland 77 K7
North Tamerton 6 B6
North Tawton 6 E5
North Third 75 F2
North Thoresby 53 F3
North Tidworth 21 F7
North Togston 71 H3
North Town Devon 6 D5
North Town Hants 22 B6
North Town W&M 22 B3
North Tuddenham 44 E4
North Uist (Uibhist a Tuath) 88 C1
North Walsham 45 G2
North Waltham 21 J7
North Warnborough 22 A6
North Watten 87 Q4
North Weald Bassett 23 H1
North Wembley 22 E3
North Wheatley 51 K4
North Whilborough 5 J4
North Wick 19 J5
North Widcombe 19 J6
North Willingham 52 E4
North Wingfield 51 G6
North Witham 42 C3
North Wootton Dorset 9 F3
North Wootton Norf 44 A3
North Wootton Som 19 J7
North Wraxall 20 B4
North Wroughton 20 E3
North Yardhope 70 E3
North Yorkshire Moors Railway NYorks YO18 7AJ 58 E1
Northacre 44 D6
Northall 32 C6
Northall Green 44 D4
Northallerton 62 D7
Northam Devon 6 C3
Northam Soton 11 F3
Northam Burrows Country Park Devon EX39 1XR 6 C2
Northampton 31 J2
Northaw 23 F1
Northay Devon 8 C4
Northay Som 8 B3
Northbay 88 B8
Northbeck 42 D1
Northborough 42 E5
Northbourne Kent 15 J2
Northbourne Oxon 21 J3
Northbridge Street 14 C5
Northbrook Hants 11 G1
Northbrook Oxon 31 F6
Northchapel 12 C4
Northchurch 22 C1
Northcote Manor 6 E4
Northcott 6 B6
Northcourt 21 J2
Northedge 51 F6
Northend B&NESom 20 A5
Northend Bucks 22 A2
Northend Warks 30 E3
Northfield Hull 59 G7
Northfield ScBord 77 H4
Northfield Som 8 B1
Northfield WMid 30 B1
Northfields 42 D5
Northfleet 24 C4
Northhouse 69 K3
Northiam 14 D5
Northill 32 E4
Northington Glos 20 A1
Northington Hants 11 G1
Northlands 53 G7
Northleach 30 C7
Northleigh Devon 6 E2
Northleigh Devon 7 K6
Northlew 6 D6
Northmoor 21 H1
Northmoor Green (Moorland) 8 C1
Northmuir 81 J5
Northney 11 J4
Northolt 22 E3
Northop (Llaneurgain) 48 B6
Northop Hall 48 B6
Northorpe Lincs 42 D4
Northorpe Lincs 43 F2
Northorpe Lincs 52 B3
Northover Som 8 D1
Northover Som 8 E2
Northowram 57 G7
Northport 9 J6
Northrepps 45 G2
Northton (Taobh Tuath) 88 E9
Northumberland Dark Sky Park N'umb 70 B4
Northumbria Craft Centre, Morpeth N'umb NE61 1PD 71 H5
Northway Glos 29 J5
Northway Som 7 K3
Northwich 49 F5
Northwick SGlos 19 J3
Northwick Som 19 G7
Northwick Worcs 29 H3
Northwold 44 B6
Northwood GtLon 22 D2
Northwood IoW 11 F5
Northwood Kent 25 K5
Northwood Mersey 48 D3
Northwood Shrop 38 D2
Northwood Green 29 G7
Northwood Hills 22 E2
Norton Glos 29 H6
Norton Halton 48 E4
Norton Herts 33 F5
Norton IoW 10 E6
Norton Mon 28 D6
Norton Notts 51 H5
Norton NSom 19 G5
Norton NYorks 58 D2
Norton N'hants 31 H2
Norton Powys 28 C2
Norton Shrop 38 D7
Norton Shrop 38 E5
Norton Shrop 39 G5
Norton Stock 62 E4
Norton Suff 34 D2
Norton Swan 17 K7
Norton SYorks 51 F4
Norton SYorks 51 H1
Norton VGlam 18 B4
Norton Wilts 20 B3
Norton WMid 40 A7
Norton Worcs 29 H3
Norton Worcs 30 B4
Norton WSuss 12 B7
Norton WSuss 12 C6
Norton Bavant 20 C7
Norton Bridge 40 A2
Norton Canes 40 C5
Norton Canon 28 C4
Norton Disney 52 B7
Norton Ferris 9 G1
Norton Fitzwarren 7 K3
Norton Green Herts 33 F6
Norton Green IoW 10 E6
Norton Green Stoke 49 J7
Norton Hawkfield 19 J5
Norton Heath 24 C1
Norton in Hales 39 G2
Norton in the Moors 49 H7
Norton Lindsey 30 D2
Norton Little Green 34 D2
Norton Malreward 19 K5
Norton Mandeville 23 J1
Norton St. Philip 20 A6
Norton Subcourse 45 J6
Norton Wood 28 C4
Norton Woodseats 51 F4
Norton-Juxta-Twycross 41 F5
Norton-le-Clay 57 K2
Norton's Cross Roads 93 D13
Norton-sub-Hamdon 8 D3
Norwell 51 K6
Norwell Woodhouse 51 K6
Norwich 45 G5
Norwich Airport 45 G4
Norwich Castle Museum & Art Gallery Norf NR1 3JU 134 Norwich
Norwich Cathedral Norf NR1 4DH 134 Norwich
Norwick 89 Q1
Norwood End 23 J1
Norwood Green GtLon 22 E4
Norwood Green WYorks 57 G7
Norwood Hill 23 F7
Norwood Park 8 E1
Noseley 42 A6
Noss Mayo 5 F6
Nosterfield 57 H1
Nosterfield End 33 K4
Nostie 83 J8
Notgrove 30 C6
Nottage 18 B4
Notting Hill 23 F3
Nottingham 41 H1
Nottingham Castle Museum & Art Gallery NG1 6EL 134 Nottingham
Nottington 9 F6
Notton Wilts 20 C5
Notton WYorks 51 F1
Nottswood Hill 29 G7
Nounsley 34 B7
Noutard's Green 29 G2
Nowton 34 C2
Nowton Park Suff IP29 5LU 34 C2
Nox 38 D4
Noyadd Trefawr 17 F1
Nuffield 21 K3
Nun Monkton 58 B4
Nunburnholme 58 E5
Nuneaton 41 F6
Nuneham Courtenay 21 J2
Nunney 20 A7
Nunnington Here 28 E4
Nunnington NYorks 58 C2
Nunnington Park 7 J3
Nunnykirk 71 F4
Nuns Quarter 93 L10
Nutt's Corner 92 H9
Nunsthorpe 53 F2
Nunthorpe Middl 63 F5
Nunthorpe York 58 B4
Nunton 10 C2
Nunwick NYorks 57 J2
Nunwick N'umb 70 D6
Nup End 33 F7
Nupend 20 A1
Nursling 10 E3
Nursted 11 J2
Nurton 40 A6
Nutbourne WSuss 11 J4
Nutbourne WSuss 12 D5
Nutfield 23 G6
Nuthall 41 H1
Nuthampstead 33 H5
Nuthurst Warks 30 C1
Nuthurst WSuss 12 E4
Nutley ESuss 13 H4
Nutley Hants 21 K7
Nutwell 51 J2
Nyadd 75 F1
Nyetimber 12 B7
Nyewood 11 J2
Nymans WSuss RH17 6EB 13 F4
Nymet Rowland 7 F5
Nymet Tracey 7 F5
Nympsfield 20 B1
Nynehead 7 K3
Nythe 8 D1
Nyton 12 C6

O

O2, The GtLon SE10 0BB 105 D7
Oad Street 24 E5
Oadby 41 J5
Oak Cross 6 D6
Oak Tree 62 D5
Oakamoor 40 C1
Oakbank 75 J4
Oakdale BCP 10 B5
Oakdale Caerp 18 E2
Oake 7 K3
Oaken 40 A5
Oakenclough 55 J5
Oakengates 39 G4
Oakenholt 48 B5
Oakenshaw Dur 62 C3
Oakenshaw WYorks 57 G7
Oakerthorpe 51 F7
Oakes 50 D1
Oakfield IoW 11 G5
Oakfield Torfaen 19 F2
Oakford Cere 26 D3
Oakford Devon 7 H3
Oakfordbridge 7 H3
Oakgrove 49 J6
Oakham 42 B5
Oakhanger 11 J1
Oakhill 19 K7
Oakington 33 H2
Oaklands Conwy 47 G7
Oaklands Herts 33 F7
Oakle Street 29 G7
Oakley BCP 10 B5
Oakley Bed 32 D3
Oakley Bucks 31 H7
Oakley Fife 75 J2
Oakley Hants 21 J6
Oakley Oxon 22 A1
Oakley Suff 35 F1
Oakley Green 22 C4
Oakley Park 37 J7
Oakridge Lynch 20 C1
Oaks 38 D5
Oaks Green 40 D2
Oaksey 20 C2
Oakshaw Ford 70 A6
Oakshott 11 J2
Oakthorpe 41 F4
Oaktree Hill 62 D7
Oakwell Hall & Country Park WYorks WF17 9LG 117 G5
Oakwood Leisure Park Pembs SA67 8DE 16 D4
Oakwoodhill 12 E3
Oakworth 57 F6
Oare Kent 25 G5
Oare Som 7 G1
Oare Wilts 20 E5
Oasby 42 D2
Oatfield 66 A2
Oath 8 C2
Oathlaw 81 K5
Oatlands 57 J4
Oban (An t-Òban) 79 K8
Obley 28 C1
Oborne 9 F3
Obthorpe 42 D4
Occlestone Green 49 F6
Occold 35 F1
Occumster 87 Q6
Oceanarium BH2 5AA 123 Bournemouth
Ochiltree 67 K1
Ochr-y-foel 47 J5
Ochtertyre P&K 80 D8
Ochtertyre Stir 75 F1
Ockbrook 41 G2
Ockeridge 29 G2
Ockham 22 D6
Ockle 78 G3
Ockley 12 E3
Ocle Pychard 28 E4
Octon 59 G2
Odcombe 8 E3
Odd Down 20 A5
Oddendale 61 H5
Oddingley 29 J3
Oddington 31 G7
Oddsta 89 P3
Odell 32 C3
Odham 6 C5
Odiham 22 A6
Odsey 33 F5
Odstock 10 C2
Odstone 41 F5
Offchurch 30 E2
Offenham 30 B4
Offerton 49 J4
Offham ESuss 13 G5
Offham Kent 23 K6
Offham WSuss 12 D6
Offley Hoo 32 E6
Offleymarsh 39 G3
Offord Cluny 33 F2
Offord D'Arcy 33 F2
Offton 34 E4
Offwell 7 K6
Ogbourne Maizey 20 E4
Ogbourne St. Andrew 20 E4
Ogbourne St. George 20 E4
Ogden Water WYorks HX2 8YA 116 B3
Oghill 90 M5
Ogle 71 G6
Oglet 48 D4
Ogmore 18 B4
Ogmore Vale 18 C2
Ogmore-by-Sea 18 B4
Ogston Reservoir Derbys DE55 6EL 51 F6
Oil Terminal 89 C8
Okeford Fitzpaine 9 H3
Okehampton 6 D6
Okehampton Camp 6 D6
Olchard 5 J3
Olchfa 17 K6
Old 31 J1
Old Aberdeen 85 P10
Old Alresford 11 G1
Old & New Towns of Edinburgh Edin 120 D2
Old Arley 40 E6
Old Basford 41 H1
Old Basing 21 K6
Old Belses 70 A1
Old Bewick 71 F1
Old Blacksmith's Shop, Gretna Green D&G DG16 5DY 69 J7
Old Blair 80 D4
Old Bolingbroke 53 G6
Old Bramhope 57 H5
Old Brampton 51 F5
Old Bridge of Urr 65 H4
Old Buckenham 44 E6
Old Burdon 62 D1
Old Burghclere 21 H6
Old Bushmills Distillery CC&G BT1 2LB 92 E2
Old Byland 58 B1
Old Cassop 62 D3
Old Church Stoke 38 B6
Old Cleeve 7 J1
Old Clipstone 51 J6
Old Colwyn 47 G5
Old Craighall 76 B3
Old Dailly 67 G4
Old Dalby 41 J3
Old Dam 50 D5
Old Deer 85 P6
Old Dilton 20 B7
Old Down SGlos 19 K3
Old Down Som 19 K6
Old Edlington 51 H3
Old Eldon 62 C4
Old Ellerby 59 H6
Old Felixstowe 35 H5
Old Fletton 42 E6
Old Ford 23 G3
Old Glossop 50 C3
Old Goginan 37 F7
Old Goole 58 D7
Old Gore 29 F6
Old Grimsby 2 B1
Old Hall 53 F1
Old Hall Green 33 G6
Old Hall Street 45 H2
Old Harlow 33 H7
Old Heath 34 E6
Old Heathfield 13 J4
Old Hill Mid Ulster 92 C8
Old Hill WMid 40 B7
Old Hurst 33 G1
Old Hutton 55 J1
Old Kea 3 F4
Old Kilpatrick 74 C3
Old Knebworth 33 F6
Old Leake 53 H7
Old Malton 58 D2
Old Mill 92 J6
Old Milton 10 D5
Old Milverton 30 D2
Old Montsale 25 G2
Old Netley 11 F3
Old Newton 34 E2
Old Philpstoun 75 J3
Old Radnor (Pencraig) 28 B3
Old Rayne 85 L8
Old Romney 15 F5
Old Royal Naval College, Greenwich GtLon SE10 9LW 105 D8
Old Scone 80 G8
Old Shields 75 G3
Old Sodbury 20 A3
Old Somerby 42 C2
Old Station, The, Tintern Parva Mon NP16 7NX 19 J1
Old Stratford 31 J4
Old Sunderlandwick 59 G4
Old Swarland 71 G3
Old Swinford 40 B7
Old Thirsk 57 K1
Old Town Cumb 55 J1
Old Town IoS 2 C1
Old Town Farm 70 D4
Old Tupton 51 F6
Old Warden 32 E4
Old Weston 32 D1
Old Windsor 22 C4
Old Wives Lees 15 F2
Old Woking 22 D6
Old Woodhall 53 F6
Old Woods 38 D3
Oldberrow 30 C2
Oldborough 7 F5
Oldbury Kent 23 J6
Oldbury Shrop 39 G6
Oldbury Warks 41 F6
Oldbury WMid 40 B7
Oldbury Court Estate Bristol BS16 2JH 100 E3
Oldbury Naite 19 K2
Oldbury on the Hill 20 B3
Oldbury-on-Severn 19 K2
Oldcastle Bridgend 18 C4
Oldcastle Mon 28 C6
Oldcastle Heath 38 D1
Oldcotes 51 H4
Oldcroft 19 K1
Oldeamere 43 G6
Oldfield 29 H2
Oldford 20 A6
Oldhall 85 J11
Oldham 49 J2
Oldham Edge 49 J2
Oldhamstocks 77 F3
Oldland 19 K4
Oldmeldrum 85 N8
Oldpark 39 F5
Oldridge 7 G6
Oldshore Beg 86 D4
Oldstead 58 B2
Oldtown 92 G8
Oldtown of Ord 85 L5
Oldwalls 17 H6
Oldways End 7 G3
Oldwhat 85 N5
Oldwich Lane 30 D1
Olgrinmore 87 P4
Oliver 69 G1
Oliver's Battery 11 F2
Ollaberry 89 M4
Ollerton ChesE 49 G5
Ollerton Notts 51 J6
Ollerton Shrop 39 F3
Olmstead Green 33 K4
Olney 32 B3
Olrig House 87 P3
Olton 40 D7
Olveston 19 K3
Olympia GtLon W14 8UX 103 G7
Omagh 91 L9
Ombersley 29 H2
Ompton 51 J6
Onchan 54 C6
Onecote 50 C7
Onehouse 34 E3
Ongar Hill 43 J3
Ongar Street 28 C2
Onibury 28 D1
Onich (Omhanaich) 79 M4
Onllwyn 27 H7
Onneley 39 G1
Onslow Green 33 K7
Onslow Village 22 C7
Oona Bridge 93 C11
Opinan High 82 H3
Opinan High 83 J1
Orange Lane 77 G6
Orbliston 84 H5
Orbost 82 C6
Orby 53 H6
Orcadia 73 K4
Orchard 73 K2
Orchard Portman 8 B2
Orchardtown 90 M4
Orcheston 20 D7
Orcop 28 D6
Orcop Hill 28 D6
Ord 82 G9
Ordhead 85 L9
Ordie 85 J10
Ordiequish 84 H5
Ordsall 51 J5
Ore 14 D6
Oreham Common 13 F5
Oreston 5 F5
Oreton 29 F1
Orford Suff 35 J4
Orford Warr 49 F3
Organford 9 J5
Orgreave 40 D4
Oritor 92 C9
Orkney Islands 89 C5
Orlestone 14 E4
Orleton Here 28 D2
Orleton Worcs 29 F2
Orleton Common 28 D2
Orlingbury 32 B1
Ormesby 63 F5
Ormesby St. Margaret 45 J4
Ormesby St. Michael 45 J4
Ormidale 73 J2
Ormiston 76 C4
Ormsaigmore 78 F4
Ormsary 73 F3
Ormskirk 48 D2
Oronsay 72 B2
Orpington 23 H5
Orrell GtMan 48 E2
Orrell Mersey 48 C3
Orrisdale 54 C4
Orroland 65 H6
Orsett 24 C3
Orsett Heath 24 C3
Orslow 40 A4
Orston 42 A1
Orton Cumb 61 H6
Orton N'hants 32 B1
Orton Longueville 42 E6
Orton Rigg 60 E1
Orton Waterville 42 E6
Orton-on-the-Hill 41 F5
Orwell 33 G3
Osbaldeston 56 B6
Osbaldwick 58 C4
Osbaston Leics 41 G5
Osbaston Shrop 38 C3
Osbaston Tel&W 38 E4
Osbaston Hollow 41 G5
Osborne 11 G5
Osborne House IoW PO32 6JX 11 G5
Osbournby 42 D2
Oscroft 48 E6
Ose 82 D6
Osgathorpe 41 G4
Osgodby Lincs 52 D3
Osgodby NYorks 58 C6
Osgodby NYorks 59 G1
Oskaig 82 F7
Osleston 40 E2
Osmaston Derby 41 F2
Osmaston Derbys 40 D1
Osmington 9 G6
Osmington Mills 9 G6
Osmondthorpe 57 J6
Osmotherley 62 E7
Osnaburgh (Dairsie) 81 K9
Ospringe 25 G5
Ossett 57 H7
Ossett Street Side 57 H7
Ossian's Grave CC&G BT44 0TG 92 H4
Ossington 51 K6
Ostend 25 F2
Osterley 22 E4
Osterley Park & House GtLon TW7 4RB 103 C8
Oswaldkirk 58 C2
Oswaldtwistle 56 C7
Oswestry 38 B3
Oteley 38 D2
Otford 23 J6
Otham 14 C2
Otherton 40 B4
Othery 8 C1
Otley Suff 35 G3
Otley WYorks 57 H5
Otter 73 H3
Otter Ferry 73 H2
Otterbourne 11 F2
Otterburn NYorks 56 D4
Otterburn N'umb 70 D4
Otterburn Camp 70 D4
Otterden Place 14 E2
Otterham 4 B1
Otterham Quay 24 E5
Otterhampton 19 F7
Ottershaw 22 D5
Otterswick 89 P4
Otterton 7 J7
Otterton Mill Devon EX9 7HG 7 J7
Otterwood 11 F4
Ottery St. Mary 7 J6
Ottinge 15 G3
Ottringham 59 J7
Oughterby 60 D1
Oughtershaw 56 D1
Oughterside 60 C2
Oughtibridge 51 F3
Oulston 58 B2
Oulton Cumb 60 D1
Oulton Norf 45 F3
Oulton Staffs 39 G3
Oulton Staffs 40 B2
Oulton Suff 45 K6
Oulton WYorks 57 J7
Oulton Broad 45 K6
Oulton Grange 40 B2
Oulton Street 45 F3
Oultoncross 40 B2
Oundle 42 D7
Our Dynamic Earth Edin EH8 8AS 126 J4
Ousby 61 H3
Ousdale 87 N7
Ousden 34 B3
Ousefleet 58 E7
Ouston Dur 62 C1
Ouston N'umb 71 F6
Out Newton 59 K7
Out Rawcliffe 55 H5
Out Skerries Airstrip 89 Q5
Outcast 55 G2
Outchester 77 K7
Outgate 60 E7
Outhgill 61 J6
Outlands 39 G3
Outlane 50 C1
Outwell 43 J5
Outwood Surr 23 G7
Outwood WYorks 57 J7
Outwoods 39 G4
Ouzlewell Green 57 J7
Ovenden 57 F7
Over Cambs 33 G1
Over ChesW&C 49 F6
Over Glos 29 H7
Over SGlos 19 J3
Over Burrows 40 E2
Over Compton 8 E3
Over Dinsdale 62 D5
Over End 50 E5
Over Green 40 D6
Over Haddon 50 E6
Over Hulton 49 F2
Over Kellet 55 J3
Over Kiddington 31 F6
Over Monnow 28 D7
Over Norton 30 E6
Over Peover 49 G5
Over Silton 62 E7
Over Stowey 7 K2
Over Stratton 8 D3
Over Tabley 49 G4
Over Wallop 10 D1
Over Whitacre 40 E6
Over Winchendon (Upper Winchendon) 31 J7
Over Worton 31 F6
Overbury 29 J5
Overcombe 9 F6
Overgreen 51 F5
Overleigh 8 D1
Overpool 48 C5
Overseal 40 E4
Overslade 31 F1
Oversland 15 F2
Oversley Green 30 B3
Overstone 32 B2
Overstrand 45 G1
Overthorpe 31 F4
Overton ChesW&C 48 E5
Overton Hants 21 J7
Overton Lancs 55 H4
Overton NYorks 58 B4
Overton Shrop 28 E1
Overton Swan 17 H7
Overton (Owrtyn) Wrex 38 C1
Overton WYorks 50 E1
Overton Bridge 38 C1
Overtown Lancs 56 B2
Overtown NLan 75 G5
Overtown Swin 20 E4
Overy 21 J2
Oving Bucks 31 J6
Oving WSuss 12 C6
Ovingdean 13 G6
Ovingham 71 F7
Ovington Dur 62 B5
Ovington Essex 34 B4
Ovington Hants 11 G1
Ovington Norf 44 D5
Ovington N'umb 71 F7
Ower Hants 10 E3
Ower Hants 11 F4
Owermoigne 9 G6
Owler Bar 50 E5
Owlpen 20 A2
Owl's Green 35 G2
Owlswick 22 A1
Owmby 52 D2
Owmby-by-Spital 52 D4
Owsleybury 11 G2
Owston 42 A5
Owston Ferry 52 B2
Owstwick 59 J6
Owthorpe 41 J2
Oxborough 44 B5
Oxcliffe Hill 55 H3
Oxcombe 53 G5
Oxen End 33 K6
Oxen Park 55 G1
Oxencombe 7 G7
Oxenhall 29 G6
Oxenholme 61 G7
Oxenhope 57 F6
Oxenpill 19 H7
Oxenton 29 J5
Oxenwood 21 G6
Oxford 21 J1
Oxford Cathedral Oxon OX1 1AB 134 Oxford
Oxford Story Oxon OX1 3AJ 134 Oxford
Oxford University Museum of Natural History Oxon OX1 3PW 134 Oxford
Oxhey 22 E2
Oxhill 30 E4
Oxley 40 B5
Oxley Green 34 D7
Oxley's Green 13 K4
Oxnam 70 C2
Oxnead 45 G3
Oxnop Ghyll 61 L7
Oxshott 22 E5
Oxspring 50 E2
Oxted 23 G6
Oxton Mersey 48 C4
Oxton Notts 51 J7
Oxton ScBord 76 C5
Oxwich 17 H7
Oxwich Green 17 H7
Oxwick 44 D3
Oykel Bridge 86 F9
Oyne 85 L8
Ozleworth 20 A2

P

Pabbay 88 E9
Packington 41 F4
Packwood 30 C1
Padanaram 81 K5
Padarn Country Park Gwyn LL55 4TY 46 D6
Padbury 31 J5
Paddington 23 F3
Paddlesworth 15 G3
Paddock 14 E2
Paddock Wood 23 K7
Paddockhole 69 H5
Paddolgreen 38 E2
Padeswood 48 B6
Padfield 50 C3
Padiham 56 C6
Padside 57 G4
Padstow 3 G1
Padworth 21 K5
Paganhill 20 B1
Pagham 12 B7
Paglesham Churchend 25 F2
Paglesham Eastend 25 F2
Paignton 5 J4
Paignton & Dartmouth Steam Railway Torbay TQ4 6AF 5 J5
Paignton Pier Torbay TQ4 6BW 5 J4
Paignton Zoo Torbay TQ4 7EU 5 J5
Pailton 41 G7
Paine's Corner 13 K4
Painscastle 28 A4
Painshawfield 71 F7
Painswick 20 B1
Pairc Shiaboist 88 H3
Paisley 74 C4
Pakefield 45 K6
Pakenham 34 D2
Palace of Holyroodhouse Edin EH8 8DX 126 J4
Palace of Westminster (Houses of Parliament) (Palace of Westminster & Westminster Abbey inc. St Margaret's Church) GtLon SW1A 0AA 105 A7
Palacerigg Country Park NLan G67 3HU 119 M1
Pale 37 J2
Palehouse Common 13 H5
Palestine 21 F7
Paley Street 22 B4
Palgowan 67 H5
Palgrave 35 F1
Pallinsburn House 77 G7
Palmarsh 15 G4
Palmers Cross 22 D7
Palmers Green 23 G2
Palmerstown 18 E4
Palnackie 65 J5
Palnure 64 E4
Palterton 51 G6
Pamber End 21 K6
Pamber Green 21 K6
Pamber Heath 21 K5
Pamington 29 J5
Pamphill 9 J4
Pampisford 33 H4
Panborough 19 H7
Panbride 81 L7
Pancrasweek 6 A5
Pancross 18 D5
Pandy Gwyn 37 F5
Pandy Mon 28 C6
Pandy Powys 37 J5
Pandy Wrex 38 A2
Pandy Tudur 47 G6
Pandy'r Capel 47 J7
Panfield 34 B6
Pangbourne 21 K4
Pannal 57 J4
Pannal Ash 57 H4
Panshanger 33 F7
Pant 38 B3
Pant Glas 36 D1
Pant Gwyn 37 H3
Pant Mawr 37 H7
Pantasaph 47 K5
Panteg 19 G2
Pantglas 37 G6
Pantgwyn Carmar 17 J3
Pantgwyn Cere 17 F1
Pant-lasau 17 K5
Panton 52 E5
Pant-pastynog 47 J6
Pantperthog 37 G5
Pant-y-dwr 27 J1
Pantyffordd 48 B7
Pant-y-ffridd 38 A5
Pantyffynnon 17 K4
Pantygasseg 19 F2
Pantygelli 28 C7
Pantymwyn 47 K6
Panxworth 45 H4
Papa Stour 89 K6
Papa Stour Airstrip 89 K6
Papa Westray 89 D2
Papa Westray Airfield 89 D2
Papcastle 60 C3
Papple 76 D3
Papplewick 51 H7
Papworth Everard 33 F2
Papworth St. Agnes 33 F2
Par 4 A5
Paradise Park, Newhaven ESuss BN9 0DH 13 H6
Paradise Wildlife Park, Broxbourne Herts EN10 7QA 23 G1
Parbold 48 D1
Parbrook Som 8 E1
Parbrook WSuss 12 D4
Parc 37 H2
Parcllyn 26 B3
Parcrhydderch 27 F3
Parc-Seymour 19 H2
Parc-y-rhôs 17 J1
Pardshaw 60 B4
Parham 35 H2
Parish Holm 68 C1
Park Aber 85 N11
Park D&S 90 M6
Park Close 56 D5
Park Corner ESuss 13 J3

Ramsey Island *Pembs* 16 A3
Ramsey Mereside 43 F7
Ramsey St. Mary's 43 F7
Ramsgate 25 K5
Ramsgate Street 44 E2
Ramsgill 57 G2
Ramsholt 35 H4
Ramshorn 40 C1
Ramsnest Common 12 C3
Ranaghan 92 C7
Ranby *Lincs* 53 F5
Ranby *Notts* 51 J4
Rand 52 E5
Rand Farm Park *Lincs* LN8 5NJ 52 E5
Randalstown 92 F7
Randwick 20 B1
Ranelly 91 L10
Rangemore 40 D3
Rangeworthy 19 K3
Ranish (Ranais) 88 K5
Rankinston 67 J2
Rank's Green 34 B7
Ranmoor 51 F4
Rannoch School 80 A5
Ranscombe 7 H1
Ranskill 51 J4
Ranton 40 A3
Ranton Green 40 A3
Ranworth 45 H4
Rapness 89 E3
Rapps 8 C3
Rascarrel 65 H6
Rash 56 B1
Rasharkin 92 E5
Rashee 92 H7
Rashwood 29 J2
Raskelf 57 K2
Rassau 28 A7
Rastrick 57 G7
Ratagan 83 K9
Ratby 41 H5
Ratcliffe Culey 41 F6
Ratcliffe on Soar 41 G3
Ratcliffe on the Wreake 41 J4
Ratford Bridge 16 B4
Ratfyn 20 E7
Rathen 85 P4
Rathfriland 93 G13
Rathillet 81 J8
Rathkeel 92 G6
Rathmell 56 D3
Ratho 75 K3
Ratho Station 75 K3
Rathven 85 J4
Ratley 30 E4
Ratling 15 H2
Ratlinghope 38 D6
Ratsloe 7 H6
Rattar 87 Q2
Ratten Row *Cumb* 60 E2
Ratten Row *Lancs* 55 H5
Rattery 5 H4
Rattlesden 34 D3
Rattray 80 G6
Raughton Head 60 E2
Raunds 32 C1
Ravenfield 51 G3
Ravenglass 60 B7
Ravenglass & Eskdale Railway (La'al Ratty) *Cumb* CA18 1SW 60 B7
Raveningham 45 H6
Raven's Green 35 F6
Ravenscar 63 K6
Ravensdale 54 C4
Ravensden 32 D3
Ravenshaw 56 E5
Ravenshayes 7 H5
Ravenshead 51 H7
Ravensmoor 49 F7
Ravensthorpe *N'hants* 31 H1
Ravensthorpe *WYorks* 57 H7
Ravenstone *Leics* 41 G4
Ravenstone *MK* 32 B3
Ravenstonedale 61 J6
Ravenstruther 75 H6
Ravensworth 62 B6
Ravernet 93 H10
Raw *F&O* 91 L12
Raw *NYorks* 63 K6
Rawcliffe *ERid* 58 C7
Rawcliffe *York* 58 B4
Rawcliffe Bridge 58 C7
Rawdon 57 H6
Rawmarsh 51 G3
Rawnsley 40 C4
Rawreth 24 D2
Rawridge 8 B4
Rawson Green 41 F1
Rawtenstall 56 D7
Rawyards 75 F4
Raydon 34 E5
Raylees 70 E4
Rayleigh 24 E2
Raymond's Hill 8 C5
Rayne 34 B6
Rayners Lane 22 E3
Raynes Park 23 F5
Reach 33 J2
Read 56 C6
Reading 22 A4
Reading Green 35 F1
Reading Street 14 E4
Reagill 61 H5
Real Mary King's Close, The *Edin* EH1 1PG 126 F4
Rearquhar 84 B1
Rearsby 41 J4
Rease Heath 49 F7
Reaveley 71 F2
Reawick 89 M8
Reay 87 M3
Reculver 25 J5
Red Ball 7 J4
Red Bull 49 H7
Red Dial 60 D2
Red Hill *Hants* 11 J3
Red Hill *Warks* 30 C3
Red Lodge 33 K1
Red Lumb 49 H1
Red Oaks Hill 33 J5
Red Point 82 H4
Red Post *Corn* 6 A5
Red Post *Devon* 5 J4
Red Rail 28 E6
Red Rock 48 E2
Red Roses 17 F4
Red Row 71 H4
Red Street 49 H7
Red Wharf Bay (Traeth Coch) 46 D4
Redberth 16 D5
Redbourn 32 E7
Redbourne 52 C3
Redbrook *Glos* 28 E7
Redbrook *Wrex* 38 E1
Redbrook Street 14 E4
Redburn *High* 83 R4
Redburn *High* 84 D6
Redburn *N'umb* 70 C7
Redcar 63 G4
Redcastle *Angus* 81 M5
Redcastle *High* 83 R6
Redcliff Bay 19 H4
Reddingmuirhead 75 H3
Reddish 49 H3
Redditch 30 B2
Rede 34 C3
Redenhall 45 G7
Redesmouth 70 D5
Redford *Angus* 81 L6
Redford *Dur* 62 A3
Redford *WSuss* 12 B4
Redgrave 34 E1
Redhill *L&C* 93 G11
Redhill *Notts* 41 H1
Redhill *NSom* 19 H5
Redhill *Surr* 23 F6
Redhill Aerodrome & Heliport 23 F7
Redhouse 73 G4
Redhouses 72 B4
Redisham 45 J7
Redland *Bristol* 19 J4
Redland *Ork* 89 C5
Redlingfield 35 F1
Redlynch *Som* 9 G1
Redlynch *Wilts* 10 D2
Redmarley D'Abitot 29 G5
Redmarshall 62 D4
Redmile 42 A2
Redmire 62 A7
Redmoor 4 A4
Rednal 38 C3
Redpath 76 D7
Redruth 2 D4
Redscarhead 76 A6
Redshaw 68 D1
Redstone Bank 16 E4
Redwick *Newport* 19 H3
Redwick *SGlos* 19 J3
Redworth 62 C4
Reed 33 G5
Reed End 33 G5
Reedham 45 J5
Reedley 56 D6
Reedness 58 D7
Reepham *Lincs* 52 D5
Reepham *Norf* 44 E3
Reeth 62 A7
Regaby 54 D4
Regil 19 J5
Regoul 84 C5
Reiff 86 B8
Reigate 23 F6
Reighton 59 H2
Reiss 87 R4
Rejerrah 3 F3
Relan 91 M13
Releath 2 D5
Relubbus 2 C5
Relugas 84 D6
Remenham 22 A3
Remenham Hill 22 A3
Rempstone 41 H3
Rendcomb 30 B7
Rendham 35 H2
Rendlesham 35 H3
Renfrew 74 D4
Renhold 32 D3
Renishaw 51 G5
Rennington 71 H2
Renton 74 B3
Renwick 61 G2
Repps 45 J4
Repton 41 F3
Rescobie 81 L5
Rescorla 4 A5
Resipole 79 J4
Resolis 84 A4
Resolven 18 B1
Respryn 4 B4
Reston 77 G4
Restormel 4 B4
Reswallie 81 L5
Reterth 3 G2
Retew 3 G3
Retford (East Retford) 51 K4
Rettendon 24 D2
Rettendon Place 24 D2
Retyn 3 F3
Revesby 53 F6
Revesby Bridge 53 G6
Rew 5 H3
Rew Street 11 F5
Rewe *Devon* 7 G6
Rewe *Devon* 7 H6
Reybridge 20 C5
Reydon 35 J1
Reydon Smear 35 K1
Reymerston 44 E5
Reynalton 16 D5
Reynoldston 17 H7
Rezare 4 D3
Rhadyr 19 G1
Rhandirmwyn 27 G4
Rhayader (Rhaeadr Gwy) 27 J2
Rhedyn 36 B2
Rheged - the Village in the Hill *Cumb* CA11 0DQ 61 F4
Rhemore 78 G5
Rhenigidale (Reinigeadal) 88 H7
Rheola 18 B1
Rhes-y-cae 47 K6
Rhewl *Denb* 38 A1
Rhewl *Denb* 47 K6
Rhewl *Shrop* 38 C2
Rhian 86 H8
Rhiconich 86 E4
Rhicullen 84 A3
Rhidorroch 83 M1
Rhifail 87 K5
Rhigos 18 C1
Rhiston 38 B6
Rhiw 36 B3
Rhiwargor 37 J3
Rhiwbina 18 E3
Rhiwbryfdir 37 F1
Rhiwderin 19 F3
Rhiwinder 18 D3
Rhiwlas *Gwyn* 37 J2
Rhiwlas *Gwyn* 46 D6
Rhiwlas *Powys* 38 B2
Rhode 8 B1
Rhodes Minnis 15 G3
Rhodesia 51 H5
Rhodiad-y-brenin 16 A3
Rhodmad 26 E1
Rhonadale 73 F7
Rhonehouse (Kelton Hill) 65 H5
Rhoose 18 D5
Rhos *Carmar* 17 G2
Rhos *NPT* 18 A1
Rhos Common 38 B4
Rhosaman 27 G7
Rhoscolyn 46 A5
Rhoscrowther 16 C5
Rhosesmor 48 B6
Rhos-fawr 36 C2
Rhosgadfan 46 D7
Rhos-goch *IoA* 46 C4
Rhosgoch *Powys* 28 A4
Rhos-hill 16 E1
Rhoshirwaun 36 A3
Rhoslan 36 D1
Rhoslefain 36 E5
Rhosllanerchrugog 38 B1
Rhosllyfgwy 46 C4
Rhosmaen 17 K3
Rhosmeirch 46 C5
Rhosneigr 46 B5
Rhosnesni 48 C7
Rhos-on-Sea 47 G4
Rhossili 17 H7
Rhosson 16 A3
Rhostrehwfa 46 C5
Rhostryfan 46 C7
Rhostyllen 38 C1
Rhos-y-bol 46 C4
Rhos-y-brithdir 38 A3
Rhosycaerau 16 C2
Rhos-y-garth 27 F1
Rhos-y-gwaliau 37 J2
Rhos-y-llan 36 B2
Rhos-y-mawn 47 G6
Rhos-y-Meirch 28 B2
R.H.S. Garden Harlow Carr *NYorks* HG3 1QB 57 H4
R.H.S. Garden Hyde Hall *Essex* CM3 8ET 24 D2
R.H.S. Garden Rosemoor *Devon* EX38 8PH 6 D4
R.H.S. Garden Wisley *Surr* GU23 6QB 22 D6
Rhu 74 A2
Rhuallt 47 J5
Rhubodach 73 J3
Rhuddall Heath 48 E6
Rhuddlan 47 J5
Rhue 83 M1
Rhulen 28 A4
Rhunahaorine 73 F6
Rhyd *Gwyn* 37 F1
Rhyd *Powys* 37 J5
Rhydargaeau 17 H3
Rhydcymerau 17 J2
Rhyd-Ddu 46 D7
Rhydding 18 A2
Rhydgaled 47 H6
Rhydlanfair 47 G7
Rhydlewis 17 G1
Rhydlios 36 A2
Rhydlydan *Conwy* 47 G7
Rhydlydan *Powys* 37 K6
Rhydolion 36 B3
Rhydowen 17 H1
Rhyd-Rosser 26 E2
Rhydspence 28 B4
Rhydtalog 48 B7
Rhyd-uchaf 37 H2
Rhyd-wen 37 J3
Rhyd-wyn 46 B4
Rhyd-y-ceirw 48 B7
Rhyd-y-clafdy 36 C2
Rhydycroesau 38 B2
Rhydyfelin *Cere* 26 E1
Rhydyfelin *RCT* 18 D3
Rhyd-y-foel 47 H5
Rhyd-y-fro 18 A1
Rhyd-y-groes 46 D6
Rhydymain 37 H3
Rhydymwyn 48 B6
Rhyd-yr-onnen 37 F5
Rhyd-y-sarn 37 F1
Rhydywrach 16 E4
Rhyl 47 J4
Rhyl Sun Centre *Denb* LL18 3AQ 47 J4
Rhymney 18 E1
Rhyn 38 C2
Rhynd 80 G8
Rhynie *Aber* 85 J8
Rhynie *High* 84 C3
Ribbesford 29 G1
Ribchester 56 B6
Ribigill 86 H4
Riby 52 E2
Riccall 58 C6
Riccarton 74 C7
Richards Castle 28 D2
Richhill 93 E12
Richings Park 22 D4
Richmond *GtLon* 22 E4
Richmond *NYorks* 62 B6
Richmond *SYorks* 51 G4
Rich's Holford 7 K2
Rickarton 81 P2
Rickerscote 40 B3
Rickford 19 H6
Rickinghall 34 E1
Rickleton 62 C1
Rickling 33 H5
Rickling Green 33 J6
Rickmansworth 22 D2
Riddell 70 A1
Riddings 51 G7
Riddlecombe 6 E4
Riddlesden 57 F5
Ridge *Dorset* 9 J6
Ridge *Herts* 23 F1
Ridge *Wilts* 9 J1
Ridge Green 23 G7
Ridge Lane 40 E6
Ridgebourne 27 K2
Ridgeway 51 G4
Ridgeway Cross 29 G4
Ridgeway Moor 51 G4
Ridgewell 34 B4
Ridgewood 13 H4
Ridgmont 32 C5
Riding Mill 71 F7
Ridham Dock 25 F5
Riding Gate 9 G2
Ridley 24 C5
Ridleywood 48 C7
Ridlington *Norf* 45 H2
Ridlington *Rut* 42 B5
Ridsdale 70 E5
Riechip 80 F6
Rievaulx 58 B1
Rift House 62 E3
Rigg 69 H7
Riggend 75 F4
Rigmaden Park 56 B1
Rigsby 53 H5
Rigside 75 G7
Riley Green 56 B7
Rileyhill 40 D4
Rilla Mill 4 C3
Rillaton 4 C3
Rillington 58 E2
Rimington 56 D5
Rimpton 9 F2
Rimswell 59 K7
Rinaston 16 C3
Ring o' Bells 48 D1
Ring of Brodgar (Heart of Neolithic Orkney) *Ork* KW16 3JZ 89 B6
Ringboy 93 M11
Ringford 65 G5
Ringinglow 50 E4
Ringland 45 F4
Ringles Cross 13 H4
Ringmer 13 H5
Ringmore *Devon* 5 G6
Ringmore *Devon* 5 K3
Ring's End 43 G5
Ringsend 92 D4
Ringsfield 45 J7
Ringsfield Corner 45 J7
Ringshall *Herts* 32 C7
Ringshall *Suff* 34 E3
Ringshall Stocks 34 E3
Ringstead *N'hants* 32 C1
Ringstead *Norf* 44 B1
Ringwood 10 C4
Ringwould 15 J3
Rinloan 84 G10
Rinsey 2 C6
Ripe 13 J6
Ripley *Derbys* 51 F7
Ripley *Hants* 10 C5
Ripley *NYorks* 57 H3
Ripley *Surr* 22 D6
Riplingham 59 F6
Ripon 57 J2
Rippingale 42 E3
Ripple *Kent* 15 J3
Ripple *Worcs* 29 H5
Ripponden 50 C1
Risabus 72 B6
Risbury 28 E3
Risby *ERid* 59 G6
Risby *Suff* 34 B2
Risca 19 F2
Rise 59 H5
Riseden 14 C4
Risegate 43 F3
Riseholme 52 C5
Riseley *Bed* 32 D2
Riseley *W'ham* 22 A5
Rishangles 35 F2
Rishton 56 C6
Rishworth 50 C1
Risinghurst 21 J1
Risley *Derbys* 41 G2
Risley *Warr* 49 F3
Risplith 57 H3
Rispond 86 G3
Rivar 21 G5
Rivenhall 34 C7
Rivenhall End 34 C7
River *Kent* 15 H3
River *WSuss* 12 C4
River Bank 33 J2
River Bridge 19 G7
River Link Boat Cruises *Devon* TQ6 9AJ 5 J6
Riverford Bridge 5 H4
Riverhead 23 J6
Riverside *Cardiff* 18 E4
Riverside *NM&D* 93 J15
Riverside Country Park *Med* ME7 2XH 24 E5
Riverside Museum & Tall Ship Glenlee *Glas* G3 8RS 118 D4
Riverton 6 E2
Riverview Park 24 C4
Riviera International Centre *Torbay* TQ2 5LZ 136 Torquay
Rivington 49 F1
Roa Island 55 F3
Roach Bridge 55 J7
Road Green 45 G6
Road Weedon 31 H3
Roade 31 J3
Roadhead 70 A6
Roadside *High* 87 P3
Roadside *Ork* 89 F3
Roadside of Kinneff 81 P3
Roadwater 7 J2
Roag 82 C6
Roast Green 33 H5
Roath 18 E4
Robert Burns Birthplace Museum *SAyr* KA7 4PQ 67 H2
Roberton *ScBord* 69 K2
Roberton *SLan* 68 E1
Robertsbridge 14 C5
Robertstown 18 D1
Roberttown 57 G7
Robeston Cross 16 B5
Robeston Wathen 16 D4
Robeston West 16 B5
Robin Hill Countryside Adventure Park *IoW* PO30 2NU 11 G6
Robin Hood *Derbys* 50 E5
Robin Hood *Lancs* 48 E1
Robin Hood *WYorks* 57 J7
Robinhood End 34 B5
Robins 12 B4
Robinsons Town 93 E10
Robinswood Hill Country Park *Glos* GL4 6SX 29 H7
Roborough *Devon* 6 D4
Roborough *Plym* 5 F4
Roby 48 D3
Roby Mill 48 E2
Rocester 40 D2
Roch 16 B3
Roch Bridge 16 B3
Roch Gate 16 B3
Rochdale 49 H1
Roche 3 G2
Rochester *Med* 24 D5
Rochester *N'umb* 70 D4
Rochester Cathedral *Med* ME1 1SX 24 D5
Rochford *Essex* 24 E2
Rochford *Worcs* 29 F2
Rock *Corn* 3 G1
Rock *N'umb* 71 H2
Rock *Worcs* 29 G1
Rock Ferry 48 C4
Rockbeare 7 J6
Rockbourne 10 C3
Rockcliffe *Cumb* 69 J7
Rockcliffe *D&G* 65 J5
Rockcliffe Cross 69 J7
Rockfield *A&B* 73 G5
Rockfield *High* 84 D2
Rockfield *Mon* 28 D7
Rockford 10 C4
Rockhampton 19 K2
Rockhead 4 A2
Rockingham 42 B6
Rockland All Saints 44 D6
Rockland St. Mary 45 H5
Rockland St. Peter 44 D6
Rockley 20 E4
Rockside 72 A4
Rockspring 92 D8
Rockstown 93 B9
Rockwell End 22 A3
Rockwell Green 7 K4
Rodborough 20 B1
Rodbourne 20 C3
Rodbridge Corner 34 C4
Rodd 28 C2
Roddam 71 F1
Rodden 9 F6
Rode 20 B6
Rode Heath 49 H7
Rodeheath 49 H6
Rodel (Roghadal) 88 F9
Roden 38 E4
Rodhuish 7 J2
Rodington 38 E4
Rodington Heath 38 E4
Rodley 29 G7
Rodmarton 20 C2
Rodmell 13 H6
Rodmersham 25 F5
Rodmersham Green 25 F5
Rodney Stoke 19 H6
Rodsley 40 E1
Rodway 19 F7
Roe Cross 49 J3
Roe Green 33 G5
Roecliffe 57 J3
Roehampton 23 F4
Roesound 89 M6
Roffey 12 E3
Rogart 87 K9
Rogate 12 B4
Rogerstone 19 F3
Rogiet 19 H3
Rokemarsh 21 K2
Roker 62 E1
Rollesby 45 J4
Rolleston *Leics* 42 A5
Rolleston *Notts* 51 K7
Rollestone 20 D7
Rolleston-on-Dove 40 E3
Rolston 59 J5
Rolstone 19 G5
Rolvenden 14 D4
Rolvenden Layne 14 D4
Romaldkirk 61 L4
Roman Bath House (Frontiers of the Roman Empire) *EDun* 119 D2
Roman Baths & Pump Room *B&NESom* BA1 1LZ 20 A5
Roman Fort (Frontiers of the Roman Empire) *Falk* 75 F3
Romanby 62 D7
Romanno Bridge 75 K6
Romansleigh 7 F3
Romesdal 82 E5
Romford *Dorset* 10 B4
Romford *GtLon* 23 J3
Romiley 49 J3
Romney Street 23 J5
Romney, Hythe & Dymchurch Railway *Kent* TN28 8PL 15 G4
Romsey 10 E2
Romsley *Shrop* 39 G7
Romsley *Worcs* 29 J1
Rona 82 G5
Ronachan 73 F5
Ronague 54 B6
Ronnachmore 72 B5
Rood End 40 C7
Rookhope 61 L2
Rookley 11 G6
Rookley Green 11 G6
Rooks Bridge 19 G6
Rook's Nest 7 J2
Rookwith 57 H1
Roos 59 J6
Roose 55 F3
Roosebeck 55 F3
Roosecote 55 F3
Rootham's Green 32 D3
Rootpark 75 H5
Ropley 11 H1
Ropley Dean 11 H1
Ropley Soke 11 H1
Ropsley 42 C2
Rora 85 Q5
Rorrington 38 C5
Roscavey 91 M10
Rose 2 E3
Rose Ash 7 F3
Rose Green *Essex* 34 D6
Rose Green *WSuss* 12 C7
Rose Hill 13 H5
Roseacre *Kent* 14 C2
Roseacre *Lancs* 55 H6
Rosebank 75 G6
Rosebrough 71 G1
Rosebush 16 D3
Rosecliston 3 F3
Rosedale Abbey 63 H7
Roseden 71 F1
Rosehearty 85 P4
Rosehill 38 D4
Roselands 13 K6
Rosemarket 16 C5
Rosemarkie 84 B5
Rosemary Lane 7 K4
Rosemeilan 91 L12
Rosemount *P&K* 80 G6
Rosemount *SAyr* 67 H1
Rosenannon 3 G2
Rosenithon 3 F6
Rosepool 16 B4
Rosevean 4 A5
Roseville 40 B6
Rosewell 76 A4
Roseworth 62 E4
Rosgill 61 G5
Roshven 79 J3
Roskhill 82 C6
Roskorwell 2 E6
Rosley 60 E2
Roslin 76 A4
Rosliston 40 E4
Rosliston Forestry Centre *Derbys* DE12 8JX 40 E4
Rosneath 74 A2
Ross *D&G* 65 G6
Ross *N'umb* 77 K7
Ross *P&K* 80 C8
Ross Priory 74 C2
Rosscor 91 F11
Rossdhu House 74 B2
Rossett 48 C7
Rossett Green 57 J4
Rosside 55 F2
Rossington 51 J3
Rosslea 91 M13
Rosslyn Chapel *Midlo* EH25 9PU 120 E6
Rossmore 10 B5
Ross-on-Wye 29 F6
Roster 87 Q6
Rostherne 49 G4
Rosthwaite *Cumb* 60 D5
Roston 40 D1
Rostrevor 93 G15
Rosudgeon 2 C6
Rosyth 75 K2
Rothbury 71 F3
Rother Valley Country Park *SYorks* S26 5PQ 111 F5
Rotherby 41 J4
Rotherfield 13 J3
Rotherfield Greys 22 A3
Rotherfield Peppard 22 A3
Rotherham 51 G3
Rothersthorpe 31 J3
Rotherwick 22 A6
Rothes 84 G6
Rothesay 73 J4
Rothiemurchus *High* PH22 1QH 84 D10
Rothienorman 85 M7
Rothiesholm 89 F5
Rothley *Leics* 41 H4
Rothley *N'umb* 71 F5
Rothney 85 L8
Rothwell *Lincs* 52 E3
Rothwell *N'hants* 42 B7
Rothwell *WYorks* 57 J7
Rotsea 59 G4
Rottal 81 J4
Rotten Row *Bucks* 22 A3
Rotten Row *WMid* 30 C1
Rottingdean 13 G6
Rottington 60 A5
Roud 11 G6
Roudham 44 D7
Rough Castle (Frontiers of the Roman Empire) *Falk* 75 G3
Rough Close 40 B2
Rough Common 15 G2
Rougham *Norf* 44 C3
Rougham *Suff* 34 D2
Rougham Green 34 D2
Roughburn 79 Q2
Roughlee 56 D5
Roughley 40 D6
Roughton *Lincs* 53 F6
Roughton *Norf* 45 G2
Roughton *Shrop* 39 G6
Round Bush 22 E2
Roundbush Green 33 J7
Roundham 8 D4
Roundhay 57 J6
Roundstreet Common 12 D4
Roundway 20 D5
Rous Lench 30 B3
Rousay 89 D4
Rousdon 8 B5
Rousham 31 F6
Rousham Gap 31 F6
Rousky 90 M8
Routenburn 73 K4
Routh 59 G5
Rout's Green 22 A2
Row *Corn* 4 A3
Row *Cumb* 55 H1
Row *Cumb* 61 H3
Row Heath 35 F7
Row Town 22 D5
Rowanburn 69 K6
Rowardennan Lodge 74 B1
Rowarth 50 C4
Rowbarton 8 B2
Rowberrow 19 H6
Rowde 20 C5
Rowden 6 E6
Rowen 47 F5
Rowfields 40 D1
Rowfoot 70 B7
Rowhedge 34 E6
Rowhook 12 E3
Rowington 30 D2
Rowland 50 E5
Rowland's Castle 11 J3
Rowlands Gill 62 B1
Rowledge 22 B7
Rowlestone 28 C6
Rowley *Devon* 7 F4
Rowley *Dur* 62 A2
Rowley *Shrop* 38 C5
Rowley Park 40 B3
Rowley Regis 40 B7
Rowly 22 D7
Rowner 11 G4
Rowney Green 30 B1
Rownhams 10 E3
Rowrah 60 B5
Rowsham 32 B7
Rowsley 50 E6
Rowstock 21 H3
Rowston 52 D7
Rowthorne 51 G6
Rowton *ChesW&C* 48 D6
Rowton *Shrop* 38 C4
Rowton *Tel&W* 39 F4
Roxburgh 77 F7
Roxby *NLincs* 52 C1
Roxby *NYorks* 63 H5
Roxhill 92 F7
Roxton 32 E3
Roxwell 24 C1
Royal Academy of Arts *GtLon* W1J 0BD 132 C3
Royal Albert Hall *GtLon* SW7 2AP 103 G7
Royal Albert Memorial Museum & Art Gallery *Devon* EX4 3RX 125 Exeter
Royal Armouries Museum, Leeds *WYorks* LS10 1LT 130 G5
Royal Artillery Barracks *GtLon* SE18 5DP 105 E8
Royal Bath & West Showground *Som* BA4 6QN 9 F1
Royal Botanic Garden *Edin* EH3 5LR 126 D1
Royal Botanic Gardens, Kew *GtLon* TW9 3AB 103 E8
Royal British Legion Village 14 C2
Royal Centre *Nott* NG1 5ND 134 Nottingham
Royal Cornwall Museum *Corn* TR1 2SJ 3 F4
Royal Festival Hall *GtLon* SE1 8XX 132 F4
Royal Highland Showground *Edin* EH28 8NB 120 A2
Royal Horticultural Halls *GtLon* SW1P 2PB 132 D6
Royal Hospital Chelsea *GtLon* SW3 4SR 103 H8
Royal Leamington Spa 30 E2
Royal Mews, Buckingham Palace *GtLon* SW1W 0QH 132 B6
Royal Naval Museum PO1 3NH 135 Portsmouth
Royal Oak 48 D2
Royal Observatory Greenwich *GtLon* SE10 8XJ 105 D8
Royal Opera House *GtLon* WC2E 9DD 132 E3
Royal Pavilion *B&H* BN1 1EE 123 Brighton
Royal Scots Regimental Museum, The *Edin* EH1 2YT 126 E5
Royal Scottish Academy *Edin* EH2 2EL 126 F4
Royal Tunbridge Wells 13 J3
Royal Victoria Country Park *Hants* SO31 5GA 96 D5
Royal Welsh Fusiliers Regimental Museum *Gwyn* LL55 2AY 46 C6
Royal Wootton Bassett 20 D3
Royal Yacht Britannia *Edin* EH6 6JJ 120 D1
Roybridge (Drochaid Ruaidh) 79 P2
Roydon *Essex* 33 H7
Roydon *Norf* 44 B3
Roydon *Norf* 44 F7
Roydon Hamlet 23 H1
Royston *Herts* 33 G4
Royston *SYorks* 51 F1
Royton 49 J2
Rozel 3 K6
Ruabon (Rhiwabon) 38 C1
Ruaig 78 B6
Ruan Lanihorne 3 F4
Ruan Major 2 D7
Ruan Minor 2 E7
Ruanaich 78 D8
Ruardean 29 F7
Ruardean Hill 29 F7
Ruardean Woodside 29 F7
Rubane 93 M10
Rubery 29 J1
Ruckcroft 61 G2
Ruckinge 15 F4
Ruckland 53 G5
Rucklers Lane 22 D1
Ruckley 38 E5
Rudbaxton 16 C3
Rudby 62 E6
Rudchester 71 G7
Ruddington 41 H2
Ruddlemoor 4 A5
Rudford 29 G6
Rudge 20 B6
Rudgeway 19 K3
Rudgwick 12 D3
Rudhall 29 F6
Rudheath 49 F5
Rudley Green 24 E1
Rudloe 20 B5
Rudry 18 E3
Rudston 59 G3
Rudyard 49 J7
Rudyard Lake *Staffs* ST13 8RT 49 J7
Rufford 48 D1
Rufford Country Park *Notts* NG22 9DF 51 J6
Rufforth 58 B4
Ruffside 61 L1
Rugby 31 G1
Rugby Football Union, Twickenham *GtLon* TW1 1DZ 103 D9
Rugeley 40 C4
Ruishton 8 B2
Ruislip 22 D3
Ruislip Gardens 22 D3
Ruislip Manor 22 E3
Rum 82 D11
Rumbling Bridge 75 J1
Rumburgh 45 H7
Rumford 3 F1
Rumleigh 4 E4
Rumney 19 F4
Rumwell 7 K3
Runcorn 48 E4
Runcton 12 B6
Runcton Holme 44 A5
Rundlestone 5 F3
Runfold 22 B7
Runhall 44 E5
Runham *Norf* 45 J4
Runham *Norf* 45 K5
Runnington 7 K3
Runsell Green 24 D1
Runshaw Moor 48 E1
Runswick Bay 63 J5
Runtaleave 80 H4
Runwell 24 D2
Ruscombe *Glos* 20 B1
Ruscombe *W'ham* 22 A4
Rush Green *GtLon* 23 J3
Rush Green *Herts* 33 F6
Rushall *Here* 29 F5
Rushall *Norf* 45 F7
Rushall *Wilts* 20 E6
Rushall *WMid* 40 C5
Rushbrooke 34 C2
Rushbury 38 E6
Rushden *Herts* 33 G5
Rushden *N'hants* 32 C2
Rushford *Devon* 4 E3
Rushford *Norf* 44 D7
Rushgreen 49 F4
Rushlake Green 13 K5
Rushmere 45 J7
Rushmere St. Andrew 35 G4
Rushmoor 22 B7
Rushock 29 H1
Rusholme 49 H3
Rushton *ChesW&C* 48 E6
Rushton *N'hants* 42 B7
Rushton *Shrop* 39 F5
Rushton Spencer 49 J6
Rushwick 29 H3
Rushy Green 13 H5
Rushyford 62 C4
Ruskie 80 B10
Ruskington 52 D7
Rusko 65 F5
Rusland 55 G1
Rusper 13 F3
Ruspidge 29 F7
Russ Hill 23 F7
Russell Green 34 B7
Russell's Green 14 C6
Russell's Water 22 A2
Russel's Green 35 G1
Rusthall 13 J3
Rustington 12 D6
Ruston 59 F1
Ruston Parva 59 G3
Ruswarp 63 J6
Rutherend 74 E5
Rutherford 76 E7
Rutherglen 74 E4
Ruthernbridge 4 A4
Ruthin (Rhuthun) *Denb* 47 K7
Ruthin *VGlam* 18 C4
Ruthrieston 85 P10
Ruthven *Aber* 85 K6
Ruthven *Angus* 80 H6
Ruthven *High* 84 B11
Ruthvoes 3 G2
Ruthwaite 60 D3
Ruthwell 69 F7
Rutland Water *Rut* LE15 8QL 42 B5
Ruyton-XI-Towns 38 C3
Ryal 71 F6
Ryal Fold 56 B7
Ryall *Dorset* 8 D5
Ryall *Worcs* 29 H4
Ryarsh 23 K6
Rydal 60 E6
Ryde 11 G5
Rydon 6 B5
Rye 14 E5
Rye Foreign 14 D5
Rye Harbour *ESuss* TN31 7TX 14 E6
Rye Harbour 14 E6
Rye Park 23 G1
Rye Street 29 G5
Ryebank 38 E2
Ryeford 29 F6
Ryehill 59 J7
Ryhall 42 D4
Ryhill 51 F1
Ryhope 62 E1
Rylands 41 H2
Rylstone 56 E4
Ryme Intrinseca 8 E3
Ryther 58 B6
Ryton *Glos* 29 G5
Ryton *NYorks* 58 D2
Ryton *Shrop* 39 G5
Ryton *T&W* 71 G7
Ryton-on-Dunsmore 30 E1

S

Sabden 56 C6
Sabden Fold 56 D6
Sackers Green 34 D5
Sacombe 33 G7
Sacombe Green 33 G7
Sacriston 62 C2
Sadberge 62 D5
Saddell 73 F7
Saddington 41 J6
Saddle Bow 44 A4
Sadgill 61 F6
Saffron Walden 33 J5
Sageston 16 D5
Saham Hills 44 D5
Saham Toney 44 C5
Saighdinis 88 C2
Saighton 48 D6
St. Abbs 77 H4
St. Agnes 2 E3
St Agnes Mining District (Cornwall & West Devon Mining Landscape) *Corn* 2 E3
St. Aidan's Winery *N'umb* TD15 2RX 77 K6
St. Albans 22 E1
St. Albans Cathedral *Herts* AL1 1BY 22 E1
St. Allen 3 F3
St. Andrews 81 L9
St. Andrew's & Blackfriars Halls *Norf* NR3 1AU 134 Norwich
St. Andrews Major 18 E4
St. Anne 3 J4
St. Anne's 55 G7
St. Ann's 69 F4
St. Ann's Chapel *Corn* 4 E3
St. Ann's Chapel *Devon* 5 G6
St. Anthony 3 F5
St. Anthony-in-Meneage 2 E6
St. Anthony's Hill 13 K6
St. Arvans 19 J2
St. Asaph (Llanelwy) 47 J5
St. Athan 18 D5
St. Aubin 3 J7
St. Audries 7 K1
St Augustine's Abbey (Canterbury Cathedral, St Augustine's Abbey, & St Martin's Church) *Kent* CT1 1PF 15 G2
St. Austell 4 A5
St. Bees 60 A5
St. Blazey 4 A5
St. Blazey Gate 4 A5
St. Boswells 76 D7
St. Botolph's Church, Boston *Lincs* PE21 6NP 43 G1
St. Brelade 3 J7
St. Breock 3 G1
St. Breward 4 A3
St. Briavels 19 J1
St. Brides 16 B4
St. Brides Major 18 B4
St. Bride's Netherwent 19 H3
St. Brides Wentlooge 19 F3
St. Bride's-super-Ely 18 D4
St. Budeaux 4 E5
St. Buryan 2 B6
St. Catherine 20 A5
St. Catherines 79 N10
St. Clears (Sanclêr) 17 F4
St. Cleer 4 C4
St. Clement *Chanl* 3 K7
St. Clement *Corn* 3 F4
St. Clether 4 C2
St. Colmac 73 J4
St. Columb Major 3 G2
St. Columb Minor 3 F2
St. Columb Road 3 G3
St. Combs 85 Q4
St. Cross South Elmham 45 G7
St. Cyrus 81 N4
St. Davids *Fife* 75 K2
St. David's (Tyddewi) *Pembs* 16 A3
St. David's *P&K* 80 E8
St. David's Hall *Cardiff* CF10 1AH 124 Cardiff
St. Day 2 E4
St. Decumans 7 J1
St. Dennis 3 G3
St. Denys 11 F3
St. Dogmaels (Llandudoch) 16 E1
St. Dogwells 16 C3
St. Dominick 4 E4
St. Donats 18 C5
St. Edith's Marsh 20 C5
St. Endellion 3 G1
St. Enoder 3 F3
St. Erme 3 F4
St. Erney 4 D5
St. Erth 2 C5
St. Erth Praze 2 C5
St. Ervan 3 F1
St. Eval 3 F2
St. Ewe 3 G4
St. Fagans 18 E4
St. Fagans National History Museum *Cardiff* CF5 6XB 99 A5
St. Fergus 85 Q5
St. Fillans 80 B8
St. Florence 16 D5
St. Gennys 4 B1
St. George *Bristol* 19 K4
St. George *Conwy* 47 H5
St. Georges *NSom* 19 G5
St. George's *Tel&W* 39 G4
St. George's *VGlam* 18 D4
St. George's Hall, Liverpool *Mersey* L1 1JJ 131 D3
St. Germans 4 D5
St. Giles' Cathedral *Edin* EH1 1RE 126 F4
St. Giles in the Wood 6 D4
St. Giles on the Heath 6 B6
St. Harmon 27 J1
St. Helen Auckland 62 B4
St. Helena 45 F4
St. Helen's *ESuss* 14 D6
St. Helens *IoW* 11 H6
St. Helens *Mersey* 48 E3
St. Helier *Chanl* 3 J7
St. Helier *GtLon* 23 F5
St. Hilary *Corn* 2 C5
St. Hilary *VGlam* 18 D4
St. Hill 13 G3
St. Ibbs 32 E6
St. Illtyd 19 F1
St. Ippollitts 32 E6
St. Ishmael 17 G5
St. Ishmael's 16 B5
St. Issey 3 G1
St. Ive 4 D4
St. Ives *Cambs* 33 G1
St. Ives *Corn* 2 C4
St. Ives *Dorset* 10 C4
St. James South Elmham 45 H7
St. John *Chanl* 3 J6
St. John *Corn* 4 E5
St. John the Baptist Church, Cirencester *Glos* GL7 2NX 20 D1
St. John's *GtLon* 23 G4
St. John's *IoM* 54 B5
St. John's *Surr* 22 C6
St. John's *Worcs* 29 H3
St. John's Chapel *Devon* 6 D3
St. John's Chapel *Dur* 61 K3
St. John's Fen End 43 J4
St. John's Hall 62 A3
St. John's Highway 43 J4
St. John's Kirk 75 H7
St. John's Town of Dalry 68 B5
St. Judes 54 C4
St. Just 2 A5
St. Just in Roseland 3 F5
St Just Mining District (Cornwall & West Devon Mining Landscape) *Corn* 2 A5
St. Katherines 85 M7
St. Keverne 2 E6
St. Kew 4 A3
St. Kew Highway 4 A3
St. Keyne 4 C4
St. Lawrence *Corn* 4 A4
St. Lawrence *Essex* 25 F1
St. Lawrence *IoW* 11 G7
St. Lawrence's Church, Eyam *Derbys* S32 5QH 50 E5
St. Leonards *Bucks* 22 C1
St. Leonards *Dorset* 10 C4
St. Leonards *ESuss* 14 D7
St. Leonards Grange 11 F5
St. Leonard's Street 23 K6
St. Levan 2 A6
St. Lythans 18 E4
St. Mabyn 4 A3
St. Madoes 80 G8
St. Margaret South Elmham 45 H7
St. Margarets *Here* 28 C5
St. Margarets *Herts* 33 G7
St. Margarets *Wilts* 21 F5
St. Margaret's at Cliffe 15 J3
St Margaret's Church (Palace of Westminster & Westminster Abbey inc. St Margaret's Church) *GtLon* SW1P 3JX 105 A7
St. Margaret's Hope 89 D8
St. Mark's 54 B6
St. Martin *Chanl* 3 J5
St. Martin *Chanl* 3 K7
St. Martin *Corn* 2 E6
St. Martin *Corn* 4 C5
St. Martin-in-the-Fields Church *GtLon* WC2N 4JH 132 E3
St. Martin's *IoS* 2 C1
St. Martins *P&K* 80 G7
St. Martin's *Shrop* 38 C2
St Martin's Church (Canterbury Cathedral, St Augustine's Abbey, & St Martin's Church) *Kent* CT1 1PW 15 G2
St. Mary 3 J6
St. Mary Bourne 21 H6
St. Mary Church 18 D4
St. Mary Cray 23 H5
St. Mary Hill 18 C4
St. Mary Hoo 24 D4
St. Mary in the Marsh 15 F5
St. Mary Magdalene Chapel, Sandringham *Norf* PE35 6EH 44 A3
St. Mary the Virgin Church, Holy Island *N'umb* TD15 2RX 77 K6
St. Mary the Virgin Church, Oxford *Oxon* OX1 4AH 21 J1
St. Mary the Virgin Church, Rye *ESuss* TN31 7HE 14 E6
St. Marychurch 5 K4
St. Mary's *IoS* 2 C1
St. Mary's *Ork* 89 D7
St. Mary's Airport 2 C1
St. Mary's Bay 15 F5
St. Mary's Church, Whitby *NYorks* YO22 4JT 63 K5
St. Mary's Grove 19 H5
St. Maughans Green 28 D7
St. Mawes 3 F5
St. Mawgan 3 F2
St. Mellion 4 D4
St. Mellons 19 F3
St. Merryn 3 F1
St. Mewan 3 G3
St. Michael Church 8 C1
St. Michael Penkevil 3 F4
St. Michael Caerhays 3 G4
St. Michael South Elmham 45 H7
St. Michaels *Fife* 81 K8
St. Michaels *Kent* 14 D4
St. Michaels *Worcs* 28 E2
St. Michael's Church, Hathersage *Derbys* S32 1AJ 50 E4
St. Michael's Mount *Corn* TR17 0HT 2 C5
St. Michael's on Wyre 55 H5
St. Mildred's Church, Whippingham *IoW* PO32 6LP 11 G5
St. Minver 3 G1
St. Monans 81 L10
St. Mungo Museum of Religious Life & Art *Glas* G4 0RH 127 H3
St. Mungo's Cathedral *Glas* G4 0QZ 127 J3
St. Neot 4 B4
St. Neots 32 E2
St. Newlyn East 3 F3
St. Nicholas *Pembs* 16 C2
St. Nicholas *VGlam* 18 D4
St. Nicholas at Wade 25 J5
St. Ninians 75 F1
St. Osyth 35 F7
St. Ouen 3 J7
St. Owen's Cross 28 E6
St. Paul's Cathedral, London *GtLon* EC4M 8AD 132 J3
St. Paul's Cray 23 H5
St. Paul's Walden 32 E6
St. Peter 3 J7
St. Peter Port 3 J5
St. Peter's 25 K5
St. Petrox 16 C6
St. Pinnock 4 C4
St. Quivox 67 H1
St. Ruan 2 E7
St. Sampson 3 J5
St. Saviour *Chanl* 3 H5
St. Saviour *Chanl* 3 K7
St. Stephen 3 G3
St. Stephens *Corn* 4 E5
St. Stephens *Corn* 6 B7
St. Stephens *Herts* 22 E1
St. Teath 4 A2
St. Thomas 7 H6
St. Tudy 4 A3
St. Twynnells 16 C6
St. Veep 4 B5
St. Vigeans 81 M6
St. Wenn 3 G2
St. Weonards 28 D6
St. Winnow 4 B5
St. Winwaloe's Church, Gunwalloe *Corn* TR12 7QE 2 D6
Saintbury 30 C5
Saintfield 93 K11
Salachail 79 M5
Salcombe 5 H7
Salcombe Regis 7 K7
Salcott 34 D7
Sale 49 G3
Sale Green 29 J3
Saleby 53 H5
Salehurst 14 C5
Salem *Carmar* 17 K3
Salem *Cere* 37 F7
Salem *Gwyn* 46 D7
Salen *A&B* 78 G6
Salen *High* 78 H4
Salendine Nook 50 D1
Salesbury 56 B6
Saleway 29 J3
Salford *CenBeds* 32 C5
Salford *GtMan* 49 H3
Salford *Oxon* 30 D6
Salford Priors 30 B3
Salfords 23 F7
Salhouse 45 H4
Saline 75 J1
Salisbury 10 C2
Salisbury Cathedral *Wilts* SP1 2EF 135 Salisbury
Salkeld Dykes 61 G3
Sallachy *High* 83 K7
Sallachy *High* 86 H9
Salle 45 F3
Salmonby 53 G5
Salperton 30 B6
Salph End 32 D3
Salsburgh 75 G4
Salt 40 B3
Salt Hill 22 C3
Salt Holme 62 E4
Saltaire 57 G6
Saltaire *WYorks* BD17 7EF 57 G6
Saltash 4 E5
Saltburn 84 B3
Saltburn-by-the-Sea 63 G4
Saltburn Cliff Lift *R&C* TS12 1DP 63 G4
Saltby 42 B3
Saltcoats *Cumb* 60 B7
Saltcoats *NAyr* 74 A6
Saltcotes 55 G7
Saltdean 13 G6
Salterbeck 60 A4
Salterforth 56 D5
Saltergate 63 J7
Salterswall 49 F6
Saltfleet 53 H3
Saltfleetby All Saints 53 H3
Saltfleetby St. Clements 53 H3
Saltfleetby St. Peter 53 H4
Saltford 19 K5
Salthaugh Grange 59 J7
Salthouse 44 E1
Saltley 40 C7
Saltmarshe 58 D7
Saltney 48 C6
Salton 58 D1
Saltrens 6 C3
Saltwell Park, Gateshead *T&W* NE9 5AX 71 H7
Saltwick 71 G6
Saltwood 15 G4
Salvington 12 E6
Salwarpe 29 H2
Salwayash 8 D5
Sambourne 30 B2
Sambrook 39 G3
Samlesbury 56 B6
Sampford Arundel 7 K4
Sampford Brett 7 J1
Sampford Courtenay 6 E5
Sampford Moor 7 K4
Sampford Peverell 7 J4
Sampford Spiney 5 F3
Samsonagh 91 H12
Samuelston 76 C3
Sanaigmore 72 A3
Sancreed 2 B6
Sancton 59 F6
Sand 19 H7
Sand Hutton 58 C4
Sandaig *A&B* 78 A6
Sandaig *High* 82 H10
Sandal Magna 51 F1
Sanday 89 F3
Sanday Airfield 89 F3
Sandbach 49 G6
Sandbank 73 K2
Sandbanks 10 B6
Sandend 85 K4
Sanderstead 23 G5
Sandford *Cumb* 61 J5
Sandford *Devon* 7 G5
Sandford *Dorset* 9 J6
Sandford *IoW* 11 G6
Sandford *NSom* 19 H6
Sandford *Shrop* 38 C3
Sandford *Shrop* 38 E2
Sandford *SLan* 75 F6
Sandford Orcas 9 F2
Sandford St. Martin 31 F6
Sandford-on-Thames 21 J1
Sandgarth 89 E6
Sandgate 15 H4
Sandgreen 65 F5
Sandhaven 85 P4
Sandhead 64 A5
Sandhills *Dorset* 8 E4
Sandhills *Dorset* 9 F3
Sandhills *Surr* 12 C3
Sandhills *WYorks* 57 J6
Sandhoe 70 E7
Sandholes 93 C9
Sandholme *ERid* 58 E6
Sandholme *Lincs* 43 G2
Sandhurst *BrackF* 22 B5
Sandhurst *Glos* 29 H6
Sandhurst *Kent* 14 C5
Sandhurst Cross 14 C5
Sandhutton 57 J1
Sandiacre 41 G2
Sandilands 53 J4

Taynuilt (Taigh an Uillt) 79 M7
Tayock 81 M5
Tayvullin 72 A3
Tayport 81 K8
Tayvallich 73 F2
Tea Green 32 E6
Tealby 52 E3
Tealing 81 K7
Team Valley 71 H7
Teanamachar 88 B2
Teangue 82 G10
Tebay 61 H6
Tebworth 32 C6
Techniquest *Cardiff* CF10 5BW 99 C6
Tedburn St. Mary 7 G6
Tedd 91 J10
Teddington *Glos* 29 J5
Teddington *GtLon* 22 E4
Tedstone Delamere 29 F3
Tedstone Wafre 29 F3
Teemore 91 K14
Teesside International Airport 62 D5
Teeton 31 H1
Teffont Evias 9 J1
Teffont Magna 9 J1
Tegryn 17 F2
Tehidy Country Park *Corn* TR14 0HA 2 D4
Teifi Marshes Nature Reserve *Pembs* SA43 2TB 16 E1
Teigh 42 B4
Teign Village 7 G7
Teigngrace 5 J3
Teignmouth 5 K3
Telford 39 F5
Telford Wonderland *Tel&W* TF3 4AY 39 G5
Telham 14 C6
Tellisford 20 B6
Telscombe 13 H6
Telscombe Cliffs 13 H6
Templand 69 F5
Temple *Corn* 4 B3
Temple *L&C* 93 J10
Temple *Midlo* 76 B5
Temple Balsall 30 D1
Temple Bar 26 E3
Temple Cloud 19 K6
Temple End 33 K3
Temple Ewell 15 H3
Temple Grafton 30 C3
Temple Guiting 30 B6
Temple Herdewyke 30 E3
Temple Hirst 58 C7
Temple Newsam *WYorks* LS15 0AE 117 M3
Temple Normanton 51 G6
Temple Sowerby 61 H4
Templecombe 9 G2
Templemoyle 90 M5
Templepatrick 92 H8
Templeton *Devon* 7 G4
Templeton *Pembs* 16 E4
Templeton Bridge 7 G4
Tempo 91 K12
Tempsford 32 E3
Ten Mile Bank 44 A6
Tenbury Wells 28 E2
Tenby (Dinbych-y-pysgod) 16 E5
Tendring 35 F6
Tendring Green 35 F6
Tenterden 14 D4
Terally 64 B6
Terling 34 B7
Tern 39 F4
Ternhill 39 F2
Terregles 65 K3
Terriers 22 B2
Terrington 58 C2
Terrington St. Clement 43 J3
Terrington St. John 43 J4
Terry's Green 30 C1
Terrydremont 92 B5
Teston 14 C2
Testwood 10 E3
Tetbury 20 B2
Tetbury Upton 20 B2
Tetchill 38 C2
Tetcott 6 B6
Tetford 53 G5
Tetney 53 G2
Tetney Lock 53 G2
Tetsworth 21 K1
Tettenhall 40 A5
Tettenhall Wood 40 A6
Tetworth 33 F3
Teversal 51 G6
Teversham 33 H3
Teviot Smokery and Water Gardens *ScBord* TD5 8LE 70 C1
Teviothead 69 K3
Tewin 33 F7
Tewkesbury 29 H5
Tewkesbury Abbey *Glos* GL20 5RZ 29 H5
Teynham 25 F5
Thackley 57 G6
Thainston 81 M3
Thakeham 12 E5
Thame 22 A1
Thames Ditton 22 E5
Thames Haven 24 D3
Thamesmead 23 H3
Thanington 15 G2
Thankerton 75 H7
Tharston 45 F6
Thatcham 21 J5
Thatto Heath 48 E3
Thaxted 33 K5
The Apes Hall 43 J6
The Bage 28 B4
The Balloch 80 D9
The Bar 12 E4
The Battery 92 H7
The Birks 85 M10
The Bog 38 C6
The Bourne 22 B7
The Bratch 40 A6
The Broad 28 D2
The Bryn 19 G1
The Burf 29 H2
The Bush 93 D10
The Butts 20 A7
The Camp 20 C1
The Chequer 38 D1
The City *Bucks* 22 A2
The City *Suff* 45 H7
The Cluster 93 E13
The Common *Wilts* 10 D1
The Common *Wilts* 20 D3
The Craigs *CC&G* 92 E5
The Craigs *High* 83 Q1
The Cronk 54 C4
The Dark Hedges *CC&G* BT53 8PX 92 F3
The Delves 40 C6
The Den 74 B5
The Den & The Glen *Aber* AB12 5FT 85 N11
The Diamond *F&O* 91 L10
The Diamond *Mid Ulster* 93 E9
The Dicker 13 J6
The Down 39 F6
The Drones 92 F4
The Drums 81 J4
The Eaves 19 K1
The English Lake District *Cumb* 60 D5
The Fingerpost 91 K11
The Flatt 70 A6
The Folly 32 E7
The Forge 28 C3
The Forstal *ESuss* 13 J3
The Forstal *Kent* 15 F4
The Forth Bridge *Fife/WLoth* EH30 9SF 75 K2
The Grange *Lincs* 53 J5
The Grange *Shrop* 38 C2
The Grange *Surr* 23 G7
The Green *Cumb* 54 E1
The Green *Essex* 34 B7
The Green *Flints* 48 B6
The Green *Wilts* 9 H1
The Grove 29 H4
The Haven 12 D3
The Headland 63 F3
The Heath 40 C2
The Herberts 18 C4
The Hermitage 23 F6
The Hill 54 E1
The Holme 57 H4
The Howe 54 A7
The Isle 38 D4
The Laurels 45 H6
The Leacon 14 E4
The Lee 22 B1
The Leigh 29 H6
The Lhen 54 C3
The Lodge 73 K1
The Lodge Visitor Centre *Stir* FK8 3SX 80 A10
The Long Kesh 93 H10
The Loup 92 E8
The Luxulyan Valley (Cornwall & West Devon Mining Landscape) *Corn* 3 H3
The Marsh 38 C6
The Moor *ESuss* 14 D6
The Moor *Kent* 14 C5
The Mumbles 17 K7
The Murray 74 E5
The Mythe 29 H5
The Narth 19 J1
The Node 33 F7
The Oval 20 A5
The Port of Hayle (Cornwall & West Devon Mining Landscape) *Corn* 2 C5
The Quarter 14 D3
The Reddings 29 J6
The Rhos 16 D4
The Rock 93 C9
The Rookery 49 H7
The Rowe 40 A2
The Sale 40 D4
The Sands 22 B7
The Sheddings 92 H6
The Shoe 20 B4
The Six Towns 92 C7
The Slade 21 J4
The Smithies 39 F6
The Spa 93 J12
The Stocks 14 E5
The Swillett 22 D2
The Thrift 33 G5
The Vauld 28 E4
The Wern 48 B7
The Wyke 39 G5
Theakston 57 J1
Thealby 52 B1
Theale *Som* 19 H7
Theale *WBerks* 21 K4
Thearne 59 G6
Theberton 35 J2
Thedden Grange 11 H1
Theddingworth 41 J7
Theddlethorpe All Saints 53 H4
Theddlethorpe St. Helen 53 H4
Thelbridge Barton 7 F4
Thelbridge Cross 7 F4
Thelnetham 34 E1
Thelveton 45 F7
Thelwall 49 F4
Themelthorpe 44 E3
Thenford 31 G4
Therfield 33 G5
Thetford *Lincs* 42 E4
Thetford *Norf* 44 C7
Thetford Forest Park *Norf* IP27 0TJ 44 C7
Thethwaite 60 E2
Theydon Bois 23 H2
Theydon Garnon 23 H2
Theydon Mount 23 H2
Thickwood 20 B4
Thimbleby *Lincs* 53 F6
Thimbleby *NYorks* 62 E7
Thingley 20 B5
Thirkleby 57 K2
Thirlby 57 K1
Thirlestane 76 D6
Thirn 57 H1
Thirsk 57 K1
Thirston New Houses 71 G4
Thirtleby 59 H6
Thistleton *Lancs* 55 H6
Thistleton *Rut* 42 C4
Thistley Green 33 K1
Thixendale 58 E3
Thockrington 70 E6
Tholomas Drove 43 G5
Tholthorpe 57 K3
Thomas Chapel 16 E5
Thomas Close 60 F2
Thompson 44 D6
Thompson's Bridge 91 J13
Thomshill 84 G5
Thong 24 C4
Thongsbridge 50 D2
Thoralby 57 F1
Thoresby 51 J5
Thoresthorpe 53 H5
Thoresway 52 E3
Thorganby *Lincs* 53 F3
Thorganby *NYorks* 58 C5
Thorgill 63 H7
Thorington 35 J1
Thorington Street 34 E5
Thorley 33 H7
Thorley Houses 33 H6
Thorley Street *Herts* 33 H7
Thorley Street *IoW* 10 E6
Thormanby 57 K2
Thornaby-on-Tees 62 E5
Thornage 44 E2
Thornborough *Bucks* 31 J5
Thornborough *NYorks* 57 H2
Thornbury *Devon* 6 B5
Thornbury *Here* 29 F3
Thornbury *SGlos* 19 K2
Thornbury *WYorks* 57 G6
Thornby 31 H1
Thorncliff 50 E1
Thorncliffe 50 C7
Thorncombe 8 C4
Thorncombe Street 22 D7
Thorncote Green 32 E4
Thorncross 11 F6
Thorndon 35 F2
Thorndon Country Park *Essex* CM13 3RZ 24 C2
Thorndon Cross 6 D6
Thorne 51 J1
Thorne St. Margaret 7 J3
Thorner 57 J6
Thorney *Bucks* 22 D4
Thorney *Notts* 52 B5
Thorney *Peter* 43 F5
Thorney *Som* 8 D2
Thorney Close 62 D1
Thorney Hill 10 D5
Thornfalcon 8 B2
Thornford 9 F3
Thorngrafton 70 C7
Thorngrove 8 C1
Thorngumbald 59 J7
Thornham 44 B1
Thornham Magna 35 F1
Thornham Parva 35 F1
Thornhaugh 42 D5
Thornhill *Cardiff* 18 E3
Thornhill *Cumb* 60 B6
Thornhill *Derbys* 50 D4
Thornhill *D&G* 68 D4
Thornhill *Soton* 11 F3
Thornhill *Stir* 80 B10
Thornhill *WYorks* 50 E1
Thornhill Lees 50 E1
Thornholme 59 H3
Thornicombe 9 H4
Thornley *Dur* 62 B3
Thornley *Dur* 62 D3
Thornley Gate 61 K1
Thornliebank 74 D5
Thornroan 85 N7
Thorns 34 B3
Thorns Green 49 G4
Thornsett 50 C4
Thornthwaite *Cumb* 60 D4
Thornthwaite *NYorks* 57 G4
Thornton *Bucks* 31 J5
Thornton *ERid* 58 D5
Thornton *Fife* 76 A1
Thornton *Lancs* 55 G5
Thornton *Leics* 41 G5
Thornton *Lincs* 53 F6
Thornton *Mersey* 48 C2
Thornton *Middl* 62 E5
Thornton *N'umb* 77 H6
Thornton *Pembs* 16 C5
Thornton *WYorks* 57 G6
Thornton Bridge 57 K2
Thornton Curtis 52 D1
Thornton Heath 23 G5
Thornton Hough 48 C4
Thornton in Lonsdale 56 B2
Thornton le Moor 52 D3
Thornton Park 77 H6
Thornton Rust 56 E1
Thornton Steward 57 G1
Thornton Watlass 57 H1
Thorntonhall 74 D5
Thornton-in-Craven 56 E5
Thornton-le-Beans 62 E7
Thornton-le-Clay 58 C3
Thornton-le-Dale 58 E1
Thornton-le-Moor 57 J1
Thornton-le-Moors 48 D5
Thornton-le-Street 57 K1
Thorntonloch 77 F3
Thornwood 23 H1
Thornylee 76 C7
Thoroton 42 A1
Thorp Arch 57 K5
Thorpe *Derbys* 50 D7
Thorpe *ERid* 59 F5
Thorpe *Lincs* 53 H4
Thorpe *Norf* 45 J6
Thorpe *Notts* 51 K7
Thorpe *NYorks* 57 F3
Thorpe *Surr* 22 D5
Thorpe Abbotts 45 F7
Thorpe Acre 41 H3
Thorpe Arnold 42 A3
Thorpe Audlin 51 G1
Thorpe Bassett 58 E2
Thorpe Bay 25 F3
Thorpe by Water 42 B6
Thorpe Constantine 40 E5
Thorpe Culvert 53 H6
Thorpe End 45 G4
Thorpe Green *Essex* 35 F6
Thorpe Green *Lancs* 55 J7
Thorpe Green *Suff* 34 D3
Thorpe Hall 58 B2
Thorpe Hesley 51 F3
Thorpe in Balne 51 H1
Thorpe in the Fallows 52 C4
Thorpe Langton 42 A6
Thorpe Larches 62 D4
Thorpe le Street 58 E5
Thorpe Malsor 32 B1
Thorpe Mandeville 31 G4
Thorpe Market 45 G2
Thorpe Morieux 34 D3
Thorpe on the Hill *Lincs* 52 C6
Thorpe on the Hill *WYorks* 57 J7
Thorpe Park *Surr* KT16 8PN 22 D5
Thorpe Row 44 D5
Thorpe Salvin 51 H4
Thorpe Satchville 42 A4
Thorpe St. Andrew 45 G5
Thorpe St. Peter 53 H6
Thorpe Street 34 E1
Thorpe Thewles 62 E4
Thorpe Tilney Dales 52 E7
Thorpe Underwood *NYorks* 57 K4
Thorpe Underwood *N'hants* 42 A7
Thorpe Waterville 42 D7
Thorpe Willoughby 58 B6
Thorpefield 57 K2
Thorpe-le-Soken 35 F6
Thorpeness 35 J2
Thorpland 44 A5
Thorrington 34 E6
Thorverton 7 H5
Thrandeston 35 F1
Thrapston 32 C1
Threapland 56 E3
Threapwood 38 D1
Threapwood Head 40 C1
Three Ashes 19 K7
Three Bridges 13 F3
Three Burrows 2 E4
Three Chimneys 14 D4
Three Cocks (Aberllynfi) 28 A5
Three Counties Showground *Worcs* WR13 6NW 29 G4
Three Crosses 17 J6
Three Cups Corner 13 K4
Three Hammers 4 C2
Three Holes 43 J5
Three Leg Cross 13 K3
Three Legged Cross 10 B4
Three Mile Cross 22 A5
Three Oaks 14 D6
Threehammer Common 45 H4
Threekingham 42 D2
Threemilestone 2 E4
Threlkeld 60 E4
Threshfield 56 E3
Threxton Hill 44 C5
Thrigby 45 J4
Thrigby Hall Wildlife Gardens *Norf* NR29 3DR 45 J4
Thringarth 61 L4
Thringstone 41 G4
Thrintoft 62 D7
Thriplow 33 H4
Throapham 51 H4
Throckenholt 43 G5
Throcking 33 G5
Throckley 71 G7
Throckmorton 29 J4
Throop 9 H5
Throphill 71 G5
Thropton 71 F3
Througham 20 C1
Throwleigh 6 E6
Throwley 14 E2
Throws 33 K6
Thrumpton *Notts* 41 H2
Thrumpton *Notts* 51 K5
Thrumster 87 R5
Thrunton 71 F2
Thrupp *Glos* 20 B1
Thrupp *Oxon* 21 F2
Thrupp *Oxon* 31 F7
Thruscross 57 G4
Thrushelton 6 C7
Thrussington 41 J4
Thruxton *Hants* 21 F7
Thruxton *Here* 28 D5
Thrybergh 51 G3
Thrybergh Country Park *SYorks* S65 4NU 111 G1
Thulston 41 G2
Thunder Bridge 50 D1
Thundergay 73 G6
Thundersley 24 E3
Thundridge 33 G7
Thurcaston 41 H4
Thurcroft 51 G4
Thurdon 6 A4
Thurgarton *Norf* 45 F2
Thurgarton *Notts* 41 J1
Thurgoland 50 E2
Thurlaston *Leics* 41 H6
Thurlaston *Warks* 31 F1
Thurlbear 8 B2
Thurlby *Lincs* 42 E4
Thurlby *Lincs* 52 C6
Thurlby *Lincs* 53 H5
Thurleigh 32 D3
Thurlestone 5 G6
Thurloxton 8 B1
Thurlstone 50 E2
Thurlton 45 J6
Thurlwood 49 H7
Thurmaston 41 J5
Thurnby 41 J5
Thurne 45 J4
Thurnham 14 D2
Thurning *Norf* 44 E3
Thurning *N'hants* 42 D7
Thurnscoe 51 G2
Thursby 60 E1
Thursden 56 E6
Thursford 44 D2
Thursford Collection *Norf* NR21 0AS 44 D2
Thursley 12 C3
Thurso (Inbhir Theòrsa) 87 P3
Thurstaston 48 B4
Thurston 34 D2
Thurston Clough 49 J2
Thurstonfield 60 E1
Thurstonland 50 D1
Thurton 45 H5
Thurvaston *Derbys* 40 D2
Thurvaston *Derbys* 40 E2
Thuxton 44 E5
Thwaite *NYorks* 61 K7
Thwaite *Suff* 35 F2
Thwaite Head 60 E7
Thwaite St. Mary 45 H6
Thwaites 57 F5
Thwaites Brow 57 F5
Thwing 59 G2
Tibbermore 80 F8
Tibberton *Glos* 29 G6
Tibberton *Tel&W* 39 F3
Tibberton *Worcs* 29 J3
Tibbie Shiels Inn 69 H1
Tibenham 45 F6
Tibshelf 51 G6
Tibthorpe 59 F4
Ticehurst 13 K3
Tichborne 11 G1
Tickencote 42 C5
Tickenham 19 H4
Tickford End 32 B4
Tickhill 51 H3
Ticklerton 38 D6
Ticknall 41 F3
Tickton 59 G5
Tidbury Green 30 C1
Tidcombe 21 F6
Tiddington *Oxon* 21 K1
Tiddington *Warks* 30 D3
Tiddleywink 20 B4
Tidebrook 13 K4
Tideford 4 D5
Tideford Cross 4 D4
Tidenham 19 J2
Tidenham Chase 19 J2
Tideswell 50 D5
Tidmarsh 21 K4
Tidmington 30 D5
Tidpit 10 B3
Tidworth 21 F7
Tiers Cross 16 C4
Tiffield 31 H3
Tigerton 81 L4
Tighnabruaich 73 H3
Tigley 5 H4
Tilbrook 32 D2
Tilbury 24 C4
Tilbury Green 34 B4
Tildarg 92 H7
Tile Hill 30 D1
Tilehurst 21 K4
Tilford 22 B7
Tilgate 13 F3
Tilgate Forest Row 13 F3
Tilgate Park *WSuss* RH10 5PQ 13 F3
Tillathrowie 85 J7
Tillers' Green 29 F5
Tilley 38 E3
Tillicoultry 75 H1
Tillietudlem 75 G6
Tillingham 25 F1
Tillington *Here* 28 D4
Tillington *WSuss* 12 C4
Tillington Common 28 D4
Tillyfourie 85 L9
Tilmanstone 15 J2
Tiln 51 K4
Tilney All Saints 43 J4
Tilney Fen End 43 J4
Tilney High End 43 J4
Tilney St. Lawrence 43 J4
Tilshead 20 D7
Tilstock 38 E2
Tilston 48 D7
Tilstone Fearnall 48 E6
Tilsworth 32 C6
Tilton on the Hill 42 A5
Tiltups End 20 B2
Timberland 52 E7
Timberland Dales 52 E6
Timbersbrook 49 H6
Timberscombe 7 H1
Timble 57 G4
Timewell 7 H3
Timperley 49 G4
Timsbury *B&NESom* 19 K6
Timsbury *Hants* 10 E2
Timsgearraidh 88 F4
Timworth 34 C2
Timworth Green 34 C2
Tincleton 9 G5
Tindale 61 H1
Tindon End 33 K5
Tingewick 31 H5
Tingley 57 H7
Tingrith 32 D5
Tingwall 89 D5
Tingwall (Lerwick Airport) 89 N8
Tinhay 6 B7
Tinney 4 C1
Tinshill 57 H6
Tinsley 51 G3
Tinsley Green 13 F3
Tintagel 4 A2
Tintagel Castle *Corn* PL34 0HE 4 A2
Tintern Parva 19 J1
Tintinhull 8 D3
Tintwistle 50 C3
Tinwald 69 F5
Tinwell 42 D5
Tippacott 7 F1
Tipps End 43 H6
Tiptoe 10 D5
Tipton 40 B6
Tipton St. John 7 J6
Tiptree 34 C7
Tiptree Heath 34 C7
Tiptree Museum *Essex* CO5 0RF 34 D7
Tirabad 27 H4
Tiraroe 91 K14
Tircur 90 L8
Tiree 78 A6
Tiree Airport 78 B6
Tirgan 92 D8
Tirley 29 H6
Tirphil 18 E1
Tirril 61 G4
Tir-y-dail 17 K4
Tisbury 9 J2
Tisman's Common 12 D3
Tissington 50 D7
Titanic Belfast BT3 9EP 121 Belfast
Titchberry 6 A3
Titchfield 11 G4
Titchmarsh 32 D1
Titchwell 44 B1
Titchwell Marsh *Norf* PE31 8BB 44 B1
Tithby 41 J2
Titley 28 C2
Titlington 71 G2
Titmore Green 33 F6
Titsey 23 H6
Titson 6 A5
Tittensor 40 A2
Tittesworth Reservoir & Visitor Centre *Staffs* ST13 8TQ 49 J7
Tittleshall 44 C3
Tiverton *ChesW&C* 48 E6
Tiverton *Devon* 7 H4
Tivetshall St. Margaret 45 F7
Tivetshall St. Mary 45 F7
Tivington 7 H1
Tixall 40 B3
Tixover 42 C5
Toab *Ork* 89 E7
Toab *Shet* 89 M11
Toberdoney 92 E3
Toberkeagh 92 F3
Tobermore 92 D7
Tobermory 78 G5
Toberonochy 79 J10
Tobson 88 G4
Tockenham 20 D4
Tockenham Wick 20 D3
Tockholes 56 B7
Tockington 19 K3
Tockwith 57 K4
Todber 9 G2
Toddington *CenBeds* 32 D6
Toddington *Glos* 30 B5
Todenham 30 D5
Todhills 69 J7
Todlachie 85 L9
Todmorden 56 E7
Todwick 51 G4
Toft *Cambs* 33 G3
Toft *Lincs* 42 D4
Toft *Shet* 89 N5
Toft Hill 62 B4
Toft Monks 45 J6
Toft next Newton 52 D4
Toftrees 44 C3
Tofts 87 R3
Toftwood 44 D4
Togston 71 H3
Tokavaig 82 G9
Tokers Green 21 K4
Tolastadh a'Chaolais 88 G4
Tolastadh Bho Thuath 88 L3
Toll Bar 51 H2
Toll of Birness 85 Q7
Tolland 7 K2
Tollard Farnham 9 J3
Tollard Royal 9 J3
Tollcross 74 E4
Toller Down Gate 8 E4
Toller Fratrum 8 E5
Toller Porcorum 8 E5
Toller Whelme 8 E4
Tollerton *Notts* 41 J2
Tollerton *NYorks* 58 B3
Tollesbury 34 D7
Tollesby 63 F5
Tolleshunt D'Arcy 34 D7
Tolleshunt Knights 34 D7
Tolleshunt Major 34 C7
Tolpuddle 9 G5
Tolvah 84 C11
Tolworth 22 E5
Tomatin 84 C8
Tombreck 84 A7
Tomchrasky (Tom Chrasgaidh) 83 N9
Tomdoun 83 M10
Tomich *High* 83 P8
Tomich *High* 84 B3
Tomintoul 84 F9
Tomnavoulin 84 G8
Ton Pentre 18 C2
Tonbridge 23 J7
Tondu 18 B3
Tonedale 7 K3
Toneel 91 H12
Tonfanau 36 E5
Tong *Kent* 14 D3
Tong *Shrop* 39 G5
Tong *WYorks* 57 H6
Tong Norton 39 G5
Tong Street 57 G6
Tonge 41 G3
Tongham 22 B7
Tongland 65 G5
Tongue 86 H4
Tongwynlais 18 E3
Tonmawr 18 B2
Tonna 18 A2
Tonnaboy 91 K13
Tonwell 33 G7
Tonyglaskan 91 K11
Tonypandy 18 C2
Tonyrefail 18 D3
Tonyteige 91 J13
Tonyvarnog 91 J14
Toome 92 E7
Toot Baldon 21 J1
Toot Hill 23 J1
Toothill *Hants* 10 E3
Toothill *Swin* 20 E3
Tooting Graveney 23 F4
Top End 32 D2
Top of Hebers 49 H2
Topcliffe 57 K2
Topcroft 45 G6
Topcroft Street 45 G6
Toppesfield 34 B5
Toppings 49 G1
Toprow 45 F6
Topsham 7 H7
Topsham Bridge 5 H5
Torbeg *Aber* 84 H11
Torbeg *NAyr* 66 D1
Torbothie 75 G5
Torbryan 5 J4
Torcross 5 J6
Tordarroch 84 A7
Tore (An Todhar) 84 A5
Torfrey 4 B5
Torksey 52 B5
Torlum 88 B3
Torlundy (Tòrr Lunndaidh) 79 N3
Tormarton 20 A4
Tormisdale 72 A5
Tormore 73 G7
Tornagrain 84 B5
Tornahaish 84 G10
Tornaveen 85 L10
Torness 83 R8
Toronto 62 B3
Torpenhow 60 D3
Torphichen 75 H3
Torphins 85 L10
Torpoint 4 E5
Torquay 5 K4
Torquhan 76 C6
Torr *CC&G* 92 H2
Torr *Devon* 5 F5
Torrance 74 E3
Torrance House 74 E5
Torre *Som* 7 J1
Torre *Torbay* 5 K4
Torridon 83 J5
Torrin 82 F8
Torrisdale *A&B* 73 F7
Torrisdale *High* 87 J3
Torrish 87 M8
Torrisholme 55 H3
Torroble 86 H9
Torry *Aber* 85 J6
Torry *Aberdeen* 85 P10
Torryburn 75 J2
Torsonce 76 C6
Torthorwald 69 F6
Tortington 12 C6
Torton 29 H1
Tortworth 20 A2
Torvaig 82 E6
Torver 60 D7
Torwood 75 G2
Torworth 51 J4
Tosberry 6 A3
Toscaig 82 H7
Toseland 33 F2
Tosside 56 C4
Tostock 34 D2
Totaig 82 B5
Tote Hill 12 B4
Totegan 87 L3
Totford 11 G1
Totham Hill 34 C7
Tothill 53 H4
Totland 10 E6
Totley 51 F5
Totnes 5 J4
Toton 41 H2
Totscore 82 D4
Tottenham 23 G2
Tottenhill 44 A4
Tottenhill Row 44 A4
Totteridge *Bucks* 22 B2
Totteridge *GtLon* 23 F2
Totternhoe 32 C6
Tottington *GtMan* 49 G1
Tottington *Norf* 44 C6
Totton 10 E3
Toulton 7 K2
Tournaig 83 J2
Tovil 14 C2
Tow Law 62 B3
Towan Cross 2 E4
Toward 73 K4
Towcester 31 H4
Towednack 2 B5
Tower Bridge Exhibition *GtLon* SE1 2UP 105 B7
Tower End 44 A4
Tower of London *GtLon* EC3N 4AB 105 B7
Towersey 22 A1
Towie 85 J9
Towiemore 84 H6
Town End *Cambs* 43 H6
Town End *Cumb* 55 H1
Town End *Mersey* 48 D4
Town Green *Lancs* 48 D2
Town Green *Norf* 45 H4
Town of Lowton 49 F3
Town Row 13 J3
Town Street 44 B7
Town Yetholm 70 D1
Towneley Hall Art Gallery & Museum *Lancs* BB11 3RQ 56 D6
Townfield 61 L2
Townhead *D&G* 65 G6
Townhead *SYorks* 50 D2
Townhead of Greenlaw 65 H4
Townhill *Fife* 75 K2
Townhill *Swan* 17 K6
Towns End 21 J6
Towns Green 49 F6
Townshend 2 C5
Towthorpe *ERid* 59 F3
Towthorpe *York* 58 C4
Towton 57 K6
Towyn 47 H5
Toynton All Saints 53 G6
Toynton Fen Side 53 G6
Toynton St. Peter 53 H6
Toy's Hill 23 H6
Trabboch 67 J1
Traboe 2 E6
Tradespark 84 C5
Trafford Centre 49 G3
Trafford Park 49 G3
Trago Mills, Newton Abbot *Devon* TQ12 6JD 5 J3
Trallong 27 J6
Trallwn 17 K6
Tram Inn 28 D5
Tranent 76 C3
Tranmere 48 C4
Trantlebeg 87 L4
Trantlemore 87 L4
Tranwell 71 G5
Trap 17 K4
Trap Street 49 H6
Traprain 76 D3
Trap's Green 30 C2
Traquair 76 B7
Trawden 56 E6
Trawscoed (Crosswood) 27 F1
Trawsfynydd 37 G2
Trealaw 18 D2
Treales 55 H6
Trearddur 46 A5
Tre-Aubrey 18 D4
Trebah Garden *Corn* TR11 5JZ 2 E6
Trebanog 18 D2
Trebanos 18 A1
Trebarrow 4 C1
Trebartha 4 C3
Trebarvah 2 E5
Trebarwith 4 A2
Trebeath 4 C2
Trebetherick 3 G1
Trebister 89 N9
Tre-boeth 17 K6
Treborough 7 J2
Trebudannon 3 F2
Trebullett 4 D3
Treburley 4 D3
Treburrick 3 F1
Trebyan 4 A4
Trecastle 27 H6
Trecott 6 E5
Trecrogo 6 B7
Trecwn 16 C2
Trecynon 18 C1
Tredaule 4 C2
Tredavoe 2 B6
Treddiog 16 B3
Tredegar 18 E1
Tredington *Glos* 29 J6
Tredington *Warks* 30 D4
Tredinnick *Corn* 3 G2
Tredinnick *Corn* 4 C5
Tredogan 18 D5
Tredomen 28 A5
Tredrissi 16 D1
Tredunnock 19 G2
Tredustan 28 A5
Tredworth 29 H7
Treen *Corn* 2 A6
Treen *Corn* 2 B5
Treesmill 4 A5
Treeton 51 G4
Trefasser 16 B2
Trefdraeth 46 C5
Trefecca 28 A5
Trefechan 18 D1
Trefeglwys 37 J6
Trefenter 27 F2
Treffgarne 16 C3
Treffynnon 16 B3
Trefgarn Owen 16 B3
Trefil 28 A7
Trefilan 26 E3
Trefin 16 B2
Treflach 38 B3
Trefnanney 38 B4
Trefnant 47 J5
Trefonen 38 B3
Trefor *Gwyn* 36 C1
Trefor *IoA* 46 B4
Treforest 18 D3
Treforest Industrial Estate 18 E3
Trefriw 47 F6
Tregadillett 4 C2
Tregaian 46 C5
Tregare 28 D7
Tregarland 4 C5
Tregarne 2 E6
Tregaron 27 F3
Tregarth 46 E6
Tregaswith 3 F2
Tregavethan 2 E4
Tregear 3 F3
Tregeare 4 C2
Tregeiriog 38 A2
Tregele 46 B3
Tregidden 2 E6
Tregiskey 4 A6
Treglemais 16 B3
Tregolds 3 F1
Tregole 4 B1
Tregonetha 3 G2
Tregonning & Gwinear Mining Districts with Trewavas (Cornwall & West Devon Mining Landscape) *Corn* 2 C5
Tregony 3 G4
Tregoodwell 4 B2
Tregoss 3 G2
Tregowris 2 E6
Tregoyd 28 A5
Tregrehan Mills 4 A5
Tre-groes 17 H1
Treguff 18 D4
Tregullon 4 A4
Tregunnon 4 C2
Tregurrian 3 F2
Tregynon 37 K6
Trehafod 18 D2
Trehan 4 E5
Treharris 18 D2
Treherbert 18 C2
Tre-hill 18 D4
Trekenner 4 D3
Treknow 4 A2
Trelan 2 E7
Trelash 4 B1
Trelassick 3 F3
Trelawnyd 47 J5
Trelech 17 F2
Treleddyd-fawr 16 A3
Trelewis 18 E2
Treligga 4 A2
Trelights 3 G1
Trelill 4 A3
Trelissick *Corn* TR3 6QL 3 F5
Trelissick 3 F5
Trellech 19 J1
Trelleck Grange 19 H1
Trelogan 47 K4
Trelowla 4 C5
Trelystan 38 B5
Tremadog 36 E1
Tremail 4 B2
Tremain 17 F1
Tremaine 4 C2
Tremar 4 C4
Trematon 4 D5
Tremeirchion 47 J5
Tremethick Cross 2 B5
Tremore 4 A4
Trenance *Corn* 3 F2
Trenance *Corn* 3 G1
Trenarren 4 A6
Trench *Tel&W* 39 F4
Trench *Wrex* 38 C2
Trencreek 3 F2
Trenear 2 D5
Treneglos 4 C2
Trenewan 4 B5
Trengune 4 B1
Trent 8 E3
Trent Port 52 B4
Trent Vale 40 A1
Trentham 40 A1
Trentishoe 6 E1
Trenwheal 2 D5
Treoes 18 C4
Treorchy 18 C2
Treowen 19 F2
Trequite 4 A3
Tre'r-ddol 37 F6
Trerhyngyll 18 D4
Tre-Rhys 16 E1
Trerulefoot 4 D5
Tresaith 26 B3
Tresco 2 B1
Trescott 40 A6
Trescowe 2 C5
Tresean 2 E3
Tresham 20 A2
Tresillian 3 F4
Tresinney 4 B2
Tresinwen 16 B1
Treskinnick Cross 4 C1
Treslea 4 B4
Tresmeer 4 C2
Tresowes Green 2 D6
Tresparrett 4 B1
Tresparrett Posts 4 B1
Tressait 80 D4
Tresta *Shet* 89 M7
Tresta *Shet* 89 Q3
Treswell 51 K5
Trethewey 2 A6
Trethomas 18 E3
Trethurgy 4 A5
Tretio 16 A3
Tretire 28 E6
Tretower 28 A6
Treuddyn 48 B7
Trevadlock 4 C3
Trevalga 4 A1
Trevalyn 48 C7
Trevanson 3 G1
Trevarnon 2 C5
Trevarrack 2 B5
Trevarren 3 G2
Trevarrian 3 F2
Trevarrick 3 G4
Trevaughan *Carmar* 16 E4
Tre-vaughan *Carmar* 17 G3
Treveighan 4 A3
Trevellas 2 E3
Trevelmond 4 C4
Trevenen 2 D6
Treverva 2 E5
Trevescan 2 A6
Trevethin 19 F1
Trevigro 4 D4
Treviscoe 3 G3
Trevivian 4 B2
Trevone 3 F1
Trevor 38 B1
Trewalder 4 A2
Trewarmett 4 A2
Trewarthenick 3 G4
Trewassa 4 B2
Trewellard 2 A5
Trewen *Corn* 4 C2
Trewen *Here* 28 E7
Trewennack 2 D6
Trewent 16 D6
Trewern 38 B4
Trewethern 4 A3
Trewidland 4 C5
Trewilym 16 E1
Trewint *Corn* 4 B1
Trewint *Corn* 4 C2
Trewithian 3 F5
Trewoon 3 G3
Treworga 3 F4
Treworlas 3 F5
Trewornan 3 G1
Treworthal 3 F5
Tre-wyn 28 C6
Treyarnon 3 F1
Treyford 12 B5
Trezaise 3 G3
Triangle 57 F7
Trickett's Cross 10 B4
Triermain 70 A7
Trillick 91 K11
Trimdon 62 D3
Trimdon Colliery 62 D3
Trimdon Grange 62 D3
Trimingham 45 G2
Trimley Lower Street 35 G5
Trimley St. Martin 35 G5
Trimley St. Mary 35 G5
Trimpley 29 G1
Trimsaran 17 H5
Trimstone 6 C1
Trinafour 80 C4
Trinant 19 F2
Tring 32 C7
Trinity *Angus* 81 M4
Trinity *Chanl* 3 K7
Trinity *Edin* 76 A3
Trisant 27 G1
Triscombe *Som* 7 H2
Triscombe *Som* 7 K2
Trislaig 79 M3
Trispen 3 F3
Tritlington 71 H4
Trochry 80 E7
Troedyraur 17 G1
Troedyrhiw 18 D1
Trofarth 47 G5
Trondavoe 89 M5
Troon *Corn* 2 D5
Troon *SAyr* 74 B7
Tropical Butterfly House, Wildlife & Falconry Centre *SYorks* S25 4EQ 111 H5
Tropical World, Roundhay *WYorks* LS8 2ER 117 L1
Trory 91 J12
Troston 34 C1
Troswell 4 C1
Trottiscliffe 24 C5
Trotton 12 B4
Trough Gate 56 D7
Troughend 70 D4
Troustan 73 J3
Troutbeck *Cumb* 60 E4
Troutbeck *Cumb* 60 F6
Troutbeck Bridge 60 F6
Trow Green 19 J1
Troway 51 F5
Trowbridge *Cardiff* 19 F3
Trowbridge *Wilts* 20 B6
Trowell 41 G2
Trowle Common 20 B6
Trowley Bottom 32 D7
Trows 76 E7
Trowse Newton 45 G5
Troy 57 H6
Trudernish 72 C5
Trudoxhill 20 A7
Trull 8 B2
Trumpan 82 C4
Trumpet 29 F5
Trumpington 33 H3
Trumps Green 22 C5
Trunch 45 G2
Trunnah 55 G5
Truro 3 F4
Truro Cathedral *Corn* TR1 2AF 3 F4
Truscott 6 B7
Trusham 7 G7
Trusley 40 E2
Trusthorpe 53 J4
Truthan 3 F3
Tubney 21 H2
Tuckenhay 5 J5
Tuckhill 39 G7
Tuckingmill 2 D4
Tuddenham *Suff* 34 B1
Tuddenham *Suff* 35 F4
Tudeley 23 K7
Tudeley Hale 23 K7
Tudhoe 62 C3
Tudweiliog 36 B2
Tuesley 22 C7
Tuffley 29 H7
Tufton *Hants* 21 H7
Tufton *Pembs* 16 D3
Tugby 42 A5
Tugford 38 E7
Tughall 71 H1
Tulleys Farm *WSuss* RH10 4PE 13 G3
Tullibardine Distillery *P&K* PH4 1QG 80 E10
Tullibody 75 G1
Tullich *A&B* 79 M9
Tullich *High* 84 C3
Tullich Muir 84 B3
Tullie House Museum & Art Gallery *Cumb* CA3 8TP 124 Carlisle
Tulliemet 80 F5
Tullintrain 90 M6
Tulloch 84 A1
Tullochgorm 73 H1
Tully 91 K13
Tullyalley 90 L5
Tullyard 90 K9
Tullybelton 80 F7
Tullycar 90 H8
Tullyconnaught 93 G12
Tullycorker 91 M11
Tullyhogue 93 D9
Tullyhogue Fort *MUlst* BT80 8UB 93 D9
Tullyhona 91 H13
Tullymacreeve 93 E14
Tullynacree 93 K12
Tullynessle 85 K9
Tullyroan Corner 93 D11
Tullyrossmearan 91 G12
Tullyveery 93 K11
Tulnacross 92 C8
Tulse Hill 23 G4
Tumble (Y Tymbl) 17 J4
Tumby 53 F7
Tumby Woodside 53 F7
Tummel Bridge 80 C5
Tummery 91 J10
Tunbridge Wells 13 J3
Tundergarth Mains 69 G5
Tunga 88 K4
Tungate 45 G3
Tunley 19 K6
Tunny 93 G9
Tunstall *ERid* 59 K6
Tunstall *Kent* 24 E5
Tunstall *Lancs* 56 B2
Tunstall *Norf* 45 J5
Tunstall *NYorks* 62 C7
Tunstall *Stoke* 49 H7
Tunstall *Suff* 35 H3
Tunstall *T&W* 62 D1
Tunstead *GtMan* 50 C2
Tunstead *Norf* 45 H3
Tunstead Milton 50 C4
Tunworth 21 K7
Tupholme 52 E6
Tupsley 28 E5
Tupton 51 F6
Tur Langton 42 A6
Turbiskill 73 F2
Turgis Green 21 K6
Turkdean 30 C7
Turleigh 20 B5
Turn 49 H1
Turnastone 28 C5
Turnberry 67 G3
Turnchapel 4 E5
Turnditch 40 E1
Turner's Green 30 C2
Turners Hill 13 G3
Turners Puddle 9 H5
Turnford 23 G1
Turnworth 9 H4
Turriff 85 M6
Turton Bottoms 49 G1
Turvey 32 C3
Turville 22 A2
Turville Heath 22 A2
Turweston 31 H5
Tutankhamun Exhibition, Dorchester *Dorset* DT1 1UW 9 F5
Tutbury 40 E3
Tutbury Castle *Staffs* DE13 9JF 40 E3
Tutnall 29 J1
Tutshill 19 J2
Tuttington 45 G3
Tutts Clump 21 J4
Tutwell 4 D3
Tuxford 51 K5
Twatt *Ork* 89 B5
Twatt *Shet* 89 M7
Twechar 75 F3
Tweedbank 76 D7
Tweedmouth 77 H5
Tweedsmuir 69 F1
Twelve Oaks 13 K4
Twelveheads 2 E4
Twemlow Green 49 G6
Twenty 42 E3
Twickenham 22 E4
Twigworth 29 H6
Twineham 13 F4
Twineham Green 13 F4
Twinhoe 20 A6
Twinstead 34 C5
Twiss Green 49 F3
Twiston 56 D5
Twitchen *Devon* 7 F2
Twitchen *Shrop* 28 C1
Twitton 23 J6
Twizell House 71 G1
Two Bridges *Devon* 5 G3
Two Bridges *Glos* 19 K1
Two Dales 50 E6
Two Gates 40 E5
Two Mills 48 C5
Twycross 41 F5
Twycross Zoo *Leics* CV9 3PX 41 F5
Twyford *Bucks* 31 H6
Twyford *Derbys* 41 F3
Twyford *Dorset* 9 H3
Twyford *Hants* 11 F2
Twyford *Leics* 42 A4
Twyford *Norf* 44 E3
Twyford *Oxon* 31 F5
Twyford *W'ham* 22 A4
Twyford Common 28 E5
Twyn Shôn-Ifan 18 E2
Twynholm 65 G5
Twyning 29 H5
Twynllanan 27 G6
Twyn-yr-odyn 18 E4
Twyn-y-Sheriff 19 H1
Twywell 32 C1
Ty Croes 46 B5
Tyberton 28 C5
Tycroes 17 K4
Tycrwyn 38 A4
Tydd Gote 43 H4
Tydd St. Giles 43 H4
Tydd St. Mary 43 H4
Tye Common 24 C2
Tye Green *Essex* 23 H1
Tye Green *Essex* 33 J6
Tye Green *Essex* 33 K7
Tye Green *Essex* 34 B6
Tyersal 57 G6
Ty-hen 36 A2
Tyldesley 49 F2
Tyle-garw 18 D3
Tyler Hill 25 H5
Tylers Green *Bucks* 22 C2
Tyler's Green *Essex* 23 J1
Tylorstown 18 D2
Tylwch 27 J1
Ty-Mawr *Conwy* 37 J1
Ty-mawr *Denb* 38 A1
Tynan 93 C12
Ty-nant *Conwy* 37 J1
Ty-nant *Gwyn* 37 J3
Tyndrum (Taigh an Droma) 79 Q7
Tyne Green Country Park *N'umb* NE46 3RY 70 E7
Tyneham 9 H6
Tynehead 76 B5
Tynemouth 71 J7
Tynewydd 18 C2
Tyninghame 76 E3
Tynron 68 D4
Tyntesfield 19 J4
Tyn-y-cefn 37 K1
Ty'n-y-coedcae 18 E3
Tyn-y-cwm 37 H7
Tyn-y-ffridd 38 A2
Ty'n-y-garn 18 B3
Tyn-y-gongl 46 D4
Tynygraig *Cere* 27 F2
Tyn-y-graig *Powys* 27 K4
Ty'n-y-groes 47 F5
Tyrella 93 K13
Tyringham 32 B4
Tyseley 40 D7
Tythegston 18 B4
Tytherington *ChesE* 49 J5
Tytherington *SGlos* 19 K3
Tytherington *Som* 20 A7
Tytherington *Wilts* 20 C7
Tytherton Lucas 20 C4
Tyttenhanger 22 E1
Ty-uchaf 37 J3
Tywardreath 4 A5
Tywardreath Highway 4 A5
Tywyn 36 E5

U

Uachdar 88 C3
Ubberley 40 B1
Ubbeston Green 35 H1
Ubley 19 J6
Uckerby 62 C6
Uckfield 13 H4
Uckinghall 29 H5
Uckington 29 J6
Uddingston 74 E4
Uddington 75 G7
Udimore 14 D6
Udley 19 H5
Udny Green 85 N8
Udston 75 F5
Udstonhead 75 F6
Uffcott 20 E4
Uffculme 7 J4
Uffington *Lincs* 42 D5
Uffington *Oxon* 21 G3
Uffington *Shrop* 38 E4
Ufford *Peter* 42 D5
Ufford *Suff* 35 G3
Ufton 30 E2
Ufton Green 21 K5
Ufton Nervet 21 K5
Ugborough 5 G5
Ugford 10 B1
Uggeshall 45 J7
Ugglebarnby 63 J6
Ugley 33 J6
Ugley Green 33 J6
Ugthorpe 63 H5
Uig *A&B* 73 K2
Uig (Uige) *High* 82 D4
Uiskevagh (Uisgebhagh) 88 C3
Ulbster 87 R5
Ulcat Row 60 F4
Ulceby *Lincs* 53 H5
Ulceby *NLincs* 52 E1
Ulceby Cross 53 H5
Ulceby Skitter 52 E1
Ulcombe 14 D3
Uldale 60 D3
Uldale House 61 J7
Uley 20 A2
Ulgham 71 H4
Ullapool (Ullapul) 83 M1
Ullenhall 30 C2
Ullenwood 29 J7
Ulleskelf 58 B6
Ullesthorpe 41 H7
Ulley 51 G4
Ulley Reservoir Country Park *SYorks* S26 3XL 111 F4
Ullingswick 28 E4
Ullinish 82 D7
Ullock 60 B4
Ullswater Steamers *Cumb* CA11 0US 60 E5
Ulpha *Cumb* 55 H1
Ulpha *Cumb* 60 C7
Ulrome 59 H4
Ulsta 89 N4
Ulster American Folk Park *F&O* BT78 5QU 90 L9
Ulster Folk & Transport Museum *A&NDown* BT18 0EU 92 K8
Ulting 24 E1
Ulva 78 F7
Ulverston 55 F2
Ulwell 10 B6
Ulzieside 68 C3
Umberleigh 6 E3
Ummer 91 K12
Unapool 86 E6
Underbarrow 61 F7
Undercliffe 57 G6
Underhill 23 F2
Underling Green 14 C3
Underriver 23 J6
Underwood *Newport* 19 G3
Underwood *Notts* 51 G7

Underwood Plym 5 F5
Undley 44 A7
Undy 19 H3
Unifirth 89 L7
Union Mills 54 C6
Union Street 14 C4
University of Glasgow Visitor Centre Glas G12 8QQ 127 B1
Unst 89 Q1
Unst Airport 89 Q2
Unstone 51 F5
Unstone Green 51 F5
Unsworth 49 H2
Unthank Cumb 61 F3
Unthank Derbys 51 F5
Up Cerne 9 F4
Up Exe 7 H5
Up Hatherley 29 J6
Up Holland 48 E2
Up Marden 11 J3
Up Mudford 8 E3
Up Nately 21 K6
Up Somborne 10 E1
Up Sydling 9 F4
Upavon 20 E6
Upchurch 24 E5
Upcott Devon 6 C6
Upcott Devon 6 D2
Upcott Here 28 C3
Upcott Som 7 H3
Upend 33 K3
Upgate 45 F4
Upgate Street Norf 44 E6
Upgate Street Norf 45 G6
Uphall Dorset 8 E4
Uphall WLoth 75 J3
Uphall Station 75 J4
Upham Devon 7 G5
Upham Hants 11 G2
Uphampton Here 28 C2
Uphampton Worcs 29 H2
Uphempston 5 J4
Uphill 19 G6
Uplands Glos 20 B1
Uplands Swan 17 K6
Uplawmoor 74 C5
Upleadon 29 G6
Upleatham 63 G5
Uplees 25 G5
Uploders 8 E5
Uplowman 7 J4
Uplyme 8 C5
Upminster 23 J3
Upottery 8 B4
Upper Affcot 38 D7
Upper Ardroscadale 73 J4
Upper Arley 39 G7
Upper Arncott 31 H7
Upper Astley 38 E4
Upper Aston 40 A6
Upper Astrop 31 G5
Upper Ballinderry 93 G10
Upper Basildon 21 K4
Upper Bayble (Pabail Uarach) 88 L4
Upper Beeding 12 E5
Upper Benefield 42 C7
Upper Bentley 29 J2
Upper Berwick 38 D4
Upper Boat 18 E3
Upper Boddam 85 L7
Upper Boddington 31 F3
Upper Borth 37 F7
Upper Boyndlie 85 P4
Upper Brailes 30 E5
Upper Breakish 82 G8
Upper Breinton 28 D4
Upper Broadheath 29 H3
Upper Broughton 41 J3
Upper Brynamman 27 G7
Upper Bucklebury 21 J5
Upper Burgate 10 C3
Upper Caldecote 32 E4
Upper Canada 19 G6
Upper Catesby 31 G3
Upper Catshill 29 J1
Upper Chapel 27 K4
Upper Cheddon 8 B2
Upper Chicksgrove 9 J1
Upper Chute 21 F6
Upper Clatford 21 G7
Upper Coberley 29 J7
Upper Colwall 29 G4
Upper Cotton 40 C1
Upper Cound 38 E5
Upper Cumberworth 50 E2
Upper Cwmbran 19 F2
Upper Dean 32 D2
Upper Denby 50 E2
Upper Denton 70 B7
Upper Derwent Reservoirs Derbys S33 0AQ 50 D4
Upper Diabaig 83 J4
Upper Dicker 13 J5
Upper Dovercourt 35 G5
Upper Dunsforth 57 K3
Upper Dunsley 32 C7
Upper Eastern Green 40 E7
Upper Egleton 29 F4
Upper Elkstone 50 C7
Upper End 50 C5
Upper Enham 21 G7
Upper Farringdon 11 J1
Upper Framilode 29 G7
Upper Froyle 22 A7
Upper Godney 19 H7
Upper Gornal 40 B6
Upper Gravenhurst 32 E5
Upper Green Essex 33 H5
Upper Green Essex 33 J5
Upper Green Mon 28 C7
Upper Green WBerks 21 G5
Upper Grove Common 28 E6
Upper Hackney 50 E6
Upper Halliford 22 D5
Upper Halling 24 C5
Upper Hambleton 42 C5
Upper Harbledown 15 G2
Upper Hardres Court 15 G2
Upper Hartfield 13 H3
Upper Hatton 40 A2
Upper Hayesden 23 J7
Upper Hayton 38 E7
Upper Heath 38 E7
Upper Heaton 50 D1
Upper Hellesdon 45 G4
Upper Helmsley 58 C4
Upper Hengoed 38 B2
Upper Hergest 28 B3
Upper Heyford N'hants 31 H3
Upper Heyford Oxon 31 F6
Upper Hill Here 28 D3
Upper Hill SGlos 19 K2
Upper Horsebridge 13 J5
Upper Howsell 29 G4
Upper Hulme 50 C6
Upper Inglesham 21 F2
Upper Kilchattan 72 B1
Upper Killay 17 J6
Upper Knockando 84 F6
Upper Lambourn 21 G3
Upper Langford 19 H6
Upper Langwith 51 H6
Upper Leigh 40 C2
Upper Ley 29 G7
Upper Loads 51 F6
Upper Longdon 40 C4
Upper Longwood 39 F5
Upper Ludstone 40 A6
Upper Lybster 87 Q6
Upper Lydbrook 29 F7
Upper Lyde 28 D4
Upper Lye 28 C2
Upper Maes-coed 28 C5
Upper Midhope 50 E3
Upper Milton 30 D7
Upper Minety 20 D2
Upper Moor 29 J4
Upper Morton 19 K2
Upper Nash 16 D5
Upper Newbold 51 F5
Upper North Dean 22 B2
Upper Norwood 23 G4
Upper Oddington 30 D6
Upper Padley 50 E5
Upper Pennington 10 D5
Upper Pollicott 31 J7
Upper Poppleton 58 B4
Upper Quinton 30 C4
Upper Ratley 10 E2
Upper Rissington 30 D6
Upper Rochford 29 F2
Upper Sanday 89 E7
Upper Sapey 29 F2
Upper Scolton 16 C3
Upper Seagry 20 C3
Upper Shelton 32 C4
Upper Sheringham 45 F1
Upper Shuckburgh 31 F2
Upper Siddington 20 D2
Upper Skelmorlie 74 A4
Upper Slaughter 30 C6
Upper Soudley 29 F7
Upper Staploe 32 E3
Upper Stoke 45 G5
Upper Stondon 32 E5
Upper Stowe 31 H3
Upper Street Hants 10 C3
Upper Street Norf 35 F1
Upper Street Norf 45 H4
Upper Street Suff 35 F5
Upper Strensham 29 J5
Upper Sundon 32 D6
Upper Swanmore 11 G3
Upper Swell 30 C6
Upper Tean 40 C2
Upper Tirkane 92 D6
Upper Thurnham 55 H4
Upper Tooting 23 F4
Upper Town Derbys 50 E6
Upper Town Derbys 50 E7
Upper Town Here 28 E4
Upper Town NSom 19 J5
Upper Tysoe 30 E4
Upper Upham 21 F4
Upper Upnor 24 D4
Upper Vobster 20 A7
Upper Wardington 31 F4
Upper Waterhay 20 D2
Upper Weald 32 B5
Upper Weedon 31 H3
Upper Welson 28 B3
Upper Weston 20 A5
Upper Whiston 51 G4
Upper Wick 29 H3
Upper Wield 11 H1
Upper Winchendon (Over Winchendon) 31 J7
Upper Witton 40 C6
Upper Woodford 10 C1
Upper Woolhampton 21 J5
Upper Wootton 21 J6
Upper Wraxall 20 B4
Upper Wyche 29 G4
Upperby 60 F1
Upperlands 92 D6
Uppermill 49 J2
Upperthong 50 D2
Upperton 12 C4
Uppertown CC&G 92 F5
Uppertown Derbys 51 F6
Uppingham 42 B5
Uppington 38 E5
Upsall 57 K1
Upsettlington 77 G6
Upshire 23 H1
Upstreet 25 J5
Upthorpe 34 D1
Upton Bucks 31 J7
Upton Cambs 32 E1
Upton ChesW&C 48 D6
Upton Corn 4 C3
Upton Corn 6 A5
Upton Devon 5 H6
Upton Devon 7 J5
Upton Dorset 9 G6
Upton Dorset 9 J5
Upton ERid 59 H4
Upton Hants 10 E3
Upton Hants 21 G6
Upton Leics 41 F6
Upton Lincs 52 B4
Upton Mersey 48 B4
Upton Norf 45 H4
Upton Notts 51 K5
Upton Notts 51 K7
Upton N'hants 31 J2
Upton Oxon 21 J3
Upton Oxon 30 D7
Upton Pembs 16 D5
Upton Peter 42 E5
Upton Slo 22 C4
Upton Som 7 H3
Upton Som 8 D2
Upton Wilts 9 H1
Upton WYorks 51 G1
Upton Bishop 29 F6
Upton Cheyney 19 K5
Upton Country Park BCP BH17 7BJ 95 B5
Upton Cressett 39 F6
Upton Crews 29 F6
Upton Cross 4 C3
Upton End 32 E5
Upton Grey 21 K7
Upton Hellions 7 G5
Upton Lovell 20 C7
Upton Magna 38 E4
Upton Noble 9 G1
Upton Park 23 H3
Upton Pyne 7 H6
Upton Scudamore 20 B7
Upton Snodsbury 29 J3
Upton St. Leonards 29 H7
Upton upon Severn 29 H4
Upton Warren 29 J2
Upwaltham 12 C5
Upware 33 J1
Upwell 43 J5
Upwey 9 F6
Upwick Green 33 H6
Upwood 43 F7
Urafirth 89 M5
Urbis, Manchester GtMan M4 3BG 133 E2
Urchfont 20 D6
Urdimarsh 28 E4
Urgha 88 G8
Urlay Nook 62 E5
Urmston 49 G3
Urpeth 62 C1
Urquhart 84 G4
Urquhart Castle High IV63 6XJ 83 R8
Urra 63 F6
Ushaw Moor 62 C2
Usher Hall Edin EH1 2EA 126 E5
Usk (Brynbuga) 19 G1
Usselby 52 D3
Usworth 62 D1
Utley 57 F5
Uton 7 G6
Utterby 53 G3
Uttoxeter 40 C2
Uwchmynydd 36 A3
Uxbridge 22 D3
Uyeasound 89 P2
Uzmaston 16 C4

V

Valley (Y Fali) 46 A5
Valley Truckle 4 B2
Valleyfield D&G 65 G5
Valleyfield Fife 75 J2
Valsgarth 89 Q1
Vange 24 D3
Vardre 17 K5
Varteg (Y Farteg) 19 F1
Vatersay (Bhatarsaigh) 88 A9
Vatten 82 C6
Vaul 78 B6
Vaynor 27 K7
Vaynor Park 38 A5
Veaullt 28 A3
Veensgarth 89 N8
Velindre Pembs 16 D2
Velindre Powys 28 A5
Vellow 7 J2
Venn 5 H6
Venn Ottery 7 J6
Venngreen 6 B4
Vennington 38 C5
Venny Tedburn 7 G6
Venterdon 4 D3
Ventnor 11 G7
Ventnor Botanic Gardens IoW PO38 1UL 11 G7
Venton 5 F5
Venton 5 F5
Venue Cymru, Llandudno Conwy LL30 1BB 47 F4
Vernham Dean 21 G6
Vernham Street 21 G6
Vernolds Common 38 D7
Verwood 10 B4
Veryan 5 G5
Veryan Green 3 G4
Vickerstown 54 E3
Victoria 3 G2
Victoria & Albert Dundee 125 Dundee
Victoria & Albert Museum GtLon SW7 2RL 103 G7
Victoria Bridge 90 K7
Vidlin 89 N6
Viewpark 75 F4
Vigo 40 C5
Vigo Village 24 C5
Villavin 6 D4
Vindobala (Frontiers of the Roman Empire) N'umb 71 G7
Vindolanda Roman Fort (Frontiers of the Roman Empire) N'umb NE47 7JN 70 C7
Vinehall Street 14 C5
Vine's Cross 13 J5
Viney Hill 19 K1
Virginia Water 22 C5
Virginstow 6 B6
Virley 34 D7
Vobster 20 A7
Voe 89 N6
Vogrie Country Park Midlo EH23 4NU 120 H5
Voirrey Embroidery Mersey CH63 6JA 112 A6
Volks Electric Railway B&H BN2 1EN 13 G6
Vow 92 E5
Vowchurch 28 C5
Voy 89 B6
Vron Gate 38 C5

W

Waberthwaite 60 C7
Wackerfield 62 B4
Wacton 45 F6
Wadbister 89 N8
Wadborough 29 J4
Waddesdon 31 J7
Waddesdon Manor Bucks HP18 0JH 31 J7
Waddeton 5 J5
Waddicar 48 C3
Waddingham 52 C3
Waddington Lancs 56 C5
Waddington Lincs 52 C6
Waddingworth 52 E5
Waddon Devon 5 J3
Waddon GtLon 23 G5
Wadebridge 3 G1
Wadeford 8 C3
Wadenhoe 42 D7
Wadesmill 33 G7
Wadhurst 13 K3
Wadshelf 51 F5
Wadworth 51 H3
Wadworth Hill 59 J7
Waen Denb 47 H6
Waen Denb 47 K6
Waen Aberwheeler 47 J6
Waen-fâch 38 B4
Waen-wen 46 D6
Wainfleet All Saints 53 H7
Wainfleet Bank 53 H7
Wainfleet St. Mary 53 H7
Wainford 45 H6
Waingroves 41 G1
Wainhouse Corner 4 B1
Wainscott 24 D4
Wainstalls 57 F7
Waitby 61 J6
Wakefield 57 J7
Wakehurst Place WSuss RH17 6TN 13 G3
Wakerley 42 C6
Wakes Colne 34 C6
Walberswick 35 J1
Walberton 12 C6
Walbottle 71 G7
Walcot Lincs 42 D2
Walcot Lincs 52 E7
Walcot NLincs 58 E7
Walcot Shrop 38 C7
Walcot Tel&W 38 E4
Walcot Green 45 F7
Walcote Leics 41 H7
Walcote Warks 30 C3
Walcott 45 H2
Walcott Dales 52 E7
Walden 57 F1
Walden Head 56 E1
Walden Stubbs 51 H1
Walderslade 24 D5
Walderton 11 J3
Walditch 8 D5
Waldley 40 D2
Waldridge 62 C2
Waldringfield 35 G4
Waldron 13 J5
Wales 51 G4
Wales Millennium Centre Cardiff CF10 5AL 99 C6
Walesby Lincs 52 E3
Walesby Notts 51 J5
Waleswood 51 G4
Walford Here 28 C1
Walford Here 28 E6
Walford Shrop 38 D3
Walford Staffs 40 A2
Walford Heath 38 D4
Walgherton 39 F1
Walgrave 32 B1
Walhampton 10 E5
Walk Mill 56 D6
Walkden 49 G2
Walker 71 H7
Walker Art Gallery, Liverpool Mersey L3 8EL 131 D3
Walker Fold 56 B5
Walkerburn 76 B7
Walkeringham 51 K3
Walkerith 51 K3
Walkern 33 F6
Walker's Green 28 E4
Walkford 10 D5
Walkhampton 5 F4
Walkingham Hill 57 J3
Walkington 59 F6
Walkwood 30 B2
Wall Corn 2 D5
Wall N'umb 70 E7
Wall Staffs 40 D5
Wall End 55 F1
Wall Heath 40 A7
Wall Houses 71 F7
Wall under Heywood 38 E6
Wallace Collection, London GtLon W1U 3BN 132 A2
Wallacehall 69 H6
Wallacetown 67 G3
Wallasey 48 B3
Wallaston Green 16 C5
Wallend 24 E4
Waller's Green 29 F5
Wallingford 21 K3
Wallington GtLon 23 F5
Wallington Hants 11 G4
Wallington Herts 33 F5
Wallington Wrex 38 D1
Wallingwells 51 H4
Wallis 16 D3
Wallisdown 10 B5
Walliswood 12 E3
Walls 89 L8
Walls of Derry D&S BT48 6PR 90 L5
Wallsend 71 J7
Wallyford 76 B3
Walmer 15 J2
Walmer Bridge 55 H7
Walmersley 49 H1
Walmley 40 D6
Walmsgate 53 G5
Walpole 35 H1
Walpole Cross Keys 43 J4
Walpole Highway 43 J4
Walpole Marsh 43 H4
Walpole St. Andrew 43 J4
Walpole St. Peter 43 J4
Walrond's Park 8 C2
Walrow 19 G7
Walsall 40 C6
Walsall Wood 40 C5
Walsden 56 E7
Walsgrave on Sowe 41 F7
Walsham le Willows 34 E1
Walshaw 49 G1
Walshford 57 K4
Walsoken 43 H4
Walston 75 J6
Walsworth 32 E5
Walter's Ash 22 B2
Walterston 18 D4
Walterstone 28 C6
Waltham Kent 15 G3
Waltham NELincs 53 F2
Waltham Abbey 23 G1
Waltham Chase 11 G3
Waltham Cross 23 G1
Waltham on the Wolds 42 A3
Waltham St. Lawrence 22 B4
Walthamstow 23 G3
Walton Bucks 32 B7
Walton Cumb 70 A7
Walton Derbys 51 F6
Walton Leics 41 H7
Walton Mersey 48 C3
Walton MK 32 B5
Walton Peter 42 E5
Walton Powys 28 B3
Walton Shrop 28 D1
Walton Som 8 D1
Walton Staffs 40 A2
Walton Suff 35 H5
Walton Tel&W 38 E4
Walton Warks 30 D3
Walton WYorks 51 F1
Walton WYorks 57 K5
Walton Cardiff 29 J5
Walton East 16 D3
Walton Elm 9 G3
Walton Hall Gardens Warr WA4 6SN 113 M5
Walton Highway 43 H4
Walton Lower Street 35 G5
Walton on the Hill 23 F6
Walton on the Naze 35 G6
Walton on the Wolds 41 H4
Walton Park D&G 65 H3
Walton Park NSom 19 H4
Walton West 16 B4
Walton-in-Gordano 19 H4
Walton-le-Dale 55 J7
Walton-on-Thames 22 E5
Walton-on-the-Hill 40 B3
Walton-on-Trent 40 E4
Walwen Flints 47 K5
Walwen Flints 48 B5
Walwick 70 E6
Walworth 62 C5
Walworth Gate 62 C4
Walwyn's Castle 16 B4
Wambrook 8 B4
Wanborough Surr 22 C7
Wanborough Swin 21 F3
Wandel 68 E1
Wandon 71 F1
Wandon End 32 E6
Wandsworth 23 F4
Wandylaw 71 G1
Wangford Suff 35 J1
Wangford Suff 44 B7
Wanlip 41 H4
Wanlockhead 68 D2
Wannock 13 J6
Wansbeck Riverside Park N'umb NE63 8TX 71 H5
Wansford ERid 59 G4
Wansford Peter 42 D6
Wanshurst Green 14 C3
Wanstrow 20 A7
Wanswell 19 K1
Wantage 21 G3
Wapley 20 A4
Wappenbury 30 E2
Wappenham 31 H4
Warblebank 60 D2
Warbleton 13 K5
Warblington 11 J4
Warborough 21 J2
Warboys 43 G7
Warbreck 55 G6
Warbstow 4 C1
Warburton 49 F4
Warcop 61 J5
Ward End 40 D7
Ward Green 34 E2
Warden Kent 25 G4
Warden N'umb 70 E7
Warden Hill 29 J6
Warden Street 32 E4
Wardington 31 F4
Wardle ChesE 49 F7
Wardle GtMan 49 J1
Wardley GtMan 49 G2
Wardley Rut 42 B5
Wardley T&W 71 J7
Wardlow 50 D5
Wardsend 49 J4
Wardy Hill 43 H7
Ware Herts 33 G7
Ware Kent 25 J5
Wareham 9 J6
Warehorne 14 E4
Waren Mill 77 K7
Warenford 71 G1
Warenton 77 K7
Wareside 33 G7
Waresley Cambs 33 F3
Waresley Worcs 29 H1
Warfield 22 B4
Wargrave Mersey 48 E3
Wargrave W'ham 22 A4
Warham Here 28 D5
Warham Norf 44 D1
Wark N'umb 70 D6
Wark N'umb 77 G7
Warkleigh 6 E3
Warkton 32 B1
Warkworth N'hants 31 F4
Warkworth N'umb 71 H3
Warland 56 E7
Warleggan 4 B4
Warley Essex 23 J2
Warley WMid 40 C7
Warley Town 57 F7
Warlingham 23 G6
Warmfield 57 J7
Warmingham 49 G6
Warminghurst 12 E5
Warmington N'hants 42 D6
Warmington Warks 31 F4
Warminster 20 B7
Warmlake 14 D3
Warmley 19 K4
Warmley Hill 19 K4
Warmsworth 51 H2
Warmwell 9 G6
Warndon 29 H3
Warners End 22 D1
Warnford 11 H2
Warnham 12 E3
Warningcamp 12 D6
Warninglid 13 F4
Warren ChesE 49 H5
Warren Pembs 16 C6
Warren House 6 E7
Warren Row 22 B3
Warren Street 14 E2
Warrenby 63 F4
Warrenpoint 93 G15
Warren's Green 33 F6
Warrington MK 32 B3
Warrington Warr 49 F4
Warsash 11 F4
Warslow 50 C7
Warsop Vale 51 H6
Warter 58 E4
Warthill 58 C4
Wartling 13 K6
Wartnaby 42 A3
Warton Lancs 55 H7
Warton Lancs 55 J2
Warton N'umb 71 F3
Warton Warks 40 E5
Warton Bank 55 H7
Warwick 30 D2
Warwick Bridge 61 F1
Warwick Castle Warks CV34 4QU 30 D2
Warwick Wold 23 G6
Warwick-on-Eden 61 F1
Wasbister 89 C4
Wasdale Head 60 C6
Waseley Hills Country Park Worcs B45 9AT 106 D8
Wash 50 C4
Wash Common 21 H5
Washall Green 33 H5
Washaway 4 A4
Washbourne 5 H5
Washbrook 19 H7
Washfield 7 H4
Washfold 62 A6
Washford Som 7 J1
Washford Warks 30 B2
Washford Pyne 7 G4
Washingborough 52 D5
Washington T&W 62 D1
Washington WSuss 12 E5
Washmere Green 34 D4
Wasing 21 J5
Waskerley 62 A2
Wasperton 30 D3
Wasps Nest 52 D6
Wass 58 B2
Wat Tyler Country Park Essex SS16 4UH 24 D3
Watchet 7 J1
Watchfield Oxon 21 F2
Watchfield Som 19 G7
Watchgate 61 G7
Watcombe 5 K4
Watendlath 60 D5
Water 56 D7
Water Eaton MK 32 B5
Water Eaton Oxon 31 G7
Water End Bed 32 E4
Water End CenBeds 32 D5
Water End ERid 58 D6
Water End Essex 33 J4
Water End Herts 23 F1
Water End Herts 32 D7
Water Newton 42 E6
Water Orton 40 D6
Water Stratford 31 H5
Water Yeat 55 F1
Waterbeach 33 H2
Waterbeck 69 H6
Watercombe 9 G6
Waterend 22 A2
Waterfall 50 C7
Waterfoot ERenf 74 D5
Waterfoot Lancs 56 D7
Waterford 33 G7
Watergate 4 B2
Waterhead Cumb 60 E6
Waterhead D&G 68 C5
Waterheath 45 J6
Waterhouses Dur 62 B2
Waterhouses Staffs 50 C7
Wateringbury 23 K6
Waterlane 20 C1
Waterloo BCP 10 B5
Waterloo Derbys 51 G6
Waterloo GtMan 49 J2
Waterloo High 82 G8
Waterloo Mersey 48 C3
Waterloo NLan 75 G5
Waterloo Norf 45 G4
Waterloo Pembs 16 C5
Waterloo P&K 80 F7
Waterloo Cross 7 J4
Waterloo Port 46 C6
Waterlooville 11 H3
Watermead Country Park Leics LE7 4PF 41 J4
Watermeetings 68 E2
Watermillock 60 F4
Watermouth Castle Devon EX34 9SL 6 D1
Waterperry Oxon OX33 1JZ 21 K1
Waterrow 7 J3
Waters Upton 39 F4
Watersfield 12 D5
Watershed Mill Visitor Centre, Settle NYorks BD24 9LR 56 D3
Watersheddings 49 J2
Waterside Aber 85 Q8
Waterside Bucks 22 C1
Waterside B'burn 56 C7
Waterside D&S 90 L5
Waterside EAyr 67 J3
Waterside EAyr 74 C6
Waterside EDun 74 E3
Watersmeet House Devon EX35 6NT 7 F1
Waterstock 21 K1
Waterston 16 C5
Waterthorpe 51 G4
Waterworld, Hanley ST1 5PU 136 Stoke-on-Trent
Watford Herts 22 E2
Watford N'hants 31 H2
Watford Park 18 E3
Wath NYorks 57 G3
Wath NYorks 57 J2
Wath Brow 60 B5
Wath upon Dearne 51 G2
Watley's End 19 K3
Watlington Norf 44 A4
Watlington Oxon 21 K2
Watnall 41 H1
Watten 87 Q4
Wattisfield 34 E1
Wattisham 34 E3
Wattlebridge 91 L14
Watton Dorset 8 D5
Watton ERid 59 G5
Watton Norf 44 D5
Watton at Stone 33 G7
Watton Green 44 D5
Watton's Green 23 J2
Wattston 75 F4
Wattstown 18 D2
Wattsville 19 F2
Waun Fawr 37 F7
Waun y Clyn 17 H5
Waunarlwydd 17 K6
Waunclunda 17 K2
Waunfawr 46 D7
Waun-Lwyd 18 E1
Wavendon 32 C5
Waverbridge 60 D2
Waverton ChesW&C 48 D6
Waverton Cumb 60 D2
Wavertree 48 C4
Wawne 59 G6
Waxham 45 J3
Waxholme 59 K7
Way Gill 56 E3
Way Village 7 G4
Way Wick 19 G5
Wayford 8 D4
Waytown 8 D5
Weacombe 7 K1
Weald 21 G1
Weald & Downland Open Air Museum WSuss PO18 0EU 12 B5
Weald Country Park Essex CM14 5QS 23 J2
Wealdstone 22 E2
Weardley 57 H5
Weare 19 H6
Weare Giffard 6 C3
Wearhead 61 K3
Wearne 8 D2
Weasenham All Saints 44 C3
Weasenham St. Peter 44 C3
Weathercote 56 C2
Weatheroak Hill 30 B1
Weaverham 49 F5
Weaverthorpe 59 F2
Webheath 30 B2
Webton 28 D5
Weddington 41 F6
Wedhampton 20 D6
Wedmore 19 H7
Wednesbury 40 B6
Wednesfield 40 B6
Weedon 32 B7
Weedon Bec 31 H3
Weedon Lois 31 H4
Weeford 40 D5
Week Devon 5 H4
Week Devon 7 F4
Week Som 7 H2
Week Orchard 6 A5
Week St. Mary 4 C1
Weeke 11 F1
Weekley 42 B7
Weel 59 G6
Weeley 35 F6
Weeley Heath 35 F6
Weem 80 D5
Weeping Cross 40 B3
Weethley 30 B3
Weeting 44 B7
Weeton ERid 59 K7
Weeton Lancs 55 G6
Weeton NYorks 57 H5
Weetwood 57 H6
Weir Essex 24 E3
Weir Lancs 56 D7
Weir Quay 4 E4
Weirbrook 38 C3
Weisdale 89 M7
Welbeck Abbey 51 H5
Welborne 44 E5
Welbourn 52 C7
Welburn NYorks 58 C1
Welburn NYorks 58 D3
Welbury 62 D6
Welby 42 C2
Welches Dam 43 H7
Welcombe 6 A4
Weldon 42 C7
Welford N'hants 41 J7
Welford WBerks 21 H4
Welford-on-Avon 30 C3
Welham Leics 42 A6
Welham Notts 51 K4
Welham Green 23 F1
Well Hants 22 A7
Well Lincs 53 H5
Well NYorks 57 H1
Well End Bucks 22 B3
Well End Herts 23 F2
Well Hill 23 H5
Well Street 23 K6
Well Town 7 H5
Welland 29 G4
Wellesbourne 30 D3
Wellhill 84 D4
Wellhouse WBerks 21 J4
Wellhouse WYorks 50 C1
Welling 23 H4
Wellingborough 32 B2
Wellingham 44 C3
Wellingore 52 C7
Wellington Cumb 60 B6
Wellington Here 28 D4
Wellington Som 7 K3
Wellington Tel&W 39 F4
Wellington Heath 29 G4
Wellington Marsh 28 D4
Wellow B&NESom 20 A6
Wellow IoW 10 E6
Wellow Notts 51 J6
Wells 19 J7
Wells Cathedral Som BA5 2UE 19 J7
Wells Green 40 D7
Wellsborough 41 F5
Wells-next-the-Sea 44 D1
Wellstyle Green 33 K7
Wellwood 75 J2
Welney 43 J6
Welsh Bicknor 28 E7
Welsh End 38 E2
Welsh Frankton 38 C2
Welsh Hook 16 C3
Welsh Mountain Zoo Conwy LL28 5UY 47 G5
Welsh Newton 28 D7
Welsh St. Donats 18 D4
Welshampton 38 D2
Welshpool (Y Trallwng) 38 B5
Welton B&NESom 19 K6
Welton Cumb 60 E2
Welton ERid 59 F7
Welton Lincs 52 D4
Welton N'hants 31 G2
Welton le Marsh 53 H6
Welton le Wold 53 F4
Welwick 59 K7
Welwyn 33 F7
Welwyn Garden City 33 F7
Wem 38 E3
Wembdon 8 B1
Wembley GtLon HA9 0WS 102 E5
Wembley 22 E3
Wembley Park 22 E3
Wembury 5 F6
Wembworthy 6 E4
Wemyss Bay 73 K4
Wenallt Cere 27 F1
Wenallt Gwyn 37 J1
Wendens Ambo 33 J5
Wendlebury 31 G7
Wendling 44 D4
Wendover 22 B1
Wendover Dean 22 B1
Wendron 2 D5
Wendron Mining District (Cornwall & West Devon Mining Landscape) Corn 2 D5
Wendy 33 G4
Wenfordbridge 4 A3
Wenhaston 35 J1
Wenlli 47 G6
Wennington Cambs 33 F1
Wennington GtLon 23 J3
Wennington Lancs 56 B2
Wensley Derbys 50 E6
Wensley NYorks 57 F1
Wensleydale Cheese Visitor Centre, Hawes NYorks DL8 3RN 56 D1
Wentbridge 51 G1
Wentnor 38 C6
Wentworth Cambs 33 H1
Wentworth SYorks 51 F3
Wenvoe 18 E4
Weobley 28 C3
Weobley Marsh 28 D3
Weoley Castle 40 C7
Wepham 12 D6
Wepre 48 B6
Wepre Country Park Flints CH5 4HL 48 B6
Wereham 44 A5
Wergs 40 A5
Wern Gwyn 36 E2
Wern Powys 28 A7
Wern Powys 38 B4
Wern Shrop 38 B2
Wernffrwd 17 J6
Wern-olau 17 J6
Wernrheolydd 28 C7
Wern-y-cwrt 19 G1
Werrington Corn 6 B7
Werrington Peter 42 E5
Werrington Staffs 40 B1
Wervil Grange 26 C3
Wervin 48 D5
Wesham 55 H6
Wessington 51 F7
West Aberthaw 18 D5
West Acre 44 B4
West Acton 22 E3
West Allerdean 77 H6
West Alvington 5 H6
West Amesbury 20 E7
West Anstey 7 G3
West Ashby 53 F5
West Ashford 6 D2
West Ashling 12 B6
West Ashton 20 B6
West Auckland 62 B4
West Ayton 59 F1
West Bagborough 7 K2
West Barkwith 52 E4
West Barnby 63 J5
West Barns 76 E3
West Barsham 44 D2
West Bay 8 D5
West Beckham 45 F2
West Benhar 75 G4
West Bergholt 34 D6
West Bexington 8 E6
West Bilney 44 B4
West Blatchington 13 F6
West Boldon 71 J7
West Bourton 9 G2
West Bowling 57 G6
West Brabourne 15 F3
West Bradford 56 C5
West Bradley 8 E1
West Bretton 50 E1
West Bridgford 41 H2
West Bromwich 40 C6
West Buckland Devon 6 E2
West Buckland Som 7 K3
West Burrafirth 89 L7
West Burton NYorks 57 F1
West Burton WSuss 12 C5
West Butsfield 62 A2
West Butterwick 52 B2
West Byfleet 22 D5
West Caister 45 K4
West Calder 75 J4
West Camel 8 E2
West Carbeth 74 D3
West Carr Houses 51 K2
West Cauldcoats 74 E6
West Chaldon 9 G6
West Challow 21 G3
West Charleton 5 H6
West Chevington 71 H4
West Chiltington 12 D5
West Chiltington Common 12 D5
West Chinnock 8 D3
West Chisenbury 20 E6
West Clandon 22 D6
West Cliffe 15 J3
West Clyne 87 L9
West Coker 8 E3
West Compton Dorset 8 E5
West Compton Som 19 J7
West Cowick 58 C7
West Cross 17 K7
West Crudwell 20 C2
West Curry 4 C1
West Curthwaite 60 E2
West Dean Wilts 10 D2
West Dean WSuss 12 B5
West Deeping 42 E5
West Derby 48 C3
West Dereham 44 A5
West Ditchburn 71 G1
West Down 6 D1
West Drayton GtLon 22 D4
West Drayton Notts 51 K5
West Edington 71 G5
West Ella 59 G7
West End Bed 32 C3
West End BrackF 22 B4
West End Caerp 19 F2
West End Cambs 43 H6
West End ERid 59 G3
West End Hants 11 F3
West End Herts 23 F1
West End Kent 25 H5
West End Lancs 55 H3
West End Lincs 53 G3
West End Norf 45 J4
West End NSom 19 H5
West End NYorks 57 G4
West End Oxon 21 H1
West End Oxon 21 J3
West End SLan 75 H6
West End Suff 45 J7
West End Surr 22 C5
West End Surr 22 E5
West End Wilts 9 J2
West End Wilts 9 J2
West End Wilts 20 C4
West End Green 21 K5
West Farleigh 14 C2
West Farndon 31 G3
West Felton 38 C3
West Firle 13 H6
West Fleetham 71 G1
West Flotmanby 59 G2
West Garforth 57 J6
West Ginge 21 H3
West Glen 73 H3
West Grafton 21 F5
West Green GtLon 23 G3
West Green Hants 22 A6
West Grimstead 10 D2
West Grinstead 12 E4
West Haddlesey 58 B7
West Haddon 31 H1
West Hagbourne 21 J3
West Hagley 40 B7
West Hall 70 A7
West Hallam 41 G1
West Halton 59 F7
West Ham 23 G3
West Handley 51 F5
West Hanney 21 H2
West Hanningfield 24 D2
West Hardwick 51 G1
West Harnham 10 C2
West Harptree 19 J6
West Harrow 22 E3
West Harting 11 J2
West Hatch Som 8 B2
West Hatch Wilts 9 J2
West Head 43 J5
West Heath ChesE 49 H6
West Heath GtLon 23 H4
West Heath Hants 21 J6
West Heath Hants 22 B6
West Heath WMid 30 B1
West Helmsdale 87 N8
West Hendon 23 F3
West Hendred 21 H3
West Heslerton 59 F2
West Hewish 19 G5
West Hill Devon 7 J6
West Hill ERid 59 H3
West Hill NSom 19 H4
West Hoathly 13 G3
West Holme 9 H6
West Horndon 24 C3
West Horrington 19 J7
West Horsley 22 D6
West Horton 77 J7
West Hougham 15 H4
West Howe 10 B5
West Howetown 7 H2
West Huntspill 19 G7
West Hyde 22 D2
West Hythe 15 G4
West Ilsley 21 H3
West Itchenor 11 J4
West Keal 53 G6
West Kennett Long Barrow (Stonehenge, Avebury & Associated Sites) Wilts SN8 1QH 20 E5
West Kennett 20 E5
West Kilbride 74 A6
West Kingsdown 23 J5
West Kington 20 B4
West Kington Wick 20 B4
West Kirby 48 B4
West Knapton 58 E2
West Knighton 9 G6
West Knoyle 9 H1
West Kyloe 77 J6
West Lambrook 8 D3
West Langdon 15 J3
West Langwell 87 K9
West Lavington Wilts 20 D6
West Lavington WSuss 12 B4
West Layton 62 B6
West Leake 41 H3
West Learmouth 77 G7
West Lees 62 E6
West Leigh Devon 5 H5
West Leigh Devon 6 E5
West Leigh Som 7 K2
West Leith 32 C7
West Lexham 44 C4
West Lilling 58 C3
West Linton 75 K5
West Liss 11 J2
West Littleton 20 A4
West Lockinge 21 H3
West Looe 4 C5
West Lulworth 9 H6
West Lutton 59 F3
West Lydford 8 E1
West Lyn 7 F1
West Lyng 8 C2
West Lynn 44 A4
West Mains 77 J6
West Malling 23 K6
West Malvern 29 G4
West Marden 11 J3
West Markham 51 K5
West Marsh 53 F2
West Marton 56 D4
West Melbury 9 H2
West Melton 51 G2
West Meon 11 H2
West Meon Hut 11 H2
West Mersea 34 E7
West Midland Safari Park & Leisure Park Worcs DY12 1LF 29 H1
West Milton 8 D5
West Minster 25 F4
West Molesey 22 E5
West Monkton 8 B2
West Moors 10 B4
West Morden 9 J5
West Morriston 76 E6
West Morton 57 F5
West Mostard 61 J7
West Mudford 8 E2
West Ness 58 C2
West Newbiggin 62 D5
West Newton ERid 59 H6
West Newton Norf 44 A3
West Norwood 23 G4
West Ogwell 5 J4
West Orchard 9 H3
West Overton 20 E5
West Panson 6 B6
West Park 48 E3
West Parley 10 B5
West Peckham 23 K6
West Pelton 62 C1
West Pennard 8 E1
West Pentire 2 E2
West Perry 32 E2
West Porlock 7 G1
West Prawle 5 H7
West Preston 12 D6
West Pulham 9 G4
West Putford 6 B4
West Quantoxhead 7 K1
West Raddon 7 G5
West Rainton 62 D2
West Rasen 52 D4
West Raynham 44 C3
West Retford 51 J4
West Rounton 62 E6
West Row 33 K1
West Rudham 44 C3
West Runton 45 F1
West Saltoun 76 C4
West Sandford 7 G5
West Sandwick 89 N4
West Scrafton 57 F1
West Shepton 19 K7
West Somerset Railway Som TA24 5BG 7 K2
West Somerton 45 J4
West Stafford 9 G6
West Stockwith 51 K3
West Stoke 12 B6
West Stonesdale 61 K6
West Stoughton 19 H7
West Stour 9 G2
West Stourmouth 25 J5
West Stow 34 C1
West Stow Country Park Suff IP28 6HG 34 B1
West Stowell 20 E5
West Stratton 21 J7
West Street Kent 14 E2
West Street Med 24 D4
West Street Suff 34 D1
West Tanfield 57 H2
West Taphouse 4 B4
West Tarbert 73 G4
West Tarring 12 E6
West Thirston 71 G3
West Thorney 11 J4
West Thurrock 23 J4
West Tilbury 24 C4
West Tisted 11 H2
West Tofts Norf 44 C6
West Tofts P&K 80 G7
West Torrington 52 E4
West Town B&NESom 19 J5
West Town Hants 11 J5
West Town NSom 19 H5
West Town Som 8 E1
West Tytherley 10 D2
West Walton 43 H4
West Wellow 10 D3
West Wembury 5 F6
West Wemyss 76 B1
West Wick 19 G5
West Wickham Cambs 33 K4
West Wickham GtLon 23 G5
West Williamston 16 D5
West Winch 44 A4
West Winterslow 10 D1
West Wittering 11 J5
West Witton 57 F1
West Woodburn 70 D5
West Woodhay 21 G5
West Woodlands 20 A7
West Worldham 11 J1
West Worlington 7 F4
West Worthing 12 E6
West Wratting 33 K3
West Wycombe 22 B2
West Yatton 20 B4
West Yell 89 N4
West Youlstone 6 A4
Westbere 25 H5
Westborough 42 B1
Westbourne BCP 10 B5
Westbourne WSuss 11 J4
Westbourne Green 23 F3
Westbrook Kent 25 K4
Westbrook WBerks 21 H4
Westbrook Wilts 20 C5
Westbury Bucks 31 H5
Westbury Shrop 38 C5
Westbury Wilts 20 B6
Westbury Leigh 20 B6
Westbury on Trym 19 J4
Westbury-on-Severn 29 G7
Westbury-sub-Mendip 19 J7
Westby Lancs 55 G6
Westby Lincs 42 C3
Westcliff-on-Sea 24 E3
Westcombe 9 F1
Westcot 21 G3
Westcott Bucks 31 J7
Westcott Devon 7 J5
Westcott Surr 22 E7
Westcourt 21 F5
Westcroft 32 B5
Westdean 13 J7
Westdowns 4 A2
Westend Town 20 A4
Wester Balgedie 80 G10
Wester Dechmont 75 J3
Wester Gruinards 83 R1
Wester Hailes 76 A4
Wester Quarff 89 N9
Wester Skeld 89 L8
Westerdale High 87 P4
Westerdale NYorks 63 G6
Westerfield 35 F4
Westergate 12 C6
Westerham 23 H6
Westerhope 71 G7
Westerleigh 19 K4
Westerloch 87 R4
Westerton Aber 85 M11
Westerton Dur 62 C3
Westerton P&K 80 D9
Westerwick 89 L8
Westfield Cumb 60 A4
Westfield ESuss 14 D6
Westfield High 87 N3
Westfield NLan 75 F3
Westfield Norf 44 D5
Westfield WLoth 75 H3
Westfield WYorks 57 H7
Westfield Sole 24 D5
Westgate Dur 61 L3
Westgate NLincs 51 K2
Westgate Norf 44 D1
Westgate N'umb 71 G6
Westgate Hill 57 H7
Westgate on Sea 25 K4
Westhall Aber 85 L8
Westhall Suff 45 J7
Westham Dorset 9 F7
Westham ESuss 13 K6
Westham Som 19 H7
Westhampnett 12 B6
Westhay Devon 8 C4
Westhay Som 19 H7
Westhead 48 D2
Westhide 28 E4
Westhill 85 N10
Westhope Here 28 D3
Westhope Shrop 38 D7
Westhorp 31 G3
Westhorpe Lincs 43 F2
Westhorpe Notts 51 J7
Westhorpe Suff 34 E2
Westhoughton 49 F2
Westhouse 56 B2
Westhouses 51 G7
Westhumble 22 E6
Westing 89 P2
Westlake 5 G5
Westlands 40 A1
Westlea 20 E3
Westleigh Devon 6 C3
Westleigh Devon 7 J4
Westleigh GtMan 49 F2
Westleton 35 J2
Westley Shrop 38 C5
Westley Suff 34 C2
Westley Heights 24 C3
Westley Waterless 33 K3
Westlington 31 J7
Westlinton 69 J7
Westloch 76 A5
Westmancote 29 J5
Westmarsh 25 J5
Westmeston 13 G5
Westmill 33 G6
Westminster 23 F4
Westminster Abbey (Palace of Westminster & Westminster Abbey inc. St Margaret's Church) GtLon SW1P 3PA 105 A7
Westminster Cathedral GtLon SW1P 2QW 132 C6
Westmuir 81 J5
Westness 89 C5
Westnewton Cumb 60 C2
Westnewton N'umb 77 H7
Westoe 71 J7
Weston B&NESom 20 A5
Weston ChesE 49 G7
Weston Devon 7 K5
Weston Devon 7 K7
Weston Dorset 9 F7
Weston Halton 48 E4
Weston Hants 11 J2
Weston Here 28 C3
Weston Lincs 43 F3
Weston Notts 51 K6
Weston NYorks 57 G5
Weston N'hants 31 G4
Weston Shrop 28 C1
Weston Shrop 38 E3
Weston Shrop 38 E6
Weston Staffs 40 B3
Weston Soton 11 F3
Weston WBerks 21 G4
Weston Bampfylde 9 F2
Weston Beggard 28 E4
Weston by Welland 42 A6
Weston Colville 33 K3
Weston Corbett 21 K7
Weston Coyney 40 B1
Weston Favell 31 J2
Weston Green Cambs 33 K3
Weston Green Norf 45 F4
Weston Heath 39 G4
Weston Hills 43 F3
Weston in Arden 41 F7
Weston Jones 39 G3
Weston Longville 45 F4
Weston Lullingfields 38 D3
Weston Park Staffs TF11 8LE 40 A4
Weston Patrick 21 K7
Weston Point 48 D4
Weston Rhyn 38 B2
Weston Subedge 30 C4
Weston Town 20 A7
Weston Turville 32 B7
Weston under Penyard 29 F6
Weston under Wetherley 30 E2
Weston Underwood Derbys 40 E1
Weston Underwood MK 32 B3
Westonbirt 20 B3
Westonbirt - The National Arboretum Glos GL8 8QS 20 B3
Westoning 32 D5
Weston-in-Gordano 19 H4
Weston-on-Avon 30 C3
Weston-on-the-Green 31 G7
Weston-on-Trent 41 G3
Weston-super-Mare 19 G5

Weston-under-Lizard 40 A4
Westonzoyland 8 C1
Westow 58 D3
Westpoint Arena, Clyst St. Mary Devon EX5 1DJ 7 H6
Westport A&B 66 A1
Westport Som 8 C2
Westra 18 E4
Westray 89 D3
Westray Airfield 89 D2
Westridge Green 21 J4
Westrigg 75 H4
Westruther 76 E6
Westry 43 G6
Westvale 48 D3
Westville 41 H1
Westward 60 D2
Westward Ho! 6 C3
Westwell Kent 14 E3
Westwell Oxon 21 F1
Westwell Leacon 14 E3
Westwick Cambs 33 H2
Westwick Dur 62 A5
Westwick Norf 45 G3
Westwick NYorks 57 J3
Westwood Devon 7 J6
Westwood Peter 42 E6
Westwood SLan 74 E5
Westwood Wilts 20 B6
Westwood Heath 30 D1
Westwoodside 51 K3
Wetham Green 24 E5
Wetheral 61 F1
Wetherby 57 K5
Wetherden 34 E2
Wetherden Upper Town 34 E2
Wetheringsett 35 F2
Wethersfield 34 B5
Wethersta 89 M6
Wetherup Street 35 F2
Wetley Abbey 40 B1
Wetley Rocks 40 B1
Wettenhall 49 F6
Wettenhall Green 49 F6
Wetton 50 D7
Wetwang 59 F4
Wetwood 39 G2
Wexcombe 21 F6
Wexham Street 22 C3
Weybourne Norf 45 F1
Weybourne Surr 22 B7
Weybread 45 G7
Weybread Street 35 G1
Weybridge 22 D5
Weycroft 8 C4
Weyhill 21 G7
Weymouth 9 F7
Weymouth Sea Life Adventure Park & Marine Sanctuary Dorset DT4 7SX 9 F6
Whaddon Bucks 32 B5
Whaddon Cambs 33 G4
Whaddon Glos 29 H7
Whaddon Glos 29 J6
Whaddon Wilts 10 C2
Whaddon Wilts 20 B5
Whaddon Gap 33 G4
Whale 61 G4
Whaley 51 H5
Whaley Bridge 50 C4
Whaley Thorns 51 H5
Whalley 56 C6
Whalsay 89 P6
Whalsay Airport 89 P6
Whalton 71 G5
Wham 56 C3
Whaplode 43 G3
Whaplode Drove 43 G4
Whaplode St. Catherine 43 G4
Wharfe 56 C3
Wharles 55 H6
Wharley End 32 C4
Wharncliffe Side 50 E3
Wharram le Street 58 E3
Wharram Percy 58 E3
Wharton ChesW&C 49 F6
Wharton Here 28 E3
Whashton 62 B6
Whatcote 30 E4
Whateley 40 E6
Whatfield 34 E4
Whatley 20 A7
Whatlington 14 C6
Whatsole Street 15 G3
Whatstandwell 51 F7
Whatton 42 A2
Whauphill 64 E6
Whaw 61 L6
Wheal Peevor (Cornwall & West Devon Mining Landscape) Corn 2 E4
Wheatacre 45 J6
Wheatcroft 51 F7
Wheatenhurst 20 A1
Wheatfield CC&G 92 B4
Wheatfield Oxon 21 K2
Wheathampstead 32 E7
Wheathill Shrop 39 F7
Wheathill Som 8 E1
Wheatley Hants 11 J1
Wheatley Oxon 21 K1
Wheatley WYorks 57 F7
Wheatley Hill 62 D3
Wheatley Lane 56 D6
Wheatley Park 51 H2
Wheaton Aston 40 A4
Wheddon Cross 7 H2
Wheelerstreet 22 C7
Wheelock 49 G7
Wheelock Heath 49 G7
Wheelton 56 B7
Wheen 81 J3
Wheldale 57 K7
Wheldrake 58 C5
Whelford 20 E2
Whelley 48 E2
Whelpley Hill 22 C1
Whelpo 60 E3
Whelston 48 B5
Whenby 58 C3
Whepstead 34 C3
Wherstead 35 F4
Wherwell 21 G7
Wheston 50 D5
Whetley Cross 8 D4
Whetsted 23 K7
Whetstone GtLon 23 F2
Whetstone Leics 41 H6
Whicham 54 E1
Whichford 30 E5
Whickham 71 H7
Whiddon 6 C5
Whiddon Down 6 E6
Whifflet 75 F4
Whigstreet 81 K6
Whilton 31 H2
Whim 76 A5
Whimble 6 B5
Whimple 7 J6
Whimpwell Green 45 H3
Whin Lane End 55 G5
Whinburgh 44 E5
Whinlatter Forest Cumb CA12 5TW 60 C4
Whinny Hill 62 D5
Whinnyfold 85 Q7
Whippingham 11 G5
Whipsnade 32 D7
Whipsnade Zoo CenBeds LU6 2LF 32 D7
Whipton 7 H6
Whirlow 51 F4
Whisby 52 C6
Whissendine 42 B4
Whissonsett 44 D3
Whisterfield 49 H5
Whistley Green 22 A4
Whiston Mersey 48 D3
Whiston N'hants 32 B2
Whiston Staffs 40 A4
Whiston Staffs 40 C1
Whiston SYorks 51 G3
Whiston Cross 39 G5
Whiston Eaves 40 C1
Whitacre Fields 40 E6
Whitacre Heath 40 E6
Whitbeck 54 E1
Whitbourne 29 G3
Whitburn T&W 71 K7
Whitburn WLoth 75 H4
Whitby ChesW&C 48 C5
Whitby NYorks 63 J5
Whitby Abbey NYorks YO22 4JT 63 K5
Whitby Lifeboat Museum NYorks YO21 3PU 63 J5
Whitbyheath 48 C5
Whitchurch B&NESom 19 K5
Whitchurch Bucks 32 B6
Whitchurch Cardiff 18 E3
Whitchurch Devon 4 E3
Whitchurch Hants 21 H7
Whitchurch Here 28 E7
Whitchurch Pembs 16 A3
Whitchurch Shrop 38 E1
Whitchurch Warks 30 D4
Whitchurch Canonicorum 8 C5
Whitchurch Hill 21 K4
Whitchurch-on-Thames 21 K4
Whitcombe 9 G6
Whitcott Keysett 38 B7
White Ball 7 J4
White Cliffs of Dover Kent CT16 1HJ 15 J3
White Colne 34 C6
White Coppice 49 F1
White Cross Corn 3 F3
White Cross Devon 7 J6
White Cross Here 28 D4
White Cross Wilts 9 G1
White End 29 H6
White Hill 9 H1
White Houses 51 K5
White Kirkley 62 A3
White Lackington 9 G5
White Ladies Aston 29 J3
White Lund 55 H3
White Mill 17 H3
White Moor 41 F1
White Notley 34 B7
White Ox Mead 20 A6
White Pit 53 G5
White Post Farm Centre, Farnsfield Notts NG22 8HL 51 J7
White Rocks 28 D6
White Roding 33 J7
White Waltham 22 B4
Whiteabbey 92 J8
Whiteash Green 34 B5
Whitebirk 56 C7
Whitebridge (An Drochaid Bhàn) 83 Q9
Whitebrook 19 J1
Whiteburn 76 D6
Whitecairn 64 C5
Whitecairns 85 P9
Whitecastle 75 J6
Whitechapel 55 J5
Whitechurch 16 E2
Whitecote 57 H6
Whitecraig 76 B3
Whitecroft 19 K1
Whitecrook 64 B5
Whitecross Corn 2 C5
Whitecross Corn 3 G1
Whitecross Dorset 8 D5
Whitecross Falk 75 H3
Whitecross NM&D 93 E13
Whitefield Devon 7 F2
Whitefield Dorset 9 J5
Whitefield GtMan 49 H2
Whitegate 49 F6
Whitegates 93 H13
Whitehall Devon 7 K4
Whitehall Hants 22 A6
Whitehall Ork 89 F5
Whitehall WSuss 12 E4
Whitehaven 60 A5
Whitehead 92 K7
Whitehill F&O 91 J11
Whitehill Hants 11 J1
Whitehill Kent 14 E2
Whitehill Midlo 76 B4
Whitehill NAyr 74 A5
Whitehills 85 L4
Whitehouse A&B 73 G4
Whitehouse A&N 92 J8
Whitehouse Aber 85 L9
Whitehouse Common 40 D6
Whitekirk 76 D2
Whitelackington 8 C3
Whitelaw 77 G5
Whitelees 74 B7
Whiteley 11 G4
Whiteley Bank 11 G6
Whiteley Green 49 J5
Whiteley Village 22 D5
Whiteleys 64 A5
Whitemans Green 13 G4
Whitemire 84 D5
Whitemoor 3 G3
Whiteness 89 M8
Whiteoak Green 30 E7
Whiteparish 10 D2
Whiterashes 85 N8
Whiterock 93 L10
Whiteshill 20 B1
Whiteside N'umb 70 C7
Whiteside WLoth 75 H4
Whitesmith 13 J5
Whitestaunton 8 B3
Whitestone A&B 73 F7
Whitestone Devon 7 G6
Whitestreet Green 34 D5
Whiteway 29 J7
Whitewell Lancs 56 B5
Whitewell Wrex 38 D1
Whiteworks 5 G3
Whitewreath 84 G5
Whitfield Here 28 D5
Whitfield Kent 15 J3
Whitfield N'hants 31 H5
Whitfield N'umb 61 J1
Whitfield SGlos 19 K2
Whitford Devon 8 B5
Whitford (Chwitffordd) Flints 47 K5
Whitgift 58 E7
Whitgreave 40 A3
Whithorn 64 E6
Whiting Bay 66 E1
Whitkirk 57 J6
Whitland (Hendy-Gwyn) 17 F4
Whitland Abbey 17 F4
Whitleigh 4 E4
Whitletts 67 H1
Whitley NYorks 58 B7
Whitley Read 22 A5
Whitley Wilts 20 B5
Whitley WMid 30 E1
Whitley Bay 71 J6
Whitley Chapel 61 L1
Whitley Heath 40 A3
Whitley Lower 50 E1
Whitley Row 23 H6
Whitlock's End 30 C1
Whitminster 20 A1
Whitmore Dorset 10 B4
Whitmore Staffs 40 A1
Whitnage 7 J4
Whitnash 30 E2
Whitnell 19 F7
Whitney-on-Wye 28 B4
Whitrigg Cumb 60 D1
Whitrigg Cumb 60 D3
Whitsbury 10 C3
Whitsome 77 G5
Whitson 19 G3
Whitstable 25 H5
Whitstone 4 C1
Whittingham 71 F2
Whittingslow 38 D7
Whittington Derbys 51 F5
Whittington Glos 30 B6
Whittington Lancs 56 B2
Whittington Norf 44 B6
Whittington Shrop 38 C2
Whittington Staffs 40 A7
Whittington Staffs 40 D5
Whittington Worcs 29 H3
Whittlebury 31 H4
Whittle-le-Woods 55 J7
Whittlesey 43 F6
Whittlesford 33 H4
Whittlestone Head 49 G1
Whitton GtLon 22 E4
Whitton NLincs 59 F7
Whitton N'umb 71 F3
Whitton Powys 28 B2
Whitton Shrop 28 E1
Whitton Stock 62 D4
Whitton Suff 35 F4
Whittonditch 21 F4
Whittonstall 62 A1
Whitway 21 H6
Whitwell Derbys 51 H5
Whitwell Herts 32 E6
Whitwell IoW 11 G7
Whitwell NYorks 62 C7
Whitwell Rut 42 C5
Whitwell Street 45 F3
Whitwell-on-the-Hill 58 D3
Whitwick 41 G4
Whitwood 57 K7
Whitworth 49 H1
Whitworth Art Gallery, Manchester GtMan M15 6ER 115 H5
Whixall 38 E2
Whixley 57 K4
Whorlton Dur 62 B5
Whorlton NYorks 62 E6
Whygate 70 C6
Whyle 28 E2
Whyteleafe 23 G6
Wibdon 19 J2
Wibsey 57 G6
Wibtoft 41 G7
Wichenford 29 G2
Wichling 14 E2
Wick BCP 10 C5
Wick Devon 7 K5
Wick (Inbhir Ùige) High 87 R4
Wick SGlos 20 A4
Wick Som 8 E1
Wick Som 19 F7
Wick VGlam 18 C4
Wick Wilts 10 C2
Wick Worcs 29 J4
Wick WSuss 12 D6
Wick John O'Groats Airport 87 R4
Wick Hill Kent 14 D3
Wick Hill W'ham 22 A5
Wick St. Lawrence 19 G5
Wicken Cambs 33 J1
Wicken N'hants 31 J5
Wicken Bonhunt 33 H5
Wickenby 52 D4
Wicker Street Green 34 D4
Wickersiack 61 H5
Wickersley 51 G3
Wicketwood Hill 41 J1
Wickford 24 D2
Wickham Hants 11 G3
Wickham WBerks 21 G4
Wickham Bishops 34 C7
Wickham Heath 21 H5
Wickham Market 35 H3
Wickham Skeith 34 E2
Wickham St. Paul 34 C5
Wickham Street Suff 34 B3
Wickham Street Suff 34 E2
Wickhambreaux 15 H2
Wickhambrook 34 B3
Wickhamford 30 B4
Wickhampton 45 J5
Wicklewood 44 E5
Wickmere 45 F2
Wickstead Park N'hants NN15 6NJ 32 B1
Wickstreet 13 J6
Wickwar 20 A3
Widcombe 20 A5
Widdington 33 J5
Widdop 56 E6
Widdrington 71 H4
Widdrington Station 71 H4
Wide Open 71 H6
Widecombe in the Moor 5 H3
Widegates 4 C5
Widemouth Bay 6 A5
Widewall 89 D8
Widford Essex 24 C1
Widford Herts 33 H7
Widford Oxon 30 D7
Widgham Green 33 K3
Widmer End 22 B2
Widmerpool 41 J3
Widnes 48 E4
Widworthy 8 B5
Wigan 48 E2
Wigan Pier GtMan WN3 4EU 48 E2
Wiganthorpe 58 C2
Wigborough 8 D3
Wiggaton 7 K6
Wiggenhall St. Germans 43 J4
Wiggenhall St. Mary Magdalen 43 J4
Wiggenhall St. Mary the Virgin 43 J4
Wiggenhall St. Peter 44 A4
Wiggens Green 33 K4
Wigginton Herts 32 C7
Wigginton Oxon 30 E5
Wigginton Shrop 38 C2
Wigginton Staffs 40 E5
Wigginton York 58 C4
Wigglesworth 56 D4
Wiggonby 60 E1
Wiggonholt 12 D5
Wighill 57 K5
Wighton 44 D2
Wightwizzle 50 E3
Wigley 10 E3
Wigmore Here 28 D2
Wigmore Med 24 E5
Wigsley 52 B5
Wigsthorpe 42 D7
Wigston 41 J6
Wigston Parva 41 G7
Wigthorpe 51 H4
Wigtoft 43 F2
Wigton 60 D2
Wigtown 64 E5
Wike 57 J5
Wilbarston 42 B7
Wilberfoss 58 D4
Wilburton 33 H1
Wilby Norf 44 E6
Wilby N'hants 32 B2
Wilby Suff 35 G1
Wilcot 20 E5
Wilcott 38 C4
Wilcrick 19 H3
Wilday Green 51 F5
Wildboarclough 49 J6
Wilde Street 34 B1
Wilden Bed 32 D3
Wilden Worcs 29 H1
Wildhern 21 G6
Wildhill 23 F1
Wildmoor 29 J1
Wildsworth 52 B3
Wilford 41 H2
Wilkesley 39 F1
Wilkhaven 84 D2
Wilkieston 75 K4
Wilksby 53 F6
Willand Devon 7 J4
Willand Som 7 K4
Willaston ChesE 49 F7
Willaston ChesW&C 48 C5
Willaston Shrop 38 E2
Willen 32 B4
Willen Lakeside Park MK MK15 9HQ 101 E3
Willenhall WMid 30 E1
Willenhall WMid 40 B6
Willerby ERid 59 G7
Willerby NYorks 59 G2
Willersey 30 C5
Willersley 28 C4
Willesborough 15 F3
Willesborough Lees 15 F3
Willesden 23 F3
Willesleigh 6 D2
Willesley 20 B3
Willett 7 K2
Willey Shrop 39 F6
Willey Warks 41 G7
Willey Green 22 C6
William's Green 34 D4
Williamscot 31 F4
Williamson Park, Lancaster Lancs LA1 1UX 55 H3
Williamthorpe 51 G6
Willian 33 F5
Willimontswick 70 C7
Willingale 23 J1
Willingdon 13 J6
Willingham 33 H1
Willingham by Stow 52 B4
Willingham Green 33 K3
Willington Bed 32 E3
Willington Derbys 40 E3
Willington Dur 62 B3
Willington Kent 14 C2
Willington T&W 71 J7
Willington Warks 30 D5
Willington Corner 48 E6
Willisham 34 E3
Willitoft 58 D6
Williton 7 J1
Willoughbridge 39 G1
Willoughby Lincs 53 H5
Willoughby Warks 31 G2
Willoughby Waterleys 41 H6
Willoughby-on-the-Wolds 41 J3
Willoughton 52 C3
Willow Green 49 F5
Willows Farm Village Herts AL2 1BB 22 E1
Willows Green 34 B7
Willsbridge 19 K4
Willslock 40 C2
Willsworthy 6 D7
Willtown 8 C2
Wilmcote 30 C3
Wilmington B&NESom 19 K5
Wilmington Devon 8 B4
Wilmington ESuss 13 J6
Wilmington Kent 23 J4
Wilmslow 49 H4
Wilnecote 40 E5
Wilney Green 44 E7
Wilpshire 56 B6
Wilsden 57 F6
Wilsford Lincs 42 D1
Wilsford Wilts 10 C1
Wilsford Wilts 20 E6
Wilsham 7 F1
Wilshaw 50 D2
Wilsill 57 G3
Wilsley Green 14 C4
Wilsley Pound 14 C4
Wilson 41 G3
Wilstead 32 D4
Wilsthorpe ERid 59 H3
Wilsthorpe Lincs 42 D4
Wilstone 32 C7
Wilton Cumb 60 B5
Wilton Here 28 E6
Wilton NYorks 58 E1
Wilton R&C 63 F5
Wilton ScBord 69 K2
Wilton Wilts 10 B1
Wilton Wilts 21 F5
Wilton House Wilts SP2 0BJ 10 B1
Wiltown 7 K4
Wimbish 33 J5
Wimbish Green 33 K5
Wimblebury 40 C4
Wimbledon 23 F4
Wimbledon All England Lawn Tennis & Croquet Club GtLon SW19 5AG 103 G10
Wimblington 43 H6
Wimborne Minster Dorset BH21 1HT 95 B3
Wimborne Minster 10 B4
Wimborne St. Giles 10 B3
Wimbotsham 44 A5
Wimpole 33 G3
Wimpole Home Farm Cambs SG8 0BW 33 G4
Wimpole Lodge 33 G4
Wimpstone 30 D4
Wincanton 9 G2
Winceby 53 G6
Wincham 49 F5
Winchburgh 75 J3
Winchcombe 30 B6
Winchelsea 14 E6
Winchelsea Beach 14 E6
Winchester 11 F2
Winchester Cathedral Hants SO23 9LS 137 Winchester
Winchet Hill 14 C3
Winchfield 22 A6
Winchmore Hill Bucks 22 C2
Winchmore Hill GtLon 23 G2
Wincle 49 J6
Wincobank 51 F3
Windermere 60 F7
Windermere Lake Cruises Cumb LA12 8AS 60 E7
Winderton 30 E4
Windle Hill 48 C5
Windlehurst 49 J4
Windlesham 22 C5
Windley 41 F1
Windmill 50 D5
Windmill Hill ESuss 13 K5
Windmill Hill Som 8 C3
Windmill Hill (Stonehenge, Avebury & Associated Sites) Wilts SN4 9NW 20 D4
Windmill Hill Worcs 29 J4
Windrush 30 C7
Windsor 22 C4
Windsor Castle W&M SL4 1NJ 137 Windsor
Windsor Green 34 C3
Windy Nook 71 H7
Windygates 81 J10
Windy Gap 93 F13
Windy-Yett 74 C5
Wineham 13 F4
Winestead 59 J7
Winewall 56 E6
Winfarthing 45 F7
Winford IoW 11 G6
Winford NSom 19 J5
Winforton 28 B4
Winfrith Newburgh 9 H6
Wing Bucks 32 B6
Wing Rut 42 B5
Wingate 62 D3
Wingates GtMan 49 F2
Wingates N'umb 71 F4
Wingerworth 51 F6
Wingfield CenBeds 32 D6
Wingfield Suff 35 G1
Wingfield Wilts 20 B6
Wingfield Green 35 G1
Wingham 15 H2
Wingham Well 15 H2
Wingmore 15 G3
Wingrave 32 B7
Winkburn 51 K7
Winkfield 22 C4
Winkfield Row 22 B4
Winkhill 50 C7
Winkleigh 6 E5
Winksley 57 H2
Winkton 10 C5
Winlaton 71 G7
Winlaton Mill 71 G7
Winmarleigh 55 H5
Winnard's Perch 3 G2
Winnersh 22 A4
Winnington 49 F5
Winscombe 19 H6
Winsford ChesW&C 49 F6
Winsford Som 7 H2
Winsham Devon 6 C2
Winsham Som 8 C4
Winshill 40 E3
Winsh-wen 17 K6
Winskill 61 G3
Winslade 21 K7
Winsley 20 B5
Winslow 31 J6
Winson 20 D1
Winsor 10 E3
Winster Cumb 60 F7
Winster Derbys 50 E6
Winston Dur 62 B5
Winston Suff 35 F2
Winston Green 35 F2
Winstone 20 C1
Winswell 6 C4
Winter Gardens NSom BS23 1AJ 137 Weston-super-Mare
Winter Gardens FY1 1HW 121 Blackpool
Winterborne Came 9 G6
Winterborne Clenston 9 H4
Winterborne Herrington 9 F6
Winterborne Houghton 9 H4
Winterborne Kingston 9 H5
Winterborne Monkton 9 F6
Winterborne Stickland 9 H4
Winterborne Whitechurch 9 H4
Winterborne Zelston 9 H5
Winterbourne SGlos 19 K3
Winterbourne Stoke 20 D7
Winterbourne WBerks 21 H4
Winterbourne Abbas 9 F5
Winterbourne Bassett 20 E4
Winterbourne Dauntsey 10 C1
Winterbourne Earls 10 C1
Winterbourne Gunner 10 C1
Winterbourne Monkton 20 E4
Winterbourne Steepleton 9 F6
Winterbrook 21 K3
Winterburn 56 E4
Wintercleugh 68 E3
Winteringham 59 F7
Winterley 49 G7
Wintersett 51 F1
Wintershill 11 G3
Winterslow 10 D1
Winterton 52 C1
Winterton-on-Sea 45 J4
Winthorpe Lincs 53 J6
Winthorpe Notts 52 B7
Winton BCP 10 B5
Winton Cumb 61 J5
Wintringham 58 E2
Winwick Cambs 42 E7
Winwick N'hants 31 H1
Winwick Warr 49 F3
Wirksworth 50 E7
Wirksworth Moor 51 F7
Wirral Country Park Mersey CH61 0HN 48 B4
Wirswall 38 E1
Wisbech 43 H5
Wisbech St. Mary 43 H5
Wisborough Green 12 D4
Wiseton 51 K4
Wishaw NLan 75 F5
Wishaw Warks 40 D6
Wisley 22 D6
Wispington 53 F5
Wissett 35 H1
Wissington 34 D5
Wistanstow 38 D7
Wistanswick 39 F3
Wistaston 49 F7
Wiston Pembs 16 D4
Wiston SLan 75 H7
Wiston WSuss 12 E5
Wistow Cambs 43 F7
Wistow NYorks 58 B6
Wiswell 56 C6
Witcham 33 H1
Witchampton 9 J4
Witchburn 66 B1
Witchford 33 J1
Witcombe 8 D2
Witham 34 C7
Witham Friary 20 A7
Witham on the Hill 42 D4
Withcall 53 F4
Withcote 42 A5
Withdean 13 G6
Witherenden Hill 13 K4
Witherhurst 13 K4
Witheridge 7 G4
Witherley 41 F6
Withern 53 H4
Withernsea 59 K7
Withernwick 59 H5
Withersdale Street 45 G7
Withersfield 33 K4
Witherslack 55 H1
Witherslack Hall 55 H1
Withiel 3 G2
Withiel Florey 7 H2
Withielgoose 4 A4
Withington Glos 30 B7
Withington GtMan 49 H3
Withington Here 28 E4
Withington Shrop 38 E4
Withington Staffs 40 C2
Withington Green 49 H5
Withington Marsh 28 E4
Withleigh 7 H4
Withnell 56 B7
Withnell Fold 56 B7
Withybrook Som 19 K7
Withybrook Warks 41 G7
Withycombe 7 J1
Withycombe Raleigh 7 J7
Withyham 13 H3
Withypool 7 G2
Witley 12 C3
Witnesham 35 F3
Witney 21 G1
Wittering 42 D5
Wittersham 14 D5
Witton Angus 81 L3
Witton Norf 45 H5
Witton Worcs 29 H2
Witton Bridge 45 H2
Witton Gilbert 62 C2
Witton Park 62 B3
Witton-le-Wear 62 B3
Wiveliscombe 7 J3
Wivelsfield 13 G4
Wivelsfield Green 13 G5
Wivenhoe 34 E6
Wiveton 44 E1
Wix 35 F6
Wixford 30 B3
Wixhill 38 E3
Wixoe 34 B4
Woburn 32 C5
Woburn Safari Park CenBeds MK17 9QN 101 H5
Woburn Sands 32 C5
Wokefield Park 21 K5
Woking 22 D6
Wokingham 22 B5
Wolborough 5 J3
Wold Newton ERid 59 G2
Wold Newton NELincs 53 F3
Woldingham 23 G6
Wolfelee 70 A3
Wolferlow 29 F2
Wolferton 44 A3
Wolfhampcote 31 G2
Wolfhill 80 G7
Wolfpits 28 B3
Wolf's Castle 16 C3
Wolfsdale 16 C3
Woll 69 K1
Wollaston N'hants 32 C2
Wollaston Shrop 38 C4
Wollaston WMid 40 A7
Wollaton 41 H2
Wollerton 39 F3
Wollescote 40 B7
Wolsingham 62 A3
Wolston 31 F1
Wolsty 60 C1
Wolvercote 21 J1
Wolverhampton 40 B6
Wolverhampton Art Gallery WMid WV1 1DU 106 B1
Wolverley Shrop 38 D2
Wolverley Worcs 29 H1
Wolvers Hill 19 G5
Wolverton Hants 21 J6
Wolverton MK 32 B4
Wolverton Warks 30 D2
Wolverton Wilts 9 G1
Wolverton Common 21 J6
Wolvesnewton 19 H2
Wolvey 41 G7
Wolvey Heath 41 G7
Wolviston 62 E4
Womaston 28 B2
Wombleton 58 C1
Wombourne 40 A6
Wombwell 51 F2
Womenswold 15 H2
Womersley 51 H1
Wonastow 28 D7
Wonersh 22 D7
Wonford 7 H6
Wonson 6 E7
Wonston 11 F1
Wooburn 22 C3
Wooburn Green 22 C3
Wood Bevington 30 B3
Wood Burcote 31 H4
Wood Dalling 44 E3
Wood Eaton 40 A4
Wood End Bed 32 D2
Wood End Bed 32 D4
Wood End Bucks 31 J5
Wood End Herts 33 G6
Wood End Warks 30 C1
Wood End Warks 40 E6
Wood End Warks 40 E7
Wood End WMid 40 B5
Wood Enderby 53 F6
Wood Green GtLon 23 G2
Wood Green Norf 45 G6
Wood Green Animal Shelter, Godmanchester Cambs PE29 2NH 33 F2
Wood Lane 38 D2
Wood Norton 44 E3
Wood Seats 51 F3
Wood Stanway 30 B5
Wood Street 45 H3
Wood Street Village 22 C6
Woodacott 6 B5
Woodale 57 F2
Woodall 51 G4
Woodbastwick 45 H4
Woodbeck 51 K5
Woodborough Notts 41 J1
Woodborough Wilts 20 E6
Woodbridge Devon 7 K6
Woodbridge Dorset 9 G3
Woodbridge Suff 35 G4
Woodburn 92 J8
Woodbury Devon 7 J7
Woodbury Som 19 J7
Woodbury Salterton 7 J7
Woodchester 20 B1
Woodchurch Kent 14 E4
Woodchurch Mersey 48 B4
Woodcombe 7 H1
Woodcote Oxon 21 K3
Woodcote Tel&W 39 G4
Woodcote Green 29 J1
Woodcott 21 H6
Woodcroft 19 J2
Woodcutts 9 J3
Woodditton 33 K3
Woodeaton 31 G7
Woodend Cumb 60 C7
Woodend N'hants 31 H4
Woodend WSuss 12 B6
Woodend Green 33 J6
Woodfalls 10 C2
Woodfield Oxon 31 G6
Woodfield SAyr 67 H1
Woodfoot 61 H5
Woodford Corn 6 A4
Woodford Devon 5 H5
Woodford Glos 19 K2
Woodford GtLon 23 H2
Woodford GtMan 49 H4
Woodford N'hants 32 C1
Woodford Som 7 J2
Woodford Bridge 23 H2
Woodford Green 23 H2
Woodford Halse 31 G3
Woodgate Devon 7 K4
Woodgate Norf 44 E4
Woodgate WMid 40 B7
Woodgate Worcs 29 J2
Woodgate WSuss 12 C6
Woodgreen 10 C3
Woodhall Invcly 74 B3
Woodhall NYorks 61 L7
Woodhall Hills 57 G6
Woodhall Spa 52 E6
Woodham Bucks 31 H7
Woodham Dur 62 C4
Woodham Surr 22 D5
Woodham Ferrers 24 D2
Woodham Mortimer 24 E1
Woodham Walter 24 E1
Woodhaven 81 K8
Woodhead Aber 85 M7
Woodhead Staffs 40 C1
Woodhenge (Stonehenge, Avebury & Associated Sites) Wilts SP4 7AR 20 E7
Woodhey 48 C4
Woodhey Green 48 E7
Woodhill Shrop 39 G7
Woodhill Som 8 C2
Woodhorn 71 H5
Woodhouse Cumb 55 J1
Woodhouse Leics 41 H4
Woodhouse WYorks 57 G7
Woodhouse WYorks 57 H6
Woodhouse WYorks 57 J7
Woodhouse Down 19 K3
Woodhouse Eaves 41 H4
Woodhouse Green 49 J6
Woodhouses GtMan 49 H2
Woodhouses Staffs 40 C5
Woodhouses Staffs 40 D4
Woodhuish 5 K5
Woodhurst 33 G1
Woodingdean 13 G6
Woodington 10 E2
Woodland Devon 5 H4
Woodland Dur 62 A4
Woodland Kent 15 G3
Woodland Head 7 F6
Woodlands Dorset 10 B4
Woodlands Hants 10 E3
Woodlands NYorks 57 J4
Woodlands Shrop 39 G7
Woodlands Som 7 K1
Woodlands Leisure Park, Dartmouth Devon TQ9 7DQ 5 J5
Woodlands Park 22 B4
Woodlands St. Mary 21 G4
Woodlane 40 D3
Woodleigh 5 H6
Woodlesford 57 J7
Woodley GtMan 49 J3
Woodley W'ham 22 A4
Woodmancote Glos 20 A2
Woodmancote Glos 20 D1
Woodmancote Glos 29 J6
Woodmancote WSuss 11 J4
Woodmancote WSuss 13 F5
Woodmancott 21 J7
Woodmansey 59 G6
Woodmansterne 23 F6
Woodmanton 7 J7
Woodmill 40 D3
Woodminton 10 B2
Woodmoor 38 B5
Woodnesborough 15 J2
Woodnewton 42 D6
Woodperry 31 G7
Woodplumpton 55 J6
Woodrising 44 D5
Woodrow 9 G3
Wood's Corner 13 K5
Woods Eaves 28 B4
Wood's Green 13 K3
Woodseaves Shrop 39 F2
Woodseaves Staffs 39 G3
Woodsend 21 F4
Woodsetts 51 H4
Woodsford 9 G5
Woodside BrackF 22 C4
Woodside CenBeds 32 D7
Woodside Cumb 60 B3
Woodside D&G 69 F6
Woodside GtLon 23 G5
Woodside Hants 10 E5
Woodside Herts 23 F1
Woodside NAyr 74 B5
Woodside P&K 80 G7
Woodside Shrop 38 C7
Woodside WMid 40 B7
Woodside Animal Farm & Leisure Park CenBeds LU1 4DG 32 D7
Woodside Green 14 E2
Woodstock Oxon 31 F7
Woodstock Pembs 16 D3
Woodthorpe Derbys 51 G5
Woodthorpe Leics 41 H4
Woodthorpe Lincs 53 H4
Woodthorpe SYorks 51 F4
Woodthorpe York 58 B5
Woodton 45 G6
Woodtown 6 C3
Woodvale 48 C1
Woodville 41 F4
Woodwall Green 39 G2
Woodwalton 43 F7
Woodwick 89 C5
Woodworth Green 48 E7
Woodyates 10 B3
Woofferton 28 E2
Wookey 19 J7
Wookey Hole 19 J7
Wookey Hole Caves & Papermill Som BA5 1BB 19 J7
Wool 9 H6
Woolacombe 6 C1
Woolage Green 15 H3
Woolage Village 15 H2
Woolaston 19 J1
Woolaston Slade 19 J1
Woolavington 19 G7
Woolbeding 12 B4
Woolcotts 7 H2
Wooldale 50 D2
Wooler 70 E1
Woolfardisworthy Devon 6 B3
Woolfardisworthy Devon 7 G5
Woolfold 49 G1
Woolfords Cottages 75 J5
Woolgarston 9 J6
Woolgreaves 51 F1
Woolhampton 21 J5
Woolhope 29 F5
Woolland 9 G4
Woollard 19 K5
Woollaton 6 C4
Woollensbrook 23 G1
Woolley B&NESom 20 A5
Woolley Cambs 32 E1
Woolley Corn 6 A4
Woolley Derbys 51 F6
Woolley WYorks 51 F1
Woolley Green Wilts 20 B5
Woolley Green W&M 22 B4
Woolmer Green 33 F7
Woolmere Green 29 J2
Woolmersdon 8 B1
Woolpit 34 D2
Woolpit Green 34 D2
Woolscott 31 F2
Woolsgrove 7 F5
Woolstaston 38 D6
Woolsthorpe 42 B2
Woolsthorpe by Colsterworth 42 C3
Woolston Devon 5 H6
Woolston Shrop 38 C3
Woolston Shrop 38 D7
Woolston Soton 11 F3
Woolston Warr 49 F4
Woolston Green 5 H4
Woolstone Glos 29 J5
Woolstone MK 32 B5
Woolstone Oxon 21 F3
Woolton 48 D4
Woolton Hill 21 H5
Woolverstone 35 F5
Woolverton 20 A6
Woolwich 23 H4
Woonton 28 C3
Wooperton 71 F2
Woore 39 G1
Wootten Green 35 G1
Wootton Bed 32 D4
Wootton Hants 10 D5
Wootton IoW 11 G5
Wootton Kent 15 H3
Wootton NLincs 52 D1
Wootton N'hants 31 J3
Wootton Oxon 21 H1
Wootton Oxon 31 F7
Wootton Shrop 28 D1
Wootton Shrop 38 C3
Wootton Staffs 40 A3
Wootton Staffs 40 D1
Wootton Bassett 20 D3
Wootton Bridge 11 G5
Wootton Common 11 G5
Wootton Courtenay 7 H1
Wootton Fitzpaine 8 C5
Wootton Green 32 D4
Wootton Rivers 20 E5
Wootton St. Lawrence 21 J6
Wootton Wawen 30 C2
Worcester 29 H3
Worcester Cathedral Worcs WR1 2LH 137 Worcester
Worcester Park 23 F5
Worcester Woods Country Park Worcs WR5 2LG 29 H3
Wordsley 40 A7
Wordwell 34 C1
Worfield 39 G6
Worgret 9 J6
Workhouse End 32 E3
Workington 60 B4
Worksop 51 H5
Worlaby Lincs 53 G5
Worlaby NLincs 52 D1
World Museum Liverpool Mersey L3 8EN 131 D3
World of Beatrix Potter Attraction Cumb LA23 3BX 60 F7
World of James Herriot, Thirsk NYorks YO7 1PL 57 K1
World's End Bucks 22 B1
Worlds End Hants 11 H3
World's End WBerks 21 H4
Worlds End WMid 40 D7
Worle 19 G5
Worleston 49 F7
Worlingham 45 J7
Worlington 33 K1
Worlingworth 35 G2
Wormald Green 57 J3
Wormbridge 28 D5
Wormegay 44 A4
Wormelow Tump 28 D5
Wormhill 50 D5
Wormingford 34 D5
Worminghall 21 K1
Wormington 30 B5
Worminster 19 J7
Wormit 81 J8
Wormleighton 31 F3
Wormley Herts 23 G1
Wormley Surr 12 C3
Wormley West End 23 G1
Wormshill 14 D2
Wormsley 28 D4
Worplesdon 22 C6
Worrall 51 F3
Worsbrough 51 F2
Worsley 49 G2
Worstead 45 H3
Worsted Lodge 33 J3
Worsthorne 56 D6
Worston 56 C5
Worswell 5 F6
Worth Kent 15 J2
Worth WSuss 13 F3
Worth Matravers 9 J7
Wortham 34 E1
Worthen 38 C5
Worthenbury 38 D1
Worthing Norf 44 D4
Worthing WSuss 12 E6
Worthington 41 G3
Worting 21 K6
Wortley Glos 20 A2
Wortley SYorks 51 F3
Wortley WYorks 57 H6
Worton NYorks 56 E1
Worton Wilts 20 C6
Wortwell 45 G7
Wothersome 57 K5
Wotherton 38 B5
Wotter 5 F4
Wotton 22 E7
Wotton Underwood 31 H7
Wotton-under-Edge 20 A2
Woughton on the Green 32 B5
Wouldham 24 D5
W.R. Outhwaite & Son Ropemakers NYorks DL8 3NT 56 D1
Wrabness 35 F5
Wrafton 6 C2
Wragby 52 E5
Wragholme 53 G3
Wramplingham 45 F5
Wrangaton 5 G5
Wrangle 53 H7
Wrangle Lowgate 53 H7
Wrangway 7 K4
Wrantage 8 C2
Wrawby 52 D2
Wraxall NSom 19 H4
Wraxall Som 9 F1
Wray 56 B3
Wrays 23 F7
Wraysbury 22 D4
Wrayton 56 B2
Wrea Green 55 G6
Wreay Cumb 60 F2
Wreay Cumb 60 F4
Wrecclesham 22 B7
Wrekenton 62 C1
Wrelton 58 D1
Wrenbury 38 E1
Wrench Green 59 F1
Wreningham 45 F6
Wrentham 45 J7
Wrenthorpe 57 J7
Wrentnall 38 D5
Wressle ERid 58 D6
Wressle NLincs 52 C2
Wrestlingworth 33 F4
Wretham 44 D6
Wretton 44 A5
Wrexham (Wrecsam) 38 C1
Wrexham Arts Centre Wrex LL11 1AU 48 C7
Wrexham Industrial Estate 38 C1
Wribbenhall 29 G1
Wrightington Bar 48 E1
Wrightpark 74 E1
Wright's Green 33 J7
Wrinehill 39 G1
Wrington 19 H5
Writhlington 19 K6
Writtle 24 C1
Wrockwardine 39 F4
Wroot 51 K2
Wrose 57 G6
Wrotham 23 K6
Wrotham Heath 23 K6
Wrotham Hill Park 24 C5
Wrottesley 40 A5
Wroughton 20 E3
Wroxall IoW 11 G7
Wroxall Warks 30 D1
Wroxeter 38 E5
Wroxham 45 H4
Wroxton 31 F4
Wstrws 17 G1
WWT London Wetland Centre GtLon SW13 9WT 103 F8
Wyaston 40 D1
Wyberton 43 G1
Wyboston 32 E3
Wybunbury 39 F1
Wych Cross 13 H3
Wychbold 29 J2
Wychnor 40 D4
Wychnor Bridges 40 D4
Wyck 11 J1
Wyck Rissington 30 C6
Wycliffe 62 B5
Wycoller 56 E6
Wycoller Country Park Lancs BB8 8SY 56 E6
Wycomb 42 A3
Wycombe Marsh 22 B2
Wyddial 33 G5
Wye 15 F3
Wyesham 28 E7
Wyfordby 42 A4
Wyke Devon 7 G6
Wyke Dorset 9 G2
Wyke Shrop 39 F5
Wyke Surr 22 C6
Wyke WYorks 57 G7
Wyke Champflower 9 F1
Wyke Regis 9 F7
Wykeham NYorks 58 E2
Wykeham NYorks 59 F1
Wyken Shrop 39 G6
Wyken WMid 41 F7
Wykey 38 C3
Wylam 71 G7
Wylde Green 40 D6
Wyllie 18 E2
Wylye 10 B1
Wymering 11 H4
Wymeswold 41 J3
Wymington 32 C2
Wymondham Leics 42 B4
Wymondham Norf 45 F5
Wyndham 18 C2
Wynford Eagle 8 E5
Wynnstay Park 38 C1
Wynyard 62 E4
Wynyard Woodland Park Stock TS21 3JG 62 D4
Wyre Forest Worcs DY14 9XQ 29 G1
Wyre Piddle 29 J4
Wyresdale Tower 56 B4
Wysall 41 J3
Wyson 28 E2
Wythall 30 B1
Wytham 21 H1
Wythburn 60 E5
Wythenshawe 49 H4
Wyton Cambs 33 F1
Wyton ERid 59 H6
Wyverstone 34 E2
Wyverstone Street 34 E2
Wyville 42 B3

Y

Y Bryn 37 H3
Y Fan 37 J7
Y Felinheli 46 D6
Y Ffôr 36 C2
Y Fron (Upper Llandwrog) 46 D7
Yaddlethorpe 52 B2
Yafford 11 F6
Yafforth 62 D7
Yalberton 5 J5
Yalding 23 K7
Yanley 19 J5
Yanwath 61 G4
Yanworth 30 B7
Yapham 58 D4
Yapton 12 C6
Yarburgh 53 G3
Yarcombe 8 B4
Yardley 40 D7
Yardley Gobion 31 J4
Yardley Hastings 32 B3
Yardro 28 B3
Yarford 8 B2
Yarkhill 29 F4
Yarlet 40 B3
Yarley 19 J7
Yarlington 9 F2
Yarm 62 E5
Yarmouth 10 E6
Yarnacott 6 E2
Yarnbrook 20 B6
Yarnfield 40 A2
Yarnscombe 6 D3
Yarnton 31 F7
Yarpole 28 D2
Yarrow ScBord 69 J1
Yarrow Som 19 G7
Yarrow Feus 69 J1
Yarrowford 69 K1
Yarsop 28 D4
Yarwell 42 D6
Yate 20 A3
Yatehouse Green 49 G6
Yateley 22 B5
Yatesbury 20 D4
Yattendon 21 J4
Yatton Here 28 D2
Yatton NSom 19 H5
Yatton Keynell 20 B4
Yaverland 11 H6
Yawl 8 C5
Yaxham 44 E4
Yaxley Cambs 42 E6
Yaxley Suff 35 F1
Yazor 28 D4
Ye Olde Pork Pie Shoppe, Melton Mowbray Leics LE13 1NW 42 A4
Yeabridge 8 D3
Yeading 22 E3
Yeadon 57 H5
Yealand Conyers 55 J2
Yealand Redmayne 55 J2
Yealand Storrs 55 J2
Yealmbridge 5 F5
Yealmpton 5 F5
Yearby 63 G4
Yearsley 58 B2
Yeaton 38 D4
Yeaveley 40 D1
Yeavering 77 H7
Yedingham 58 E2
Yelford 21 G1
Yell 89 N4
Yelland Devon 6 C2
Yelland Devon 6 D6
Yelling 33 F2
Yelvertoft 31 G1
Yelverton Devon 5 F4
Yelverton Norf 45 G5
Yenston 9 G2
Yeo Mill 7 G3
Yeo Vale 6 C3
Yeoford 7 F6
Yeolmbridge 6 B7
Yeomadon 6 B5
Yeovil 8 E3
Yeovil Country Park Som BA20 1QZ 8 E3
Yeovil Marsh 8 E3
Yeovilton 8 E2
Yerbeston 16 D5
Yesnaby 89 B6
Yesterday's World, Battle ESuss TN33 0AQ 14 C6
Yetholm Mains 70 D1
Yetlington 71 F2
Yetminster 8 E3
Yettington 7 J7
Yetts o'Muckhart 80 F10
Yew Green 30 D2
Yielden 32 D2
Yieldshields 75 G5
Ynys 36 E2
Ynys Tachwedd 37 F6
Ynysboeth 18 D2
Ynysddu 18 E2
Ynyshir 18 D2
Ynyslas 37 F6
Ynysmaerdy 18 D3
Ynysmeudwy 18 A1
Ynystawe 17 K5
Ynyswen 18 C2
Ynysybwl 18 D2
Yockenthwaite 56 E2
Yockleton 38 C4
Yokefleet 58 E7
Yoker 74 D4
York 58 C4
York Castle Museum YO1 9SA 137 York
York Dungeon YO1 9RD 137 York
York Minster YO1 7HH 137 York
Yorkletts 25 G5
Yorkley 19 K1
Yorkshire Museum YO1 7FR 137 York
Yorkshire Sculpture Park WYorks WF4 4LG 50 E1
Yorton 38 E3
Yorton Heath 38 E3
Youldon 6 B5
Youldonmoor Cross 6 B5
Youlgreave 50 E6
Youlthorpe 58 D4
Youlton 57 K3
Young's End 34 B7
Yoxall 40 D4
Yoxford 35 H2
Ysbyty Cynfyn 27 G1
Ysbyty Ifan 37 H1
Ysbyty Ystwyth 27 G1
Ysceifiog 47 K5
Ysgubor-y-coed 37 F6
Ystalyfera 18 A1
Ystrad 18 C2
Ystrad Aeron 26 E3
Ystrad Meurig 27 G2
Ystrad Mynach 18 E2
Ystradfellte 27 J7
Ystradffin 27 G4
Ystradgynlais 27 G7
Ystradowen Carmar 27 G7
Ystradowen VGlam 18 D4
Ystumtuen 27 G1
Ythanwells 85 L7
Ythsie 85 N7

Z

Zeal Monachorum 7 F5
Zeals 9 G1
Zelah 3 F3
Zennor 2 B5
Zouch 41 H3
ZSL London Zoo GtLon NW1 4RY 102 H6

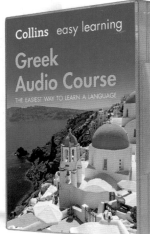

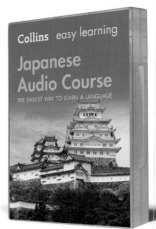

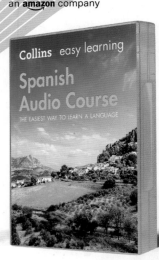

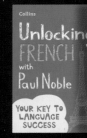